Mediterranean Archaeologies of Insularity in an Age of Globalization

Mediterranean Archaeologies of Insularity in an Age of Globalization

edited by

Anna Kouremenos and Jody Michael Gordon

OXBOW | books
Oxford & Philadelphia

Published in the United Kingdom in 2020 by
OXBOW BOOKS
The Old Music Hall, 106–108 Cowley Road, Oxford OX4 1JE

and in the United States by
OXBOW BOOKS
1950 Lawrence Road, Havertown, PA 19083

Paperback Edition: ISBN 978-1-78925-344-3
Digital Edition: ISBN 978-1-78925-345-0 (ePub)

A CIP record for this book is available from the British Library

Library of Congress Control Number: 2020937150

Printed in the United Kingdom by Short Run Press

Typeset by Versatile PreMedia Services (P) Ltd

For a complete list of Oxbow titles, please contact:

UNITED KINGDOM
Oxbow Books
Telephone (01865) 241249
Email: oxbow@oxbowbooks.com
www.oxbowbooks.com

UNITED STATES OF AMERICA
Oxbow Books
Telephone (610) 853-9131, Fax (610) 853-9146
Email: queries@casemateacademic.com
www.casemateacademic.com/oxbow

Oxbow Books is part of the Casemate Group

Front cover: Sanctuary of Apollo Hylates, Kourion, Cyprus. (Photo: Jody Michael Gordon)
Back cover: Aerial view of the Carthailac precinct from Torre d'en Galmés. (Photo courtesy of Amalia Pérez-Juez)

Contents

Preface

In March 2014, the editors met in person for the first time during a panel Anna had organized for the 24th Theoretical Roman Archaeology Conference (TRAC) at the University of Reading in the United Kingdom. The title of the panel was *Insularity and Identity in the Roman Mediterranean* and after a morning of insightful discussion, we soon discovered that our research focused on similar themes. Not only were we examining various aspects of insularity in two large islands in the eastern Mediterranean during the Roman period – Crete and Cyprus – but we were also concerned with how modern scholars view such topics as insular identities and cross-cultural connectivity. We also agreed that new modes of analysis were needed to better understand how hyper-connected islands like Crete and Cyprus were integrated into empires like Rome's, and so we were drawn into debating the theoretical issue surrounding the topic of island archaeology that loomed large at those same RAC and TRAC meetings, *i.e.* globalization.

After discussing for several months over email how island archaeology might be enhanced by a globalization approach, we decided to explore the topic further by organizing a panel for the 118th Archaeological Institute of America (AIA) annual meeting in Toronto, Canada that solicited papers from scholars concerning aspects of identity and globalization processes on various Mediterranean islands. Because globalization occurs during eras of punctuated connectivity, we decided that the best way to shed light on how enhanced levels of social interaction created new Mediterranean islander identities was to focus our panel on a diachronic approach. Consequently, in this resulting volume, specific eras of ancient Mediterranean history known for their increased connectivity and the islands where such connections occurred have been analyzed from a globalization perspective that examines networking, cultural diversity, and multiple processes of social change.

As we read and edited this volume's chapters, several of our long-held assumptions about the ancient Mediterranean were challenged, both because of the diachronic and geographically diverse perspectives that the papers provided and due to the expansion of our knowledge about specific island archaeologies. Moreover, throughout the editorial process, a few questions kept coming to the fore: is globalization an appropriate theoretical mode for analyzing the formation of ancient islander identities? If so, can globalization theory be uniformly applied across the islands of the Mediterranean or is it only useful for the study of certain groups of islands at specific historical moments? This ongoing theoretical debate can be witnessed across the volume's chapters and is especially addressed in the Afterword by P. Nick Kardulias, a scholar who has frequently grappled with the nature of social change in the Mediterranean region over the long-term. As a result, the reader is encouraged to reflect on his/her own position on the applicability of a globalization approach to Mediterranean island archaeology after reading the chapters herein.

This volume is based on the aforementioned AIA panel, yet its topics have been supplemented by invited contributions from scholars working on additional islands. As with all edited volumes, the completion of each chapter required dedication and patience as well as the input of several individuals without whose expertise, suggestions for improvement, and patience this volume would not have been possible. In addition to the authors of the papers in this volume, who share our passion for and interest in understanding island life, we are grateful to P. Nick Kardulias for his input and willingness to take on the task of writing the Afterword. We extend our sincere gratitude to Erica Angliker, Erin Walcek Averett, Scott Gallimore, Dennis Joch, Matthias Kalisch, Becky Martin, Anthony Russell, Michael Vickers, and Bill Weir for their comments and suggestions in improving the various papers. Thanks are also due to Brandon Olson for providing a map for the Introduction, and we would like to recognize Rebecca Sweetman, Justin Walsh, Tamar Hodos, Peter van Dommelen, Andrea Roppa, David Hernandez, Carrie Fulton, and Kevin Fisher for discussions relating to this volume and the original AIA panel. Finally, we are indebted to the editorial team at Oxbow Books, particularly to Julie Gardiner and Jessica Scott, for their advice and patience in producing this volume.

Anna Kouremenos and Jody Michael Gordon

About the Authors

Anna Kouremenos received her D.Phil. in Archaeology from the University of Oxford with a thesis on houses and identity in Roman Crete and is currently Lecturer in Archaeology at the University of Tübingen. She is the editor and author of numerous volumes and papers on topics dealing with the history and archaeology of the Hellenistic East and Roman Greece, insularity and identity, migration and mobility in the Graeco-Roman world, archaeological theory, and the reception of antiquity.

Jody Michael Gordon is an Associate Professor of Humanities and Social Sciences at Wentworth Institute of Technology in Boston, MA where he teaches classes on ancient history, art and architecture, and classical reception. He received his Ph.D. in Classical Archaeology from the Department of Classics at the University of Cincinnati and has authored several book chapters and articles on the archaeology of Roman and Early Christian Cyprus.

Anthony Russell received his doctorate from the University of Glasgow. His research interests include the Middle and Late Bronze Age in the central Mediterranean, cross-cultural consumption, materiality, globalization, and intangible heritage. For the past nine years he has been involved in culture resource management in both Scotland and western Canada.

Evi Gorogianni is Professor of Instruction at the Department of Anthropology of the University of Akron. She is the co-editor of *Beyond Thalassocracies: Understanding Processes of Minoanisation and Mycenaeanisation in the Aegean* (co-edited with P. Pavúk and L. Girella 2016) and several papers on Minoanization and its materiality, migration (especially women's mobility), and archaeological practice in Greek archaeology. Her latest on-going project is the study of the MBA ceramic assemblage discovered recently under the classical theatre of Karthaia on Kea.

Charles Barnett graduated from Macquarie University, Sydney, with a Ph.D. titled *Cultural Integration, Social Change and Identities in Late Iron Age and Roman Liburnia*. He currently holds a position at Macquarie's Higher Degree Research Office. His research interests include the history and archaeology of Late Iron Age and Early Roman Europe, particularly the study of identities and socio-cultural developments in colonial and provincial contexts, and with an emphasis on the Adriatic region.

Marina Ugarković is an archaeologist from Split, Croatia. In 2015 she was awarded a Ph.D. from the University of Zagreb for a thesis on the burial customs of Issa, an ancient Greek city in central Dalmatia. Currently, she holds a tenured research position at the Institute of Archaeology in Zagreb, Croatia. Her research interests include Mediterranean archaeology, with emphasis on the Adriatic and material culture of the Hellenistic period, Greeks and locals in Dalmatia, necropolises and the archaeology of death and burial rites, pottery studies, cultural identities and interaction, processes of cultural hybridization.

Leigh Anne Lieberman is a classical archaeologist who examines how and why artifacts and spaces were recycled and repurposed in the ancient world with a particular focus on the material culture of Sicily, Sardinia, and the southern Italian peninsula. She earned a B.A. and M.A. in Classics from The Johns Hopkins University, and an M.A. and Ph.D. from the Department of Art and Archaeology at Princeton University. She has taught at the Intercollegiate Center for Classical Studies in Rome, Claremont McKenna College, Pitzer College, and Scripps College, and she is currently the Director of The Digital Humanities Initiative at The Claremont Colleges.

Lindsey A. Mazurek is Assistant Professor in the Department of Classical Studies at the University of Indiana, Bloomington and co-director of the Mediterranean Connectivity Initiative. She received her Ph.D. in Art History from Duke University. Her work focuses on connectivity, transcultural exchange, and mobility in the Hellenistic and Roman Mediterranean. Together with Cavan Concannon, she edited *Across the Corrupting Sea: Post-Braudelian Approaches to the Ancient Eastern Mediterranean* (2016).

Alexander J. Smith is Assistant Professor of Anthropology at The College at Brockport – SUNY. He received his Ph.D. from the Joukowsky Institute for Archaeology and the Ancient World at Brown University in 2015, studying the Late Iron Age of the Balearic Islands. He is currently a co-director of the Sinis Archaeological Project in West Central Sardinia and the director of Frost Town Archaeology in Western New York. His research interests include island identity in the Western Mediterranean, archaeological survey, and the historical archaeology of New York State.

Jane E. Francis holds a Ph.D. in Classical Archaeology from Bryn Mawr College and is Associate Professor in the Department of Classics, Modern Languages and Linguistics at Concordia University in Montreal. Her research focuses on the Roman period on Crete, including ceramics, sculpture, fabric analysis, ancient beekeeping, and landscape archaeology.

William R. Caraher is Associate Professor in History at the University of North Dakota. He received his Ph.D. in Ancient History at Ohio State University, has directed archaeological projects in Cyprus, and worked extensively in Greece. He is the co-author of *Pyla-Koutsopetria I: Archaeological Survey of An Ancient Coastal Town* (2014) with R. Scott Moore and David K. Pettegrew, and *The Oxford Handbook of Early Christian Archaeology* (2019) with David K. Pettegrew and Tom Davis. He is also Director and Publisher of *The Digital Press at the University of North Dakota* and is Editor of the *North Dakota Quarterly*.

P. Nick Kardulias is the Marian Senter Nixon Professor of Classical Civilization and Professor of Anthropology and Archaeology at the College of Wooster (USA). His research interests include the analysis of stone tools as they relate to the study of agriculture and craft specialization in ancient cultures, and the use of world-systems analysis and evolutionary theory in archaeological contexts. He has directed projects in Greece, Cyprus, and the United States. Recent publications include *The Ecology of Pastoralism* (editor; 2015) and *Lithics Past and Present: Perspectives on Chipped Stone Studies in Greece* (co-editor; 2016).

Abstracts

Nuragic Networking? Assessing Globalization and Glocalization in a Late Bronze Age Sardinian Context

Anthony Russell

The Late Bronze Age in Sardinia represented the height of prehistoric connectivity on the island, as represented by the presence of several exotic materials and finished products. While the raw number of extra-insular objects or perceived influences is significantly less than 1st millennium BCE connections on the island (*i.e.* with Phoenicians, Greeks and eventually, Romans), can this conspicuous connectivity nonetheless benefit from a globalization framework of analysis, in the way that later periods have? In other words, can a globalization perspective help us to understand either material impacts, or changes in the structure or functioning of Nuragic society during the Late Bronze Age? How does such a perspective compare to the more established world systems model of contact? Employing two widespread Late Bronze Age objects as a case study, Late Helladic pottery and copper oxhide ingots, it is argued that while some concepts derived from globalization studies have interpretive potential (*e.g.* 'glocalization'), a broader globalization framework seems a bad fit for the level of contact during this period in Sardinia, where local consumption choices and responses to inter-island social pressures are more likely to have influenced material expressions and social change.

Mobility and Globalization: The View from the Bronze Age Cyclades

Evi Gorogianni

Even though the degree of interconnectedness that the world experiences today may be unprecedented, evidence from many past cultures challenges the assumption that globalization is a modern phenomenon, especially if one adopts a broader definition that does not necessitate reference to modern economic systems. The Aegean of the MBA and the LBA bears almost all the hallmarks of an ancient globalization. Indeed, from the beginning of the MBA, the already connected Aegean archipelago experienced a surge of interaction and connectivity between long distance locales. This connectivity seems to have promoted the creation of a global culture that shaped (but did not define) the way or the degree to which inhabitants of these communities regarded themselves as closely tied to, or positioned far away from, decision-making centers. Material culture tells this story very eloquently.

The present paper explores various categories of objects (imported pottery, locally produced pottery, and the evidence for textile production) from the Middle and Late Bronze Age site of Ayia Irini, a small gateway community on the island of Kea (Greece). This particular community is of interest because the analysis of its material culture demonstrates the simultaneous operation of the paradoxical yet complimentary tendencies of cultural homogenization and the creation of alterity and interculturality. Moreover, the author advocates for the expansion of the list of possible processes beyond trade and exchange that contributed to the globalization of the Aegean. Even though trade and exchange were significant forces in the integration of this globalized context, the social integration of this mini world was most likely also due to a continuous low-level migration and the planned articulation of a kinship network based on marital alliances.

Globalization Processes and Insularity on the Dalmatian Islands in the Late Iron Age

Charles Barnett and Marina Ugarković

The Iron Age eastern Adriatic communities played an integral part in the shaping of the Adriatic cultural seascape. Their connectivity to wider Mediterranean networks was increased through the establishment of sea-trade routes connecting Greece to settlements in the Po valley around the 5th century BCE, the foundation of Greek colonies on central Dalmatian islands in the 4th century BCE, and increasing Roman commercial and political interaction in the eastern Adriatic from the 3rd century BCE. The islands off the coast of modern-day Dalmatia acted as nodes on these routes, helping integrate coastal and hinterland areas into the social and economic sphere of trans-Mediterranean networks. Globalizing influences on these islands encouraged integration in both indigenous and colonial communities. This paper discusses the integration of the Adriatic into Mediterranean-wide economic and socio-political networks in the Iron Age. The available archaeological evidence from the central and southern Dalmatian islands is analysed to develop a picture of how different communities reacted to globalizing processes during this period. Material from Greek and local settlements on the central Dalmatian islands suggests a variety of cultural experiences resulted from increasing connectivity during the Late Iron Age. The insular character of these communities certainly impacted their level of interaction with globalizing networks, leading to localized preferences and cultural repertoires.

Apollo Archegetes as a Globalizing Divinity: Numismatic Iconography and the Memory of Sicilian Naxos

Leigh Anne Lieberman

After their foundations in the Archaic period, the settlements of Sicily came to be occupied by mixed communities that were well-positioned to participate in a global culture, resilient in the face of challengers but negotiable among allies. This chapter examines the impact that globalizing processes had on the Sicilian Naxians and their settlement by focusing in particular on the creative manipulation of numismatic iconography by several Sicilian communities.

The first Greek settlement on the island, Naxos, simultaneously marked both a physical periphery of the Greek world and a cultural center for Sicilian Greek identity. But, despite this sense of cultural capital, Naxos was targeted by Syracuse in the 5th century BCE; the settlement was first depopulated by Hieron I of Syracuse in the early 5th century (Diod. Sic. 11.49.1–2; 76.3) and, after a period of recovery, ultimately destroyed by Dionysius I of Syracuse at the end of the century (Diod. Sic. 14.14.1–2; 15.2). At this time, the territory of the Naxians was occupied by the neighboring indigenous Sikels, but the site of their settlement was never formally revived (Diod. Sic. 14.15.3). Scholars have largely relied on this historical framework to understand the fate of Naxos and its citizens but have been less concerned with understanding how the Naxians and their neighbors coped with these pivotal transitions. This chapter targets precisely this question by examining how and why the iconographies of specific divinities, namely Dionysus and Apollo, were exploited in response to the depopulation and destruction of Naxos by the Naxians themselves, their neighbors, and those claiming Naxian heritage.

Balearic Indigeneity in a Global Mediterranean: Considering Circular Domestic Structures of Late Iron Age Menorca

Alexander Smith

Over the past 20 years, Menorcan megalithic houses dating to the Late Talayotic Culture (roughly the end of the 6th to 1st centuries BCE) have been subject to multiple excavation campaigns, resulting in a wealth of information regarding Late Iron Age domestic architecture and practices. Exhibiting both a circular ground plan and megalithic construction methods, the material culture in many of these structures can be dated to as late as the 1st centuries BCE or CE.

This study will argue that in the face of increased exposure to external influences indigenous elements within these household structures were emphasized or hyperbolized, pointing to a sense of indigenous identity or indigeneity among the islanders. Such elements included circular ground plans, hypostyle halls, and megalithic roof supports that referenced cult sites, all of which were associated with large, elite dwellings. During this period much of Menorca's extra-island interaction stemmed from Carthaginian and Roman contacts as the island was gradually exposed to and integrated into the networks of these global powers. As a whole, the domestic evidence showcases a culture that was persistent during a time of change in the western Mediterranean, but also self-referential and creative, emphasizing its local traditions while utilizing foreign material culture. In considering themes of globalization and the local experience through the lens of Late Talayotic Menorca, this study will conclude by discussing the concept of indigeneity from an anthropological perspective and its potential application to Mediterranean archaeology in the Late Iron Age.

Fashioning a Global Goddess: The Representation of Isis across Hellenistic Seascapes

Lindsey A. Mazurek

In this paper, I take a seascape-oriented approach to the study of island and mainland port connections in the Hellenistic Mediterranean that reconfigures the idea of a 'region'. When Greek devotees began to worship the Egyptian goddess Isis in the late 4th century BCE, they chose to develop new images of the goddess. Most popular among these was a distinctive costume that featured a mantle knotted between the breasts to create an X-pattern, a type that Jan Eingartner has called the *Knotenpalla*. The first examples of this type, dating to the mid-Hellenistic period, were thought to come from the islands of Delos and Rhodes, but another has been found at Amphipolis, suggesting a new way of considering island and mainland connectivity in the Hellenistic period.

I begin my essay by examining the role of the port in antiquity. I argue that ports could both enable and restrict connectivity and propose that we consider ports through the metaphor of the valve: able to permit, restrict, and redirect cultural flows. Next, I define the *Knotenpalla* and trace the type's cultic and social meanings. Through formal analysis, I argue that the mid-Hellenistic types from Delos, Rhodes, and Amphipolis form a cohesive enough group to suggest that their Isiac communities had a relationship with each other. I conclude by suggesting that these connections were built by migration, but also help us understand the active role geography played in community formation. Comparing these statuettes with a regional example from Beroia, I argue that the disjuncture between Isis' representation at Hellenistic sites in Macedonia indicates that sea-based forms of regionality could have been as, or in some cases, more, influential to cultural and religious development as land-based regions. This case study helps us reposition ports as parts of island networks and see the shores of the Mediterranean more clearly as part of seascapes.

Globalization and Insularity in (Dis)Connected Crete

Jane E. Francis

The position of Crete on the intersection of cultural and trade routes and its merger with Cyrenaica into a Roman province in the 30s BCE should have ensured its swift and thorough engagement with Mediterranean politics, economy, and lifestyle. This did not happen, and the archaeological record indicates very little acknowledgment of the Roman presence for nearly a century. This paper examines the material evidence for Crete's response to Roman rule, when and how it occurred, and to what degree the island became 'Roman'. Different types of sites – urban, rural, Roman colony, administrative capital, pre-existing Greek settlements – preserve markedly different evidence, and it is clear that individual histories, prior alliances, site functions, locations, and access to resources exerted greater influence on the island's development than did the implantation of Roman rule. Crete's transformation into a Roman province was thus not uniform but governed by a myriad of forces both internal and external: insularity and adherence to earlier practices can be observed alongside more globalized, outward-looking pursuits. Crete offers an opportunity to observe these two seemingly opposing forces in a single area, and to develop a more nuanced interpretation of Roman power.

From the Land of the Paphian Aphrodite to the Busy Christian Countryside: Globalization, Empire, and Insularity in Early and Late Roman Cyprus

Jody Michael Gordon and William R. Caraher

During the Early (c. 30 BCE –293 CE) and Late Roman (c. 293–649 CE) periods, the island of Cyprus was integrated into two different Mediterranean empires, the Roman and the Byzantine. In both eras, the island's location on maritime routes stretching from Egypt, to the Aegean, to Byzantium and Rome, assured that Cypriots would be integrated into global networks of socio-economic interaction as connectivity ebbed and flowed vis-à-vis imperial expansion. Yet, the island's *longue durée* features, such as its location, resources, and deep cultural history, and each empire's changing social practices (such as the transition from paganism to Christianity) and geopolitical goals, forced Cypriots to engage dynamically with globalized networks in ways that made sense both at home and abroad. If insularity can be seen as a form of identity that islanders actively create and modify over time, archaeological remains can serve as markers of the different ways that Cypriots identified themselves within complex global networks. This chapter's goal is to explore archaeologically how Cypriot culture changed in the face of globalizing pressures during two of the most connected periods in the island's history. Through a comparative analysis of ceramics, coins, and architecture, we show how long-term geographical factors and short-term social structures can reveal differences between globalization episodes and can also shed light on how these forces influenced Cypriots as they negotiated their identities across a range of local and global networks.

Chapter 1

Introduction

Jody Michael Gordon and Anna Kouremenos

Throughout the history of the Mediterranean region, connectivity between peoples has always been a driving force of social change (Fig. 1). During certain periods, such mobility and cross-cultural interaction was facilitated through terrestrial road networks in coastal regions. However, it was arguably the Mediterranean Sea's maritime networks that transformed its fragmented regions into one of the most connected and culturally creative in world history.[1] Technological innovations in ship design and navigation from the Neolithic period onwards allowed people to venture out from coastal farming villages to trade their foodstuffs for natural resources, from obsidian to copper to marble.[2] Such early voyages also compressed space and time in revolutionary ways.[3] Resources located hundreds of miles away that once took weeks to acquire could now be accessed in days. Moreover, peoples who once lived separate, isolated lives at great distances from each other were now connected in ways that could be either socially beneficial or, more often, disruptive. Although geography, climate, and natural resources always affected the contours of Mediterranean life, the sea's ability to connect the 'frogs around a pond' (to use Plato's phrase in *Phaedo* 109b) who populated its shores may have played an even greater role in shaping the region's historical and cultural trajectories.[4]

Venturing out into the wine-dark sea in antiquity could be a precarious and dangerous affair. Ancient mariners had to trust their ships as well as their navigation skills, knowledge of reefs, winds, and currents, and often had to invoke providence to escape the fury of storms or the predations of pirates. Given such essential skills and dangers, it is no wonder that Odysseus and Aeneas as *iactati alto* became two of the region's archetypal heroes.[5] Yet the benefits of connectivity, especially in terms of trade and political hegemony, seem to have outweighed the risks.[6] As Pericles famously stated about Athens' 5th-century BCE naval empire, 'Μέγα γὰρ τὸ τῆς θαλάσσης κράτος' ('Command of the sea is a powerful thing').[7]

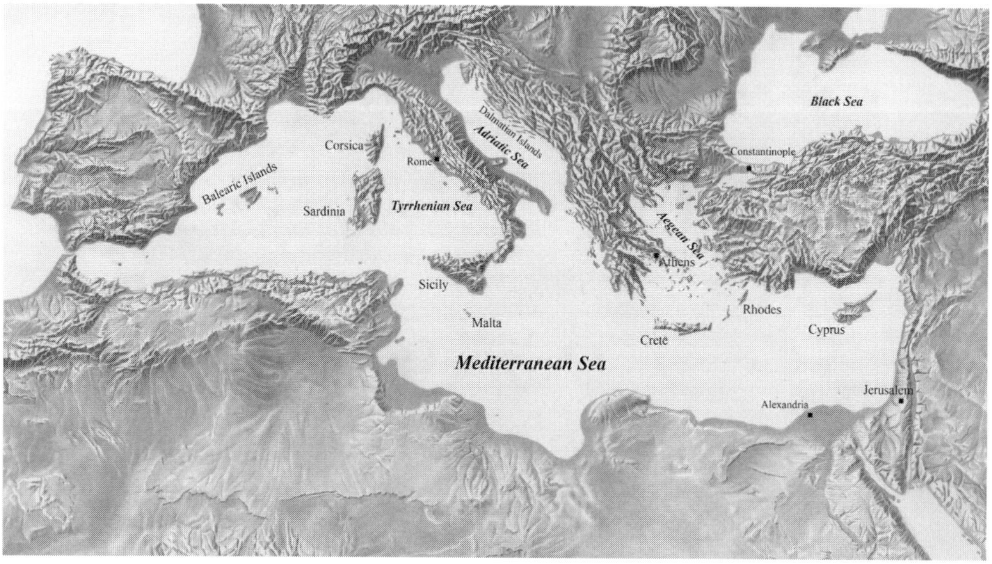

Figure 1: Map of the Mediterranean with major islands (Brandon Olson).

For people living around the pre-modern Mediterranean, sea travel was the technological advance that allowed groups to control resources and spheres of influence through the ability to rapidly move from region to region and to respond to competitive political or economic threats and environmental risks.[8] As a result, the historical and archaeological evidence suggests that the post-Neolithic Mediterranean was periodically overflowing with ships, even if most sailors had to travel short distances and frequently seek refuge in the closest protected anchorage depending on the wind and weather.[9] Many seafarers thus traveled within sight of land, so that terrestrial safe havens could be easily accessed. Although the Mediterranean's coasts contained emporia, such as Piraeus or Naukratis, where seafarers could both trade their wares or wait until the wind changed, the sea was also dotted with literally hundreds of maritime stopping points where sailors could engage in cabotage and make new economic and cultural connections.[10] Most prominent among these points were the hundreds of islands that dot the wine-dark sea.[11]

The Mediterranean is marked by islands of various sizes, from the matchbox-continent 'big five' of Sicily, Sardinia, Cyprus, Corsica, and Crete, to the mid-range islands of Rhodes, Lesbos, Majorca, or Euboea, to the archipelagos, such as the Cyclades, the Maltese chain, or the Dalmatian islands, to the smaller stopping locations like Pantelleria or Antikythera.[12] Given the large number of islands, in the pre-modern era when sea travel was the most efficient form of mobility, these sea-girt landmasses facilitated connectivity, human-to-human networking, and the social benefits that could attend such exchanges of materials and ideas.[13] According to Broodbank, 'by virtue of their location in the midst of the sea, and the startling fact that they enjoy over a third of the total coastline, islands play a dramatically greater role in Mediterranean history than their size (in sum less than 5% of the basin's land area) would lead us to anticipate.'[14]

At the same time, the great variation in island size, their resources, and locations vis-à-vis trade routes and continental landmasses also affected the islanders' influence on historical developments.[15] Depending on their biogeographical value as well as their perceived socio-cultural roles (*e.g.* as sanctuaries, like Delos), Mediterranean islands can be situated on a connectivity spectrum that stretches from relative isolation from hegemonic political and economic systems on the one pole and nearly complete integration into such systems on the other.[16] However, as both Broodbank and Constantakopoulou suggest for most Mediterranean islands, 'the aggregate trend through time has certainly been towards integration'.[17] In Constantakopoulou's study of the cultural-political dynamics of the 5th-century BCE Aegean, the author refers to the insular phenomenon of 'interaction, integration, and connectivity' as the 'dance of the islands', a metaphorical image that evokes constant motion, recurrent rhythms, interpersonal contact, and the exchange of emotions and ideas.[18] From this perspective, ancient Mediterranean islands seem like the ideal places to study the effect of connectivity on cultural change.[19] But why is this issue so pressing in both an archaeological and sociological sense and what theoretical precepts can be brought to bear to understand how connectivity affects island life? These questions are central to the goals of this volume and will be addressed from a range of viewpoints in the chapters that follow.

Mediterranean Archaeologies of Insularity in an Age of Globalization explores how comparative archaeologies of insularity can contribute to dialogues on the social impact of ancient Mediterranean connectivity.[20] The volume is inspired by our current episteme, one in which we can no longer view Mediterranean history as the sum of a series of regional, quasi-evolutionary developments. Instead, we are inspired to view the history *of* the Mediterranean world as the result of a dynamic series of cross-cultural interconnections – driven by human actions *and* environmental forces – that cyclically pushed groups to interact with each other. This paradigmatic framework for analyzing Mediterranean antiquity is symptomatic of our present state of globalization.[21] Today, culture, politics, economics, and other social spheres are interconnected through technology at a level unprecedented in world history. People's decisions in one part of the world almost immediately impact individuals and groups in another. The shrinking of time and space on a global level initiates processes of socio-cultural change that produce both winners and losers. Globalization is a process that reveals the causes and effects of increased intercommunal connectivity, and how such changes affect people's lives.

As many chapters in this volume specifically suggest, enhanced connectivity affects people's notions of culture and identity across a multi-scalar playing field where multi-directional interactions can occur on the micro (*e.g.* local or insular level), intermediate (*e.g.* central-place, urban or emporium context), and macro levels (global or imperial).[22] Although 'culture' is a notoriously slippery term to define, Martin's historically-contingent and practice-oriented definition suggests that it involves:

> a dynamic structuring system in which individuals participate to a greater or lesser extent in 'shared beliefs, values, customs, behaviors, and artifacts,' which are used by, 'members of a society...to cope with their world and with one another and that are transmitted from generation to generation through learning.'[23]

It is within such cultural contexts, which are transformed by connectivity, that identities are formed through human and accompanying material interactions, the latter of which have serious implications for the interpretive power of archaeology. In terms of defining identity, Díaz-Andreu and Lucy define it as, 'individuals' identification with broader groups on the basis of differences socially sanctioned as significant'.[24] Yet they also suggest that identity is 'inextricably linked to the sense of belonging. Through identity we perceive ourselves, and others see us, as belonging to certain groups and not others'. Finally, they argue that 'identities are constructed through interaction between people and the process by which we acquire and maintain our identities requires choice and agency'.[25]

Globalization is an inherently connective and interactive process that prompts people to choose how their cultures are shaped and their identities – including, for islanders, one's sense of belonging to an island society – are defined. As such, contemporary globalization reveals trends and criteria that can also be witnessed in the past when levels of contact between people increased. In archaeological terms, changes in the material culture record often indicate punctuated moments when cultures and identities were reformulated in response to new types of connections. Thus, although the term 'globalization' may appear to only reflect today's hyperconnected world, more recently, some scholars have begun to detect symptoms of globalization in past societies, even if the scale was not specifically 'global' in the present sense.[26]

If globalization as a theoretical concept can be applied to past societies, the archaeological study of social change on Mediterranean islands through a globalizing lens seems particularly relevant. This is because the historical and archaeological evidence for terrestrial and especially maritime connectivity in the ancient Mediterranean detectable through shipwreck, ceramic, architectural, numismatic, and sculptural evidence, is abundant.[27] It reveals that islands were often involved in a 'dance' of connectivity facilitated by both the conduit of the Mediterranean itself and the people who actively plied its waters for political, economic, or even religious purposes. For Horden and Purcell, 'islands are places of strikingly enhanced exposure to interaction and are central to the history of the Mediterranean'; they are '"in the swim" of communications'.[28]

It is not surprising then that at several points in its history, the archaeological evidence for cultural integration, especially on islands, increases, illustrating that the Mediterranean underwent cyclic episodes of heightened connectivity that produced archaeological remains bearing the hallmarks of globalization processes. These processes can include glocalization, grobalization or other modes of social interaction across a spectrum from external acculturation to local resistance.[29] As Broodbank has argued, 'if island archaeology is to become as rigorous, challenging and creative as it should be, there is arguably a need to think harder about when and why specific approaches are properly predictable'.[30] In our current age, we feel that the application of globalization theory to the study of ancient Mediterranean island life seems particularly prescient, not only because it can shed new light on how islanders shaped their insular identities (or notions of 'insularity'), but also because novel insights into how increased connectivity can affect people's lives may help guide decision-making within our own globalized world.[31]

With these ideas in mind, this volume brings together archaeologists working on different Mediterranean islands and a range of material culture types to examine how insularities changed during eras when connectivity increased.[32] Each chapter situates a specific island within the context of the globalizing forces that conditioned its era and utilizes archaeological material to reveal how islanders shaped their notions of insularity at the liminal nexus of local and global influences. With the exception of Corsica, all of the 'big five' islands are represented, while archipelagos, such as the Balearic and Dalmatian, and smaller islands, like Delos and Kea, are also included, providing a range of island biogeographical features and encompassing the east-to-west breadth of the Mediterranean. In addition, the volume also covers a wide chronological range from the Middle Bronze Age to the Late Roman period to reveal how the value of long-term features that influence connectivity, such as an island's strategic location or resource base, can change over time as social conditions are altered.[33] Finally, the volume presents an Afterword that synthesizes its key themes and emphasizes how a globalization approach to studying the material culture of these unique sea-girt places can illuminate how scholars think about cultural change in the past and present.

Overall, the goal of this volume is not to provide a handbook about how to *do* island archaeology or about how insularities change in prescriptive and predictable ways. Instead, by diachronically examining a range of island types within a geographical context that witnessed fluctuating levels of unity and connectivity, this volume presents a pluralistic discourse that sheds light on how islanders adapt to cross-cultural integration, and how globalization processes have affected, and will continue to affect, people's lives.

Globalizing the Ancient Mediterranean

> Epiphanios became famous throughout Egypt, and the bishops sought to make him a bishop. And God guided Epiphanios ... And we returned to our own country and entered the monastery of the great Hilarion. But the great Hilarion had left the monastery because of the considerable annoyance which he suffered and sailed to Cyprus, to the places around Paphos ... And God guided Epiphanios to Cyprus.[34]
>
> *Vita of St Epiphanios*

Figure 2: Saint Epiphanios of Salamis (Österreichische Nationalbibliothek; public domain).

During the latter half of the 4th century CE, a young Christian monk from the Holy Land named Epiphanios sailed for the island of Cyprus in order to seek out the anchorite, Hilarion (Fig. 2). After meeting the sage, Epiphanios decided he should return to the Levantine ports of Ascalon and Gaza in order to spread Orthodoxy. When he asked Hilarion for advice about his travels, the monk told him that he would be safe by sea if he sailed for Salamis on Cyprus' east coast as opposed to Palestine. Epiphanios, however, decided to ignore Hilarion's advice and took the first boat to Ascalon. This ship was almost immediately ravaged by storms, and despite Epiphanios' best intentions, the waves and currents tossed him ashore at Salamis, exactly as Hilarion had requested. God, the Mediterranean, and the island of Cyprus seemed to be working in mysterious, interconnected, ways. When he arrived in Salamis, he encountered a council of Cypriot bishops convened to select a new bishop for the town. Miraculously, Epiphanios was recognized for his piety and made bishop.

From this island port town, Epiphanios would go on to become archbishop of Cyprus and a Church Father known far and wide for his efforts to root-out heresy. In fact, the bishop's fervor for Orthodoxy and holiness would take him from his Cypriot island home to most corners of the Late Roman maritime world. He was a friend of St Jerome, who called him the '*pentaglossos*' since he spoke Greek, Latin, Hebrew, Aramaic, and Coptic. He traveled to Rome to cure the sister of emperor Honorius, and sailed to Constantinople to treat the emperor Theodosius I. By the end of his life, to quote Claudia Rapp, the 'geographical scope of Epiphanios' efforts on behalf of Orthodoxy thus encompassed the entire Mediterranean'.[35]

This concise biography of Epiphanios presents the 21st-century reader with an image of a life that is, at first glance, exotic and far removed from our present experience. Epiphanios lived over 1600 hundred years ago as a religious sage who spent his time debating church doctrine and using miracles to cure the sick. Like the apostles before him, he is depicted iconographically as a stern bearded saint who travels extensively to rein in heresy, a project that was explicated in his extant treatise, *The Panarion*, which was read throughout Christendom. From a modern perspective, Epiphanios' hagiography reveals a quasi-mythical Mediterranean world where saints performed miracles that ultimately led to the ecumenical triumph of Orthodoxy.

From another perspective, however, Epiphanios' peripatetic and multicultural existence as an islander who sought to communicate with a much wider world also reflects the multicultural lives of a significant percentage of the world's population today. Take the travel writer, Pico Iyer (1957–present), for example. In his review of Iyer's *Autumn Light*, Philip Lopate describes Iyer's decision to take up residence on an island in the following terms:

> Born in England to Indian parents who later moved to Santa Barbara, California, he attended graduate school at Oxford and Harvard and then went to work for Time magazine. On a Tokyo stopover while returning from a trip to Hong Kong, he was enchanted to find 'a world suddenly intimate and human-scaled. ... By the time I boarded my plane in early afternoon, I'd decided to leave my comfortable-seeming job in New York City and move to Japan.'[36]

Here we are presented with the geographically dynamic biography of a person whose identity is composed of a mix of cultural influences. As a child of the postcolonial and technologically accelerated world of the late 20th century, he is raised by Eastern parents, educated in Western schools, and works for an influential current affairs magazine in New York, the heart of capitalism, only to abandon this existence to return to an island in the East. As a result, his worldview is a composite of his many experiences in England, America, and Japan, and he is now able to share his thoughts from his island home instantly through online articles, e-books, or YouTube Ted Talks.[37] Arguably, Iyer is a prime example of a 'global citizen'. His identity has been formed during a historical era where the twain of East and West have connected through the technology of jet engines and the internet. More importantly, Iyer is the product of a world where the primary process of social change has come to be known as globalization.

Thomas Friedman, in his seminal work on modern globalization, *The Lexus and the Olive Tree*, concisely defines globalization in the following manner:

> it is the inexorable integration of markets, nation-states and technologies to a degree never witnessed before – in a way that is enabling individuals, corporations, and nation-states to reach around the world farther, faster, deeper and cheaper than ever before, and in a way that is enabling the world to reach into individuals, corporations and nation-states farther, faster, deeper, cheaper than ever before.[38]

This is the globalization that most of us, including Pico Iyer, have come to recognize as simply a part of 21st-century life. A process whereby space and time have become compressed to the point where the entire planet seems integrated, especially in terms of near-instantaneous data and capital flows, intercontinental travel, and the internationalization of popular culture from McDonalds to *Star Wars*. One can now visit a Disney theme park in America, Europe, or Asia, and buy a Coca-Cola on every continent. Indeed, contemporary globalization leaves characteristic material remains that will mark our particular phase of the Anthropocene.[39] Modern globalization is also a process of change that goes 'farther, faster, and cheaper' than ever before, and that leaves no one untouched, whether they are an individual, a corporation, or a nation-state. Most people now sit at the end of a node, whether in an airport, or an iPhone, that is connected to a myriad of flight routes or online social networks.

Sometimes, this enhanced connectivity can have positive effects. To quote Kwame Anthony Appiah, we have 'come to a point where each of us can realistically imagine contacting any other of our six billion conspecifics and sending that person something worth having: a radio, an antibiotic, a good idea'.[40] Thus globalization can improve people's lives by making them healthier, wealthier, and perhaps even more democratic. On the other hand, Friedman cautions that there is no way to escape modern globalization; this 'inexorable integration' affects us all, and it has produced 'a powerful backlash from those brutalized or left behind by this new system'.[41] Indeed, people affected by proxy wars, wealth inequality, terrorism, refugee migration, the loss of local culture, and climate change are all suffering the stresses of postmodern worldwide integration, stresses that could lead to immense geopolitical unrest and an uncertain global future. As a result, the study of globalization and its toll on humanity is an urgent sociological problem that all academic disciplines should address, including archaeology.[42]

If we have all been affected by globalization in the 21st century, as Friedman suggests, how has this process influenced archaeological scholarship? Over the last 30 years, scholars of antiquity have explored archaeological topics from post-processual perspectives that are skeptical of positivist and predictable modes of cultural development and that recognize the role played by human agency within specific geohistorical contexts as crucial to understanding material remains. Such pluralistic approaches have arguably been spurred on by a theoretical paradigm shift influenced by the experiences of scholars living in an age of globalization.

This phenomenon has been effectively addressed in terms of ancient Mediterranean archaeology by Ian Morris beginning in the early 2000s, when he introduced a new explanatory model of how the ancient Mediterranean world functioned, following the publication of Horden and Purcell's *The Corrupting Sea* (2000).[43] In this kaleidoscopic work that attempted to provide an early history of the Mediterranean region following Fernand Braudel's pioneering example for the Renaissance (*The Mediterranean and the Mediterranean World in the Age of Philip II* [1972]), Horden and Purcell painted a picture of a dynamic maritime world seething with life where connectivity facilitated by human agency helped to support the development of microregions, from the Adriatic to the Sahel, which all faced similar levels of precarity.[44] This perspective offered a more integrated, unified, and global view of Mediterranean social change than previous perspectives that stressed isolated regional development and relative long-term stagnation.

Morris argued that this significant re-envisioning of Mediterranean life was possible because 'globalization has changed the way academics think' and that 'historians of the pre-modern Mediterranean are seeing in their sources the same kinds of phenomena that they experience in their daily lives'.[45] He also reasoned that a 'connectedness model' of ancient Mediterranean history is valuable because 'it reveals new dimensions of antiquity and gives antiquity new significance for understanding the world around us'.[46] Yet, Morris' support for this novel perspective also came with some caveats, namely that Mediterranean connectedness was a process that involved states as well as individuals, and that, like all processes of cross-cultural interaction, it could create socially positive or negative consequences. Like Friedman, Morris highlighted the fact that increased integration could produce 'powerful backlashes' (*e.g.* revolts, wealth inequality, or religious persecution) even as an empire like Rome could provide a level of political stability that served as a metaphorical 'rising tide that lifted all Mediterranean boats' for more than two centuries during the *Pax Romana*.

Since 2009, Morris' connectedness model has witnessed a rise in academic adherents as archaeologists have attempted to push the globalization analogy further by examining how the material evidence for mobility and increased connectivity reshaped ancient Mediterranean cultures.[47] Tamar Hodos in the *Routledge Companion to Archaeology and Globalization* has defined globalization as 'processes of increasing connectivities that unfold and manifest as social awareness of these connectivities'.[48] For the Roman period in particular, Pitts and Versluys state that globalization involves, 'processes by which localities and people become increasingly interconnected and interdependent'.[49] A more detailed set of criteria for identifying past globalization episodes has been outlined by Justin Jennings.[50] He suggests that globalization processes are occurring if all of the following phenomena are present: time-space compression, deterritorialization, standardization, unevenness, homogenization, cultural heterogeneity, and the re-embedding of local culture.

Based on these definitions, globalization seems to involve connecting regions and their peoples in interdependent ways that result in novel forms of social awareness that change is happening. A key word here is interdependent, since globalization includes the cultivation of a sense of belonging reified through the conscious connecting (or disconnecting) of an individual(s) or group(s) to a system or network often for some benefit to the individual(s)/group(s) within the context of local lived space. This observation does not necessarily rule out unconscious globalization through quotidian practices as well, but globalizing experiences often seem to be shaped by conscious, and often strategic, activities especially when bigger structural systems are involved, such as integrating empires or religious ideologies.[51]

If globalization entails active 'manifestations' of 'social awareness' of connectivity, and if we can posit that material culture not only reflects the residue of past interactions and people's *mentalités*, but also actively shapes them, then we can suggest that archaeological remains can shed light on past globalizations.[52] Indeed, a 'dramatic punctuation' of material finds dating to a particular era and type, and found within a specific context, might be a tell-tale sign that increased connectivity is occurring. We may not know exactly *who* is manipulating the objects, but we can often prove that a larger number, or a more diverse array, of objects are appearing in new places or are being manipulated in different, and historically original, ways.[53] For globalized archaeologies, materiality and mobility are key to revealing levels of connectivity.[54]

A globalization approach to archaeological materials, especially with regard to well-connected islands, is also valuable for its ability to incorporate the internal and external forces that characterize social encounters during globalized eras. As both Jennings and Hodos have argued, globalization is a process that – paradoxically – results in *both* social homogenization and heterogenization; phenomena that are often visible in the material remains from the same historical moment or even spatial context. Globalization is thus valuable for the analysis of historical scenarios, like the Hellenistic or Roman periods, where imperial integration is often seen as a top-down, acculturative process. A globalization approach, on the other hand, can accommodate and reveal the agency of both colonizer and colonized, as several of the papers in this volume argue.

Increased connectivity between social groups produces highly variable results. Globalization requires connectivity, but such connections can happen in myriad ways that produce many of the globalizing indicators highlighted by Jennings. As a result, the diversity of forms of globalized interaction also leaves room for many modes of social change, from acculturative processes, such as grobalization, to hybridizing processes, such as glocalization, or even outright attempts to resist or ignore connectivity and integration altogether, as a few of the case studies in this volume suggest. Archaeologies of globalization are thus concerned with active social interactions and recursive or disruptive practices, from simple cabotage between individuals to complex colonial encounters between islanders and empires.[55] Arguably, it is these events and processes that combine with the changing meaning of insular biogeographies to reshape island cultures and identities.

Given the archaeological evidence for increased connectivity to new and diverse commercial and cultural networks throughout Mediterranean history, we suggest that a globalization approach to the evidence provides a particularly pluralistic and flexible approach to understanding processes of cultural change. At the same time, we also appreciate that the application of globalization theory to antiquity has also been critiqued both because of its presentist inspiration (*e.g.* that the concept of 'global' did not exist until Magellan or the advent of capitalism) and because some regions (and even some Mediterranean islands) were sometimes able to escape increased levels of connectivity for long-periods of time.[56] We thus leave it up to the reader to decide which aspects of globalization theory seem most applicable to both island and terrestrial archaeology.

This point brings us back to St Epiphanios, an islander positioned at the crux of local and global forces, whose life was transformed by the 'farther, faster, deeper and cheaper' levels of connectivity that characterized the Early Christian Mediterranean.

Just as Pico Iyer identifies Japan as his home today, Epiphanios may have identified himself first and foremost as the Archbishop of Cyprus. However, as an islander and a Christian leader, who was born in the Holy Land and spoke five languages, Epiphanios was able to integrate himself into a range of maritime networks that compressed space and time and allowed the saint to connect with many other religious leaders far removed from his bishopric. He was a global citizen living in an interconnected Mediterranean world who was ideally suited to participate in shared globalizing cultural practices, precisely because *he was an islander*. It is unsurprising then that the archaeology of his adopted home of Cyprus reveals architectural remains of global influences from Constantinople and the Holy Land, as well as the continuity of local traditions in ceramics, mosaics, and sculptural display. People like Epiphanios, much like Pico Iyer today, were agents of connectivity between people and places. They were the ones who made or mobilized the objects that granted people a 'social awareness of these connectivities'. In this sense, ancient Mediterranean islanders, due to the similarity of their 'global' experiences, have a great deal to teach us about how increased levels of connectivity can both positively and negatively affect people's lives.

Globalized Archaeologies of Insularity: A Pluralist Perspective

> I have sailed the islands – first in the Adriatic, then in the Ionian and the Aegean – seeking out similarities and differences, comparing Sicily with Corsica, Majorca with Minorca. I have not put in at every port, however; I have spent most of my time at the mouths of rivers. Getting to know the length and breadth of the Mediterranean is no easy task.[57]
>
> Predrag Matvejević, *Mediterranean: A Cultural Landscape*

As the Croatian writer Predrag Matvejević poetically argued, the region's islands provide insights into the differences and similarities that can be evoked by the fragmented seascapes of the 'corrupting sea'. Although one often imagines the generic Mediterranean islandscape as typified by 'gentle breezes, lemon trees, golden oranges, myrtles, and laurels', the actual biogeography of the region's islands as well as the sea's currents and seasonal winds creates a maritime geography that is most often marked by difference.[58] In the island world of the Mediterranean, Sicily *is* quite different from Corsica in terms of its natural resources, its proximity to the European mainland, and its local *histoire événementielle*. Yet, at certain times in their history, these seemingly disparate islands have also shared similarities in political rule (*e.g.* the Roman empire), economic connections (to the Greeks), and religious beliefs (Christianity).[59]

Such cultural congruencies are particularly evident in the archaeological remains dating to historical periods when connectivity to the extra-insular world markedly increased, and islanders were united with people of distant coasts by material and physical bonds stretching across land and sea. During such eras, when long-distance traders arrived with new items for trade and unfamiliar languages could be heard on coastal breakwaters, islanders, and especially those living in port cities, likely felt a sense of belonging to a wider cultural world.[60] Indeed, negotiating similarity and difference is part of what it means to be an islander; it is a part of the 'island paradox' of being actively separated from wider cultural trends at some moments and more connected to them at others.[61]

The volume's first chapters focus on one of the earliest periods of increased connectivity in the Mediterranean, the Middle and Late Bronze Ages (c. 2000–1000 BCE).[62] In the eastern Mediterranean, the Minoans of Crete expanded their cultural influence throughout the southern Aegean, while Mycenaean aristocrats based at Pylos and Tiryns interacted with external traders, such as those who sailed on the famously cosmopolitan Ulu Burun ship.[63] In the West, incredible and idiosyncratic cultural developments were occurring in places like Sardinia, where the Nuragic civilization built massive stone towers and leveraged the island's mineralogical resources to link the island into Mediterranean-wide trade routes that stretched as far east as Cyprus.[64]

Within this dynamic context, Russell's article on Late Bronze Age Sardinia explores how such new levels of connectivity may have affected local social developments within the Tyrrhenian maritime zone. Interestingly, through an analysis of imports such as Late Helladic pottery and Cypriot oxhide ingots, he reveals that although Sardinians were clearly integrated into regional trade and knowledge networks, the local desire for external contacts and their material expressions seems to have been limited. Globalizing materials, such as Late Helladic pots, appear to have been used for strictly local purposes and, if emulation of any sort occurred, its effects were extremely limited or led to hybridizing glocalization at best. In the case of Sardinia, perhaps the island's relative distance from continental shores limited the strength of connectivity and allowed for a degree of local insular development.[65]

Gorogianni's article on the globalizing influences of Minoan culture on Middle and Late Bronze Age Kea offers an interpretation on how connectivity affected Bronze Age island life. In the Aegean scenario, it seems that paradoxical local and global pressures – pressures typical of islands like Kea in the 'swim of communications' between the Mycenaean and Minoan worlds – affected the nature of material culture.[66] Through an analysis of imported and local pottery as well as loomweights and spindle whorls, Gorogianni reveals an 'intense entanglement of the local, global, and regional' where low-level migration, most likely of women associated with textile production, was a key agent of social change. In short, when seen through a globalization lens, Kea cannot be seen as simply a Minoan colony. The island's location on a well-plied trading route and its connectivity to mainland, Cycladic, and Cretan influences transformed the site into a complex crucible of cross-cultural development.

Another major phase of Mediterranean connectivity occurred following the establishment of Greek colonies during the Late Iron Age.[67] By the 6th–4th centuries BCE, Greek city-states could be found in such regions as Olbia in the Crimea, Cyrene in Libya, and Massalia in France.[68] Greek pottery and religious symbolism were exported by mariners and colonizers throughout the Mediterranean, and these globalizing materials disrupted local cultural practices and power dynamics, especially on strategically-located islands.[69] It should be pointed out that the study of connectivity in this era has often been approached from the colonialist perspective of top-down Hellenization, which privileges the cultural meaning of Greek, versus locally-produced, materials.[70] However, a globalization approach that leaves room for negotiated cultural dialogues between a range of agents, expands our interpretive understanding of how Greek material culture traveled and was integrated into processes of cultural change unique to connected insular contexts.

Barnett and Ugarković's study of the archaeology of the Dalmatian islands offers a fascinating insight into the influence of Greek culture within the context of another of the Mediterranean's fragmented seas, the Adriatic. It also examines how an archipelago of islands located on a major sea route can result in different, localized responses to globalizing influences. Through the analysis of archaeological remains from the islands of Pharos, Issa, Korčula, and Brač, the authors show that each group of islanders selectively drew on Greek 'globalizing styles and cultural practices, adopting them according to local preferences in a way that incorporated both global and local sets in processes that were driven by contemporary geostrategic, cultural, economic and political contexts'.

Even as such connections between the Greek and Dalmatian worlds were at work in the Adriatic, the island of Sicily, the Mediterranean's largest insular landmass, was also experiencing a period of intra-insular social and political upheaval.[71] Lieberman's analysis of the numismatic imagery from Sicilian Naxos over the 5th and 4th centuries BCE illustrates the semiotic power of Greek religious iconography within the specific ethnic and cultural politics of a large and fragmented island. She shows that through the manipulation of numismatic images related to Dionysos and Apollo, Sicilians could transform symbols that originally represented the expansion of Greek culture by Naxians on the local level, to images that symbolized Greek Sicily on a 'global' level, especially in terms of the cult of Apollo Archegetes. Through her diachronic analysis of cultural change in eastern Sicily, Lieberman exposes the tension between local vs. global cultural forces and polis vs. island-wide identities on an agriculturally fertile island located at the nexus of eastern and western trading networks.

The latter half of the 1st millennium BCE was also a period of social development in the Balearic Islands, and especially on the island of Menorca.[72] During Late Talayotic times, this far western, sub-continental island group was externally influenced by both the Carthaginians and the Roman Republic. Based on the evidence from domestic architecture, Smith suggests that local Menorcan elites responded to outside contacts by actively engaging their indigeneity. Thus, although globalizing forces were regionally present, especially in nearby Ibiza and on the mainland, the imperial agendas of Carthage and Rome may have deemed the island unworthy of economic integration – at least until after the Third Punic War – due to its lack of natural resources and its distance from the Iberian coast. This geohistorical situation permitted a socio-political phenomenon that allowed for local insular expressions of identity even in the face of regional globalizing pressures. The Menorcan situation reveals that it is easy for islanders to practice indigeneity if their island lacks the biogeographical lures that attract participants into global networks.

Based on the archaeological evidence for amphorae, epigraphy, and artistic styles, the island world of the Hellenistic *oikoumene* in the eastern Mediterranean was clearly a locus of intense maritime connectivity.[73] Although, borders were constantly being drawn and redrawn between the warring kingdoms of the *diadochoi*, in cultural terms, a globalizing religious and aesthetic worldview was established that facilitated cross-cultural interaction and mobility of materials, especially within the maritime world.[74]

Mazurek's study of Isiac statuary returns us to the 'dance' of the Aegean island world. It is particularly instructive in terms of understanding how enhanced maritime connectivity can collapse space and time and lead to globalized cultural processes. Her seascape analysis of the transmission of sculptural types for Isis from Rhodes to Delos to the mainland port of Amphipolis reveals how sea travel allowed the Amphipolitans 'to identify themselves as part of a trans-oceanic network rather than (perhaps in addition to) a Macedonian one'. This study provides strong evidence for the influence of enhanced connectivity on local cultural practices and the roles that islands play as connecting sinews in networks that stretch from continents even to the middle of maritime environments, like Delos, situated as it is, in the middle of the Cyclades.[75]

The last, and perhaps most unified, phases of ancient Mediterranean history are those of the Roman and Late Roman periods. According to Ian Morris, during the latter half of the 1st millennium BCE, 'Rome overcame all rivals uniting the [Mediterranean] basin politically in the 2nd and 1st centuries BCE. By 200 CE Rome provided a security system that affected economics, society, and culture in the Mediterranean, the Near East, and temperate Europe.'[76] This vision of a united and dynamic *Mare Nostrum* thriving under the *Pax Romana* is supported by the maritime archaeological evidence, which shows that the high-point for dated shipwrecks is from the 1st century BCE through the 1st century CE.[77] During Early Roman times, the Mediterranean's port cities from Taracco to Rome to Ephesus to Caesarea Maritima to Alexandria were thriving metropoleis thronged with traders from distant ports trading garum, wine, olive oil, or marble statues.[78] Maritime connectivity, and the islands where sailors stopped on their journeys, played a key role in disseminating elements of an elite Roman imperial culture that could be shared yet modified in many of the Mediterranean's fragmented regions. Although the dominant paradigm for understanding the spread of a Roman *koine* culture has been the theory of Romanization, scholars like Hingley, Kousser, and Versluys have recently argued that cultural unity could be created from diversity through the local manipulation of Roman material culture's symbolic value in context.[79] A globalization approach that examines how connectivity caused people to interact and adopt, reject, or hybridize materials such as statues, mosaics, or coins helps to transcend simplistic acculturative models of cultural change and to shed light on the true complexity of identity negotiation during the High Empire.

After the Third Century Crisis, the greater Mediterranean remained somewhat connected through the globalizing power of Christianity, a new religion that unified practitioners, like St Epiphanios, from Spain to the Holy Land.[80] Yet, following Constantine's shift of the imperial capital to Constantinople and the establishment of new religious pilgrimage routes that led to the Holy Land, pre-Byzantine maritime trading patterns were altered and the eastern Mediterranean in particular entered an era of increased economic prosperity that supported a 'busy Roman countryside'.[81] It is true that the idea of a 'global' Christian world likely existed, but in reality, the ceramic and shipwreck evidence suggests that different globalizing processes may have begun to emerge in the eastern and western sectors of the Mediterranean basin.[82] Islanders still played a key role in this Late Roman maritime world, however, with the advent of Arab raiders into the Mediterranean by the mid-7th century, their position would shift from that of locations in the 'swim of communications' to that of an insular system of border states that functioned as 'middle ground' between Arab, Byzantine, and European networks.[83]

The volume's final two chapters are set within this hyper-connected maritime world of the Early and Late Roman eastern Mediterranean. Francis' study of Crete within the early Roman empire examines a range of archaeological materials from ceramics to architecture to statuary to explore how becoming Roman on Crete was a gradual and contextually dependent process.[84] Although globalizing forces eventually led to the construction of impressive villas and baths by local elites in well-connected port cities by the 1st and 2nd centuries CE, this process was not rapid and took several generations following the Roman conquest. Moreover, the island's large size created regional modes of 'becoming Roman' as rural areas or sites that were less connected to major ports preserved Hellenistic burial customs or traditional modes of architectural construction.[85] Greek, as opposed to Latin, also remained the dominant language throughout the island for the entire Early Roman period, and although the island was part of a single province together with Cyrenaica, there seems to have been scanty cultural contact between the regions, likely due to the open sea. For Francis, Crete, as an island connected to Roman trade routes but still marked by long-standing cultural traditions and a diverse topography, was both globalized *and* insular depending on social and spatial context.

Gordon and Caraher's paper diachronically and comparatively examines the influence of connectivity on the Mediterranean's third largest island, Cyprus, during the Early and Late Roman periods. For Gordon, Early Roman Cyprus seems to have been affected by heightened connectivity in similar ways to Crete. Following the Roman takeover in 30 BCE, some elements of imperial culture, such as bronze coins, proclaimed the empire's influence over the island, but few other artifacts illustrate a rapid transition to Roman cultural norms. When this transition did begin to occur during the reigns of Tiberius and Claudius, the process was still gradual. The creation of hybrid coin types that mixed Greek legends and images of local religious sites with the emperor's image, the construction of podium temples at ancient sanctuaries, and the possible development of locally-produced red-slipped ceramic shapes known as Cypriot sigillata, are all indicators of the gradual adoption of some common materials found throughout the Roman world. Clearer signs of globalization are present in Cyprus' connected port cities by the 2nd century CE when mosaic and marble-clad villas were constructed by local elites. On the other hand, Cyprus' interior sites that were less connected to maritime networks exhibit forms of material culture more attuned with long-term Cypriot practices. Due to Cyprus' large size and its location on key east–west shipping routes between Rome and Alexandria, Cypriots living under Roman rule, like Cretans, experienced different levels of connectivity depending on the islandscape they inhabited. As a result, these islanders were exposed to different levels of globalizing influences, which affected how they constructed their notions of insularity. In Late Antiquity, Cyprus' long-term architectural traditions and its autocephalous church created what Caraher refers to as 'distinct places' that were linked to global cultural practices, but also influenced by intra-insular trends. As has been their fate throughout history, Cypriots living in Late Roman times remained connected to external influences from the Near East, Anatolia, and the Hellenic world, a connectivity that seems even more striking when contrasted with the island's more disconnected role as a boundary zone during the Early Middle Ages.[86]

Kardulias' Afterword brings together several of the volume's main themes and highlights how heightened levels of connectivity throughout antiquity have often created unifying cultural similarities on many of the Mediterranean's biogeographically diverse islands. In terms of insularity, he emphasizes the 'island paradox' whereby islanders can be connected or disconnected from wider social and cultural influences depending on island location, size, and resources. He also views globalization as a process which leads to economic and cultural homogenization but can also be used as a theoretical lens for studying the past when connectivity, especially between islanders and external groups, resulted in altered cultural contexts and new conceptions of insularity. For Kardulias, globalization provides a framework to examine 'the general features that tied together various groups through trade, exchange of styles, and other practices that highlight commonalities, while at the same time pointing out the variation and idiosyncratic nature of the individual cultures and sites involved in complex networks'. He points out that globalization, although particularly felt on connected islands, can be explored in an 'expansive' way that looks at an array of connections stretching from insular hinterlands to coasts to other islands or continents. He also underlines the increasing homogeneity of culture and Mediterranean unity archaeologically witnessed in later historical periods when kingdoms and empires, such as those of the *diadochoi*, Rome, or Byzantium entered the Mediterranean arena. Through the application of globalization theory to Mediterranean island archaeology, Kardulias recognizes archaeology's social power to help us better understand how connectivity can affect human existence.

As the case studies presented in this volume suggest, ancient connectivity, like that of today, had the potential to irrevocably transform people's lives in positive and negative ways. Moreover, because of the integration of islands into ancient sea routes, islanders who inhabited liminal coastscapes were often inordinately affected by cross-cultural interactions. Take for example, St Paul, arguably Early Christianity's greatest *islomane*.[87] As described in *Acts*, he began his mission on Cyprus, but also visited Samothrace, Lesbos, Samos, Kos, Rhodes, Crete, Sicily, and Malta. As someone who had frequently lived on islands, he understood the paradoxical nature of being connected to others even when separated by the ambivalent boundary of the sea. As a Roman citizen, writing in Greek during the 1st century CE, he also likely felt the tension of being part of a larger global state, a regional Christian community, as well as a person from Tarsus in Anatolia. Thus, in his first letter to the Corinthians, when he said, 'For now we see through a glass, darkly' he was speaking as a globalized islander; as someone who knew that the world we see reflected today is an imperfect reflection of what the future might hold, especially if one lives on an island in an interconnected sea like the Mediterranean.[88]

Although the diachronic *periplous* offered here may only permit us to compare the past to the present as 'through a glass, darkly', we posit that archaeological explorations of ancient globalization, especially in interconnected places like islands, have the potential to make us think deeply about the pros and cons of connectivity.[89] Archaeology, then, seems like it has an informative and predictive role to play in helping modern populations negotiate the positive effects and negative 'backlashes' that increased connectivity may impose on people, both now and in the future. We anticipate that the studies in this volume will contribute to this vital discourse.

Notes

1 For the fragmentation of the Mediterranean, see Braudel 1972, 108; Horden and Purcell 2000, 77–79; Rainbird 2007, 79. For the sea's role as a connective sinew between regions, see Horden and Purcell 2000, 133; Arnaud and de Souza 2006; Schäfer 2016; Manning 2018.
2 Or even as early as the Paleolithic; see Strasser *et al.* 2010; Dawson 2013; Knapp 2013, 46–47.
3 Leidwanger and Knappett 2018, 3.
4 For the edges of the Mediterranean world, see Broodbank 2013, 56.
5 Watkins and Ryerson 2014, 1–2.
6 Constantakopoulou 2007, 135; Broodbank 2016.
7 Manning 2018; Hanink 2019, 19–21.
8 Braudel 1972, 23–24; Broodbank 2013, 19–20.
9 Braudel 1972, 103–104; Leidwanger and Knappett 2018, 1–2.
10 Horden and Purcell 2000, 126.
11 For a concise discussion of the study of island archaeology in the Mediterranean, see Cherry *et al.* 1991, 9–10.
12 For the term 'matchbox continent', see Held 1989.
13 For the role of islands in ancient Mediterranean Sea routes, see Arnaud 2005. Network theory has often been effectively applied to the study of heightened connectivity and cultural change in the ancient Mediterranean. For a review of such approaches, see Malkin *et al.* 2007; Malkin *et al.* 2009; Knappett 2011; Malkin 2011; Alberti and Sabatini 2013; Knappett 2013; Tartaron 2013; Knappett 2017; Broodbank 2018; Leidwanger and Knappett 2018.
14 Broodbank, 2013, 78.

15 In the case of Cyprus, for example, see Counts and Iacovou 2013.
16 Renfrew and Wagstaff 1982, 2; Broodbank 2000, 19; Bevan and Connelly 2013, 5.
17 Broodbank 2000, 10; Constantakopoulou 2007, 2.
18 Constantakopoulou 2007, 2.
19 For other recent volumes focused on comparative island archaeologies in the Mediterranean, see Broodbank 2000; Constantakopoulou 2005; van Dommelen and Knapp 2010; Cadogen *et al.* 2012; Michaelides 2013; Kouremenos 2018a; Zavagno *et al.* 2019; Cau Ontiveros and Mas Florit 2019.
20 For a brief discussion of how to approach comparative island archaeologies, see also Campbell and Conolly 2008.
21 See Morris 2005.
22 Harris 2005, 3–20.
23 Bates and Plog 1990, 7; Martin 2017, 16.
24 Díaz-Andreu and Lucy 2005, 1.
25 Díaz-Andreu and Lucy 2005, 1–2. See also Watkins and Ryerson 2014, 5.
26 See in particular the chapters in Hodos 2017a.
27 Rainbird 2007; Broodbank 2013, 26–36.
28 Horden and Purcell 2000, 76.
29 Hodos 2017b.
30 Broodbank 2000, 7.
31 For a concise definition of insularity as a social identity and its relationship to time and space, see Knapp 2008, 18, 22–24.
32 *cf.* Abulafia's (2011, xvii) division of Mediterranean history into five distinct periods marked by when the sea was 'by varying degrees integrated into a single commercial, cultural, and even (under the Romans) political zone'. This volume covers what equates to the final phase of his 'First Mediterranean' (22,000–1000 BCE) as well as most of his 'Second Mediterranean' (1000 BCE–600 CE).
33 For a discussion of the value of integrating a long-term geographical approach to an interactionist connective one, see Horden and Purcell 2000, 36–43. See also Knapp and van Dommelen 2010, 13 for the value of a diachronic and geographically pluralist approach to studying connectivity, materiality, and cultural change in the Mediterranean.
34 *Vita of St Epiphanios* 30 (344A–B); 32; Pohlsander 1999, 16.
35 Rapp 2015, 32. For more on St Epiphanios' biography, see Kim 2015.
36 Lopate 2019.
37 Iyer 2013.
38 Friedman 1999, 9.
39 Pitts and Versluys 2015, 14.
40 Appiah 2006, xii–xiii.
41 Friedman 1999, 9.
42 For an archaeological discussion of the human death toll caused by mass refugee migration see De Léon 2015 and the articles in Hamilakis 2017. For an archaeological analysis of how oil production has altered the human landscapes of the northern United States, Caraher 2016.
43 Morris 2005.
44 Horden and Purcell 2000, 9–49. See also Harris 2005.
45 Morris 2005, 40. For two of the more thoughtful sociological approaches to current issues in globalization theory, see Appadurai 1996 and Pieterse 2004.
46 Morris 2005, 51.
47 The following is a selection of works that have recently applied globalization theory to archaeological data in the Mediterranean and Near East: Hingley 2005; LaBianca and Scham 2006; Sweetman 2007; Hitchner 2008; Hodos 2010; Jennings 2011; Boozer 2012; Pitts and Versluys 2015; Hodos 2017a.

48 Hodos 2017b. For the stress on connectivity as a force of social change in the past and present, see LaBianca and Scham 2006.
49 Pitts and Versulys 2015, 11.
50 Jennings 2017, 14–15.
51 Stein 2005, 26–27.
52 Binliff 1991, 10–13.
53 For more on the complex ways that objects were transported and circulated in the ancient Mediterranean, see Fulton 2017.
54 For the importance of materiality and mobility to archaeologies of connectivity and globalization, see van Dommelen and Knapp 2010; Concannon and Mazurek 2016; Kiriatzi and Knappett 2016; Leidwanger and Knappett 2018. For a deeper discussion of the 'unstable terrain of interrelationships between sociality, temporality, spatiality, and materiality' and 'our material lifeworld and its recursive shaping of our human experience', see Meskell 2005, 2.
55 For cabotage, see Mazurek 2016, 42–43. For the archaeology of colonial encounters, see van Dommelen 1998; Gosden 2004; Stein 2005; Dietler 2010.
56 For general critiques of the application of globalization theory to the past and archaeological research in the Mediterranean, see Counts 2008, 3–4; Pitts and Versluys 2015, 8–10; Robertson 2017, 54–64.
57 Matvejević 1999, 7.
58 For an English translation of Goethe's song 'Kennst du das Land?' from *Wilhelm Meisters Lehrjahr*, see Goethe 2020, 18 January.
59 For a brief introduction to Roman Corsica, see Mary 2018; for a study of Roman Sicily, see Wilson 1990.
60 Reger 2016, 17.
61 Knapp 2008, 19–22.
62 Broodbank 2013, 373–383.
63 Broodbank 2013, 399–402; Tartaron 2013, 26.
64 van Dommelen 1998; Dyson and Rowland 2007.
65 For a related analysis of Bronze Age Sicily, see Russell 2017.
66 Gorogianni *et al.* 2016.
67 Malkin 2011; Lucas *et al.* 2019.
68 Dietler 1998.
69 Walsh 2014.
70 Dietler 2010, 46; Chrubasik and King 2017.
71 Hodos 2010; De Angelis 2016.
72 See also Santacreu 2017.
73 Gibbins 2001; Constantakopoulou 2017, 9.
74 Eiring and Lund 2005; Fenn and Römer-Strahl 2013; Chaniotis 2018.
75 Constantakopoulou 2017.
76 Morris 2005, 44.
77 Wilson 2011.
78 Gordon 2018.
79 Hingley 2005; Kousser 2008, 81–110; Versluys 2015, 152–67.
80 Dark 2007.
81 Rautman 2000; Pettegrew 2007.
82 Leidwanger 2017.
83 Michaelides *et al.* 2013; Zavagno 2017; 2018.
84 A conclusion that is also echoed in Gallimore 2019. For further recent research on Roman Crete, see Francis and Kouremenos 2016; Kouremenos 2018b.

85 For the concept of 'becoming Roman', see Woolf 1998.
86 Zavagno 2017.
87 Lawrence Durrell (1953, 15–16), himself a frequent Mediterranean islander, defined 'islomanes' as people 'who find islands somehow irresistible. The mere knowledge that they are on an island, a little world surrounded by the sea, fills them with an indescribable intoxication'.
88 I Corinthians 13:12, King James Version. The full passage is: 'For now we see through a glass, darkly; but then face to face: now I know in part; but then shall I know even as also I am known.'
89 See also LaBianca and Scham 2006, 5; Broodbank 2013, 44–53.

Bibliography

Abulafia, D. (2011) *The Great Sea: A Human History of the Mediterranean.* London: Allen Lane.
Alberti, M.E. and Sabatini, S. (eds) (2013) *Exchange Networks and Local Transformations: Interaction and Local Change in Europe and the Mediterranean from the Bronze Age to the Iron Age.* Oxford: Oxbow Books.
Appadurai, A. (1996) *Modernity at Large. Cultural Dimensions of Globalisation.* Minneapolis: University of Minnesota Press.
Appiah, K.A. (2006) *Cosmopolitanism: Ethics in a World of Strangers.* 1st edn. New York: W.W. Norton.
Arnaud, P. (2005) *Les routes de la navigation antique: Itinéraires en Méditerranée.* Paris: Éditions Errance.
Arnaud, P. and de Souza, P. (eds) (2016) *The Sea in History Volume 1: The Ancient World.* Woodbridge: The Boydell Press.
Bates, D.G. and Plog, F. (1990) *Cultural Anthropology.* New York: McGraw-Hill.
Bevan, A. and Conolly, J. (2013) *Mediterranean Islands, Fragile Communities and Persistent Landscapes.* Cambridge: Cambridge University Press.
Bintliff, J.L. (1991) *The Annales School and Archaeology.* Leicester: Leicester University Press.
Boozer, A. (2012) Globalizing Mediterranean Identities: The Overlapping Spheres of Greek, Egyptian and Roman Worlds at Tremithus. *Journal of Mediterranean Archaeology* 25(2), 219–242.
Braudel, F. (1972) *The Mediterranean and the Mediterranean World in the Age of Philip II.* Translated by S. Reynolds. 1st edn. New York: Harper & Row.
Broodbank, C. (2000) *An Island Archaeology of the Early Cyclades.* Cambridge: Cambridge University Press.
Broodbank, C. (2013) *The Making of the Middle Sea: A History of the Mediterranean from the Beginning to the Emergence of the Classical World.* Oxford: Oxford University Press.
Broodbank, C. (2016) The Transmitting Sea: A Mediterranean Perspective. In *Human Mobility and Technological Transfer in the Prehistoric Mediterranean*, edited by E. Kiriatzi and C. Knappett. Cambridge: Cambridge University Press, 18–30.
Broodbank, C. (2018) Does Island Archaeology Matter? In *Regional Approaches to Social Complexity: Studies in Honour of John F. Cherry*, edited by A. Knodell and T. Leppard. Sheffield: Equinox, 188–206.
Cadogen, G., Iacovou, M., Kopaka, K. and Whitley, J. (2012) *Parallel Lives: Ancient Island Societies in Crete and Cyprus: Papers Arising from the Conference in Nicosia Organized by the British School at Athens, the University of Crete and the University of Cyprus, in November-December 2006.* British School at Athens Studies 20. London: The British School at Athens.
Campbell, M. and Conolly, J. (2008) Preface: Comparative Island Archaeologies. In *Comparative Island Archaeologies*, edited by J. Conolly and M. Campbell, iii–v. BAR International Series 1829. Oxford: Archaeopress.
Caraher, W.R. (2016) The Archaeology of Man Camps: Contingency, Periphery, and Late Capitalism. In *The Bakken Goes Boom: Oil and the Changing Geographies of Western North Dakota*, edited by W.R. Caraher and K. Conway. Grand Forks: Digital Press at the University of North Dakota, 181–198.
Cau Ontiveros, M.Á. and Mas Florit, C. (eds) (2019) *Change and Resilience: The Occupation of Mediterranean Islands in Late Antiquity.* Joukowsky Institute Publication 9. Oxford: Oxbow Books.

Chaniotis, A. (2018) *Age of Conquests: The Greek World from Alexander to Hadrian.* Cambridge, MA: Harvard University Press.

Cherry, J.F., Davis, J.L. and Mantzourani, E. (1991) *Landscape Archaeology as Long-Term History: Northern Keos in the Cycladic Islands from Earliest Settlement until Modern Times.* Monumenta Archaeologica 16. Los Angeles: UCLA Institute of Archaeology.

Chrubasik, B and King, D. (eds) (2017) *Hellenism and the Local Communities of the Eastern Mediterranean: 400 BCE–250 CE.* Oxford: Oxford University Press.

Concannon, C.W. and Mazurek, L.A. (eds) (2016) *Across the Corrupting Sea: Post-Braudelian Approaches to the Ancient Eastern Mediterranean.* London: Routledge.

Constantakopoulou, C. (2005) Proud to Be an Islander: Island Identity in Multi-Polis Islands in the Classical and Hellenistic Aegean. *Mediterranean Historical Review* 20(1), 1–34.

Constantakopoulou, C. (2007) *The Dance of the Islands: Insularity, Networks, the Athenian Empire and the Aegean World.* Oxford: Oxford University Press.

Constantakopoulou, C. (2017) *Aegean Interactions: Delos and its Networks in the Third Century.* Oxford: Oxford University Press.

Counts, D.B. (2008) Master of the Lion: Representation and Hybridity in Cypriote Sanctuaries. *American Journal of Archaeology* 112(1), 3–27.

Counts, D.B. and M. Iacovou (2013) New Approaches to the Elusive Iron Age Kingdoms of Cyprus: An Introduction. *Bulletin of the American Schools of Oriental Research* 370, 1–13.

Dark, K. (2006) Globalizing Late Antiquity: Models, Metaphors and the Realities of Long-Distance Trade and Diplomacy. *Reading Medieval Studies*, XXXII, 3–14.

Dawson, H. (2013) *Mediterranean Voyages: The Archaeology of Island Colonisation and Abandonment.* Walnut Creek, Left Coast Press.

De Angelis, F. (2016) *Archaic and Classical Greek Sicily: A Social and Economic History.* New York: Oxford University Press.

De León, J. (2015) *The Land of Open Graves: Living and Dying on the Migrant Trail.* Oakland, California: University of California Press.

Díaz-Andreu, M., and Lucy, S. (2005) Introduction. In *Archaeology of Identity: Approaches to Gender, Age, Status. Ethnicity and Religion*, edited by M. Díaz-Andreu, S. Lucy, S. Babic and D.N. Edwards. London: Routledge, 1–12.

Dietler, M. (1998) Consumption, Agency, and Cultural Entanglement: Theoretical Implications of a Mediterranean Colonial Encounter. In *Studies in Culture Contact: Interaction, Culture Change, and Archaeology*, edited by J. Cusick. Center for Archaeological Investigations Occasional Paper 25. Carbondale: Southern Illinois University.

Dietler, M. (2010) *Archaeologies of Colonialism: Consumption, Entanglement, and Violence in Ancient Mediterranean France.* Berkeley: University of California Press.

Durrell, L. (1953) *Reflections on a Marine Venus: A Companion to the Landscape of Rhodes.* London: Faber and Faber.

Dyson, S.L. and Rowland, R.J. (2007) *Archaeology and History in Sardinia from the Stone Age to the Middle Ages: Shepherds, Sailors, and Conquerors.* Philadelphia: University of Pennsylvania Museum of Archaeology and Anthropology.

Eiring, J. and Lund, J. (eds) (2004) *Transport Amphorae and Trade in the Eastern Mediterranean. Acts of the International Colloquium at the Danish Institute at Athens, September 26–29, 2002.* Monographs of the Danish Institute at Athens, 5. Athens: The Danish Institute at Athens.

Fenn, N. and Römer-Strehl, C. (eds) (2013) *Networks in the Hellenistic World. According to the Pottery in the Eastern Mediterranean and Beyond.* BAR International Series, S2539. Oxford: Archaeopress.

Francis, J.E. and Kouremenos, A. (2016) *Roman Crete: New Perspectives.* Oxford: Oxbow Books.

Friedman, T. (1999) *The Lexus and the Olive Tree. Understanding Globalization.* New York: Farrar, Straus and Giroux.

Fulton, C. (2017) Agents of Appropriation. In *Rome, Empire of Plunder: The Dynamics of Cultural Appropriation,* edited by M. Loar, C. MacDonald and D. Padilla Peralta. Cambridge: Cambridge University Press, 194–213.

Gallimore, S. (2019) An Island in Crisis? Reconsidering the Formation of Roman Crete. *American Journal of Archaeology* 123(4), 589–617.

Gibbins, D. (2001) Shipwrecks and Hellenistic Trade. In *Hellenistic Economies*, edited by Z. Archibald, J. Davies, V. Gabrielsen and G.J. Oliver. London: Routledge, 205–232.

Goethe, J.W. von. (2020) 18 January. Mignon's Song ['Do you know the land?']. Translated by R. Wigmore. *Oxford Lieder.* https://www.oxfordlieder.co.uk/song/907.

Gordon, J.M. (2018) Transforming Culture on an Insula Portunalis: Port Cities as Central Places in Early Roman Cyprus. In *Central Places and Un-Central Landscapes: Political Economies and Natural Resources in the Longue Durée,* edited by G. Papantoniou and A.K. Vionis. *Land* 7(4) https://doi.org/10.3390/land7040155.

Gorogianni, E., Pavúk, P. and Girella, L. (2016) *Beyond Thalassocracies: Understanding Processes of Minoanisation and Mycenaeanisation in the Aegean.* Oxford: Oxbow Books.

Gosden, C. (2004) *Archaeology and Colonialism: Cultural Contact from 5000 BC to the Present.* Topics in Contemporary Archaeology. Cambridge: Cambridge University Press.

Hamilakis, Y. (2017) Archaeologies of Forced and Undocumented Migration. *Journal of Contemporary Archaeology* 3(2), 121–139.

Hanink. J. (trans.) (2019) *How to Think about War: An Ancient Guide to Foreign Policy: Speeches from the History of the Peloponnesian War.* Princeton, New Jersey: Princeton University Press.

Harris, W.V. (2005) The Mediterranean and Ancient History. In *Rethinking the Mediterranean*, edited by W.V. Harris. Oxford: Oxford University Press, 1–44.

Held, S. (1989) Colonization Cycles on Cyprus 1: The Biogeographic and Paleontological Foundations of Early Prehistoric Settlement. *Report of the Department of Antiquities, Cyprus*, 7–28.

Hingley, R. (2005) *Globalizing Roman Culture: Unity, Diversity and Empire.* London: Routledge.

Hitchner, B. (2008) 27 June. Globalization Avant la Lettre: Globalization and the History of the Roman Empire. *New Global Studies* 2(2): http://www.degruyter.com/view/j/ngs.2008.2.2/ngs.2008.2.2.1034/ngs.2008.2.2.1034.xml?format=INT.

Hodos, T. (2010) Globalization and Colonization: A View from Iron Age Sicily. *Journal of Mediterranean Archaeology* 23(1), 81–106.

Hodos, T. (ed.) (2017a) *The Routledge Handbook of Archaeology and Globalization.* London: Routledge.

Hodos, T. (2017b) Globalization: Some Basics. An Introduction to *The Routledge Handbook of Archaeology and Globalization.* In *The Routledge Handbook of Archaeology and Globalization*, edited by T. Hodos. London: Routledge, 3–11.

Horden, P. and Purcell, N. (2000) *The Corrupting Sea: A Study of Mediterranean History.* Malden, MA: Blackwell Publishing.

Iyer, P. (2013) Where is Home? Filmed in June 2013 in Edinburgh, Scotland. TED video 13:49. https://www.ted.com/talks/pico_iyer_where_is_home?language=en.

Jennings, J. (2011) *Globalizations and the Ancient World.* Cambridge: Cambridge University Press.

Jennings, J. (2017) Distinguishing past globalizations. In *The Routledge Handbook of Archaeology and Globalization*, edited by T. Hodos. London: Routledge, 12–28.

Kiriatzi, E. and Knappett, C. (eds) (2016) *Human Mobility and Technological Transfer in the Prehistoric Mediterranean.* Cambridge: Cambridge University Press.

Kim, Y.R. (2015) *Epiphanius of Cyprus: Imagining an Orthodox World.* Ann Arbor: University of Michigan Press.

Knapp, A.B. (2008) *Prehistoric and Protohistoric Cyprus: Identity, Insularity, and Connectivity.* Oxford: Oxford University Press.

Knapp, A.B. (2013) *The Archaeology of Cyprus: From Earliest Prehistory through the Bronze Age.* Cambridge: Cambridge University Press.

Knapp, A.B. and van Dommelen, P. (2010) Material Connections: Mobility, materiality, and Mediterranean identities. In *Material Connections in the Ancient Mediterranean: Mobility, Materiality and Mediterranean Identities*, edited by P. van Dommelen and A.B. Knapp. London: Routledge, 1–18.

Knappett, C. (2011) *An Archaeology of Interaction: Network Perspectives on Material Culture and Society.* Oxford: Oxford University Press.

Knappett, C. (ed.) (2013) *Network Analysis in Archaeology: New Approaches to Regional Interaction.* Oxford: Oxford University Press.

Knappett, C. (2017) Globalization, Connectivities and Networks: An Archaeological Perspective. In *The Routledge Handbook of Archaeology and Globalization*, edited by T. Hodos. London: Routledge, 29–41.

Kousser, R.M. (2008) *Hellenistic and Roman Ideal Sculpture: The Allure of the Classical.* Cambridge: Cambridge University Press.

Kouremenos, A. (ed.) (2018a) *Insularity and Identity in the Roman Mediterranean.* Oxford: Oxbow Books.

Kouremenos, A. (2018b) In the Heart of the Wine-Dark Sea: Cretan Insularity and Identity in the Roman Period. In *Insularity and Identity in the Roman Mediterranean*, edited by A. Kouremenos. Oxford: Oxbow Books, 41–64.

LaBianca, Ø. and Scham, S. (eds) (2006) *Connectivity in Antiquity: Globalization as a Long-term Historical Process.* London: Equinox.

Leidwanger, J. and Knappett, C. (eds) (2018) *Maritime Networks in the Ancient Mediterranean World.* Cambridge: Cambridge University Press.

Lopate, P. (2019) Pico Iyer Reflects on a Quarter-Century of Life in Japan. Review of *Autumn Light: Season of Fire and Farewells,* by Pico Iyer. *New York Times,* April 22, 2019. Accessed January 18, 2020. (https://www.nytimes.com/2019/04/22/books/review/picoiyer-autumn-light-memoir-japan.html).

Lucas, J., Murray, C.A. and Owen, S. (eds) (2019) *Greek Colonization in Local Contexts: Case Studies in Colonial Interactions.* Oxford: Oxbow Books.

Malkin, I. (2011) *A Small Greek World: Networks in the Ancient Mediterranean.* Greeks Overseas. Oxford: Oxford University Press.

Malkin, I., Constantakopoulou, C. and Panagopoulou, K. (2007) Preface: Networks in the Ancient Mediterranean. *Mediterranean Historical Review* 22(1), 1–9.

Malkin, I., Constantakopoulou, C. and Panagopoulou, K. (eds) (2009) *Greek and Roman Networks in the Mediterranean.* London: Routledge.

Manning, J.G. (2018) *The Open Sea: The Economic Life of the Ancient Mediterranean World from the Iron Age to the Rise of Rome.* Princeton: Princeton University Press.

Martin, S.R. (2017) *The Art of Contact: Comparative Approaches to Greek and Phoenician Art.* 1st edn. Philadelphia: University of Pennsylvania Press.

Mary, J-B. (2018) Etudes et constat préliminaire des implantations fortifies de Corse du second âge du Fer au changement d'ère. Le cas de la region Centre-Ouest de la Corse. *Insularity and Identity in the Roman Mediterranean*, edited by A. Kouremenos. Oxford: Oxbow Books, 165–198.

Matvejevic, P. (1999) *Mediterranean: A Cultural Landscape.* Translated by Michael Henry Heim. Berkeley and Los Angeles: University of California Press.

Mazurek, L.A. (2016) Material and Textual Narratives of Authenticity: Creating Cabotage and Memory in the Hellenistic Eastern Mediterranean. In *Across the Corrupting Sea: Post-Braudelian Approaches to the Ancient Eastern Mediterranean*, edited by C.W. Concannon and L.A. Mazurek. London: Routledge, 39–64.

Meskell, L. (2005) Introduction: Object Orientations. In *Archaeologies of Materiality*, edited by L. Meskell. Oxford: Blackwell, 1–17.
Michaelides, D., Pergola, P. and Zanini, E. (eds) (2013) *The Insular System of the Early Byzantine Mediterranean: Archaeology and History*. Oxford: Archaeopress.
Morris, I. (2005) Mediterraneanization. In *Mediterranean Paradigms in Classical Antiquity*, edited by I. Malkin. Oxford, Routledge, 30–55.
Pettegrew, D. (2007) The Busy Countryside of Late Roman Corinth: Interpreting Ceramic Data Produced by Regional Archaeological Surveys. *Hesperia* 76(4), 743–784.
Pieterse, J.N. (2004) *Globalization and Culture: Global Mélange*. Oxford: Rowman and Littlefield.
Pitts, M. and Versluys, M.J. (eds) (2015) *Globalisation and the Roman World: World History, Connectivity and Material Culture.* Cambridge: Cambridge University Press.
Pohlsander, H. (1999) *Greek Texts of the Fourth to Thirteenth Centuries.* Sources for the History of Cyprus 7. Altamont: Greece and Cyprus Research Center, SUNY Albany.
Rainbird, P. (2007) *The Archaeology of Islands.* Cambridge: Cambridge University Press.
Rapp, C. (2014) Christianity in Cyprus in the Fourth to Seventh Centuries: Chronological and Geographical Frameworks. In *Cyprus and the Balance of Empires: Art and Archaeology from Justinian I to the Coeur de Lion*, edited by T. Davis and C.A. Stewart. Archaeological Reports 20. Boston: American Schools of Oriental Research, 29–38.
Rautman, M. (2000) The Busy Countryside of Late Roman Cyprus. *Report of the Department of Antiquities, Cyprus*, 317–331.
Reger, G. (2016) Nodes of Sea and Sand: Ports, Human Geography, and Networks of Trade. In *Ancient Ports: The Geography of Connections. Proceedings of an International Conference at the Department of Archaeology and Ancient History, Uppsala University, 23–25 September 2010*, edited by K. Höghammer, B. Alroth and A. Lindhagen. Boreas: Uppsala Studies in Ancient Mediterranean and Near Eastern Civilizations 34. Uppsala: Uppsala Universitet, 9–36.
Renfrew, C. and Wagstaff, M. (1982) *An Island Polity: The Archaeology of Exploitation in Melos.* Cambridge: Cambridge University Press.
Robertson, R. (2017) Globalization Thinking and the Past. In *The Routledge Handbook of Archaeology and Globalization*, edited by T. Hodos. London: Routledge, 54–65.
Russell, A. (2017) Sicily without Mycenae: A Cross-cultural Consumption Analysis of Connectivity in the Bronze Age Central Mediterranean. *Journal of Mediterranean Archaeology* 30(1), 59–83.
Santacreu, D.A. (2017) The Times They Were a-Changing: Cultural Encounters, Social Transformations and Technological Change in Hand-Made Pottery from Mallorca (Spain). *Journal of Mediterranean Archaeology* 30(1), 105–131.
Schäfer, C. (ed.) (2016) *Connecting the Ancient World: Mediterranean Shipping, Maritime Networks and their Impact.* Rahden/Westf.: Verlag Marie Leidorf.
Stein, G. (ed.) (2005) *The Archaeology of Colonial Encounters: Comparative Perspectives.* School of American Research Advanced Seminar Series. Santa Fe: School of American Research Press.
Strasser, T.F., Panagopoulou, E., Runnels, C.N., Murray, P.M., Thompson, N., Karkanas, P.,McCoy, F.W. and Wegmann, K.W. (2010) Stone Age Seafaring in the Mediterranean: Evidence from the Plakias Region for Lower Palaeolithic and Mesolithic Habitation of Crete. *Hesperia* 79(2), 145–190.
Sweetman, R.J. (2007) Roman Knossos: The Nature of a Globalized City. *American Journal of Archaeology* 111.1, 61–81.
Tartaron, T. (2013) *Maritime Networks in the Mycenaean World.* Cambridge: Cambridge University Press.
van Dommelen, P. (1998) *On Colonial Grounds: A Comparative Study of Colonialism and Rural Settlement in First Millennium BC West Central Sardinia.* Archaeological Studies Leiden University 2. Leiden: Faculty of Archaeology, University of Leiden.
van Dommelen, P. and Knapp, A.B. (eds) (2010) *Material Connections in the Ancient Mediterranean: Mobility, Materiality and Mediterranean Identities.* London: Routledge.

Versluys, M.J. (2015) Roman Visual Material Culture as Globalising *Koine*. In *Globalisation and the Roman World: World History, Connectivity and Material Culture*, edited by M. Pitts and M.J. Versluys. Cambridge: Cambridge University Press, 141–174.

Vionis, A.K. and Papantoniou, G. (2019) Economic Landscapes and Transformed Mindscapes in Cyprus from Roman Times to the Early Middle Ages. In *Change and Resilience: The Occupation of Mediterranean Islands in Late Antiquity*, edited by M.Á. Cau Ontiveros and C. Mas Florit. Joukowsky Institute Publication 9. Oxford: Oxbow Books, 257–284.

Walsh, J. St P. (2014) *Consumerism in the Ancient World: Imports and Identity Construction*. New York, NY: Routledge.

Watkins, J. and Reyerson, K. (2016) Mediterranean Identities in the Premodern Era: Entrepôts, Islands, Empires. In *Mediterranean Identities in the Premodern Era: Entrepôts, Islands, Empires*, edited by J. Watkins and K. Reyerson. London: Routledge, 1–11.

Wilson, A. (2011) Developments in Mediterranean shipping and maritime trade from the Hellenistic period to AD 1000. In *Maritime Archaeology and Ancient Trade in the Mediterranean*, edited by D. Robinson and A. Wilson. Oxford Centre for Maritime Archaeology 6. Oxford: Institute of Archaeology, University of Oxford, 33–60.

Wilson, R.J.A. (1990) *Sicily under the Roman Empire: The Archaeology of a Roman Province, 36 BC–AD 535*. Warminster: Aris & Phillips.

Woolf, G. (1998) *Becoming Roman: The Origins of Provincial Civilization in Gaul*. Cambridge: Cambridge University Press.

Zavagno, L. (2017) *Cyprus Between Late Antiquity and the Early Middle Ages (ca. 600–800): An Island in Transition*. Birmingham Byzantine and Ottoman Studies. Oxford: Routledge.

Zavagno, L. (2018) 'Islands in the Stream': Toward a New History of the Large Islands of the Byzantine Mediterranean in the early Middle Ages *ca*. 600–*ca*. 800' *Mediterranean Historical Review* 33(2), 149–177.

Zavagno, L., Darley, R. and Jarrett, J. (2019) Editorial. *Al-Masāq* 31(2), 129–139.

Chapter 2

Nuragic Networking? Assessing Globalization and Glocalization in a Late Bronze Age Sardinian Context

Anthony Russell

Sardinia is the second largest island in the Mediterranean and has been a place of human occupation since at least the Upper Paleolithic period (c. 9600 BCE).[1] Nuragic society across the island flourished during the latter half of the 2nd millennium BCE, resulting in a demographic boom, and the construction of thousands of stone towers (nuraghi) that are the most conspicuous archaeological remnant of this era (Table 1 and Fig. 3). This boom, which took place at the beginning of the local Late Bronze Age,[2] was already on the wane by the end of the LBA (or Final Bronze Age) at the close of the 2nd millennium BCE, resulting in a partial dispersal of the island's population away from the tower sites, and an appeal to new sources of power and influence.[3]

It was previously believed that this ubiquitous and distinct monumental building phase was the result of the insularity of the island's population, which resulted in an Easter Island-like extreme building period.[4] Extensive archaeological investigations over the last century, however, have shown that Sardinia's perceived isolation was overstated, and nearly every phase of Sardinian prehistory has yielded evidence for extra-insular contact, involving both foreign materials on the island, as well as Sardinian objects abroad. The LBA, in fact, represents the high watermark for evidence of contact on the island in the pre-colonial period. Given this connectivity, it was inevitable that scholars would question how much of an impact extra-insular peoples, objects, and ideas contributed to either the boom or bust phases of LBA Nuragic society.

In the past fifteen years there has been a growing trend of investigating ancient connectivity through the lens of modern globalization studies. Such analyses have yielded fruitful reconstructions of interaction between disparate societies in the past, particularly for colonial and imperial historical scenarios in the Mediterranean

Table 1: Relative chronology synchronisms for the central Mediterranean, the Aegean, and Cyprus (adapted from Russell and Knapp 2017, 4).

	Sardinia	Cyprus	Aegean	Italy
1500BC		LC I	LH II	
1450	MBA 2			
1400			LH IIIA	MBA Appenine
1350	MBA 3	LC IIA - IIC (early)		
1300				
1250			LH IIIB	Bronzo Recente
1200	LBA: Bronzo Recento		LH IIIB/C	
1150		LC IIC (late) - IIIA		
1100		LC IIIB	LH IIIC	Bronzo Finale
1050				
1000	LBA: Bronzo Finale	Iron Age	Sub-Mycenaean	
950				Iron Age
900				

during the 1st millennium BCE.[5] Given the evidence for contact in the LBA, however, can such a framework help to inform us on the conspicuous connectivity of this earlier time period?

The present study begins with a brief overview of the material record of LBA Sardinia, and a quick sketch of how prehistorians believe Nuragic society was organized. Following that, there is a discussion of what globalization means in a cultural context, what features we should expect to see in the past, and what the advantages of such a framework are compared to world systems models. The ideas generated in that discussion will then be applied to the archaeological record of LBA Sardinia to assess the applicability of a globalization perspective on Nuragic communities. Two 'globalized' Mediterranean commodities will be employed as a case study: Late Helladic pottery and copper oxhide ingots. This study concludes with the appraisal

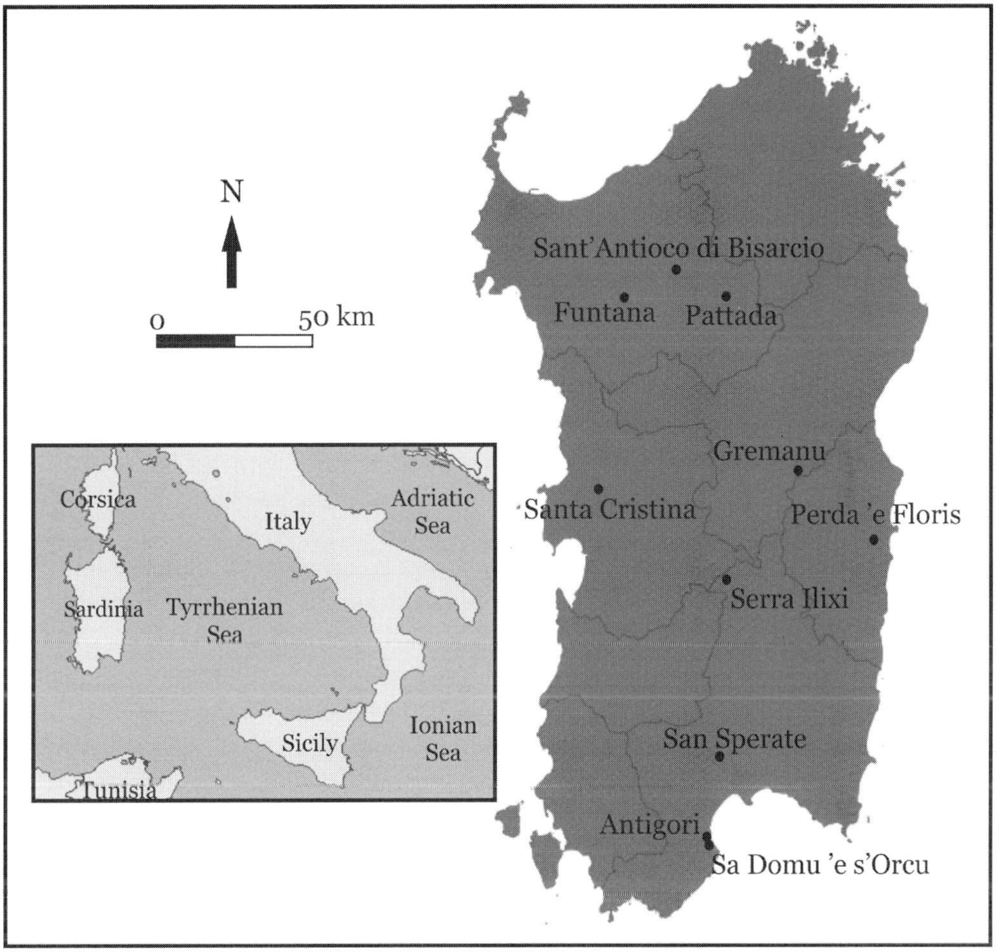

Figure 3: Map of Sardinia showing sites mentioned in the text. Inset: Sardinia's position within the central Mediterranean (author's image).

that, while discrete instances of 'glocalization' may be interpreted within specific contexts, overall globalization is not a useful framework for interpreting Sardinia's less intensive connectivity in the late 2nd millennium BCE.

Nuragic Sardinia: The People of the Towers

Sardinia's island nature certainly affected the type of contact its communities had with their Mediterranean contemporaries, but this goes beyond simply acknowledging that all external connections would have been maritime in nature. Both its size and its placement within the Mediterranean in relation to other land masses played a role in Sardinian connectivity. Sardinia's significant size and its relative abundance of the means of subsistence (arable soils, pasture land, timber, stone, metallic ores, and fresh water sources) would have made it much more self-sufficient and less prone to shortages or droughts than other, smaller islands and archipelagos (*e.g.* Malta, the Aeolian Islands).[6] As shown on the map (Fig. 1), Sardinia defines the western edge of the Tyrrhenian Sea, with the closest landmass being Corsica to its north, across a short strait of about 12 km. Beyond Corsica, however, Sardinia is relatively isolated from the next closest mainland of Tunisia (c. 180 km), the Italian peninsula (c. 190 km) and the south coast of France (c. 275 km). In combination, this self-sufficiency and relative distance from everywhere but Corsica, meant that both the need to interact with the rest of the Mediterranean world, as well as the opportunity to do so, would have been more circumscribed for Sardinia than for other islands. This is not to suggest that Sardinia was poorly placed to take advantage of maritime exchange networks entirely, or that self-sufficiency was a comprehensive disincentive for interaction. Non-Sardinians may have sought out contact with the island because of their own particular needs, and any ships exploiting the east–west networks that stretched from the Levant to Spain[7] would have found Sardinia a convenient stopping point, particularly its southern coast. It may even be possible to interpret one such 'southern' route via the presence of Sardinian pottery at Kommos (southern Crete), at Cannatello (southern Sicily), and the presence of eastern Mediterranean material at Cannatello and Nuraghe Antigori (southern Sardinia).[8]

Sardinia's natural sea borders also delimit the extent of the Nuragic culture, which was remarkably consistent island-wide. Aside from some predictable overlaps with nearby Corsica,[9] Sardinian material culture stands distinct from its Mediterranean neighbors. This does not necessarily mean a single, well-defined and self-aware Sardinian ethnic group existed in the Bronze Age. It seems probable, however, that such shared material expressions and lifeways would have allowed Nuragic communities to recognize a difference between communing with other Sardinian settlements versus interaction with non-islanders. Therefore, Nuragic Sardinians would have drawn a distinction between traditional, local material expressions and those materials, ideas, and influences that were the by-product of extra-insular connectivity.

A discussion of the archaeology of LBA Sardinia necessarily begins with a description of its most ubiquitous feature, the nuraghi themselves. Nuraghi are conical towers constructed of courses of dry stone masonry, which often rise two or three stories, with stairways incorporated into the thickness of the walls.[10] The exact number of nuraghi that were constructed during the Bronze Age is not certain, although 7,000 is the most commonly quoted estimate.[11] They are found in every ecological zone of the island, and no region is completely free from their presence. Nuraghi sites are typically comprised of a single tower surrounded by smaller buildings, usually referred to as *capanne* or 'huts'.[12] Over the course of the LBA, some nuraghi develop into more complex multi-towered structures, occasionally including an encircling wall with towers of its own (Fig. 4). These most complex nuraghi look like proper fortresses, and include hut structures both within and outside of the walls. In these complex sites

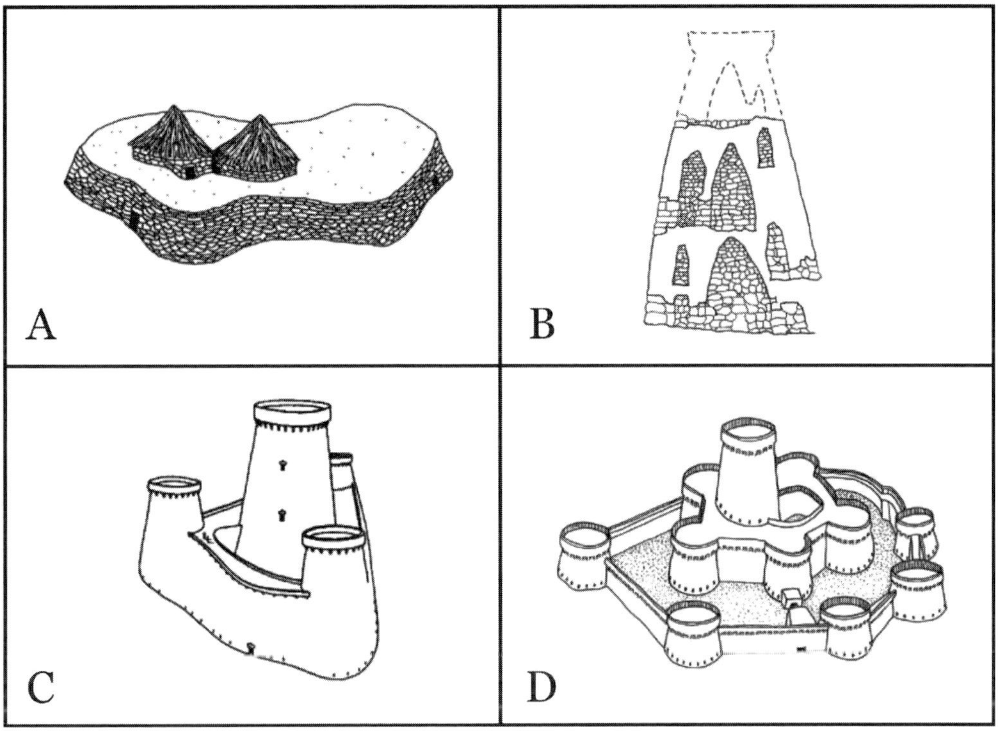

Figure 4: Levels of nuraghe complexity. A: Early Bronze Age proto-nuraghe; B: single-tower nuraghe; C: multi-towered nuraghe; D: fortress-like multi-towered core, with surrounding antemural wall and towers (adapted from Russell 2010, 108).

huts are often grouped together in clusters of 5–6 buildings around a central shared space. While many of these fortress-like nuraghi developed out of single-tower sites, at least a few of them appear to have been planned as such from scratch.[13]

The simple single-towered communities were the most common type of settlement, with multi-towered complexes representing about 30% of the total of known sites.[14] The towers, although multi-functional, were first and foremost residences. Within single-tower sites a social hierarchy is generally believed to have existed, which at its most basic would have involved an upper-status family who lived in the tower, and their subordinates who inhabited the surrounding huts.[15] At the more architecturally complex sites, further sub-ranks have been proposed, with those families living in the hut compounds within the walls believed to have held higher status than those living in the ante-mural huts.[16] The proliferation of nuraghi over the course of the LBA is often explained as the result of social fissioning, involving the descendants of elite families venturing out to develop their own tower communities in emulation of their parents' status.[17] The inter-visibility of many tower sites in several regions may be an indication of such social fissioning, resulting in clan control over an increasing territory.[18] Within such clan-based 'cantons'[19] it is easy to envision a scenario where some tower sites became more complex and influential through competition and rivalry with their related neighbors.

There has been some debate regarding the source of wealth and power for the elite tower-dwelling rulers, with some scholars proposing that extra-insular connections lead to the greater accumulation of wealth and status. In these scenarios, it is generally thought that the Sardinian elites traded metallic ores to overseas merchants in exchange for foreign exotica.[20] Archaeologically, however, this correlation has been difficult to prove, as the more complex nuraghi do not exhibit any superior stockpiles of ore, nor have they yielded more foreign objects or influences than single tower sites.[21] Even assessing how much certain ore sources were exploited during the LBA is impossible to say, as subsequent mining in later time periods tends to destroy earlier evidence of use. A more likely scenario for the LBA is that wealth was based on land, agricultural resources, labor, and livestock. This seems to be borne out by the presence of the most complex nuraghi in good agricultural and pasture areas, with only multi-towered Nuraghe Antigori on the coast.[22]

Regardless of their sources of wealth, Sardinian elites only managed to exert regional levels of authority at best, and there was no single ruler for the island. The relationship between the most complex sites has been justifiably referred to by Blake as 'acephalous cohesion',[23] where communities were in competition with each other, leading to an emulation of formal features and lifeways, and likely conflict over territory. The latter is indicated by both the extreme popularity of the nuraghe as site-type, the development of more fortress-like settlements over time, and the possible destruction of certain sites at the end of the LBA, leading to episodes of both re-building and abandonment.[24]

As mentioned in the introduction, Sardinia in the LBA was a connected island, with evidence for contact with the Italian mainland, Corsica, Sicily, the Aeolian Islands, Spain, France, the Aegean islands and the Greek mainland, Cyprus, and perhaps the Levant.[25] Baltic amber has also been found on the island, which may have reached Sardinia via eastern Mediterranean agents.[26] The evidence for contact involves not only foreign objects found in Sardinian contexts, but also Sardinian materials (*e.g.* obsidian, pottery, and certain metallurgical forms) recovered from extra-insular locations. Two key imports, which will be discussed further in the context of possible globalization scenarios, are Late Helladic pottery and copper oxhide ingots.

Late Helladic (LH) pottery refers to a repertoire of painted, wheelmade pottery that became popular in the Mediterranean during the 2nd millennium BCE, spreading out from its initial development in the Aegean region (Table 1). These pots became so popular, in fact, that certain areas (*e.g.* Cyprus, the Levant, southern Italy) began to produce their own regional varieties of them. In southern Italy, along with the spread of the pottery itself, the specific technologies regarding how to make it (involving clay selection, levigation, wheel-fashioning, and firing) were also introduced, resulting in the co-presence of genuine imports, and closely copied 'imitations'.[27] Given that such a transfer of technologies probably required face-to-face instruction by potters familiar with these techniques, it is likely that people from the Aegean had settled (at least temporarily or seasonally) in peninsular Italy.[28]

There is significantly less LH pottery in Sardinia than in southern peninsular Italy. It has been recovered from 12 sites, all of which, except for Nuraghe Antigori, have yielded 10 or fewer sherds. At Antigori, the sherd count is approximately 200,[29] and includes examples that are locally made (Fig. 5). The pottery has been classified as LH IIIB1–LH IIIC, although only a single sherd seems to demand an LH IIIC date, giving the bulk of the data a chronological spread of 1300–1150 BCE.[30] It is unclear how many actual vessels are represented by this sherd count, or how many of them represent imports, although petrographic analysis of a selection of the data set suggests that half of it was made on Sardinia.[31] Unlike the scenario in southern Italy, however, there does not appear to have been a concomitant technological transfer. The locally made examples were likely handmade or formed on a slow wheel, and are a darker color than the imports, suggesting a different clay selection strategy, levigation technique, and firing pattern. Further, the painted designs on the locally made copies are much cruder that those seen on imported LH ware.[32] All of this suggests there was no co-presence of foreign potters and local artisans at Antigori.

Metalworking on Sardinia is primarily known from finished goods, often found in buried hoards, but also in tombs and domestic contexts. There is very little primary evidence for ore extraction or even smelting, and it is largely accepted that later, more intensive mining activities obliterated any indication of Bronze Age or earlier exploitation of copper on the island.[33] Nevertheless, enough finished bronzes and

Figure 5: Late Helladic pottery sherds from Nuraghe Antigori. Left: locally made pot; right: imported Aegean-made pot (adapted from Russell 2011, 173).

copper bun ingots have had provenience analyses performed on them to be confident that much of the metal used was locally sourced.[34] Even within the corpus of finished objects there is secondary evidence of Sardinian metallurgy in the form of smithing tools found in hoards. Much of this evidence involves broken tools (*i.e.* in founders hoards), and it is possible that some of these tools were imported to the island as scrap metal. Still, enough examples of tongs, coal shovels, and hammers have been found to make it a safe assumption that some of them were used by Sardinian smiths.[35]

Copper oxhide ingots are so-called because of their easily recognizable shape, reproduced both in the ingots themselves and in iconography (Fig. 6). Sardinia is particularly conspicuous in the spread of these ingots, with approximately 180 examples known from over 30 find spots. This stands in stark contrast to their central Mediterranean neighbors, where the recovered examples range from a few (Sicily, Aeolian Islands, Corsica) to none (peninsular Italy, Malta). Most of the examples from Sardinia are fragmentary, although seven whole examples have been recovered.[36] Many scholars consider the island of Cyprus to have been the source of most of the Sardinian oxhide ingots.[37] While there has been a healthy debate on the validity of certain sourcing techniques and their ability to precisely pinpoint copper ore sources,[38] it is a certainty that the oxhide ingot form hails from the eastern Mediterranean, and would have been introduced to Sardinia during the LBA. Indeed, only three oxhide ingot fragments of the dozens analyzed have yielded a chemical signature consistent with a Sardinian source. Moreover, all three were found in a single hoard at the site of Sedda Ottinnara di Pattada.[39] Regardless of their sourcing, production, or technology transfer scenario, LH pottery and copper oxhide ingots represent instances of 'globalized' materials circulating in LBA Sardinia, and will be assessed as such.

Along with the debates regarding the provenience of certain objects, there has been a concomitant debate regarding the impact of foreign objects, ideas, and people upon the structure and functioning of Nuragic society. Such debates are too involved to delve into here, but they roughly align into 'maximalist' and 'minimalist' camps, with the former promoting a broader, longer lasting impact of foreign stimuli upon Nuragic society, while the latter tend to favor endogenous factors when interpreting social change. Maximalists are more willing to accept the physical presence of outsiders in Sardinia, and argue for the systematic nature of the connections they represent.

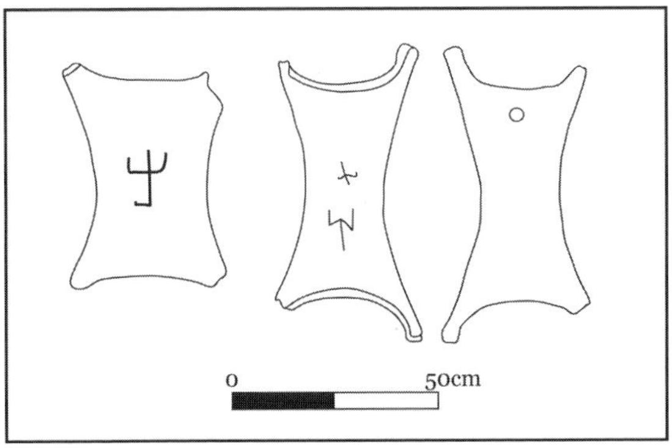

Figure 6: Schematic drawing of three of the five copper oxhide ingots found near the nuraghe at Serra Ilixi, showing dimensions and founders markings (author's image).

Minimalists tend to interpret LBA extra-insular connections as casual, situational, and often indirect.

By the end of the 2nd millennium BCE, there are clear signs of the disruption of Nuragic society. The development of the fortress-like settlements suggests perceived threats and pressures, either internal or external, and by the end of the LBA there are instances of site abandonment (both permanent and temporary), the rebuilding of damaged towers and walls, the spread of new open settlement types (*i.e.* not featuring towers), and the suggestion of new sources of power and authority.[40] The latter can be seen both in the development of some towers from domestic to more ritualistic functioning, the towers themselves accruing some kind of symbolic meaning,[41] as well as in the introduction of a new class of monument, the sacred well or spring.

These sacred wells may have developed out of water cult practices that existed during the Middle Bronze Age.[42] There are not many examples compared to the nuraghi, with about 60 sites known, dating to both the Late Bronze and Early Iron Age.[43] While there is considerable variety in the forms such buildings take, the most monumental types usually involve a stone-lined pit, which is capped with a conical (or nuraghe-like) stone structure varying between 3–13 m in height.[44] This construction is occasionally subterranean, but more often is built upon level ground or into the side of a hill. Often a small enclosed forecourt is situated in front of the entrance, creating a kind of *temenos* precinct for the performance of cult-related activity.[45] In some sacred wells, deposits of animal bones, pottery, and votive offerings have been found, hinting at certain activities such as communal feasting.[46] Many of these ritual complexes occupy liminal areas between Nuragic settlements, suggesting that they were shared between different communities. While places to make votive deposits might seem likely areas to find foreign materials, only two sites (Santa Cristina and Perda 'e Floris) have yielded extra-insular objects.[47] Re-use and rebuilding, as well as looting, however, may be impairing our perception of standard practices at these sites.

This combination of the development of sacred well sites and the 'sacralization' of the towers has been interpreted as reflecting new, competing sources of authority, possibly in an environment when tower elites no longer provided stable security for their people. This may have involved an elite response to changing ideologies of authority, as traditional leaders sought to justify their positions by adopting 'religious' identities, and promoted the tower as a 'sacred' symbol itself. In some scholars' views, the position of Nuragic leader would never have been completely comfortable, constantly requiring re-negotiation and interpretation.[48]

Given this brief sketch of LBA Nuragic society, the opportunities for applying a globalization model are twofold. First, can we argue that a globalized Mediterranean world helped develop or promote the demographic boom and extreme monumentalization of Nuragic society? What role would globalized forms like LH pottery or copper oxhide ingots have performed in such a scenario? Secondly, did extra-insular connectivity in any way contribute to the decline of Nuragic society, including the spread of new ideologies, and new sources of authority? Before this analysis, however, it is important to state explicitly what is meant by 'globalization' from a cultural-material perspective, and to explicate what we would expect to see in the archaeological record in order for such a model to have descriptive or predictive force.

Globalization as an Interactionist Model

Before attempting to define globalization, it is perhaps useful to discuss why archaeology needs yet another '-ization'. One clear benefit is that it facilitates comparisons with interactions in modern world, the way in which cross-cultural encounters play out today, and the impact on the parties involved. These are scenarios that can be directly observed, recorded and theorized about. Such an analogy is useful to archaeology in general; in the present study, where prehistoric societies are involved, it is particularly beneficial, as the archaeological record is the primary source of evidence, and by its nature is partial and ambiguous. The ability to judicially compare features of modern interaction to past societies at the very least provides alternative 'narratives' about the ancient world.[49]

In the past I have employed contemporary ethnographies in my research in an attempt to understand material culture patterning in the LBA central Mediterranean. Of particular use was the concept of cross-cultural consumption, which emphasizes 'the logic by which goods are *received* (acquired, understood and employed)'.[50] This was an important first step in counteracting the dominant binary and unidirectional 'complex core vs simplistic periphery' narratives that have dominated the interpretation of culture contact in the central Mediterranean. Specific ethnographies explored included the reception of Barbie dolls in the Yucatan peninsula,[51] the consumption of Coca Cola in Argentina[52] and Trinidad,[53] and the performance of beauty pageants in Belize.[54] These studies, however, are not just discrete ethnologies, they are expressions of experiencing a globalized world. Is it possible to broaden the scope of analysis from localized instances of cross-cultural consumption, to a larger framework of globalization in the ancient world?

Globalization is one of those terms for which one has a general idea of its meaning, although a specific definition proves harder to formulate. Indeed, those who study modern globalization have found more areas of discrepancy than consensus.[55] Part of the problem involves the use of the term within different disciplines, resulting in competing ideas regarding how long-term a process it has been, what parties are involved, or what the resulting features of globalization are.[56] The challenge is to find a definition that on the one hand is flexible enough to encompass both the modern and ancient world, while on the other hand is specific enough to: 1) stand distinct from other interactionist models; and 2) still have descriptive and predictive force. The first obstacle to overcome in the present study, then, is to come up with a working definition of globalization that will facilitate analysis of cross-cultural interactions in LBA Sardinian society.

Within the broader concept of globalization studies, the first point of departure is that for archaeological purposes a broader cultural – and not strictly economic – globalization is implicated. As a result, archaeologists can explore areas that are not restricted to trade and commerce, even if those are the specific initial motivations for contact, such as religion, arts and crafts, cuisine, and social organization. This allows us to look at globalization as a long-term process, and not just a by-product of modern neo-liberal economic policies.[57] Within all disciplinary traditions, Nederveen Pieterse has identified four areas of consensus, three of which are directly applicable to the present study: globalization is shaped by technological change; it involves more than just state-level agents; and its spread or impact is uneven.[58] These features allow for a distinction between globalization and other interactionist models. For example, unlike world systems theory,[59] globalization recognizes the actions of non-elite and non-state actors as potential generators of social change. Furthermore, world systems tend to concentrate on international-scale economics and levels of political integration, but are less concerned with the reception of cultural materials and messages.[60] World systems models are often explained in very binary terms: core vs periphery; elite 'A' directly interacting with elite 'B'. This results in a simplified portrayal of the contact scenario, and can omit obscure key 'players' involved.[61]

Jennings further specifies that globalization involves 'complex connectivity' that yields an 'array of social changes that are associated with the formation of global culture'.[62] While at one time this 'global culture' was described as a homogenizing force,[63] more recently the resulting global 'mélange' is characterized by heterogeneities.[64] This recognizes the creative potential of the consumers of global culture to pervert the expectations or meanings of globalized objects, practices, or ideas so that they fit more comfortably within local systems of value. Such a process of foreign-exotic assimilation is referred to as 'glocalization',[65] where the articulation of the experience of consuming globalized material may be only superficially similar across cultural boundaries, while a closer examination reveals local variety. As Hodos has succinctly stated: 'shared practices are not the same as identically replicated ones'.[66]

In fact, one possible outcome of globalization is resistance, or 'culture clash', whereby the boundaries between cultural units becomes more distinct and defined.[67] This clash could be expressed by the outright rejection of the globalized forms, resulting in a fragmentation that Barber has referred to as 'jihad'.[68] Another outcome of such a clash, however, sees the external stimuli assimilated, undergoing creative re-contextualizations intended to naturalize the foreign, thus preserving and solidifying the consumers' distinct identities within the globalized environment.[69] As a result, the present study must look at the contextual scenarios at play in both the consuming and producing/exporting parties (and recognizing that this could represent more than just two groups involved), when interpreting possible material assimilations.

Connectivity in a Bronze Age Sardinian context is not an all-or-none scenario. Given its size and island nature, it is to be expected that some parties or communities were more involved in extra-insular networks than others. For example, we could expect the communities of coastal Sardinia to be more conspicuously 'connected' to the greater Mediterranean world than remoter, inland areas.[70] This doesn't exclude the interior of the island from involvement, as coastal sites could operate as global 'gateways',[71] re-distributing foreign goods and ideas to the hinterland. Instead, there might be a predictable drop-off in evidence the further we move from the coast. Furthermore, certain communities of practice like metallurgists, potters, and other craftspeople may be more susceptible to the flow of materials, technologies, and practices than other groups.

With these interpretive challenges in mind, globalization for the present study is defined as a network of connectivity that exists between disparate communities, whereby:

- The connection is established through the long distance spread of raw materials, commodities, ideologies, technologies, and/or people.[72]
- Those living within the affected communities experience a feeling of global 'compression';[73] a sense of the world shrinking, where what would at first have seemed distant and exotic becomes recognized as an authentic part of the local experience (see Mazurek in this volume). In such an intensively connected scenario interdependencies are created.[74]
- Such recognition of this connection and its impact is not restricted to the elite classes, even if in many instances they stand to benefit materially more than their subordinates.
- The reception of globalized forms leads to shared practices, albeit ones that are reproduced differently via a process of 'glocalization', where the objects, technologies, or practices involved could be assimilated as much as their consumers are.
- Technological transfers are particularly implicated in the spread of globalized forms, and often have a key part to play in reshaping social norms, although such technologies will still be socially embedded.[75] In some scenarios, it may be possible to interpret how the technological expedience of new methods and practices is able to counter the cultural conservatism of specific communities of practice.
- The spread and impact of globalized forms will be uneven in space and time, given the varying levels of participation within such networks, differing levels of social complexity involved, and dynamic power relations.[76]

This definition should provide a decent entry point to begin analyzing the cultural interactions at play in LBA Sardinia. It is specific enough to distinguish such an approach from other interactionist models, while at the same time is flexible enough to facilitate comparisons between the present and the past. It is not so flexible, however, that it will automatically impose an interpretation of globalization where such a model is not warranted.

Nuragic Sardinia: A Globalized Society?

One of the running themes of the present volume is the impact of globalization on island societies specifically. It was mentioned at the outset that the notion of an isolated, 'insular' Nuragic society has been significantly downscaled by archaeological investigations of the past century. It is nevertheless certain that Sardinia being an island conditioned the kinds of connectivity that existed. Its particular positioning in the central Mediterranean, farther away from the more complex and intensively connected societies of the eastern Mediterranean than its neighbors in Sicily, the Aeolian Islands, and southern peninsular Italy, impacted both who was involved as well as the intensity of these connections.

Among the various sources of evidence for contact during the LBA, LH pottery and copper oxhide ingots represent two of the best candidates for globalized cultural forms. Both had a broad (nearly pan-Mediterranean) diffusion, they influenced local technologies in certain regions, and both material types existed throughout the extent of the time period. These objects and their possible impacts will be analyzed against the criteria provided for globalization outlined in the previous section, followed by a broader discussion of whether globalization can be said to have affected the development of Nuragic society, the social disruptions at the end of the LBA, or any shared identity of Nuragic peoples.

When it comes to LH pottery, it is clear that Nuraghe Antigori is the only site for which we can discuss a possible globalized community. The approximately 200 sherds recovered from this site is much more than what is typically found in Sardinian contexts,[77] and includes both actual imports and a version of LH pottery produced locally. This unique situation does not prevent us from exploring a globalization scenario, since an uneven impact is one of its defining features. Given the lack of island-wide political authority in LBA Sardinia, and the presumed level of regional autonomy, an uneven impact is perhaps what we should expect to encounter. The use of LH pottery may have been restricted to the elite at Antigori, given it has only been recovered from within the tower complex, although this multi-towered site is unusual in its layout, sitting atop a 177 m, steeply sloped hill,[78] with no physical place for the surrounding village of huts found at other nuraghi. It is possible, therefore, that subaltern classes also lived within the complex, and took part in any practices associated with LH pottery. The location of the finds, spread out in two of the towers and in four other 'rooms', would also suggest that access to these pots was not strictly controlled.

The principal investigator classified Nuraghe Antigori as a Mycenaean gateway community, and it was certainly well placed on the south coast of the island to function as such, given the aforementioned 'route of the islands'.[79] There is also an appreciable drop-off in LH pottery beyond coastal Antigori, as would be expected between a gateway community and its hinterland. The investigator also insisted upon the physical presence of Mycenaean agents at the site,[80] although it is not clear from the material assemblage why this was necessary. I have argued elsewhere that the actual pottery consumption patterns seen at Antigori more closely resemble the scenario encountered in southern Italy than that in the Aegean. This pattern includes: the presence of imported and locally-made LH pottery; commonalities in the shape repertoire, with a decided preference for table wares; similar design motifs found on the painted decoration of the pots; a shared set of provenience results for the imported examples; and the accompanying introduction of a new class of grey ware pottery.[81] Such shared features may suggest that the connection was with southern Italian agents rather than directly with Aegean naval merchants. From a globalization perspective, of course, it does not matter if 'Mycenaean' ships sailed all the way to Sardinia, or if the introduction of LH pottery was mediated through southern Italian communities. In either case the residents of Antigori were incorporated into the wider global network of the consumption and production of LH pottery via a distant extra-insular connection.

It is with the actual production of LH pottery at Antigori, however, where obstacles to a globalization framework start to appear. The spread of technology has been identified as one feature that could act as a globalization facilitator, with the potential to impact the functioning of local communities. At Antigori, unlike the situation in southern Italy, local copies of LH pottery were not produced using the same technology as the genuine Aegean imports. While scholars could posit the presence of Aegean potters on the peninsula, and discuss the social impact of a switch from a domestic to a workshop level of industry,[82] at Antigori no such technological transfer occurred. The production of local LH pots falls within the technological ambit of traditional handmade Sardinian pottery, including hand forming the vessels, clay selection and treatment, and firing techniques. Where there was no corresponding tradition to draw from, as was the case for painting pottery, the Sardinian potters improvised, resulting in darker colors, and more crudely executed designs than the genuine imports. It seems likely, then, that no industrial overhaul occurred as a result of the reception and consumption of LH pottery at Antigori. While a lack of technological transmission on its own does not preclude the community of Nuraghe Antigori from involvement in a globalized world, it does condition the intensity and type of contact experienced. This raises the question of the value or meaning of this pottery for the islanders who made and consumed it, and how similar or different it was from consumers in the Aegean or southern Italy.

Did the users of LH pottery at the site experience any sense of global compression through its introduction? This is difficult to assess. The prominence of tableware shapes has suggested the introduction of collective feasting, and perhaps eastern Mediterranean style wine drinking at Antigori, as indicated by the inclusion of kraters and drinking cups associated with this practice.[83] There is some evidence that Sardinians were already a wine drinking people by the LBA, and public feasting has been attested in both tower and other, ritualized contexts.[84] How much did existing social practice change through the introduction of new pottery forms? One piece of supplementary evidence from Antigori that might indicate a new, culturally significant symbol is a small lead object recovered from a cave context within the complex. It has been interpreted as a votive double-axe, and evidence of the establishment of an Aegean cult at the site.[85] Such an interpretation is not corroborated by any other finds from the cave, however, and others have suggested the object may in fact represent the hull of a boat (when viewed upside-down), and thus perhaps an indication of a new source of wealth or authority (*i.e.* the control of sea-borne exchange). In either case, this is a lot of interpretive weight to place upon an isolated, ambiguous object.

Regardless of the uncertain effect the consumption or production of LH pottery had on the residents of Nuraghe Antigori, it is clear that from a broader islander perspective that the presence of this globalized form had little to no impact on the lives of Nuragic communities. Beyond this coastal settlement, and perhaps nearby Nuraghe Sa Domu'e s'Orcu, there is practically no evidence for the use or spread of LH pottery, and its impact seems extremely localized to the Sarroch seaside area. There would have been no sense of a compressed world, nor a recognition of a shared practice of drinking or feasting with communities in the Aegean or eastern Mediterranean. Unlike in southern Italy, the reception of LH pottery was not accompanied by technological changes to ceramic industry on the island, and into the Early Iron Age the production of local pottery continues with a high level of continuity to the LBA, at least until the more widespread adoption of a slow wheel, associated with later examples of grey ware pottery.[86]

If there was no attempt to popularize this type of pottery and the practices associated with it beyond Nuraghe Antigori, then why did the people living there attempt to make a local variety at all? It could have been simply a matter of taste for certain individuals living there, who recognized that they could not rely on a consistent stream of imports to meet local consumption needs. Another possibility is that they never intended to act as an entrepôt for their hinterland or beyond, but were using these pots as a message directed outwards to potential exchange partners. By conspicuously consuming goods well known to mobile agents from other parts of the Mediterranean, the people of Nuraghe Antigori could convey the message that they were open to new ideas and practices, while at the same time providing a sense of the familiar to foreign maritime merchants.[87]

Copper oxhide ingots represent quite a different diffusion and technological scenario. Whereas Sardinia had a more circumscribed spread of LH pottery than its central Mediterranean neighbors, it has yielded significantly more oxhide ingot evidence than any other part of the region. This has led some scholars to suggest a close relationship between Sardinia and the eastern Mediterranean, especially Cyprus.[88] Seven whole and approximately 180 fragments of copper oxhide ingots have been recovered from 35 sites.[89] This stands in sharp contrast to the situation in Sicily (two fragments known from two sites), the Aeolian Islands (about 10 fragments from a single context), Corsica (one whole ingot) or peninsular Italy and Malta, where no such evidence has been found.[90] Given this clear distribution bias in favor of Sardinia, it is not surprising that a particular connection between the island and Cyprus has been proposed.

Along with the ingots, there has also been evidence for metallurgical tools that resemble Cypriot (or more broadly eastern Mediterranean) prototypes, possibly indicating shared technological practices. These tools include tongs (seven), coal shovels (four), and hammers (three). Furthermore, finished bronze objects, such as miniature tripod stands (four), daggers (two), fibulae (one), and mirrors (two) have been compared to Cypriot types.[91] The majority of these objects have been dated to the 13th–10th centuries BCE. While this might not seem like a large corpus of evidence for the entire island over a 300 year period, it should be acknowledged that metal artifacts are more susceptible to recycling and re-use, and thus are never preserved in as great amounts as other artifact types like pottery.

One stumbling block to the suggestion of an enduring Cypriot presence on the island is the lack of unambiguous Cypriot finds beyond the ingots themselves. For example, very little Cypriot pottery has been found in Sardinia for this period. Only three sites have yielded possible Cypriot pottery fragments, none of which included any Cypriot metal finds.[92] Theoretically, of course, the presence of foreign metal objects does not need to indicate the presence of foreign agents from their region of production any more than the presence of LH pottery in Antigori needs to be interpreted as a Mycenaean presence at that site. Many of the perceived similarities between smithing tools are fairly generic, and the specific function these implements performed may preclude distinctive stylistic aspects that can be easily attributed to a geographic craft tradition.[93]

One intriguing idea concerning oxhide ingots is that they accrued social meaning in Sardinia beyond that of a functional, convertible raw material to be exploited. Lo Schiavo has suggested a symbolic meaning for oxhide ingots, due to their presence with 'votive' materials in hoards.[94] More recently, Blake has proposed that the distributional bias of oxhide ingots in Sardinia may represent a preservational quirk: in other parts of the central Mediterranean copper ingots may have been valued strictly as a commodity to be converted into other objects, while in Sardinia they maintained a kind of cultural capital, requiring at least fragments of ingots to be preserved or offered.[95] While the votive nature of certain hoard contexts could be debated, it is true that some oxhide ingot finds have been recovered from less ambiguous ritual contexts, such as the fragments recovered from a well sanctuary at Perda 'e Floris,[96] or the fragments located within the sanctuary site of Gremanu o Madau.[97] The two whole ingots found together beneath the pavement of the central tower of Nuraghe Sant'Antioco di Bisarcio also do not fit the profile of typical utilitarian founder's hoards, and are more likely ritually significant foundation deposits.[98] While an ingot fragment may seem like an unusual ritual offering, such particalization of exotic items has been interpreted in recent interactionist studies as being both a representation of the whole, as well as signaling formalized relations between parties.[99]

How much of this metallurgical evidence benefits from a globalization interpretation? Due to the unequal spread of metallic ores across the Mediterranean, being involved in metallurgy in the LBA meant being a part of wider networks for the movement of raw material, finished objects, recycled objects, technological flows, and perhaps even skilled labor by necessity.[100] Metallurgy does not appear to have been as prone to formal conservatism as other crafts like pottery. Presumably the technological benefits of adopting new forms in weaponry, armor, and other tools outweighed traditionalist concerns. In this, Sardinian smiths certainly engaged in a broader community of practice, one that encompassed several parts of the Mediterranean. This might preclude the interpretation of a specific relationship with Cyprus, but from a globalization perspective it does not matter with whom Sardinian smiths directly interacted. It could be argued that the more agents involved, the easier it is to promote an interpretation of a globalized network.

How much did the developments in metallurgy actually affect Nuragic society beyond a specific community of practicing metal workers? The copper industry does not appear to have impacted the power structures of LBA Sardinia – all Nuragic settlements seem to have practiced a local-needs level of metalworking, and the more complex nuraghi have not yielded either surplus stockpiles of ingots or greater amounts of finished metal objects than simple mono-tower sites. The idea that external traders came to Sardinia to gain access to the island's metallic resources is at least tempered by the fact that Nuragic communities were willing to accept imported copper ingots. Even a possible special social value placed on the oxhide ingot form should be qualified. There are no parallels in Sardinia to the 'Enkomi Ingot God' figurine from Cyprus,[101] and its value as a symbol of wealth and power was almost certainly more circumscribed.

Three intriguing pieces of evidence, however, may indicate experiencing a compressed, connected world, and a shift in functioning of Nuragic communities. These are the three oxhide fragments from Sedda Ottinnara di Pattada that yielded a local Sardinian provenience. If this assignment is correct, it has implications on the functioning of Nuragic society, in that it could represent a shift from subsistence level copper exploitation to the intentional generation of copper surpluses for export. This can be implied because the oxhide ingot form in the Mediterranean is strongly associated with bulk exchange and transportation, especially by ship. Oxhide ingots have been found in great numbers in eastern Mediterranean shipwrecks, most notably the Ulu Burun wreck,[102] and their shape is pragmatically well suited to loading and unloading in ship holds, and increased ease of shifting as ballast.[103] If Nuragic communities were attempting to emulate the oxhide shape, it is tempting to consider their possible participation (or at least intention to participate) in bulk copper networking. Again, this is a lot of interpretive weight to place on three ingot fragments, and the imperfect way they were cast (overly porous compared to imported ingots)[104] might indicate that this is another instance of glocalization in a particular Nuragic community. Therefore, much like the production of LH pottery at Antigori, metallurgists at Pattada had the impetus to copy a foreign form, but not the requisite technological information to reproduce that form accurately. It is also worth mentioning that Pattada is not a coastal site (Fig. 1), so any straightforward connection to extra-insular shipping is uncertain. Given that the fragments were found in a hoard context, however, it may be that they were originally cast elsewhere. For the present these three fragments represent an intriguing, if uncorroborated, hint of Sardinia's desire to participate in globalized networks.

From a broader island-wide perspective, it is difficult to associate either LH pottery or copper oxhide ingots with either the growth in complexity of Nuragic sites, or the demographic boom associated with the ubiquitous spread of tower sites over the course of the LBA. Nor does the spread of these objects seem to have played a hand in the disruptions seen at the end of the LBA, the growth of new open settlements, or the development of new sanctuary sites. The increasing scarcity of local resources such as land, labor, livestock and timber are more likely to have played a role as destabilizing elements and threats to the control of traditional tower-dwelling elites. Access to, and control of the spread of foreign materials, and any associated practices with them, does not appear to have been a key factor in the boom and bust of Nuragic Sardinia.[105]

Conclusion: Size Matters?

This study has followed a pattern familiar to those who research interactions in the Bronze Age Mediterranean: the impact of contact with the east upon the west. The two case studies explored, LH pottery and copper oxhide ingots, fit comfortably within this narrative of unidirectional influences from a complex eastern Mediterranean 'core', to a less stratified, technologically inferior 'periphery'. The reasons for this are largely pragmatic: in the Late Bronze Age evidence for connections with other parts of the Mediterranean is more limited, and consequently much more has been written about these east–west connections. Different case studies from other prehistoric time periods, however, such as the spread of megalithic architecture in the Neolithic,[106] or the diffusion of bell beakers in the Early Bronze Age,[107] would have produced quite different lines on a map, and more heavily implicated the western Mediterranean (and temperate Europe). Such examinations might produce quite different conclusions about Sardinia's place in a globalized world.

Following a traditional east-to-west pattern, however, does not mean we need to rehash common assumptions about either the superiority of eastern 'high culture', or that the power dynamic strongly favored eastern mobile agents.[108] By adopting a more nuanced globalization perspective we can move beyond the assumptions of passive acculturation upon Sardinian Nuragic society, and engage in a discussion of local motivations and systems of value. It also allows us to question the power dynamics of interaction between the two regions, disputing the assumption that the eastern 'exporters' had complete control in any contact scenario. Sardinia's particular insular features (size, resources, and placement within the Mediterranean) suggest that Nuragic communities would only have had to trade with outsiders to satisfy their own particular needs, even if such network traffic was significantly less 'busy' beyond southern peninsular Italy. Nevertheless, the general low-level of intensity of contact with the east, and the particularly circumscribed impacts it had on Nuragic society island-wide, must qualify any interpretation of Sardinia as part of a wider, globalized Mediterranean.

Is being in a globalized world restricted to places that have larger, urban or 'proto-urban' centers? Classen has investigated the impact of global hypermarkets (*i.e.* large shops that are a combination of supermarket and department store) in the primarily agricultural district of northwest Argentina.[109] This region, however, also has cities and towns with several thousand residents and consumers, which operate as useful network nodes for the conduction of information and technology flows, international products, and mobile labor forces. Certainly, the issue of scale is one interpretive obstacle to the straightforward comparison of modern and ancient globalizations. Even within the scope of the LBA, there are large discrepancies in settlement sizes between the urban and proto-urban centers of the eastern Mediterranean and the villages of the central-west. Because of this, Iacono cautions that we should not expect the same number of imports in the central Mediterranean (specifically LH pottery) because there are much fewer consumers to make use of them. The greater proportion of imports to southern Italy compared to the relatively small communities where they have been found could mean they potentially had a larger impact in such a setting than in the larger urban centers of the east.[110]

Even with this important proviso, however, the Nuragic communities of LBA Sardinia seem largely outside of this globalized world in both space and time. Geographically, the effective range of the network involving the consumption and production of LH pottery seems to recede beyond the communities in southern peninsular Italy. While Sardinia is certainly part of the pan-Mediterranean network of metallic ores, finished bronze objects, and technological information flows, this community of practice seems to have had a very limited impact on the functioning of Nuragic society. The control of ore sources or metallurgy in general does not appear to have been an important source of wealth and power in the growth of Nuragic communities, and all sites seem to have practiced metalwork for their own use, without the drive to create surpluses.[111] The three 'local' oxhide ingots from the Pattada hoard are the only indication that any attempt was made to produce copper beyond local demand. In chronological terms, the rise and recession of Nuragic society during the LBA seems largely dependent on emic factors, rather than any impact of globalized commodities, technological transfers, or ideological exchanges. In the 1st millennium BCE, with the physical co-presence of new peoples (Phoenicians), there is more scope to explore Nuragic Sardinia in a globalized and colonized Mediterranean world.[112]

Beyond the issue of the intensity of contact representing a key obstacle in any straightforward comparison of modern globalization and LBA Sardinian interactions,

I return to the idea that globalization networks create 'interdependencies' between the communities so affected.[113] It is hard to interpret such dependencies either on the part of Sardinian consumers of globalized forms, or on the parties who interacted with them. Any social strategy of accruing power or influence via extra-insular connections must have been extremely localized (*e.g.* Anigori), if it existed at all. As for the foreign demand for Sardinian copper, that has been largely assumed but not proven. It is difficult to see any eastern Mediterranean polities being dependent on such a commodity when the switch to an iron-based economy was already underway during Sardinia's Late Bronze Age.

Even if an overarching globalization framework represents an uneven fit for the functioning of LBA Nuragic society, the analysis of specific instances of 'glocalization' do benefit from comparisons to modern global encounters, even if such local articulations had a short period of existence, like the consumption and production of LH pottery at Antigori. Furthermore, an interpretation of the more restricted functioning of a smaller community of practice, like metalworkers in Sardinia, may be usefully informed by the impact of technological and information flows that are a key feature of living in a modern, compressed world. That such globalized practices failed to generate broader social impacts within the islander communities of Nuragic Sardinia has more to do with the largely autonomous, regional operations of those communities, than any significant degree of isolation experienced by the island's occupants during the Late Bronze Age.

Notes

1 Webster 1996, 44.
2 Henceforth LBA, called the Recent Bronze Age by Sardinian prehistorians.
3 Campus *et al.* 2010, 67–68.
4 Blake 2015, 96.
5 *e.g.* Hingley 2005; Hodos 2010; Versluys 2014; Jennings 2017.
6 Webster 2015, 10–11.
7 What Broodbank (2013, 465) refers to as the 'route of the isles'.
8 Russell and Knapp 2017, 21.
9 Webster 2015, 9.
10 Webster 1996, 92.
11 Webster 1996, 91; Blake 2015, 97.
12 Dyson and Rowland 2007, 68.
13 Lilliu 1988, 502; Usai 1995, 254.
14 Webster 2015, 87.
15 Blake 2015, 96–97.
16 Lilliu 1988, 576.
17 Perra 1997, 59–60.
18 Gallin 1989, 52.
19 Lilliu 1988, 574–575.
20 Lo Schiavo 2003a, 28; Blake 2008, 6.
21 Blake 2015, 98.
22 Webster 2015, 99.

23 Blake 2015.
24 Webster 2015, 84; Campus *et al.* 2010, 67.
25 Giardino 1995; Lo Schiavo 2003a; Vianello 2005, 140–58.
26 Negroni Catacchio 1989, 660; Blake 2015, 102–103.
27 Jones *et al.* 2014, 452.
28 Jones *et al.* 2014, 451–453; Kiriatzi and Andreou 2016, 146–149.
29 Russell 2011, 172. In contrast, some sites in southern Italy have yielded several hundreds to multiple thousands of sherds; see Blake 2008, 9–12.
30 Webster 1996, 140; Vianello 2005, 215.
31 Jones and Day 1987, 266–68.
32 Russell 2010, 117.
33 Webster 1996, 136; see also Webster 2015, 96 for more recent smelting evidence from Nuraghe Funtana.
34 Begemann *et al.* 2001, 68–69; Russell and Knapp 2017, 10.
35 Lo Schiavo *et al.* 1985, 22–28.
36 Webster 2015, 126.
37 Stos-Gale and Gale 1992, 333; Begemann *et al.* 2001.
38 Budd *et al.* 1995; Knapp 2000.
39 Begemann *et al.* 2001, 57.
40 Perra 1997, 63–64; Tronchetti 2015, 269; Webster 2015, 107.
41 As seen in the development of miniature tower models, Blake 1997.
42 Ugas 2005, 84–85.
43 Webster 2015, 189.
44 Dyson and Rowlands 2007, 85.
45 Webster 2015, 189.
46 Webster 1996, 148.
47 Russell 2011, 149.
48 Usai 1995, 257.
49 *e.g.* the application of globalization theory on Roman Crete in Sweetman 2007.
50 Howes 1996, 2, emphasis original.
51 Macdougal 2003; Russell 2011, 47.
52 Classen 1996; Russell 2017, 65.
53 Miller 2001; Russell 2016, 158.
54 Wilk 1995; Russell 2016, 158.
55 Nederveen Pieterse 2015, 8–24.
56 Nederveen Pieterse 2015, 16; Jennings 2017, 12.
57 Nederveen Pieterse 2015, 21–22.
58 Nederveen Pieterse 2015, 9.
59 Wallerstein 1974; Parkinson and Galaty 2009, 8–9.
60 Pitts and Versluys 2014, 8.
61 Nederveen Pieterse 2015, 78.
62 Jennings 2011, 2.
63 *i.e.* the 'coca-colonization' of the modern world, Howes 1996, 3.
64 Hodos 2010, 81–82; Pitts and Versluys 2014, 13.
65 Hodos 2010, 83; Nederveen Pieterse 2015, 54.
66 Hodos 2010, 82.
67 Hodos 2010, 82.
68 Barber 1995; Howes 1996, 6.
69 Hodos 2010, 82. See also van Dommelen 1998, 42, for an example of Punic-Roman interaction in Sardinia.

70 Gordon 2018, 6.
71 Polanyi 1963, 30; see also Mazurek in this volume.
72 Jennings 2017, 13.
73 Hodos 2010, 81.
74 Sweetman 2007, 65; Pitts and Versluys 2014, 11.
75 Nederveen Pieterse 2015, 10.
76 Nederveen Pieterse 2015, 13–14.
77 Russell 2011, 171–72. Combined, the other 11 Sardinian sites that have LH pottery evidence have yielded only 39 sherds. Nuraghe Sa Domu 'e s'Orcu, located 4 km south of Antigori, has produced the next most contextual pottery, with 6 sherds recovered. Webster 1996, 140.
78 Lilliu 1988, 399.
79 Broodbank 2013, 465.
80 Ferrarese Ceruti 1997, 273; *contra* Lilliu 1988, 401.
81 Russell 2010, 116–117.
82 Borgna and Levi 2015, 117.
83 Webster 1996, 140.
84 Webster 2015, 112.
85 Ferrarese Ceruti 1980, 392.
86 Webster 2015, 166.
87 Doonan (2001, 160–161) has used such an explanation for new architectural forms seen on coastal Sicily in the Bronze Age, arguing that such novel constructions and practices may themselves be the product of inter-community competition.
88 Lo Schiavo 2001; Lo Schiavo and Campus 2013.
89 Russell and Knapp 2017, 8.
90 Lo Schiavo 2008, 229–34, 241; Russell and Knapp 2017, 16–17.
91 Lo Schiavo *et al.* 1985.
92 Vagnetti 2001, 80–81; Vianello 2005, 165. One of the sites, a tomb near San Sperate, also produced a cylinder seal, which could be of Cypriot manufacture, Lo Schiavo 2003a, 16–17.
93 Russell and Knapp 2017, 11.
94 Lo Schiavo 2003b, 121.
95 Blake 2015, 102.
96 Vianello 2005, 127.
97 Lo Schiavo 2005, 321–322.
98 Lo Schiavo 2005, 319. Founder's hoards are typically characterised by a collection of used or damaged metal objects and other recycled scrap metal (*e.g.* oxhide ingot fragments), hidden by smiths to be used in their foundries at a later date.
99 Chapman 2000; Blake 2015, 102; Campbell 2016.
100 Knapp 2008, 77–81; Russell 2011, 179.
101 Knapp 2008, 277–79.
102 Patton 1996, 173. Two hundred oxhide ingots were recovered from this single shipwreck.
103 The idea that the shape was meant to represent a particular weight or value of copper is undermined by the wide variety of weights encountered, even within the same cargo, Knapp 2008, 310.
104 Begemann *et al.* 2001, 57–58.
105 Webster 2015, 138–139.
106 Such as a recent examination of megalithic burials in Schulz Paulsson 2019.
107 Webster 2015, 34–35.
108 Dietler 2005, 56.
109 Classen 1996.

110 Iacono 2015, 260.
111 Blake 2015, 98.
112 van Dommelen 2005; Hayne 2016.
113 Pitts and Versluys 2014, 11.

Bibliography

Barber, B.R. (1995) *Jihad vs. McWorld: How Globalism and Tribalism are Reshaping the World.* New York: Ballantine Books.

Begemann, F., Schmitt-Strecker, S., Pernicka, E. and Lo Schiavo, F. (2001) Chemical Composition and Lead Isotopy of Copper and Bronze from Nuragic Sardinia. *European Journal of Archaeology* 4, 43–85.

Blake, E. (2005) Late Bronze Age Sardinia: Acephalous Cohesion. In *The Cambridge Prehistory of the Bronze and Iron Age Mediterranean*, edited by A.B. Knapp and P. van Dommelen. New York: Cambridge University Press, 96–108.

Blake, E. (2008) The Mycenaeans in Italy: A Minimalist Position. *Papers of the British School of Rome* 76, 1–34.

Blake, E. (1997) Strategic Symbolism: Miniature Nuraghi of Sardinia. *Journal of Mediterranean Archaeology* 10, 151–164.

Borgna, E. and Levi, S.T. (2015) The Italo-Mycenaean Connection. Some Considerations on the Technological Transfer in the Field of Pottery Production. In *The Transmission of Technological Knowledge in the Production of Ancient Mediterranean Pottery*, edited by W. Gauss, G. Klebinder-Glauss and C. von Rüden. Vienna: Österreichisches Archäologisches Institut, 115–138.

Broodbank, C. (2013) *The Making of the Middle Sea. A History of the Mediterranean from the Beginning to the Emergence of the Classical World.* Oxford: Oxford University Press.

Budd, P., Pollard, A.M., Scaife, C. and Thomas, R.G. (1995) Oxhide Ingots, Recycling and the Mediterranean Metals Trade. *Journal of Mediterranean Archaeology* 8.1, 1–32.

Campbell, L. (2016) Proportionalising Practices in the Past: Roman Fragments Beyond the Frontier. In *Creating Material Worlds. The Uses of Identity in Archaeology*, edited by E. Pierce, A. Russell, A. Maldonado and L. Campbell, 215–239. Oxford: Oxbow Books.

Campus, F., Leonelli, V. and Lo Schiavo, F. (2010) La Transizione Culturale dall'Età del Bronzo all' Età del Ferro nella Sardegna Nuragica in Relazione con l'Italia Tirrenica. *Bollettino di Archeologia On Line*, www.archeologia.beniculturali.it/pages/pubblicazioni.html.

Chapman, J. (2000) *Fragmentation in Archaeology: People, Places and Broken Objects in the Prehistory of South Eastern Europe.* London: Routledge.

Classen, C. (1996) Sugar Cane, Coca-Cola and Hypermarkets: Consumption and Surrealism in the Argentine Northwest. In *Cross-Cultural Consumption. Global Markets, Local Realities*, edited by D. Howes. New York: Routledge, 39–54.

Dietler, M. (2005) The Archaeology of Colonization and the Colonization of Archaeology. In *The Archaeology of Colonial Encounters: Comparative Perspectives*, edited by G.J. Stein. Santa Fe: School of American Research Press, 33–68.

Doonan, O. (2001) Domestic Architecture and Settlement Planning in Early and Middle Bronze Age Sicily: Thoughts on Innovation and Social Process. *Journal of Mediterranean Archaeology* 14.2, 159–188.

Dyson, S. and Rowland, R. (2007) *Archaeology and History in Sardinia from the Stone Age to the Middle Ages: Shepherds, Sailors and Conquerors.* Philadelphia: University of Pennsylvania Museum of Archaeology.

Ferrarese Ceruti, M.L. (1997) Ceramica Micenea in Sardegna (Nota Preliminare). In *Archeologia della Sardegna Preistorica e Protostorica*, edited by A. Antona and F. Lo Schiavo. Nuoro: Poliedro, 269–276.

Ferrarese Ceruti, M.L. (1980) Micenei in Sardegna! *Rendiconti della Accademia Nazionale dei Lincei* 8.35, 391–393.

Gallin, L.J. (1989) *Architectural Attributes and Inter-Site Variation. A Case Study: The Sardinian Nuraghi.* Unpublished PhD dissertation, Department of Anthropology, University of California, Los Angeles.

Giardino, C. (1995) *Il Mediterraneo Occidentale fra XIV ed VII Secolo a.C: Cerchie Minerarie e Metallurgiche. The West Mediterranean between the 14th and 8th Centuries BC: Mining and Metallurgical Spheres.* British Archaeological Reports International Series 612. Oxford: Tempus Reparatum.

Gordon, J.M. (2018) Transforming Culture on an Insula Portunalis: Port Cities as Central Places in Early Roman Cyprus. *Land* 7.4, 1–28.

Hayne, J. (2016) Drinking Identities and Changing Ideologies in Iron Age Sardinia. In *Creating Material Worlds. The Uses of Identity in Archaeology*, edited by E. Pierce, A. Russell, A. Maldonado and L. Campbell. Oxford: Oxbow Books, 105–134.

Hingley, R. (2005) *Globalizing Roman Culture: Unity, Diversity and Empire.* London: Routledge.

Hodos, T. (2010) Globalization and Colonization: A View from Iron Age Sicily. *Journal of Mediterranean Archaeology* 23.1, 81–106.

Howes, D. (1996) Introduction: Commodities and Cultural Borders. In *Cross-Cultural Consumption. Global Markets, Local Realities*, edited by D. Howes. New York: Routledge, 1–16.

Iacono, F. (2015) Feasting at Roca: Cross-Cultural Encounters and Society in the Southern Adriatic during the Late Bronze Age. *European Journal of Archaeology* 18, 259–281.

Jennings, J. (2017) Distinguishing Past Globalizations. In *The Routledge Handbook of Archaeology and Globalization*, edited by T. Hodos. London: Routledge, 12–28.

Jennings, J. (2011) *Globalizations and the Ancient World.* Cambridge: Cambridge University Press.

Jones, R.E. and Day, P. (1987) Aegean-type Pottery on Sardinia: Identification of Imports and Local Imitations by Chemical Analysis. In *Studies in Sardinian Archaeology* 3. *Nuragic Sardinia and the Mycenaean World*, edited by M.S. Balmuth. British Archaeological Reports International Series 387. Oxford: British Archaeological Reports, 257–269.

Jones, R.E., Levi, S.T., Bettelli, M. and Vagnetti, L. (2014) *Italo-Mycenaean Pottery: The Archaeological and Archaeometric Dimensions.* Incunabula Graeca 103. Rome: Consiglio Nazionale delle Ricerche.

Kiriatzi, E. and Andreou, S. (2016) Mycenaean and Mycenaeanising Pottery across the Mediterranean: A Multi-Scalar Approach to Technological Mobility, Transmission and Appropriation. In *Human Mobility and Technological Transfer in the Prehistoric Mediterranean*, edited by E. Kiriatzi and C. Knappett. Cambridge: Cambridge University Press, 128–153.

Knapp, A.B. (2008) *Prehistoric and Protohistoric Cyprus. Identity, Insularity, and Connectivity.* Oxford: Oxford University Press.

Knapp, A.B. (2000) Archaeology, Science-Based Archaeology and the Mediterranean Bronze Age Metals Trade. *European Journal of Archaeology* 3, 31–56.

Lilliu, G. (1988) *La Civilità dei Sardi dal Paleolitico all'Età dei Nuraghi.* Torino: Nuova Edizioni Rai Radiotelevisione Italiana.

Lo Schiavo, F. (2008) Oxhide Ingots in the Central Mediterranean: Recent Perspectives. In *Aegean Metallurgy in the Bronze Age*, edited by I. Tzachili. Athens: Ta Pragmata Publications, 227–245.

Lo Schiavo, F. (2005) Oxhide Ingots, Cyprus and Sardinia. In *Archaeometallurgy in Sardinia from the Origins to the Beginning of the Early Iron Age*, edited by F. Lo Schiavo, A. Giumlia-Mair, U. Sanna and R. Valera. Monographies Instrumentum 30. Montagnac: Éditions Monique Mergoil, 305–331.

Lo Schiavo, F. (2003a) Sardinia between East and West: Interconnections in the Mediterranean. In *ΠΛΟΕΣ ... Sea Routes ... Interconnections in the Mediterranean 16th–6th c. BC*, edited by N.C. Stampolidis and V. Karageorghis. Athens: A.G. Leventis Foundation, 15–33.

Lo Schiavo, F. (2003b) The Problem of Early Tin from the Point of View of Nuragic Sardinia. In *The Problem of Early Tin*, edited by A. Giumlia-Mair and F. Lo Schiavo. British Archaeological Reports International Series 1199. Oxford: Archaeopress, 121–132.

Lo Schiavo, F. (2001) Late Cypriot Bronzework and Bronzeworkers in Sardinia, Italy and Elsewhere in the West. In *Italy and Cyprus in Antiquity: 1500–450 BC*, edited by L. Bonfante and V. Karageorghis. Nicosia: Costakis and Leto Severis Foundation, 131–152.

Lo Schiavo, F. and Campus, F. (2013) Metals and Beyond: Cyprus and Sardinia in the Bronze Age Mediterranean Network. *Pasiphae* 7, 147–158.

Lo Schiavo, F., Vagnetti, L. and Macnamara, E. (1985) Late Cypriot Imports to Italy and their Influence on Local Bronzework. *Papers of the British School of Rome* 53, 1–71.

Macdougall, J.P. (2003) Traditional Commodities as Local Cultural Icons: Barbie Dolls in Mexico. *Journal of Popular Culture* 37, 257–275.

Miller, D. (2001) Coca-Cola: A Sweet Black Drink from Trinidad. In *Consumption*, edited by D. Miller. Critical Concepts in the Social Sciences IV. London: Routledge, 388–406.

Negroni Catacchio, N. (2016) L'ambra Produzione e Commerci nell'Italia Preromana. In *Italia Omnium Terrarum Parens*, edited by C. Ampolo, D. Briquel, P. Càssola Guida, B. D'Agostino, C. De Simone, A. La Regina, V. La Rosa, M. Lejeune, M. Lombardo, N. Negroni Catacchio, N.F. Parise, R. Peroni, A.L. Prosdocimi and G. Pugliese Carratelli. Milano: Libri Scheiwiller, 659–696.

Nederveen Pieterse, J. (2015) *Globalization and Culture. Global Mélange*. Lanham, Maryland: Rowman and Littlefield.

Parkinson, W.A. and Galaty, M.L. (2009) Introduction: Interaction and Ancient Societies. In *Archaic State Interaction: The Eastern Mediterranean in the Bronze Age*, edited by W.A. Parkinson and M.L. Galaty. Santa Fe: School for Advanced Research Press, 3–28.

Patton, M. (1996) *Islands in Time. Island Sociogeography and Mediterranean Prehistory*. London: Routledge.

Perra, M. (1997) From Deserted Ruins: An Interpretation of Nuragic Sardinia. *Europeae* 3.2, 49–76.

Pitts, M. and Versluys, M.J. (2014) Globalisation and the Roman World: Perspectives and Opportunities. In *Globalisation and the Roman World: World History, Connectivity, and Material Culture*, edited by M. Pitts and M.J. Versluys. Cambridge: Cambridge University Press, 3–31.

Polanyi, K. (1963) Ports of Trade in Early Societies. *Journal of Economic History* 23, 30–45.

Russell, A. (2017) Sicily without Mycenae: a Cross-Cultural Consumption Analysis of Connectivity in the Bronze Age Central Mediterranean. *Journal of Mediterranean Archaeology* 30.1, 59–83.

Russell, A. (2016) We are not You. Being Different in Bronze Age Sicily. In *Creating Material Worlds. The Uses of Identity in Archaeology*, edited by E. Pierce, A. Russell, A. Maldonado and L. Campbell. Oxford: Oxbow Books, 153–174.

Russell, A. (2010) Foreign Materials, Islander Mobility and Elite Identity in Late Bronze Age Sardinia. In *Material Connections in the Ancient Mediterranean. Mobility, Materiality and Identity*, edited by P. van Dommelen and A.B. Knapp. London: Routledge.

Russell, A. (2011) *In the Middle of the Corrupting Sea. Cultural Encounters in Sicily and Sardinia between 1450-900 BC*. Unpublished PhD dissertation, Department of Archaeology, University of Glasgow, Glasgow, UK.

Russell, A. and Knapp, A.B. (2017) Sardinia and Cyprus: An Alternative View on Cypriotes in the Central Mediterranean. *Papers of the British School at Rome* 85, 1–35.

Schulz Paulsson, B. (2019) Radiocarbon Dates and Bayesian Modeling Support Maritime Diffusion Model for Megaliths in Europe. *Proceedings of the Academy of Sciences of the United States of America*: Online edition: https://www.pnas.org/content/early/2019/02/05/1813268116.

Stos-Gale, Z.A. and Gale, N.H. (1992) New Light on the Provenience of the Copper Oxhide Ingots Found on Sardinia. In *Sardinia in the Mediterranean: A Footprint in the Sea*, edited by R.H. Tykot and T.K. Andrews. Monographs in Mediterranean Archaeology 3. Sheffield: Sheffield Academic Press, 317–346.

Sweetman, R.J. (2007) Roman Knossos: The Nature of a Globalized City. *American Journal of Archaeology* 111, 61–81.

Tronchetti, C. (2015) Cultural Interactions in Iron Age Sardinia. In *The Cambridge Prehistory of the Bronze and Iron Age Mediterranean*, edited by A.B. Knapp and P. van Dommelen. New York: Cambridge University Press, 266–284.

Ugas, G. (2005) *L'Alba dei Nuraghi*. Cagliari: Fabula.

Usai, A. (1995) Nota sulla Società della Sardegna Nuragica e sulla Funzione dei Nuraghi. In *Settlement and Economy in Italy 1500 BC–AD 1500. Papers of the Fifth Conference of Italian Archaeology*, edited by N. Christie. Oxbow Monographs 41. Oxford: Oxbow Books, 253–259.

Vagnetti, L. (2001) Some Observations on Late Cypriot Pottery from the Central Mediterranean. In *Italy and Cyprus in Antiquity: 1500–450 BC*, edited by L. Bonfante and V. Karageorghis. Nicosia: Costakis and Leto Severis Foundation, 77–96.

van Dommelen, P. (2005) Colonial Interactions and Hybrid Practices. In *The Archaeology of Colonial Encounters: Comparative Perspectives*, edited by G.J. Stein. Santa Fe: School of American Research Press, 109–141.

van Dommelen, P. (1998) Punic Persistence: Colonialism and Cultural Identities. In *Cultural Identity in the Roman Empire*, edited by R. Laurence and J. Berry. New York: Routledge, 25–48.

Versluys, M.J. (2014) Understanding Objects in Motion: An Archaeological Dialogue on Romanization. *Archaeological Dialogues* 21, 1–20.

Vianello, A. (2005) *Late Bronze Age Mycenaean and Italic Products in the West Mediterranean: A Social and Economic Analysis*. British Archaeological Reports, International Series 1439. Oxford: Archaeopress.

Wallerstein, I. (1974) *The Modern World System I: Capitalist Agriculture and the Origins of the European World-Economy in the Sixteenth Century*. New York: Academic Press.

Webster, G.S. (2015) *The Archaeology of Nuragic Sardinia*. Monographs in Mediterranean Archaeology 14. Sheffield: Equinox Publishing Ltd.

Webster, G.S. (1996) *A Prehistory of Sardinia, 2300–500 BC*. Monographs in Mediterranean Archaeology 5. Sheffield: Sheffield Academic Press.

Wilk, R. (1995) Learning to be Local in Belize: Global Systems of Difference. In *Worlds Apart. Modernity through the Prism of the Local*, edited by D. Miller. London: Routledge, 110–133.

Chapter 3

Mobility and Globalization: The View from the Bronze Age Cyclades

Evi Gorogianni

To Isa Rodriguez Soto and Mira Mohsini, thank you

Introduction

In 1997, a two-headed Trojan horse (Fig. 7) was installed at the US–Mexican border by artist Marcos Ramírez Erre.[1] The artist bestowed the instantly recognizable Greek mythological symbol of invasion (through less than upfront means) with a transparent body and two heraldic heads, one looking towards Mexico and the other pointing to the US. These attributes were meant to underscore the cultural exchange and the bonds of mutual dependency between the two countries that are forged on a border crossed by 50,000 people per day.[2] The sculpture also emphasized the permeability of borders, which are never unidirectional, and the ambiguities generated by popular media treatments of the topic of US–Mexico relations. Overall, the artwork served as a potent reminder for the effects, intended or not, of a meeting of cultures in a globalized context.

For decades, globalization, often interchangeably used alongside the terms Westernization or Americanization,[3] was considered to be a process of cultural homogenization that erodes local identity and traditions in exchange for the seductive trappings of urban Western comforts. The modern world poignantly disproves this popular set of assumptions. Globalization itself (instead of just homogenizing the world over) has proven to be a breeding ground for cultural heterogeneity and even dissonance. As Néstor García Canclini[4] notes, even when generalized directional flows may allude to the erosion of local and/or national identities, other processes enact 'an articulated fragmentation of the world that reorders differences and inequalities without eradicating them' resulting in the construction of new transnational communities or new emergent local traditional narratives.

Figure 7: 'Toy-an-Horse Toy an Horse', a two-headed replica of the Trojan Horse overlooking the two sides of the US-Mexican border from its vantage point at the cross-checkpoint at San Ysidro (courtesy of Mr Ramírez Erre).

The modern context is an endless source of inspiration when scholars and scientists approach the past, and globalization is no exception, as Jody Michael Gordon and Anna Kouremenos succinctly underlined in the introduction and elsewhere.[5] Globalization, as a structural and appropriately scaled conceptual framework, has been used for a few decades now to analyze past interaction and help interpret its effects.[6] Two interrelated features are considered essential for identifying past globalizations[7]: a surge in connectivity and the creation of a global culture. The *surge of complex connectivity* (especially among long-distance locales), usually manifests in the archaeological record as the flow of cultural products or practices coupled with 'wider changes within a conceptual or experiential world',[8] which triggers cultural change and leads to the creation of a *global culture* that is consciously embraced by the participating communities. These two phenomena, *i.e.* surge in complex connectivity and the creation of a global culture, are further correlated with increased standardization and homogeneity coupled with the deterritorialization of cultural traits, but also with inherent vulnerability of all the participants to the exchange network.[9]

One such globalized context was the Aegean archipelago during the Middle and Late Bronze Age.[10] Evidence indicates that the Aegean was a theater of interregional and/or intercultural contact since the early Bronze Age (or perhaps even earlier)[11] and was unquestionably integrated, albeit marginally, within the eastern Mediterranean and Near Eastern world system.[12] In the 2nd millennium BCE, flows intensified considerably, both within the Aegean but also with the rest of the eastern Mediterranean. This intensification is partly due to the introduction of a new technology in shipbuilding, the sailboat.

Instead of the paddle, which was used to propel their longboats and canoes,[13] Cycladic mariners adopted the square sail, oars, and the steering oar as the means of propelling larger watercraft by the end of the Early Bronze Age (EBA hereafter).[14] These innovations, probably introduced from Egypt and/or the Near East via Crete,[15] had wide-ranging repercussions for maritime activity. The new sailing craft shrunk distances (increasing the possible day's range from about 20–50 km to c. 100–150 km), massively improved flexibility in the travel direction (especially against the prevailing winds), and increased cargo capacity.[16] As a result, Aegean communities experienced the phenomenon of time-space compression.[17] The Aegean and, more importantly for our purposes, the Cycladic communities, who were previously the purveyors of goods and knowledge, became more accessible, and certainly more vulnerable, to individuals or groups that owned the sailing ships. Indeed, during the end of the EBA there is archaeological evidence for increased concern about violence – nucleation in concert with the abandonment and/or fortification of settlements,[18] which lends support to a reversal of Cycladic fortunes and a general restructuring of Aegean ways of life.

On some islands, a more nucleated habitation pattern replaces the dispersed communities that dotted the islands (and the mainland).[19] The EB II 'small world' pattern of interactions is abandoned for another that emphasizes navigation along a north/south axis and prioritized coastal locales with good anchorage, close to good agricultural lands, and access to desirable resources. The new ships were able to supply the needs of a burgeoning elite class on Crete with not only metals, which were the primary trade product since the EBA, but also other exotic products, such as wool textiles, saffron, unguents, and obsidian as well as other volcanic stones.[20] In turn, trade and exchange brought to the islands a number of products, the most archaeologically detectable of which is imported pottery. More crucially, these connective forces also brought a new symbolic language of power and imported technologies (*e.g.* the fast potter's wheel, the upright loom, Linear A writing, a system of weights and measures, tripod cooking), which ultimately transformed Aegean culture and everyday experience, and resulted in the forging of a Pan-Aegean *koine*. This widespread cultural change has often been called 'Minoanization'[21] and bears all the strengths and weaknesses of other '-izations'.[22]

Interest in Minoanization has resulted in the application of a number of different approaches over the years,[23] of which the most recent is influenced by globalization. The application of the globalization studies' theoretical framework has made apparent certain aspects for which previous frameworks (thalassocracy, colonization, acculturation, hybridity, etc.) were not as successful in accounting for the whole picture. Therefore, globalization studies bring to light the realization that we cannot understand the processes and experiences that affect people and their things in the contemporary world or in the archaeological past if we regard cultures as homogeneous, unchanging, and firmly anchored and delineated in space. Nor can we understand cultural interaction if we give into cultural relativism and approach globalization merely as a process of fragmentation and heterogenization and 'dispute that any sort of homogeneous system ever existed, and reject the distinction, between universal signatures and particular localities'.[24] Instead, a much more productive approach is to come to terms with the paradoxical and often contradictory assemblage of processes, phenomena, and agencies that constitute globalization and examine not only its homogenizing propensities but also alterity, interculturality, and the tensions between the local and the global.[25]

I have argued elsewhere that we need to venture beyond the macro-level and adopt more reflexive and flexible strategies for exploring cultural change during periods of heightened connectivity, because macro-level approaches, no matter how illustrative they may be, obscure the agency of individuals and objects that ultimately are the decisive factors in this process.[26] Moreover, in the case of Minoanization, the length of the phenomenon makes it improbable that one model can explain all permutations that occurred over time for more than three centuries. Detailed analysis of the phenomenon indicates that various cultural media were affected by this process in different ways and at differential speeds, a realization that obliges us to entertain different avenues of transmission (*e.g.*, adoption of pottery styles, technologies, dress codes, and architectural forms require very different transmission processes).[27] Thus, over the last decade scholars have been attentive to processes at the micro-level in an attempt to humanize the phenomenon[28] and have sought possible explanations that involve agency and local involvement within the general process of acculturation.

The present paper is very much in line with the approach outlined above and therefore sheds light on the human landscape of the globalized Aegean by discussing various categories of objects and practices and exploring their implications for the people that used and produced them. In this endeavor, the material record examined comes from Ayia Irini, a site on the Cycladic island of Kea (Fig. 8).

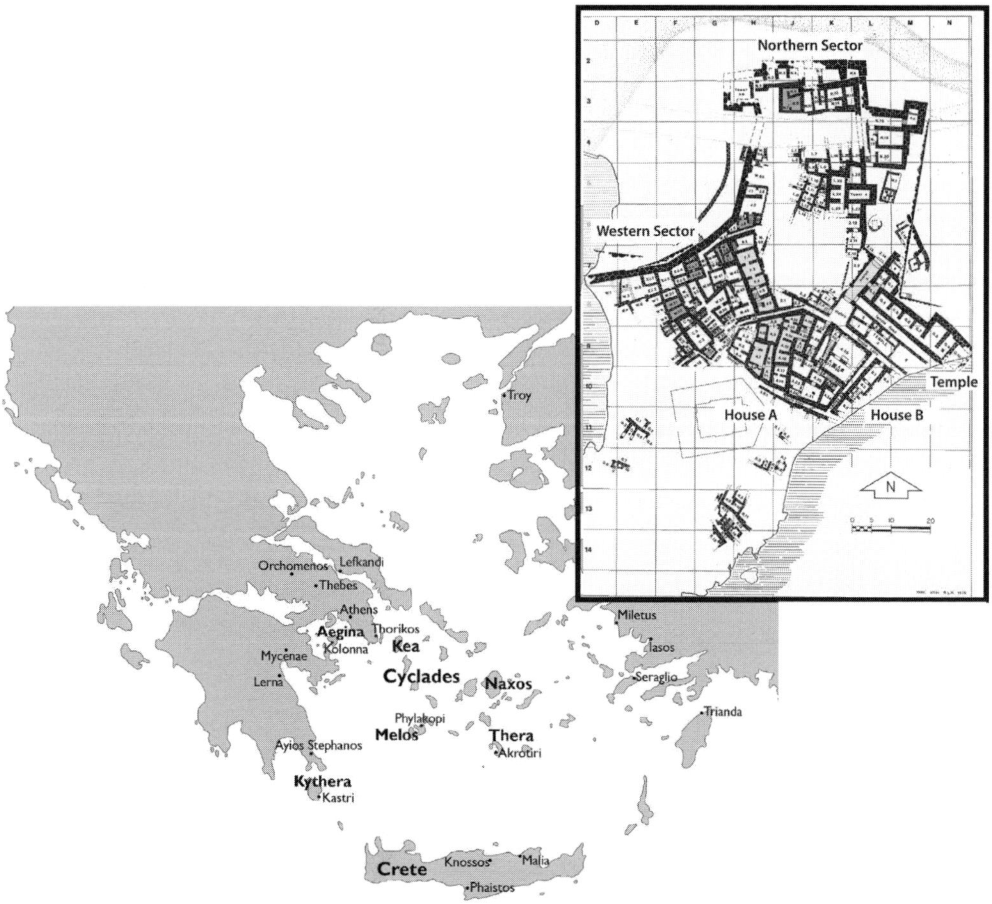

Figure 8: Map of the Aegean and the plan of the site of Ayia Irini on Kea (map by B. Trail; site plan after Schofield 2011, plate 2).

Kea is the one of the largest Cycladic islands[29] and the closest to the Greek Mainland in terms of geographical distance, which curiously seems to stretch and contract over time as the island experienced inclusion and exclusion from the various networks that prevailed at different time periods. During the Middle and Late Bronze Age, Kea and its sole major site, Ayia Irini, stood in a border zone, *i.e.* at the edge of the Minoanized world and culturally close to Cretan communities while at the same time in close association with communities on the Mainland shore that did not identify culturally as a part of the Minoan world.[30] Ayia Irini itself was a border town, where another version of Ramírez Erre's two-headed and transparent Trojan horse could have been set up. The community's material culture eloquently tells the story of a simultaneous adoption of the 'globalized' culture (*i.e.* cultural homogenization) and the creation of alterity through local adaptations and adjustments.[31]

The material culture categories examined in this paper are imported pottery, locally produced pottery, and the evidence for textile production from the Northern Sector of Ayia Irini (Fig. 9), which has been the author's research focus.[32] This paper also advocates for the expansion of the list of possible processes that contributed to the globalization of the Aegean beyond trade and exchange. Even though trade and exchange were significant forces in the integration of this globalized context, the social integration of this mini-world was most likely also due to a continuous low-level migration and the planned articulation of a kinship network based on marital alliances (for a similar phenomenon during the Hellenistic period, see Mazurek in this volume).

Imports

Imports, or non-local objects found displaced in assemblages away from the place of manufacture, have long attracted the attention of scholars as tangible indicators of either movement of people, trade, or exchange. In any consideration of displaced objects, there are a number of interpretive possibilities that should be entertained. Were they consumer goods, loot, gifts in a gift exchange, private property, or various combinations of the options listed? Recently, some scholars have problematized modern and past perceptions of 'foreign' and imports/exports,[33] cautioning us that perhaps distinctions modern researchers make may not have been applicable in the past. Moreover, not all kinds of imports are made the same, and each of them carries variable interpretive implications.

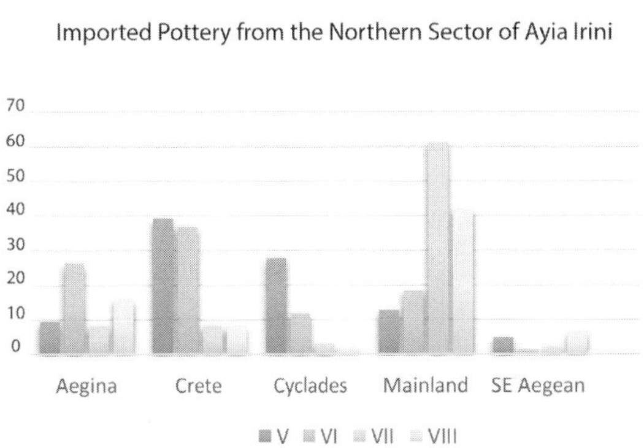

Figure 9: Quantitative representation (percentages) of imported ceramics by region. For raw counts, see Table 2.

Nevertheless, imports remain a significant gauge of interaction, particularly imported pottery, which has been an interpretive conundrum for scholars because of its sheer ubiquity. Its importance in the archaeological literature has ranged from an expensive luxury to a low-value commodity used only as ballast in ships; however, lately the scholarly consensus, at least in the Aegean context, is that pottery was not a high-value or prestige good, nor necessarily one controlled by palatial centers. Even in the Mycenaean case, in which archaeological data is complemented by documentary evidence, the involvement of the palaces in pottery production (let alone distribution) seems to have been tangential at best, with very few exceptions.[34] This laisser-faire attitude of the palaces stood despite the fact that consumption of Mycenaean fine wares increased substantially throughout the Aegean and eastern Mediterranean. Nevertheless, pottery as a commodity was not without value. According to Sherratt,[35] most often the intensification of demand in the acquisition of high-value resources (*e.g.* metals), which seems to be the primary motivation for long-distance trade and exchange, creates a ripple effect of diversification of transported commodities. Alongside the high-value commodities, which were tightly controlled, cargoes also tend to include goods with high or purely added value (such as pottery) which create an 'unofficial' and largely undocumented aspect of the overall trade activity.[36] Thus, pottery was a product that could produce a profit at the margin, which made it an important cargo in its own right.[37]

Given this framework, the consideration of imported pottery at Ayia Irini becomes a particularly insightful topic. It has often been underlined that Ayia Irini's reason for existence and prosperity was the interest in the metal resources at nearby Lavrion, particularly in cerussite and galena, or more commonly silver and lead.[38] From the time of its reestablishment in MC II (c. 1800 BCE) until its abandonment during LM IB/LH II (c. 1525–1400 BCE; see Table 2), Ayia Irini seems to have functioned as the main hub for the transshipment of mined and processed ores, the distribution of which was widespread in the Aegean.[39] Even though it is reasonable to assume that some of the imported wares might have been the private property of occasional migrants or gifts to influential people at the site, it is very likely that its bulk might have been the result of the kind of trade model that Sherratt advances, consumed by the 'elites' or heads of households at Ayia Irini. Ships sailing to Ayia Irini would bring imported pottery, both container vessels filled with products and vessels to be traded in their own right. Of course, as Sherratt points out, products like pottery, with purely added value, have little commonly recognized value in their own right and depend on a nexus of associations with elite symbols and practices, which then creates demand for them.[40] Therefore, imported pottery may serve as a barometer of sorts for the integration of this particular site with the rest of the Aegean world and provide qualitative and quantitative insights into its degree of connectivity.

For this exercise, the imported ceramic assemblage from the Northern Sector,[41] an area of the site which was first inhabited in the late MBA (MM IIIA, c. 1700 BCE) (see Table 2), was put to the test.[42] In summing up the diachronic importation trends portrayed in Fig. 9, we observe that imports from Crete early on are a significant

Table 2: Chronological chart for periodization at Ayia Irini, Kea.

Ayia Irini	*Relative chronology*	*Suggested dates BCE*
Period IV	MB II	1800–1700
Period V	MB III	1700–1600
Period VI	LB I	1600–1525
Period VII	LB II	1525–1400
Period VIII	LB III/LH IIIA	1400–1300

presence in the imported assemblage of Ayia Irini, showing as over one third of the imported wares in Periods V and VI (*i.e.* early Neopalatial period), but seem to decrease over time, a trend that becomes much more marked after Period VI, and results in less than 10% in Period VII (*i.e.* late Neopalatial period). Diachronically, the assemblage also presents some other interesting trends that supplement and contextualize perhaps the big picture of import decline. In the Period VI (LM IA) the proportion of imports from a North-central Cretan origin increased dramatically to the detriment of imports from other Cretan locales (Table 3), possibly indicating intensification (and increasing exclusivity?) in the relationship between North-central Crete and Ayia Irini. Imports from the Cyclades (mainly the Southern Cyclades, but also other production centers, albeit to a lower degree) also seem to gradually decline over time, starting from one-third of the assemblage (28%) and dropping to very low levels (2%) in Period VIII (*i.e.* LH IIIA or 1400–1300 BCE). In Period V, open and closed vessels are equally well-represented and included both Minoanising and traditional Cycladic shapes, whereas in the next period almost all of the assemblage is composed of open shapes.

Aeginetan imports (Fig. 9) seem to fluctuate diachronically in the Northern Sector; they peak in Period VI (c. 1600–1525 BCE) and decline significantly in Period VII (c. 1525–1400 BCE), only to increase slightly in Period VIII (c. 1400–1300 BCE). Conversely, products from workshops on the Greek Mainland, which were present since the re-establishment of the settlement in Period IV,[43] become increasingly better represented in the imported assemblage,[44] increasing 100% over the previous period (61%) during Period VII and continuing in Period VIII. Last but not least, there is a limited but consistent relationship with the Southeast Aegean.

Therefore, if imported pottery is the weathervane for affiliations (either real or desired), the elites of Ayia Irini clearly shift their affiliations over time. Whereas Crete, and especially North-central Crete, is a focal point for about two centuries (1700–1525 BCE, or the early Neopalatial period), in Period VII (c. 1525–1400 BCE, of LM IB) Ayia Irini elites prefer to look elsewhere. The connections with Central Greece, which never seem to go out of fashion, are more intense in Period VII (LH II/LM IB), while the Northeast Peloponnese seems to become an area of substantial interest after Period VII. At the present time, these shifts in connectivity cannot be firmly correlated with specific

Table 3: Quantitative data derived from the assemblage of imported pottery of the Northern Sector of Ayia Irini on Kea. The data in this table underline the relationships represented in Figure 2.

Region	*V (raw)*	*V (%)*	*VI (raw)*	*VI (%)*	*VII (raw)*	*VII (%)*	*VIII (raw)*	*VIII (%)*
Aegina	20	10	20	26	8	8	10	16
Crete (North-central)	56	27	28	37	7	7	4	6
Crete (assorted)	26	12	0	0	1	1	1	2
Southern Cyclades	47	22	7	9	3	3	1	2
Cyclades (assorted)	11	5	2	3	0	0	0	0
Mainland (North)	23	11	10	13	31	32	10	16
Mainland (South)	4	2	4	5	20	20	16	26
Mainland	0	1	0	0	9	0	0	0
Mainland/Kythera	3	0	0	0		9	0	0
Southeast Aegean	10	5	1	1	2	2	4	6
Unknown	9	4	3	4	11	11	16	26
Crete North-central or Mainland	0	0	1	1	6	6	0	0
Total	209		76		98		62	

processes. However, there seems to be a loose correlation with the rise and the waning fortunes of Cretan as well as the Mainland palatial polities. This correlation needs further investigation taking into consideration potential environmental changes (related to the eruption of the Thera volcano but also to other causes) and changes in the productivity of the Lavrion mines, which might have been declining, among other factors.[45]

Local Ceramic Production

An interesting question is how closely these trends compare to emulation in the ceramics manufactured locally. Recent research shows that local potters follow a similar but divergent trajectory.[46] In Period IV (c. 1800–1700 BCE, which was not discussed above due to a near absence in the Northern Sector), potters on site adhere to contemporary Cycladic and Aeginetan traditions in shape-repertoire and technology. Only a minuscule percentage (2%) of the assemblage drew its inspiration from Minoan shapes and was manufactured with Minoan derived technology, *i.e.* the fast potter's wheel.[47] In the succeeding Period V (c. 1700–1600 BCE), although preferences at the dinner table (*i.e.* open shapes) seem to favor equally open shapes of Minoan inspiration and the ones of the Cyclado-Aeginetan-Helladic tradition, the rest of the assemblage used for pouring, cooking, and other mundane uses seems to be firmly rooted in the Minoan tradition.[48] This variability is particularly intriguing and suggests the 'introduction of another "new technology" in everyday domestic life that further supports the introduction of immigrants from Crete and especially women within the community of existing residents at Ayia Irini',[49] based on the assumption that they are the ones choosing the technological devices for food preparation.[50]

Ceramic trends established in the 17th-century BCE (Period V) are sustained and intensified in the following two periods, VI and VII. Minoan shapes seem to gain in popularity even though they never thoroughly eclipse their Cyclado-Aeginetan counterparts, while the potter's wheel seems to be the preferred manufacturing method, albeit used in combination with coiling.[51] The range of emulated shapes during Periods VI and VII (early Neopalatial period) is narrower in all but the Minoanizing specialty shapes, while the preferred cups on the dinner table continue the local Minoanizing tradition. Despite this continuity in the use of Minoanizing shapes, there are traces of a disjunction. The popular ogival or S-shaped cup, which is the preferred shape for drinking on Crete, is peculiarly absent from the ceramic assemblage of Period VII. As indicated elsewhere, this subtle differentiation might betray that the dining table fashions of the Mainland (also Minoanized to an extent) are the most influential at this time.

This short and very condensed summary speaks about a few different processes at work that are conflated in discussions of ceramic assemblages: fashions in fine wares (which usually change relatively rapidly, *i.e.* every one or two generations) and producers' preferences in technology, whether we are referring to the vase maker or the cook. Even though fashions in shapes or decoration schemes for fine wares follow more closely the trends that are observed in imported wares sought by the heads of households, the technological methods used by producers reveal a different network of affiliations to communities of practice, familial traditions, and even migratory flows through the Aegean.

More specifically, as argued recently, pottery production at Ayia Irini was most likely practiced at the level of a household industry, not unlike metallurgy, textile production, manufacture of aromatics, etc. There is good evidence for multiple units of production at Ayia Irini from its re-foundation during Period IV and well into Period VII, although there is also evidence for increasing standardization in the production of specific shapes and the introduction of the fast potter's wheel.[52] The latter technological device and its corresponding technological culture were imported from Crete. As has been argued elsewhere, this introduction presupposes either the migration of Cretan-trained potters to the island or a long apprenticeship away from 'home' for Keian potters and subsequent maintenance of ties with the specific community of practice.[53] At the same time, the use of the potter's wheel never became exclusive to other manufacturing methods, with a combination method including coil building and rotational kinetic energy being the most popular method in Period VII.[54] All in all, the picture that is emerging is one that includes a constant (albeit slow) flow of craft producers who traveled through the Aegean and participated in a community of practice. These same craft producers, when settled, then practice their particular brand of craft in communication with other potters in the town, and pass the knowledge of their craft from generation to generation which ultimately results in a blending between the local and the non-local.[55]

The same blending of 'constellations of practice' can be seen in another sector of production, food preparation, which constitutes another important marker of mobility and ethnic/cultural diversity.[56] In a recent paper that gathered and summarized the evidence for cooking practices at Ayia Irini,[57] two major cooking technological packages were used by local cooks. The first was a Cretan one, which included three tripod shapes, jugs, jars, and trays, and a flat-bottomed tray,[58] and the second was a Cyclado-Mainland one which included a wide-mouthed jar with rounded profile and a pedestaled or rounded bottom (Fig. 10). There are two major differences between these two technological approaches. The first one lies in the spatial relationship between the vessel and the coals of the hearth, with the tripod vessels sitting over the coals (*i.e.* no need for a fixed hearth), whereas the wide-mouthed jars were nestled in the coals[59] or deposited in the periphery of the hearth. As for the second one, it regards the type of dishes that might have been produced with these vessels. Whereas both traditions produced stews in their respective shapes with deep bowl and restricted openings, the Cretan tradition made it possible to make flatbreads or sauté foods in the shallow pans of the baking dishes or trays (Fig. 10).

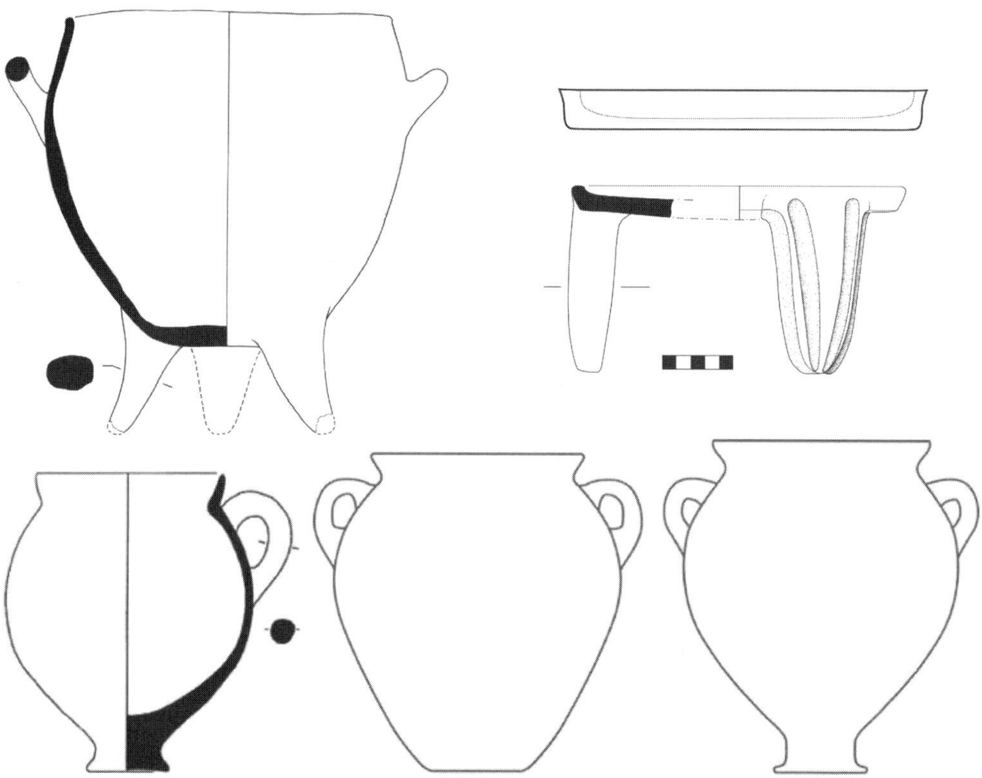

Figure 10: Repertoire of cooking shapes discussed in the paper. Upper portion: Cretan cooking shapes; Lower portion: Mainland style cooking jars (after Gorogianni et al. *2017).*

Both technological approaches to cooking seem to appear during Period IV.[60] Table 4 shows that the presence of Mainland-style cooking pots dominates the culinary landscape of the town during its initial phases. During Period IV, however, Mainland-style cooking pots seem to coexist in the same deposits with Cretan-style pots even since the earliest subphase (IVa). The coexistence of these cooking traditions persists throughout Period IV, but the balance between them gradually shifts in favor of the Cretan tradition. The ratio of Cretan-style cooking pots vs. Mainland-style pots increases steadily during Period IV (see Table 4), until in Period V there are no recorded instances of Mainland-style cooking pots, either locally produced or imported from Aegina.[61] Mainland-style cooking pots reappear in Period VI (during which admittedly the sample to date is seriously restricted) and VII. However, unlike in the earlier periods, there is no single instance of co-presence of the aforementioned two cooking traditions in the same space.

Even though there is no strict co-presence, it is equally valid that there is no strict definition of areas or houses for that matter in which cooks exclusively used one of these cooking traditions in any period of the site. Three illustrative examples support this claim: a) House A Rooms 15, 16, and 17; b) Northern Sector Rooms N.10, N.11, and N.12; and c) Northeast Bastion Rooms N.19/17 and N.20 (see Fig. 11).[62] In every one of these cases, cooking pots of the two traditions were stored or used in the adjacent and communicating spaces, which comprised the cooking quarters of the house.

Table 4: Survey of cooking vessels from Ayia Irini Periods IV through VII.

Period (or phase)	*No of deposits*	*MS-CJ pres.*	*Non-local MS-CJ*	*CICA pres.*	*Non-local CICA*	*Co-pres.*	*MS-CJ no.*	*CICA no.*	*Ratio of CICA / MS-CJ*
Iva	12	11		2		1	59	5	0.1
Ivb	22	19		11		9	106	27	0.3
Ivc	11	9		6		5	25	19	0.8
V	15	0	0	15	2[1]	0	0	47	0.0
VI	7	2	2[2]	5	1[3]	0	2	11	5.5
VII	20	10	10[4]	10	2[5]	0	11	16	1.5

Abbreviations: MS-CJ: Mainland Style Cooking Jar; CICA: Cretan Inspired Cooking Apparatus. Sources: *Period IV deposits*: Overbeck 1989. N.B. only single-phase deposits have been selected for inclusion in this chart; shaded cells represent the absence of data on provenance. *Period V deposits*: Davis 1986. *Period VI and VII*: for House A, see Cummer and Schofield 1984; for Western Sector, see Schofield 2011; for MS see Bikaki 1984; for the Northern Sector: data from the Ayia Irini Northern Sector Archaeological Project; Area B: Abell 2014b. [1] Provenance: one probably from Crete and the other one from Southern Cyclades; [2] Provenance: most likely Aeginetan; [3] Provenance: most likely from Central Cyclades; [4] Provenance: most likely Aeginetan; [5] Provenance: one probably from Aegina and the other one from the Cyclades.

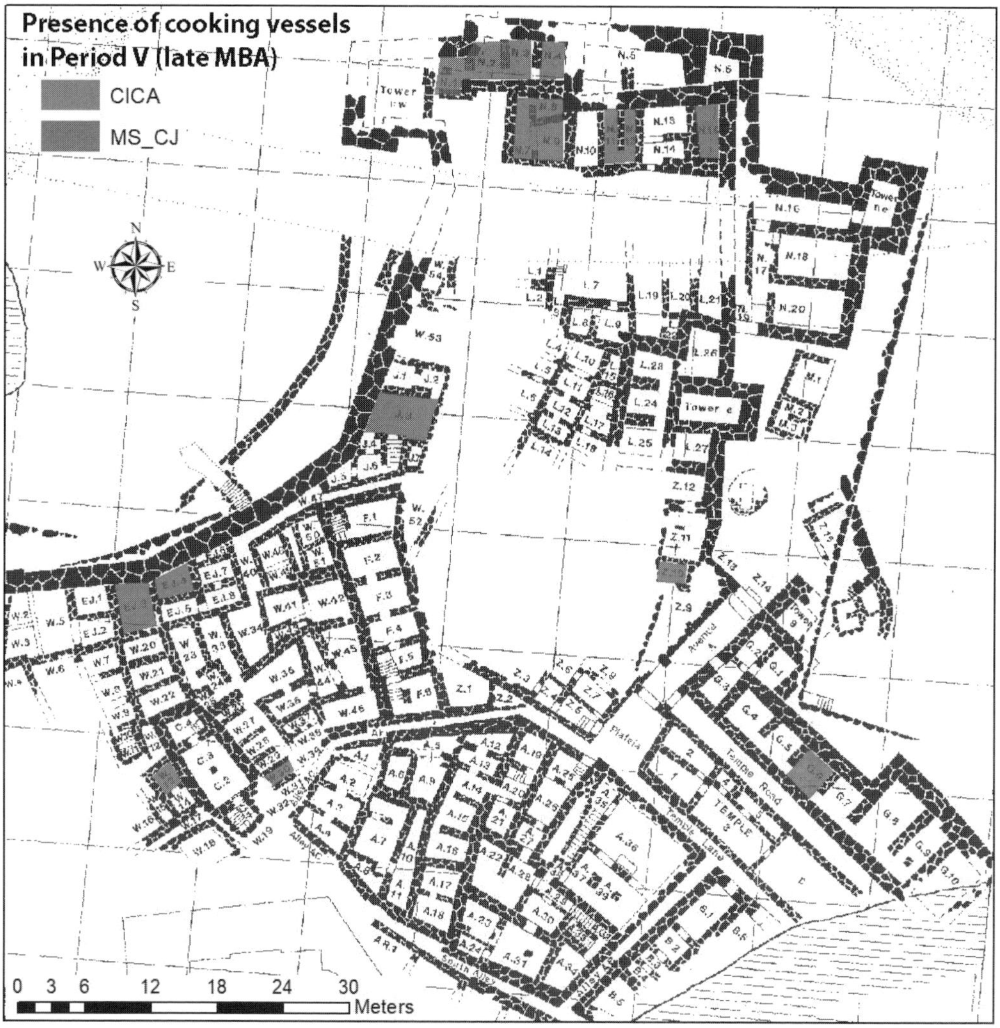

Figure 11: Spatial distribution of cooking jars (based on data in Gorogianni et al. *2017).*

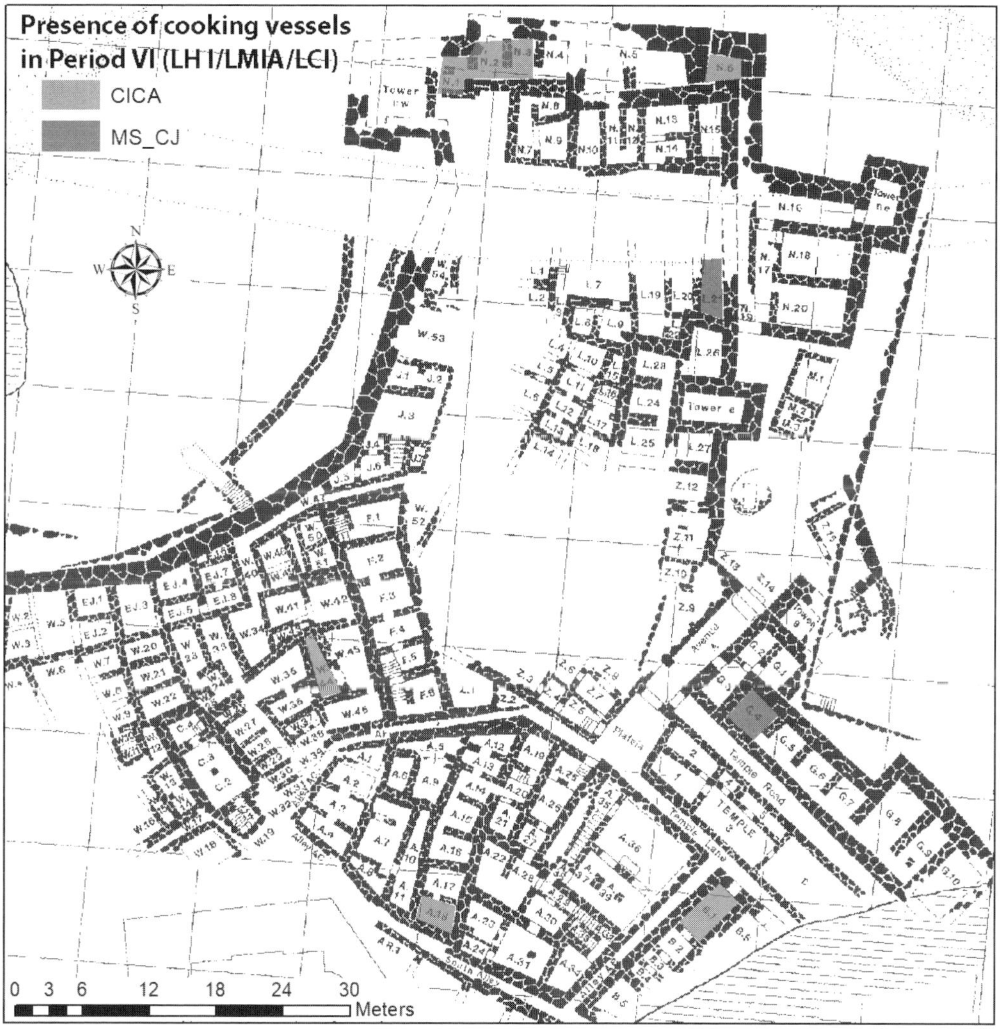

Figure 11: (Continued)

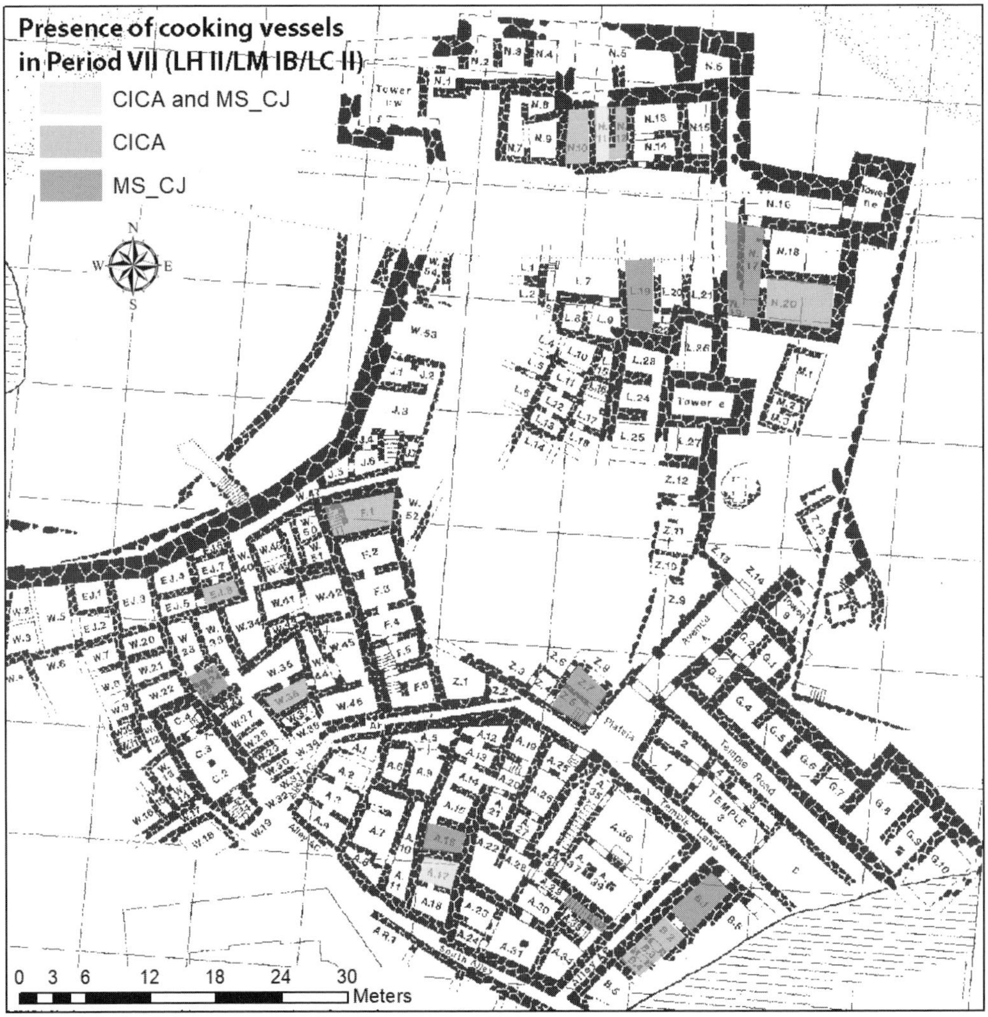

Figure 11: Spatial distribution of cooking jars (based on data in Gorogianni et al. 2017). (Continued)

Textile Hints

Apart from pottery, another commodity that seems to have been used for exchange during the Bronze Age (and later) was textiles.[63] Barber[64] has connected the intensification and elaboration of textile production during the Bronze Age, as well as their use for the signification of class and social status, with the growing demand for metals, which probably intensified in the MBA Aegean along with the development of state-level communities on Crete. Barber's observation certainly resonates in the case of Minoan Crete where, since the Protopalatial period, there is a marked interest in the centralized administration of textile production[65] that continues into the Mycenaean period both on Crete[66] and on the Mainland.[67]

The production of textiles involves various implements depending on the particular technology used (*i.e.* the type of loom) or the type of fabric needed to be produced. In the Minoan world, the production of textiles entailed: a) a device for the production of thread, which involved a dropped, whorl-weighted spindle or some other archaeologically undetectable device,[68] and b) the warp-weighted loom and loomweights in an assortment of types including spherical, discoid, and cuboid weights.[69] These textile tools are most often manufactured in terracotta, but also sometimes in stone and other raw materials, albeit much less frequently.

Of all these tools, loomweights and spindle whorls have been found in MBA and LBA Aegean contexts beyond Crete,[70] which categorically supports the diffusion of the particular technological device used by Cretan weavers to other parts of the Aegean. However, not all types of loomweights were favored in non-Cretan contexts. The discoid type, which is the 'most typical Minoan loomweight'[71] was the type primarily adopted and used in Aegean communities. This type was most often manufactured from the same raw materials as the locally produced pottery even though it remains to be ascertained who produced these artifacts, *i.e.* the potter or the weaver.[72] Despite the predominance of the locally manufactured discoid loomweights, according to Cutler,[73] there is a low but consistent percentage of the discoid loomweights that were not manufactured locally, but rather transported there from other places (much like Minoanizing pottery, which was not produced on Crete but exchanged widely).

Textile production in the ancient Mediterranean is inextricably connected to the female sphere, so the deterritorialization of textile tools from their place of manufacture usually reveals some form of exchange that involves women. On the one hand, it indicates a correlated mobility of their users in the context of intermarriage, migration, and/or slavery, since they rarely have intrinsic value except to their user.[74] On the other hand, especially for textile tools that have intrinsic or symbolic value (*i.e.* ones made in luxurious or exotic materials or decorated), the recovery of these objects in locations away from the place of manufacture supports the status of these objects as gifts appropriate for female recipients.[75]

At Ayia Irini, loomweights of the discoid variety are present already from the earliest phase of the re-foundation of the site, *i.e.* Period IVa,[76] and continue to be used until the abandonment of the site in LH III (Fig. 12).[77] Overall, more than a thousand

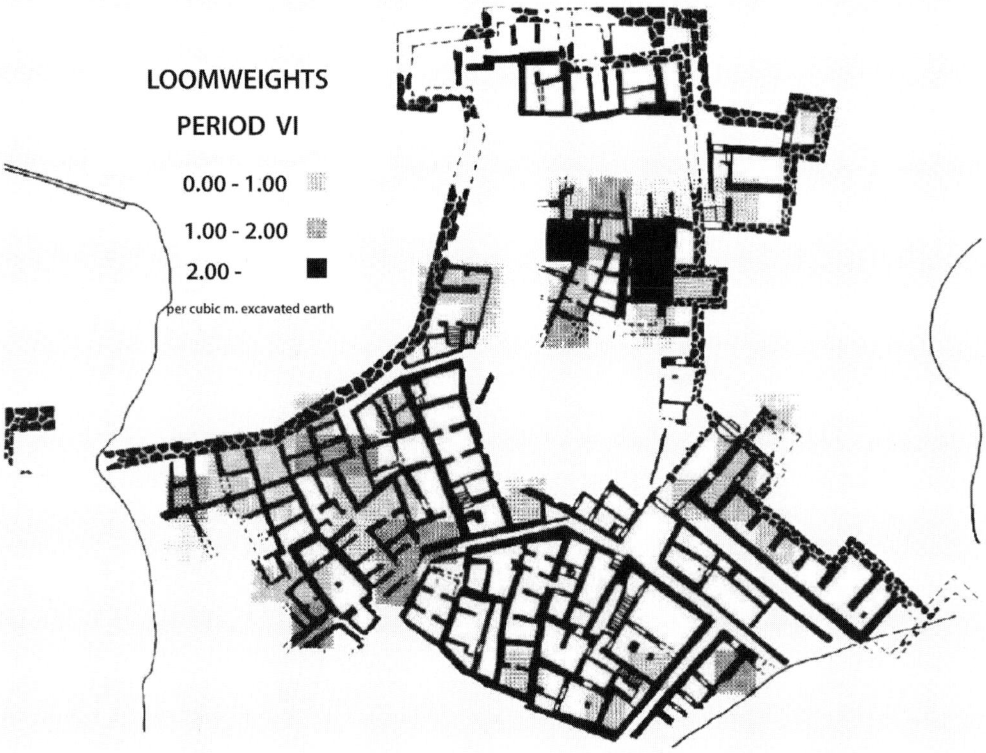

Figure 12: Densities of loom weights at LC I Ayia Irini (from Davis 1984, fig. 3; courtesy of J.L. Davis). Densities were calculated per cubic meter of excavated earth.

terracotta (as well as stone and bone) artifacts were recovered from almost all buildings and all periods.[78] None of the concentrations of loomweights seem to plausibly represent an *in situ* loom,[79] though the study of textile tools is still in progress.[80] Moreover, most of the spaces, except for the unpublished Area L[81] during LC I, have not produced large enough concentrations to support the presence of a workshop. This means that textile production was an important household industry at the site.[82]

The Northern Sector is no exception. Tables 5 and 6 summarize the data from a selected sample of 62 loomweights from single period deposits and 24 spindle whorls respectively.[83] The data show that about 11% to 18% of the loomweights had been fashioned in non-local clays.[84] In Period V, Aegina (and another unknown source) is the provenance for a few of the textile tools, and therefore their associated weavers, whereas in Period VII the range of places includes not only Aegina but also Crete, the Southern Cyclades (*i.e.* Melos and/or Thera), and Naxos. The sample of spindle whorls is more restricted than the loomweights and this evidence seems to indicate a preference for locally made spindle whorls. The only exception in this pattern are two spindle whorls (about 18%) in Period VII deposits, which seem to have been

Table 5: Suspected provenance of loomweights from the Northern Sector of Ayia Irini, based on macroscopic inspection (data from the Ayia Irini Northern Sector Archaeological Project).

	V%	VI%	VII%
Local	86.7	88.9	81.6
Unknown	6.7	11.1	2.6
Aeginetan	6.7	0	5.3
North-central Crete	0	0	2.6
Cretan-Assorted	0	0	2.6
Southern Cyclades	0	0	2.6
Naxian	0	0	2.6
Total imported	13.4	11.1	18.4
Total no loomweights	15	9	38

Table 6: Suspected provenance of spindle whorls from the Northern Sector of Ayia Irini, based on macroscopic inspection (data from the Ayia Irini Northern Sector Archaeological Project).

	V %	VI%	VII%
Local	100	100	70
Unknown	0	0	10
Aeginetan	0	0	10
Central Greece	0	0	10
Total imported	0	0	30
Total no spindle whorls	10	4	10

manufactured elsewhere (*i.e.* Aegina and Central Greece). This range of sources is not dissimilar to the range observed in contemporary imported pottery, which was also subjected to the same program of ceramic fabric analyses (see above).

Discussion

The Aegean of the MBA and the LBA bears almost all the hallmarks of an ancient globalization.[85] Indeed, from the beginning of the MBA, the already connected Aegean archipelago experiences a surge in interaction and connectivity between long distance locales, something most likely facilitated by the introduction of the square sail technology in maritime travel. This connectivity seems to have promoted the creation of a global culture or a Pan-Aegean *koine* at the local level,[86] as well as a formal and stylistic Pan-Mediterranean one.[87] Alongside this broader trend towards cultural homogenization and standardization, studies have shown that the phenomenon of globalization furthers the creation of cultural heterogeneity, *i.e.* glocalization, as different locales pursue different avenues of mixing global trends with their local idiom.

The present paper explored these trends in the material culture of the Northern Sector of Ayia Irini on the island of Kea (Greece), a small gateway community on the northwestern part of the Cyclades and not far from the Attic and Euboean shores. This border zone highlights the simultaneous adoption of the Pan-Aegean global culture and the creation of alterity by embracing the global and making it work for the local context.[88] Several examples of this process from Ayia Irini underline the creation of alterity within a general, gradual, and diffuse trend of cultural 'homogenization', which can be observed in the material culture of Ayia Irini and in the other major hubs in the Aegean's maritime network (*e.g.* Akrotiri, Phylakopi, Ialysos, Miletos, and others), albeit in different configurations. So, for example, at Ayia Irini the locally produced pottery, even though heavily influenced by Minoan fashions, never fully conforms with the expectations associated with a 'pure' Minoan assemblage.

However, the goal of this paper is not only to demonstrate these fairly obvious aspects of Ayia Irini's archaeological record, but also to explore the conduits and agents of this integration by shedding light on the human landscape of the town. At the beginning of the paper, Ramírez Erre's transparent two-headed Trojan horse served as a metaphor for cultural exchange, which is infused with relationships of mutual dependence and multidirectional influence without eradicating the power differentials that may exist in an exchange relationship. People, objects, and ideas are equally important parts of this equation,[89] and in the case of past globalizations, objects have admittedly been preeminent in discussions,[90] no doubt because of their visibility in the archaeological record. However, if the modern context has shown us anything it is that mobility is an integral part of the human condition[91] and of the phenomenon of globalization.[92] Thus, it follows that surges in connectivity, as well as the articulation of inequalities within the connected space (due to social, political, and economic factors, as well as other types of destabilizing influences), may favor a related surge in the intensity of human mobility.

For the last couple of decades, the cultural integration of the Aegean has been explored with a variety of explanatory models in which mobility was a side note (if it was discussed at all), purportedly because of its elusive archaeological signature as well as a reactionary distaste towards migrationism, which is not unique to Aegean archaeology.[93] Most recently, the reintroduction of human mobility as a factor contributing to culture change has reemerged in archaeological discourse[94] and the present paper joins these efforts utilizing data from the Northern Sector of Ayia.

Within the context of this ancient globalization, the culture of Ayia Irini was transformed in ways that signal the operation of low-grade migration as well as of cultural fusion responsive to Minoan, Cycladic, and Mainland cultural traditions (or at least a subset of them) to differing degrees. Figure 13, which summarizes the relationships across the artifactual categories from the Northern Sector discussed in the paper, highlights the diachronic continuity of contact and mobility between the

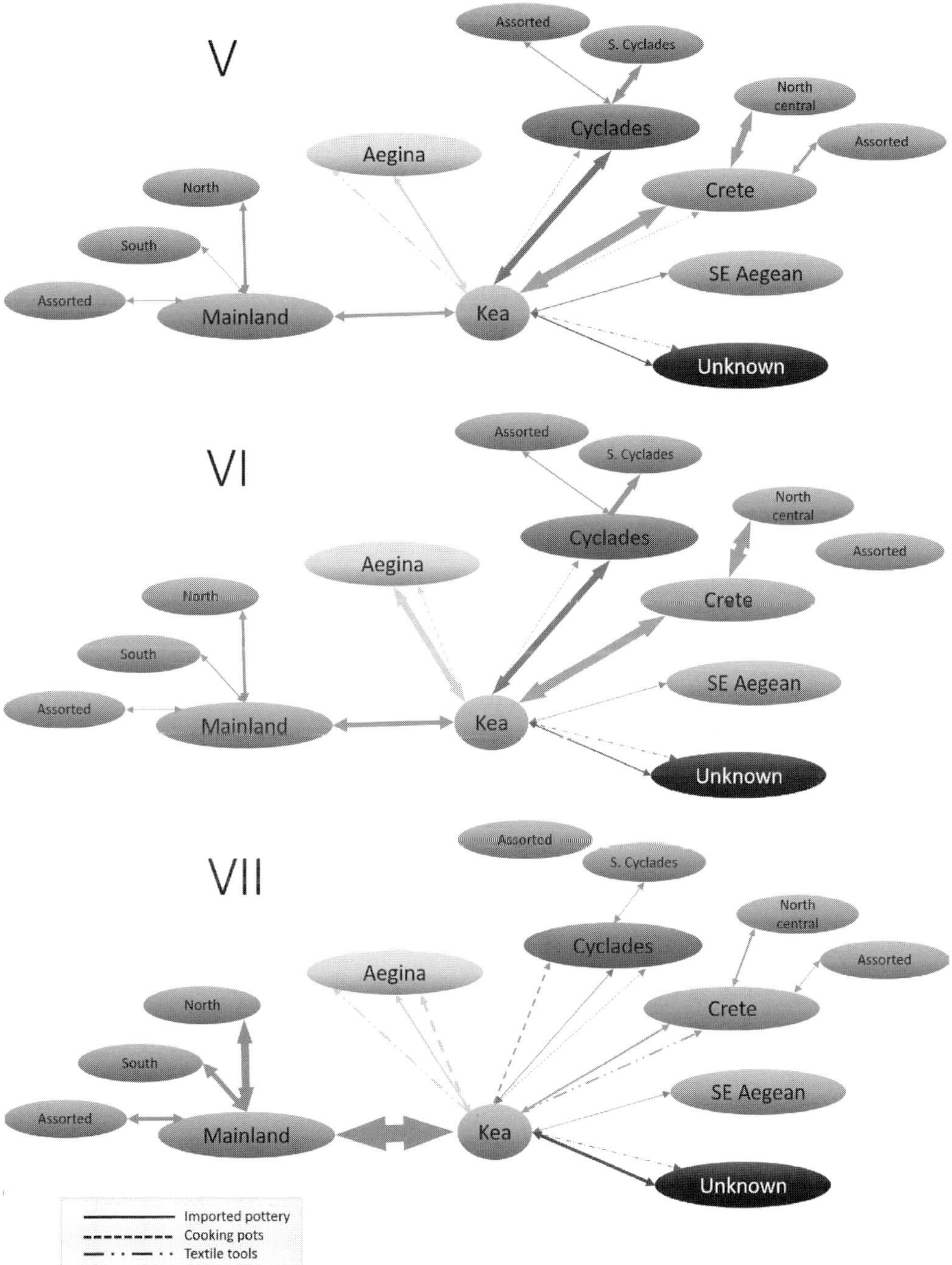

Figure 13: Visualization of the relationships between various parts of the Aegean and Kea, attested in the material culture of the Northern Sector.

Ayia Irini community and Aegina, the Cyclades (mainly Melos, Thera, and Naxos), as well as other unspecified locales.

The prevalence of the Minoan cultural element is unquestionable, especially during the period that spans from the end of the MBA to the middle of the LBA. However, at this point in the history of the discourse, to accord to the Minoan cultural element an *a priori* dominance would obscure the rich tapestry of interactions in the complex transregional network that linked the Aegean communities and, as the data from Ayia Irini shows, propagated Minoan culture. It would also obscure the various cultural adaptations that can be explained through the nuanced use of the phenomenon of deterritorialization,[95] and, in the case of Ayia Irini, mutual cultural assimilation among groups or individuals, all of which landed at Ayia Irini at one point or another where they were 'naturalized'.[96]

A particularly illustrative case is the adoption of the Cretan technology (tripod cooking pots, baking pans, etc.) for food preparation, a category of culture that is particularly interesting for the purposes of this paper, since it is one of the most accepted indices for the presence of migrants who preserve their domestic habitus within the confines of the household.[97] Starting as early as the 18th century BCE (Period IV, or MM II), the tripod cooking technology seems to have been introduced to the settlement by migrants, and by the beginning of the next period, it seems to be the most popular technology among the cooks at Ayia Irini. The diffusion of the technology to the rest of the population of this small town could be envisioned, but this was not a localized phenomenon. A 17th-century BCE (Period V, or MM IIIA) import of a tripod cooking pot from the southern Cyclades shows that Ayia Irini is not unique in its adoption of this new cooking technology, and also that the adoption of the technology was bolstered by similar developments at other sites with which Ayia Irini was connected. This pattern seems to conform well with it being regarded as a 'complex contagion', which is the process of transmission mainly of trends, traits, technologies, or political views, in which their adoption usually requires more than one cases of exposure.[98]

However, the adoption of a new cooking technology and weaving technology requires that we reserve a place in our explanatory models for human mobility, and especially the mobility of women, since in the Aegean context (and in many other cultures) they are in charge of food preparation and textile production. In both cases, it is reasonably clear that the introduction of these technologies is not the outcome of a mere trade or exchange relationship and this is one of the rare cases in which we can disambiguate the methodological trilemma in distinguishing among migration, trade, and diffusion.[99]

Women are usually considered immobile, or at least more immobile than men who are the default gender for traders, diplomats, soldiers of fortune, and other mobile categories. However, women were not immobile in traditional societies nor in the ancient world, and should be added to the categories of mobile groups who ultimately foster the integration of regions. There are multiple reasons for which women may take to the road, including religion and ritual, slavery (and war captives), and exogamous marriage. Exogamous marriage requires special focus since it is an overlooked aspect of regional and interregional integration.[100]

In a recent collection of papers, Voss and Casella (2012) remind us of the often overlooked aspects of colonialism.[101] These are the effects of colonialism, expansionism and even political consolidation on sex, gender(ing), and the 'tense and tender ties'[102] that bind political, institutional, economic, emotive, affectional, and familial aspects of the social lives that unfolded in both the metropole and colony.[103] Even though in the Aegean it has been argued convincingly that perhaps we are dealing with a context in which coloniality may have existed with or without the presence of colonies per se,[104] it would nevertheless be interesting to explore other ways in which this *ecumene* was integrated, and if cultural changes reverberated or were transmitted through it.

In other parts of the world, marital alliances (and their manipulation) are documented to have been one of the primary instruments for political expansion and consolidation. The Inca case, among many others, is indeed thought-provoking.[105] Prior to the consolidation of Inca control over the basin around Cusco, which over time grew into the administrative center of the state and later of the empire, Inca rulers chose as their principal wives the daughters of non-Inca elites within the Cusco valley. However, after the transformation to a state-level society, the preferred marriage partners changed to daughters of their political peers in the regions surrounding the Cusco Basin. This change in the pattern of marriage exchange shows that the choice of the principal wife was 'one means of consolidating political support' for the realization of their goals, which ultimately led to the formation of the Inca empire.[106]

More recently, Barbara Mills argued convincingly for intermarriage (and migration) being an important vector of ceramic change and cultural transmission in the American Southwest.[107] Mills draws from ethnographic accounts and archaeological data to articulate the role of exogamous unions acting as bridges between communities, which enhances the opportunities for the spread of innovation by producing and consuming 'boundary objects', *i.e.* objects which also act as bridges between practices and communities. Mills' argument resonates with the Aegean case in which the mobility of craftspeople has been convincingly demonstrated.[108]

If intermarriage, at least at the elite level, did not exist in the Aegean, then the region would have been unusal within the wider context of the Mediterranean since there is plenty of evidence that indicates such marital exchanges were not unusual in the rest of the Bronze Age Mediterranean and Near East, areas with which the Aegean had contacts. The complex politics of the eastern Mediterranean urged even the most introverted of kingdoms, such as Egypt, to engage in the exchange of spouses that formed and consolidated political alliances. The strongest evidence for these dynastic alliances come from the Amarna letters.[109] The Amarna documents shed more light not only to the practice of exogamy among the dynastic families of the eastern Mediterranean but also its complexities.

Could a similar scenario have happened in the Aegean during the Middle and the Late Bronze Age? Admittedly, solid evidence for the Aegean is hard to come by, but there are two pieces of evidence that provide food for thought. In the thorough re-examination of the princely burials of Grave Circle A at Mycenae, Nafplioti found that at least three individuals of the eleven that she subjected to strontium isotope ratio ($^{87}Sr/^{86}Sr$) analysis may have been non-local (and most of them female), though the evidence is not unproblematic.[110] One of them, the central burial in Grave III, which dates probably to LH I,[111] merits particular mention.[112] Not only did it belong to an individual that may have been a non-local female, but also one that was significantly richer than the other two male burials in the same grave.[113] This was probably the burial of a non-local elite female, who married into the Mycenaean ruling family, thus consolidating political relationships between Mycenae and her homeland, which are further emphasized symbolically with the inclusion of one of her offspring who was interred on her chest encased in gold.[114]

Similar nuances of intermarriage between Aegean elites are preserved of course in the mythological corpus of Ancient Greece (*i.e.* in the Homeric poems) as well as in the local myths of the Cycladic island of Kea. According to a local tale recorded by the poet Bacchylides (1.112–128), the Keian princess Dexithea was 'tamed' by none other than King Minos of Crete. Their union started a local royal lineage with their son Euxantios who had the right to claim a share of his father's estate after his father's death (and didn't, see Pindar, *Pae.* 4.1– 53). Thus, even though the evidence for intermarriage is not substantial at face value, nevertheless, the above cases indicate that intermarriage contributed to the Aegean configuration of power and that we are limiting the scope of our interpretive possibilities by not engaging with the topic.

Epilogue

The present paper illustrated the human landscape that belies the archaeological record of Ayia Irini, on Kea, a site that was an important node in the Aegean network during the MBA and the LBA. The interrogation of various artifactual categories, such as imported pottery, locally produced pottery, and the evidence for textile production makes apparent a number of interesting take-aways. On the one hand, even though the community was unquestionably imbued by Minoan 'ways of doing things', proclaiming it a Minoan colony disregards strong evidence for intense entanglement between the local, the global, and the regional. Figure 7 indicates that the connections established by imported pottery are supported by associated evidence of mobility that seem to have integrated this *ecumene*. The only case in which the evidence from the cooking pots or the textile production equipment is relatively 'silent' about the mobility is the mainland. This does not mean that the mainland was separate from this integrated whole, as other lines of evidence strongly emphasize the embeddedness of Ayia Irini in its regional context, a context that includes Attica and Boeotia.[115] The incipient picture is a border community accessible to people from different parts of the Aegean, another place where 'the whole world teaches and learns'.[116] A significant component of the teaching and learning, as I have argued, was done by women whose life trajectories led them to Ayia Irini (which is in no way unique), as migrant slaves or spouses. Their mobility, a largely unexplored topic whose tip of the iceberg this paper merely grazed, emerges as a vector for the simultaneous production of homogeneous cultural forms and alterity, and as such deserves further research.

Notes

1 Ramírez Erre 1997.
2 Ramírez Erre 1997; see also García Canclini 2014, 32–34.
3 Hodos 2017, 3.
4 García Canclini 2014, 24–38.
5 Gordon 2018a; 2018b; Kouremenos 2018.
6 Malkin *et al.* 2009; Jennings 2011; Malkin 2011; *e.g.* Hodos 2014; Versluys 2014; Hodos 2015; Versluys and Pitts 2015; Jennings 2017.
7 Jennings 2011, 21–32; Hodos 2017; Jennings 2017.
8 Hodos 2017, 4.
9 Jennings 2011, 21–32; 2017.
10 Knappett 2017; for another globalization, see Sweetman this volume.
11 Broodbank 2016, 24–26.
12 Feldman 2006, 8–9 et passim; Sherratt 2009; Cline 2015.
13 Broodbank 2000, 98–99; 2013a, 327–329.
14 Wachsmann 1998; Broodbank 2000, 342–347; Tartaron 2013, 51–53.
15 Wedde 2000, 76–80; Carter 2006; Broodbank 2010.
16 Broodbank 2000, 345–347 and table 12; 2013a, 290–292, 373–375, 464–466.
17 Harvey 1990; see also Hodos 2017, 4; Jennings 2017, 14.
18 Broodbank 2000, 320–349; 2008; 2010; 2013b, 540; Wiener 2013, 582–584.
19 Cherry 1982; Davis and Cherry 1990; Cherry *et al.* 1991.
20 Davis 1979, 146–148.
21 Hägg and Marinatos 1984; Broodbank 2004; Laffineur and Greco 2005; Whitelaw 2005; Berg 2007; Davis and Gorogianni 2008; MacDonald *et al.* 2009; Gorogianni *et al.* 2016b.
22 The term 'Minoanization' derives from the adjective 'Minoan', which was initially used by Sir Arthur Evans primarily with chronological connotations. Its usage, however, was extended to the culture and the people of Crete during the Bronze Age. Therefore, the usage of the term erroneously promotes the impression of homogeneity and the existence of a monolithic entity (much like a modern state), which for a long time colored the discourse of Minoanization, especially for the proponents of the 'Minoan thalassocracy' inspired by Thucydides. Despite the serious drawbacks of this ambiguous term, no satisfactory alternatives have been proposed. For a more detailed discussion with relevant references, see Broodbank 2004, 50–53; Davis and Gorogianni 2008, n. 1; Girella *et al.* 2016, 2–3; Knappett 2017, 29–30.
23 See Girella *et al.* 2016.
24 Boozer 2012, 220.
25 Robertson 1995.
26 Gorogianni 2016.
27 Gorogianni 2016.
28 Berg 2007; Hilditch 2008; Brysbaert 2011; Cutler 2011; Knappett 2011; Gorogianni *et al.* 2015; Abell and Hilditch 2016; Cutler 2016; Gorogianni 2016; Gorogianni *et al.* 2016a.
29 Broodbank 2000, fig. 14.

30 Davis and Gorogianni 2008. For cultural distancing of Attic communities, see Papadimitriou 2010, 249–254 with earlier references. See also several papers on MBA and LBA Attica in Wright *et al.* forthcoming.
31 Gorogianni 2016; *cf.* Nikolakopoulou and Knappett 2016.
32 The Northern Sector of Ayia Irini has been the focus of the author's research since 2004 and most recently the locus of an interdisciplinary collaborative project, the Ayia Irini Northern Sector Archaeological Project (AINSAP). AINSAP was codirected by Dr R.D. Fitzsimons and the author.
33 Cline 2005; Laffineur 2005; Panagiotopoulos 2012.
34 Sherratt 1999, 173–4; Thomas 2005, 540; Shelton 2010, 193; Shelmerdine 2013.
35 Sherratt 1999.
36 Sherratt 1999, 175–177.
37 Sherratt 1999, 179.
38 Gale *et al.* 2009.
39 Gale 1998; Stos-Gale 2000; Gale and Stos-Gale 2008; Gale *et al.* 2009; Kayafa 2010, 710.
40 Sherratt 1999, 185–185.
41 The suggested provenance of imported ceramics is based on the characterization and petrographic analysis by Dr J. Hilditch. For the special challenges that the material of Ayia Irini presents because its excavation, see Gorogianni 2013; 2016, 140; Gorogianni and Abell forthcoming.
42 See also Gorogianni and Abell forthcoming.
43 Overbeck 1989.
44 Comparatively, the mainland imports at Akrotiri are minimal. Knappett and Nikolakopoulou (2008, 7) note that in the deposits that are roughly equivalent to Period V (MM IIIA), in 131 complete vessels, there were 23 Cretan vases and only 4 of other provenance.
45 Bassiakos and Tselios 2012.
46 Gorogianni 2016, 140–144; Gorogianni *et al.* 2016a.
47 Abell and Hilditch 2016; Gorogianni *et al.* 2016a.
48 Gorogianni 2016, 144 and table 8.3a.
49 Gorogianni 2016, 141.
50 For a complimentary perspective, see Russell in this volume.
51 Gorogianni *et al.* 2016a.
52 Davis and Lewis 1985; Abell 2014b; Abell and Hilditch 2016; Gorogianni *et al.* 2016a; Abell and Gorogianni 2018.
53 Abell and Hilditch 2016; Gorogianni *et al.* 2016a.
54 Abell and Hilditch 2016; Gorogianni *et al.* 2016a.
55 Gorogianni 2016; see also Lis *et al.* 2018; Abell and Gorogianni forthcoming.
56 Hastorf 1998; Hamilakis 1999; Joyner 2007; Ben-Shlomo *et al.* 2008; Karageorghis and Kouka 2011.
57 Gorogianni *et al.* 2017.
58 Betancourt 1980; Barnard and Brogan 2003; Rutter 2004; Rutter and Van de Moortel 2006; Barnard and Brogan 2011.
59 Lis 2015, 105.
60 Overbeck 1989; Abell 2014a.
61 Davis 1986.
62 It should be noted that the absence or relative rarity of locally produced Mainland-style cooking pots is especially marked, which may be due to the fact that they were discriminated against during the post-excavation processing, as opposed to the super diagnostic and virtually indestructible tripod leg (for the archaeological practices of the Ayia Irini excavations, see Gorogianni 2008; 2013).

63 Gleba 2014, 83–89.
64 Barber 2007, 177–178.
65 Militello 2007; Burke 2010, 43–49.
66 Killen 1984; 2007.
67 Chadwick 1988; Nosch 2003; Nosch *et al.* 2006; Burke 2010, 66–76; Olsen 2014.
68 Tzachili 1997, 125–129; Burke 2010, 50.
69 Burke 2010, 50–59.
70 Cutler 2016, 173.
71 Burke 2010, 56. See also, Carington Smith 1975, 275.
72 See Quercia and Foxhall 2014, 70.
73 Cutler 2012; 2016, 175; forthcoming.
74 Barber 1991, 299; Cutler 2012; 2016; Gorogianni *et al.* 2015; see also D'Ercole 2011; Quercia and Foxhall 2014, 73.
75 Gleba 2014, 89–91.
76 Overbeck 1989; Abell 2014a.
77 Cutler 2016.
78 Davis 1984; Cutler 2012; Gorogianni *et al.* 2015; Cutler 2016, 175; Cutler forthcoming.
79 Davis 1984, 161, note 11.
80 Cutler forthcoming.
81 Davis 1984, 161.
82 Davis 1984; Schofield 1990. No matter how important textile production was, it probably never attained the scale of intensity that has been suggested for Akrotiri (Tzachili 1990; 1997; 2007). There, the exceptionally high numbers of loomweights found in specific houses in combination with complimentary evidence from Linear A documents and the presence of lead weights suggest 'the likelihood that textiles were being produced for exchange beyond the household at Akrotiri' (Cutler 2016, 176 with relevant references).
83 The assemblage of artifacts connected to textile production have been studied by Joanne Cutler Cutler forthcoming; 2016 and the author. The characterization of the artifacts was done by Dr Jill Hilditch.
84 Cutler 2011; Gorogianni *et al.* 2015; Cutler 2016.
85 See Jennings 2011, 20–32; Hodos 2017; Jennings 2017.
86 Davis and Gorogianni 2008.
87 Feldman 2006.
88 A phenomenon often called glocalization. For glocalization, see Robertson 1995; Ritzer 2003; Inda and Rosaldo 2008.
89 Hodder 2012; 2016.
90 *e.g.* Knappett and Nikolakopoulou 2008.
91 Castles *et al.* 2014, 84–100; van Dommelen 2014; see also Hamilakis 2016.
92 Appadurai 1996; Hannerz 1997; Inda and Rosaldo 2008.
93 See *e.g.* Hannerz 1997; Hakenbeck 2008. A rare exception to this trend was K. Branigan's and E. Schofield's attempts (Branigan 1981; Schofield 1983; Branigan 1984; Schofield 1984) to think through the Aegean evidence and somewhat operationalize archaeological identification of mobility (mainly as colonization) that skirted the 'traditional' conceptualization of migration as a tidal wave that brought with it sweeping cultural changes for the Mediterranean of historic times, see Boardman 1999; Muller 2013.
94 See *e.g.* Abell 2014a; Gorogianni *et al.* 2015; Gorogianni 2016; Gorogianni *et al.* 2016a; Kiriatzi *et al.* 2016; Mokrišová 2016; Nikolakopoulou and Knappett 2016; Knappett 2018; Lis *et al.* 2018; Cutler forthcoming.
95 Hernàndez i Martí 2006.
96 Abell 2014a; Gorogianni 2016; Abell and Gorogianni forthcoming.

97 Burmeister 2000, 542.
98 See Kiriatzi *et al.* 2016; Knappett 2018. For the concept of complex contagion, see Centola and Macy 2007; Centola 2015; Manzo *et al.* 2018.
99 Burmeister 2000, 542.
100 Deagan 1985; Coldstream 1993; Day 2004; Loman 2004; Voss 2008; Mustafa *et al.* 2013; Mills 2018.
101 Casella and Voss 2012, 1.
102 Stoler 2001.
103 Casella and Voss 2012, 1.
104 Knappett and Nikolakopoulou 2008.
105 Covey 2003, 348; D'Altroy 2003, 53–65.
106 Covey 2003, 348.
107 Mills 2018.
108 See *e.g.* Abell 2014a; Gorogianni *et al.* 2015; Gorogianni 2016; Gorogianni *et al.* 2016a; Mokrišová 2016; Nikolakopoulou and Knappett 2016; Knappett 2018; Lis *et al.* 2018; Cutler forthcoming.
109 Moran 1992; Cohen and Westbrook 2000; see also Meier 2000.
110 Nafplioti 2009.
111 Kilian-Dirlmeier 1986, 161–176.
112 Laffineur 1989, 236; Graziadio 1991, 436–437; Papazoglou-Manioudaki *et al.* 2010, 169. The central burial is Stamatakis' burial 'M' and 'MYC2, III' in Nafplioti and Musgrave's referencing system (Papazoglou-Manioudaki *et al.* 2010, 169); for identification of this burial as a non-native to Mycenae, see Nafplioti 2009, 289. The mere choice to have her interred in Grave Circle A makes her special since the male-to-female burial ratio (73% males, 20% females, and 7% adults of unknown sex, see Papazoglou-Manioudaki *et al.* 2010, 214) shows that only exceptional women of the family were buried there.
113 Dickinson 1977, 49; Graziadio 1991, 436–437; Papazoglou-Manioudaki *et al.* 2010, 160–161. She was buried with two diadems, one on her head and another one on her chest, and most of the grave furnishings belonged to her, including a gold and silver pin with a fertility scene and a series of miniature toilet vases (Papazoglou-Manioudaki *et al.* 2010, 160–161).
114 This elite female might have been from the region of eastern Euboea, southeast Attica, the western Cyclades or central Crete, since her strontium isotope ratio falls in the range represented in these regions (Nafplioti 2011, 1568–1569).
115 Gorogianni *et al.* forthcoming. See also papers on the MBA and LBA Attica in Wright *et al.* forthcoming.
116 From Jorge Amado's novel *Tent of Miracles* (1971), as quoted in Hannerz 1997, 7.

Bibliography

Abell, N.D. (2014b) *Reconsidering a Cultural Crossroads: A Diachronic Analysis of Ceramic Production, Consumption, and Exchange Patterns at Bronze Ayia Irini, Kea, Greece.* Ph.D., Cincinnati: University of Cincinnati.

Abell. N.D. (2014a) Migration, Mobility, and Craftspeople in the Aegean Bronze Age: A Case Study from Ayia Irini on the Island of Kea. *World Archaeology* 46, 4, 551–568.

Abell, N.D. and Gorogianni, E. (2018) Pottery Production on Late Bronze Age Kea: Organizational Perspectives. Paper delivered in the *19th International Congress of Classical Archaeology*. Cologne/Bonn.

Abell, N.D. and Gorogianni, E. (2019) The Past in Practice: Craft Producers and Material Culture Change at Ayia Irini, Kea. In *MNHMH/MNEME. Past and Memory in the Aegean Bronze Age. Proceedings of the 17th International Aegean Conference, University of Udine, Department of*

Humanities and Cultural Heritage Ca' Foscari University of Venice, Department of Humanities, 17–21 April 2018, edited by E. Borgna, I. Caloi, F. Carinci and R. Laffineur. Aegeaeum 43. Leuven: Peeters, 655–658.

Abell, N.D. and Hilditch, J. (2016) Adoption and Adaptation in Pottery Production Practices: Investigating Cycladic Community Interactions through the Ceramic Record of the Second Millennium BC. In *Beyond Thalassocracies. Understanding Processes of Minoanisation and Mycenaeanisation in the Aegean*, edited by E. Gorogianni, P. Pavúk and L. Girella. Oxford: Oxbow Books, 155–171.

Appadurai, A. (1996) Disjunction and Difference in the Global Cultural Economy. In *Modernity at Large: Cultural Dimensions of Globalization*, edited by J.X. Inda and R. Rosaldo. Minneapolis: University of Minnesota Press, 27–47.

Barber, E.J.W. (1991) *Prehistoric Textiles: The Development of Cloth in the Neolithic and Bronze Ages with Special Reference to the Aegean*. Princeton, N.J.: Princeton University Press.

Barber, E.J.W. (2007) Weaving the Social Fabric. In *Ancient Textiles: Production, Craft and Society. Proceedings of the First International Conference on Ancient Textiles, held at Lund, Sweden, and Copenhagen, Denmark, on March 19–23, 2003*, edited by C. Gillis and M.-L.B. Nosch. Oxford: Oxbow Books, 173–178.

Barnard, K.M. and Brogan, T.M. (2003) *Mochlos IB: Period III. Neopalatial Settlement on the Coast: The Artisans' Quarter and the Farmhouse at Chalinomouri. The Neopalatial Pottery*. Prehistory Monographs 8. Philadelphia: INSTAP Academic Press.

Bernard, K.M. (2011) Pottery of the Late Neopalatial Periods at Mochlos. In *LM IB Pottery: Relative Chronology and Regional Differences. Acts of a Workshop Held at the Danish Institute at Athens in Collaboration with the INSTAP Study Center for East Crete, 27–29 June 2007*, edited by T.M. Brogan and E. Hallager. Monographs of the Danish Institute at Athens 11. Athens: Danish Institute at Athens, Vol. 2, 427–444.

Bassiakos, Y. and Tselios, T. (2012) On the Cessation of Local Copper Production in the Aegean in the 2nd Millennium BC. In *Eastern Mediterranean Metallurgy and Metalwork in the Second Millennium BC: A conference in honour of James D. Muhly, Nicosia, 10th–11th October 2009*, edited by V. Kassianidou and G. Papasavvas. Oxford: Oxbow Books, 151–161.

Ben-Shlomo, D., Shai, I., Zukerman, A. and Maier, A.M. (2008) Cooking Identities: Aegean Style Cooking Jugs and Cultural Interaction in Iron Age Philistia and Neighboring Regions. *American Journal of Archaeology* 112(2), 225–246.

Berg, I. (2007) *Negotiating Island Identities: The Active Use of Pottery in the Middle and Late Bronze Age Cyclades*. Gorgias Dissertations 31. Piscataway, NJ: Gorgias Press.

Betancourt, P.P. (1980) *Cooking Vessels from Minoan Kommos: A Preliminary Report*. UCLA Occasional Paper 7. Los Angeles: UCLA Institute of Archaeology.

Boardman, J. (1999) *The Greeks Overseas: Their Early Colonies and Trade*. 4th edn. New York: Thames and Hudson.

Boozer, A.L. (2012) Globalizing Mediterranean Identities: The Overlapping Spheres of Egyptian, Greek and Roman Worlds at Trimithis. *Journal of Mediterranean Archaeology* 25, 2, 219–242.

Branigan, K. (1981) Minoan Colonialism. *The Annual of the British School at Athens* 76, 23–33.

Branigan, K. (1984) Minoan Community Colonies in the Aegean. In *The Minoan Thalassocracy. Myth and Reality. Proceedings of the Third International Symposium at the Swedish Institute in Athens, 31 May–5 June 1982*, edited by R. Hägg and N. Marinatos. SkrAth 4° XXXII. Stockholm: Paul Åströms Förlag, 49–53.

Broodbank, C. (2000) *An Archaeology of the Early Cyclades*. Cambridge: Cambridge University Press.

Broodbank, C. (2004) Minoanization. *Proceedings of the Cambridge Philological Society* 50, 46–91.

Broodbank, C. (2008) The Early Bronze Age in the Cyclades. In *The Cambridge Companion to the Aegean Bronze Age Shelmerdine*, edited by C.W. Shelmerdine. Cambridge: Cambridge University Press, 47–76.

Broodbank, C. (2010) 'Ships a-sail from over the rim of the sea': voyaging, sailing and the making of Mediterranean societies c. 3500–500 BC. In *The Global Origins of Seafaring*, edited by A. Anderson, J. Barrett and K. Boyle. Cambridge: McDonald Institute for Archaeological Research, 249–264.

Broodbank, C. (2013a) *The Making of the Middle Sea: A History of the Mediterranean from the Beginning to the Emergence of the Classical World*. Oxford: Oxford University Press.

Broodbank, C. (2013b) 'Minding the Gap': Thinking About Change in Early Cycladic Island Societies from a Comparative Perspective. *American Journal of Archaeology* 117, 4, 535–543.

Broodbank, C. (2016) The Transmitting Sea: A Mediterranean Perspective. In *Human Mobility and Technological Transfer in the Prehistoric Mediterranean*, edited by E. Kiriatzi and C. Knappett. British School at Athens Studies in Greek Antiquity. Cambridge: Cambridge University Press, 18–30.

Brysbaert, A. (ed.) (2011) *Tracing Prehistoric Social Networks through Technology: A Diachronic Perspective on the Aegean*. Routledge Studies in Archaeology 3. London and New York: Routledge.

Burke, B. (2010) *From Minos to Midas: Ancient Cloth Production in the Aegean and in Anatolia*. Ancient Textiles Series 7. Oxford: Oxbow Books.

Burmeister, S. (2000) Archaeology and Migration: Approaches to an Archaeological Proof of Migration. *Current Anthropology* 41, 4, 539–567.

Carington Smith, J. (1975) *Spinning, Weaving and Textile Manufacture in Prehistoric Greece - from the Beginning of the Neolithic to the End of the Mycenaean Ages; with Particular Reference to the Evidence Found on Archaeological Excavations*. Ph.D., University of Tasmania.

Carter, R. (2006) Boat remains and maritime trade in the Persian Gulf during the sixth and fifth millennia BC. *Antiquity* 80, 52–63.

Casella, E.C. and Voss, B.L. (2012) Intimate Encounters. An Archaeology of Sexuality within Colonial Worlds. In *The Archaeology of Colonialism: Intimate Encounters and Sexual Effects*, edited by B.L. Voss and E.C. Casella. New York: Cambridge University Press.

Castles, S., Haas, H. de, and Miller, M.J. (2014) *The Age of Migration: International Population Movements in the Modern World*. 5th edn. Basingstoke: Palgrave Macmillan.

Centola, D. (2015) The Social Origin of Networks and Diffusion. *American Journal of Sociology* 120, 5, 1295–1338.

Centola, D. and Macy, M. (2007) Complex Contagions and the Weakness of Long Ties. *American Journal of Sociology* 113, 3, 702–734.

Chadwick, J. (1988) The Women of Pylos. In *Texts, Tablets and Scribes. Studies in Mycenaean Epigraphy and Economy Offered to Emmett L. Bennett, Jr.*, edited by J.-P. Olivier and T.G. Palaima. Minos Supplement 10. Salamanca: Ediciones Universidad de Salamanca, 43–95.

Cherry, J.F. (1982) A Preliminary Definition of Site Distribution on Melos. In *An Island Polity: The Archaeology of Exploitation in Melos*, edited by A.C. Renfrew and J.M. Wagstaff. Cambridge and New York: Cambridge University Press, 10–23.

Cherry, J.F., Davis, J.L. and Mantzourani, E. (1991) Prehistoric Northern Keos: Analysis and Interpretation of the Survey Finds. In *Landscape Archaeology as Long-Term History. Northern Keos in the Cycladic Islands From Earliest Settlement to Modern Times*, edited by J.F. Cherry, J.L. Davis and E. Mantzourani. Monumenta Archaeologica 16. Los Angeles: UCLA Institute of Archaeology, 217–232.

Cline, E.H. (2005) The Multivalent Nature of Imported Objects in the Ancient Mediterranean World. In *Emporia: Aegeans in the Central and Eastern Mediterranean. Proceedings of the 10th International Aegean Conference/10e Rencontre égéenne internationale, Athens, Italian School of Archaeology, 14–18 April 2004*, edited by R. Laffineur and E. Greco. Aegaeum 25. Liège and Austin: Université de Liège, Histoire de l'art et archéologie de la Grèce antique and University of Texas at Austin, Program in Aegean Scripts and Prehistory, 45–51.

Cline, E.H. (2015) Preliminary Thoughts on Abundance vs. Scarcity in the Ancient World: Competition vs. Cooperation in Late Bronze Age Trade across the Aegean and Eastern Mediterranean. In *Policies of Exchange: Political Systems and Modes of Interaction in the Aegean and the Near East in the 2nd Millennium BCE. Proceedings of the International Symposium at the University of Freiburg Institute for Archaeological Studies, 30th May–2nd June 2012*, edited by B. Eder and R. Pruzsinszky. Oriental and European Archaeology. Vienna: Austrian Academy of Sciences Press, 209–219.

Cohen, R. and Westbrook, R. (eds) (2000) *Amarna Diplomacy: The Beginnings of International Relations*. Baltimore: Johns Hopkins University Press.

Coldstream, J.N. (1993) Mixed Marriages at the Frontiers of the Early Greek World. *Oxford Journal of Archaeology* 12, 1, 89–107.

Covey, R.A. (2003) A Processual Study of Inka State Formation. *Journal of Anthropological Archaeology* 22, 333–357.

Cutler, J. (2011) *Crafting Minoanisation: Textiles, Crafts Production and Social Dynamics in the Bronze Age Southern Aegean*. Ph.D., London: University College London.

Cutler, J. (2012) Ariadne's Thread: The Adoption of Cretan Weaving Technology in the Wider Southern Aegean in the Mid-Second Millennium BC. In *KOSMOS. Jewellery, Adornment and Textiles in the Aegean Bronze Age*, edited by M.-L.B. Nosch and R. Laffineur. Aegeaeum 31. Liège: Université de Liège, Histoire de l'art et archéologie de la Grèce antique, 145–154.

Cutler, J. (2016) Fashioning Identity: Weaving Technology, Dress and Cultural Change in the Middle and Late Bronze Age Southern Aegean. In *Beyond Thalassocracies. Understanding Processes of Minoanisation and Mycenaeanisation in the Aegean*, edited by E. Gorogianni, P. Pavúk and L. Girella, 172–185. Oxford: Oxbow Books.

Cutler, J. (forthcoming) *Crafting Minoanisation: Textiles, Crafts Production and Social Dynamics in the Bronze Age Southern Aegean*. Ancient Textiles 33. London: Oxbow Books.

D'Altroy, T.N. (2003) *The Incas. The Peoples of America*. Malden, MA, Oxford, Carlton, Victoria: Blackwell.

Davis, J.L. (1979) Minos and Dexithea: Crete and the Cyclades in the Later Bronze Age. In *Papers in Cycladic Prehistory*, edited by J.L. Davis and J.F. Cherry. UCLAMon 14. Los Angeles: UCLA Institute of Archaeology, 143–157.

Davis, J.L. (1984) Cultural Innovation and the Minoan Thalassocracy at Ayia Irini, Keos. In *The Minoan Thalassocracy. Myth and Reality. Proceedings of the Third International Symposium at the Swedish Institute in Athens, 31 May–5 June 1982*, edited by R. Hägg and N. Marinatos. SkrAth 4° XXXII. Stockholm: Paul Åströms Förlag, 159–165.

Davis, J.L. (1986) *Ayia Irini: Period V*. Keos V. Mainz on Rhine: Philipp von Zabern Verlag.

Davis, J.L. and Cherry, J.F. (1990) Spatial and Temporal Uniformitarianism in Late Cycladic I: Perspectives from Kea and Milos on the Prehistory of Akrotiri. In *Thera and the Aegean World III. Vol. 1: Archaeology. Proceedings of the Third International Congress, Santorini, Greece, 3–9 September 1989*, edited by D.A. Hardy, C.G. Doumas, J.A. Sakellarakis and P.M. Warren. London: The Thera Foundation, 185–200.

Davis, J.L. and Gorogianni, E. (2008) Potsherds from the Edge: Defining the Limits of Minoanized Areas of the Aegean. In *Horizon Ορίζων. A Colloquium on the Prehistory of the Cyclades, Cambridge 25-28 March 2004*, edited by N. Brodie, J. Doole and G. Gavalas. McDonald Institute Monographs. Cambridge: McDonald Institute for Archaeological Research, 379–388.

Davis, J.L. and Lewis, H.B. (1985) Mechanization of Pottery Production: A Case Study from the Cycladic Islands. In *Prehistoric Production and Exchange: The Aegean and Eastern Mediterranean*, edited by A.B. Knapp and T. Stech. UCLA Monograph 24. Los Angeles and Berkeley: University of California Press, 79–92.

Day, P.M. (2004) Marriage and Mobility: Traditions and the Dynamics of the Pottery System in Twentieth Century East Crete. In *Pseira VIII: The Archaeological Survey of Pseira Island. Part 1*, edited by P.P. Betancourt, C. Davaras and R. Hope Simpson. Prehistory Monographs 11. Philadelphia, PA: INSTAP Academic Press, 105–142.

Deagan, K. (1985) Spanish-Indian Interaction in Sixteenth-century Florida and Hispaniola. In *Cultures in Contact: The Impact of European Contacts on Native American Cultural Institutions, AD 1000–1800*, edited by W.W. Fitzhugh. Washington, D.C.: Anthropological Society of Washington, 281–318.

D'Ercole, M.C. (2011) Sharing New Worlds: Mixed Identities Around the Adriatic (Sixth to Fourth Centuries BCE). In *Cultural Identity in the Ancient Mediterranean*, edited by E.S. Gruen. Los Angeles: Getty Research Institute, 428–452.

Dickinson, O.T.P.K. (1977) *The Origins of Mycenaean Civilisation.* SIMA 49. Göteborg: Paul Åströms Förlag.

van Dommelen, P. (2014) Moving On: Archaeological Perspectives on Mobility and Migration. *World Archaeology* 46, 4, 477–483.

Feldman, M.H. (2006) *Diplomacy by Design: Luxury Arts and an 'International Style' in the Ancient Near East, 1400–1200 BCE.* Chicago and London: University of Chicago Press.

Gale, N.H. (1998) The Role of Kea in Metal Production and Trade in the Late Bronze Age. In *Kea-Kythnos: History and Archaeology. Proceedings of an International Symposium Kea-Kythnos. 22–25 June 1994*, edited by L.G. Mendoni and A. Mazarakis-Ainian. Meletimata 27. Paris and Athens: Diffusion de Boccard; Research Centre for Greek and Roman Antiquity, National Hellenic Research Foundation, 737–758.

Gale, N.H. and Stos-Gale, Z. (2008) Changing Patterns in Prehistoric Cycladic Metallurgy. In *Horizon Ορίζων. A Colloquium on the Prehistory of the Cyclades, Cambridge 25–28 March 2004*, edited by N. Brodie, J. Doole and G. Gavalas. McDonald Institute Monographs. Cambridge: McDonald Institute for Archaeological Research, 387–408.

Gale, N.H., Kayafa, M. and Stos-Gale, Z.A. (2009) Further Evidence for Bronze Age Production of Copper from Ores in the Lavrion Ore District, Attica, Greece. In *Proceedings of the 2nd International Conference: Archaeometallurgy in Europe*, edited by A. Giumlia-Mair, P. Craddock, A. Hauptmann, J. Bayley, M. Cavallini, G. Garagnani, B. Gimour, S. La Niece, W. Nicodemi and T. Rehren. Milan: Associazione Italiana di Metallurgia, 158–176.

García Canclini, N. (2014) *Imagined Globalization.* Translated by G. Yudice. Durham and London: Duke University Press.

Girella, L., Gorogianni, E. and Pavúk, P. (2016) Introduction: Methodological Considerations. In *Beyond Thalassocracies. Understanding Processes of Minoanisation and Mycenaeanisation in the Aegean*, edited by E. Gorogianni, P. Pavúk and L. Girella. Oxford: Oxbow Books, 1–14.

Gleba, M. (2014) Cloth Worth a King's Ransom Textile Circulation and Transmission of Textile Craft in the Ancient Mediterranean. In *Knowledge Networks and Craft Traditions in the Ancient World. Material Crossovers*, edited by K. Rebay-Salisbury, A. Brysbaert and L. Foxhall. Routledge Studies in Archaeology 13. Oxford: Routledge, 83–103.

Gordon, J.M. (2018a) Insularity and Identity in Roman Cyprus: Connectivity, Complexity, and Cultural Change. In *Insularity and Identity in the Roman Mediterranean*, edited by A. Kouremenos. Oxford and Philadelphia: Oxbow Books, 4–40.

Gordon, J.M. (2018b) Transforming Culture on an Insula Portunalis: Port Cities as Central Places in Early Roman Cyprus. *Land* 7 4: 155.

Gorogianni, E. (2008) *Creation Stories: The Archaeological Site of Ayia Irini, Kea and the Production of Archaeological Knowledge.* Ph.D., Cincinnati: Cincinnati.

Gorogianni, E. (2013) Site in Transition: John L. Caskey, Ayia Irini and Archaeological Practice in Greek Archaeology. *Aegean Archaeology* 10 (2009–2010), 105–120.

Gorogianni, E. (2016) Keian, Kei-noanised, Kei-cenaeanised? Interregional Contact and Identity in Ayia Irini, Kea. In *Beyond Thalassocracies. Understanding Processes of Minoanisation and Mycenaeanisation in the Aegean*, edited by E. Gorogianni, P. Pavúk and L. Girella. Oxford: Oxbow Books, 136–154.

Gorogianni, E. (2017) Aegean Fusion Cuisine: Ayia Irini, Kea as Cultural 'Middle Ground'. In *Cooking Vessels to Cultural Practices in the Late Bronze Age Aegean*, edited by J. Hruby and D. Trusty. Oxford: Oxbow Books, 57–71.

Gorogianni, E. and Abell, N.D. (forthcoming) Insularity and Cosmopolitanism in Ayia Irini, Kea. In *Island, Mainland, Coastland & Hinterland Ceramic Perspectives on Connectivity in the Ancient*

Mediterranean, Conference at the University of Amsterdam, February 1-3, 2013, edited by J. Hilditch, A. Kotsonas, C. Beestman-Kruijshaar, M. Revello Lami, S. Rückl and S. Ximeri. Amsterdam: Amsterdam University Press.

Gorogianni, E., Abell, N.D. and Hilditch. J. (2016a) Reconsidering Technological Transmission: The Introduction of the Potter's Wheel at Ayia Irini, Kea, Greece. *American Journal of Archaeology* 120, 2, 195–220.

Gorogianni, E., Abell, N.D. and Hilditch, J. (forthcoming) Kea and Attica: Revisiting Connections in the Middle and Late Bronze Age. In *Athens and Attica in Prehistory International Conference Athens, 27–31 May 2015*, edited by J.C. Wright, N. Polychronakou-Sgouritsa, N. Papadimitriou, S. Fachard, and E. Andrikou. Athens: American School of Classical Studies at Athens; University of Athens.

Gorogianni, E., Cutler, J. and Fitzsimons, R.D. (2015) Something Borrowed, Something New: Possible Archaeological Evidence for Foreign Brides as Catalysts for Acculturation at Ayia Irini, Kea. In *'NOSTOI' Indigenous Culture, Migration, and Integration in the Aegean Islands and Western Anatolia during the Late Bronze and Early Iron Age. Research Center for Anatolian Civilizations (RCAC) of Koç University in Istanbul, March 31st–April 3rd 2011*, edited by N. Stampolidis, Ç. Maner and K. Kopanias. Istanbul: Research Center for Anatolian Civilizations (RCAC) of Koç University in Istanbul, 853–886.

Gorogianni, E., Pavúk, P. and Girella, L. (eds) (2016b) *Beyond Thalassocracies. Understanding Processes of Minoanisation and Mycenaeanisation in the Aegean*. Oxford: Oxbow Books.

Graziadio, G. (1991) The Process of Social Stratification at Mycenae in the Shaft Grave Period: A Comparative Examination of the Evidence. *AJA* 95, 403–440.

Hägg, R. and Marinatos, N. (eds) (1984) *The Minoan Thalassocracy: Myth and Reality. Proceedings of the Third International Symposium at the Swedish Institute in Athens, 31 May–5 June, 1982*. SkrAth 4° XXXII. Göteborg: Paul Åströms Förlag.

Hakenbeck, S. (2008) Migration in Archaeology: Are We Nearly There Yet? *Archaeological Review from Cambridge 2008*, 2, 9–26.

Hamilakis, Y. (1999) Food Technologies/Technologies of the Body: The Social Context of Wine and Olive Oil Production and Consumption in Bronze Age Crete. *World Archaeology* 35, 1, 38–54.

Hamilakis, Y. (2016) Archaeologies of Forced and Undocumented Migration. *Journal of Contemporary Archaeology* 3, 2, 121–139.

Hannerz, U. (1997) Flows, Boundaries and Hybrids: Keywords in Transnational Anthropology (Original title: Fluxos, fronteiras, híbridos: palavras-chave da antropologia transnacional). *Mana* 3, 1, 7–39.

Harvey, D. (1990) *The Condition of Postmodernity: An Enquiry into the Origins of Cultural Change*. Cambridge, MA: Blackwell.

Hastorf, C.A. (1998) The Cultural Life of Early Domestic Plant Use. *Antiquity* 72, 773–782.

Hernàndez i Martí, G.M. 2006. The Deterritorialization of Cultural Heritage in a Globalized Modernity. *Journal of Contemporary Culture* 1, 92–107.

Hilditch, J. (2008) *Reconstructing Technical Choice, Social Practice and Networks of Exchange in the Middle Bronze Age of the Cyclades: The Ceramic Perspective*. D.Phil., Exeter: University of Exeter.

Hodder, I. (2012) *Entangled: An Archaeology of the Relationships between Humans and Things*. Chichester and Malden, MA: Wiley-Blackwell.

Hodder, I. (2016) *Studies in Human-Thing Entanglement*. Vol. 17. self publishing online. http://www.ian-hodder.com/books/studies-human-thing-entanglement.

Hodos, T. (2014) Stage Settings for a Connected Scene. Globalization and Material-culture Studies in the Early First Millennium BCE Mediterranean. *Archaeological Dialogues* 21, 1, 24–30.

Hodos, T. (2015) Global, Local and in Between: Connectivity and the Mediterranean. In *Globalisation and the Roman World: World History, Connectivity and Material Culture*, edited by M.J. Versluys and M. Pitts. New York: Cambridge University Press, 240–253.

Hodos, T. (2017) Globalization: Some Basics. An Introduction to The Routledge Handbook of Archaeology and Globalization. In *The Routledge Handbook of Archaeology and Globalization*, edited by T. Hodos. Routledge Handbooks. London and New York: Routledge, 3–11.

Inda, J.X. and Rosaldo, R. (2008) Tracking Global Flows. In *The Anthropology of Globalization: A Reader*, edited by J.X. Inda and R. Rosaldo. 2nd edn. Malden, MA, Oxford, Carlton, Victoria: Blackwell Publishing, 3–46.

Jennings, J. (2011) *Globalizations and the Ancient World*. Cambridge: Cambridge University Press.

Jennings, J. (2017) Distinguishing Past Globalizations. In *The Routledge Handbook of Archaeology and Globalization*, edited by T. Hodos. Routledge Handbooks. London and New York: Routledge, 12–28.

Joyner, L. (2007) Cooking Pots as Indicators of Cultural Change, a Petrographic Study of Byzantine and Frankish Cooking Wares from Corinth. *Hesperia* 76, 183–227.

Karageorghis, V. and Kouka, O. (eds) (2011) *On Cooking Pots, Drinking Cups, Loomweights and Ethnicity in Bronze Age Cyprus and Neighbouring Regions: An International Archaeological Symposium held in Nicosia, November 6th–7th 2010*. Nicosia: The A.G. Leventis Foundation.

Kayafa, M. (2010) Middle Helladic Metallurgy and Metalworking: Review of the Archaeological and Archaeometric Evidence from the Peloponnese. In *Mesohelladika. Μεσοελλαδικά: La Grèce continentale au Bronze Moyen. Η ηπειρωτική Ελλάδα στη Μέση εποχή του Χαλκού. The Greek Mainland in the Middle Bronze Age. Actes du colloque international organisé par l'École française d'Athènes, en collaboration avec l'American School of Classical Studies at Athens et le Netherlands Institute in Athens, Athènes, 8–12 mars 2006*, edited by A. Philippa-Touchais, G. Touchais, S. Voutsaki and J. Wright. BCH Supplement 52. Athènes: École française d'Athènes, 701–711.

Kilian-Dirlmeier, I. (1986) Beobachtungen zu der Schachtgräbern von Mykenai und zu der Schmuckbeigaben mykenischer Männergräber. *Jahrbuch des romisch-germanischen Zentralmuseums Mainz* 33, 156–198.

Killen, J.T. (1984) The Textile Industries at Pylos and Knossos. In *Pylos Comes Alive: Industry and Administration in a Mycenaean Palace*, edited by C.W. Shelmerdine and T. Palaima. New York: Fordham University, 49–63.

Killen, J.T. (2007) Cloth Production in Late Bronze Age Greece: The Documentary Evidence. In *Ancient Textiles: Production, Craft and Society. Proceedings of the First International Conference on Ancient Textiles, held at Lund, Sweden, and Copenhagen, Denmark, on March 19–23, 2003*, edited by C. Gillis and M.-L.B. Nosch. Ancient Textile Series 1. Oxford: Oxbow Books, 50–58.

Kiriatzi, E., Knappett, C., Knappett, C. and Kiriatzi, E. (2016) Technological Mobilities: Perspectives from the Eastern Mediterranean – An Introduction. In *Human Mobility and Technological Transfer in the Prehistoric Mediterranean*. British School at Athens Studies in Greek Antiquity. Cambridge: Cambridge University Press, 1–17.

Knappett, C. (2011) *An Archaeology of Interaction: Network Perspectives on Material Culture and Society*. New York and Oxford: Oxford University Press.

Knappett, C. (2017) Globalization, Connectivities, and Networks: An Archaeological Perspective. In *The Routledge Handbook of Archaeology and Globalization*, edited by T. Hodos. Routledge Handbooks. London and New York: Routledge, 29–41.

Knappett, C. (2018) From Network Connectivity to Human Mobility: Models for Minoanization. *Journal of Archaeological Method and Theory* 25, 974–995.

Knappett, C. and Nikolakopoulou, I. (2008) Colonialism without Colonies? A Bronze Age Case Study from Akrotiri, Thera. *Hesperia* 77, 1–42.

Kouremenos, A. (ed.) (2018) *Insularity and Identity in the Roman Mediterranean*. Oxford: Oxbow Books.

Laffineur, R. (1989) Mobilier funéraire et hiérarchie sociale aux cercles des tombes de Mycènes. In *Transition: Le monde égéen du bronze moyen au bronze récent*, edited by R. Laffineur. Aegaeum 3. Liège: Histoire de l'art et archéologie de la Grèce antique. Universitè de l'Etat à Liège, 227–238.

Laffineur, R. (2005) Imports/Exports in the Eastern Mediterranean: For a Specific Methodology. In *Emporia: Aegeans in the Central and Eastern Mediterranean. Proceedings of the 10th International Aegean Conference/10e Rencontre égéenne internationale, Athens, Italian School of Archaeology, 14–18 April 2004*, edited by R. Laffineur and E. Greco. Aegaeum 25. Liège and Austin: Université de Liège, Histoire de l'art et archéologie de la Grèce antique and University of Texas at Austin, Program in Aegean Scripts and Prehistory, 53–58.

Laffineur, R. and Greco, E. (eds) (2005) *Emporia: Aegeans in the Central and Eastern Mediterranean. Proceedings of the 10th International Aegean Conference/10e Rencontre égéenne internationale, Athens, Italian School of Archaeology, 14–18 April 2004*. Aegaeum 25. Liège and Austin: Université de Liège, Histoire de l'art et archéologie de la Grèce antique and University of Texas at Austin, Program in Aegean Scripts and Prehistory.

Lis, B. (2015) From Cooking Pots to Cuisine. Limitations and Perspectives of Ceramic-based Approach. In *Ceramics, Cuisine and Culture: The Archaeology and Science of Kitchen Pottery in the Ancient Mediterranean World*, edited by M. Spataro and A. Villing. Oxford: Oxbow Books, 104–114.

Lis, B., Rückl, Š. and Choleva, M. (2018) Mobility in the Bronze Age Aegean: The Case of Aeginetan Potters. In *The Transmission of Technical Knowledge in the Production of Ancient Mediterranean Pottery. Proceedings of the International Conference at the Austrian Archaeological Institute at Athens 23rd–25th November 2012*, edited by W. Gauss, G. Klebinder-Gauss and C. von Rüden. Sonderschriften 54. Vienna: Österreichisches Archäologisches Institut, 63–75.

Loman, P. (2004) *Mobility of Hellenistic Women*. Ph.D. thesis, Nottingham: University of Nottingham. http://eprints.nottingham.ac.uk/11684/1/Loman_thesis_incl_authors_note.pdf.

MacDonald, C.F., Hallager, E. and Niemeier, W.-D. (eds) (2009) *The Minoans in the Central, Eastern and Northern Aegean – New Evidence: Acts of a Minoan Seminar 22–23 January 2005 in Collaboration with the Danish Institute at Athens and the German Archaeological Institute at Athens*. Monographs of the Danish Institute at Athens 8. Athens: The Danish Institute at Athens.

Malkin, I. (2011) *A Small Greek World: Networks in the Ancient Mediterranean*. Oxford: Oxford University Press.

Malkin, I., Constantakopoulou, C. and Panagopoulou, K. (eds) (2009) *Greek and Roman Networks in the Mediterranean*. London and New York: Routledge.

Manzo, G., Gabbriellini, S., Roux, V. and M'Mbogori, F.N. (2018) Complex Contagions and the Diffusion of Innovations: Evidence from a Small-N Study. *Journal of Archaeological Method and Theory*.

Meier, S.A. (2000) Diplomacy and International Marriages. In *Amarna Diplomacy: The Beginnings of International Relations*, edited by R. Cohen and R. Westbrook. Baltimore and London: Johns Hopkins University Press, 165–173.

Militello, P. (2007) Textile Industry and Minoan Palaces. In *Ancient Textiles: Production, Craft and Society. Proceedings of the First International Conference on Ancient Textiles, held at Lund, Sweden, and Copenhagen, Denmark, on March 19–23, 2003*, edited by C. Gillis and M.-L.B. Nosch. London: Oxbow Books, 36–45.

Mills, B.J. (2018) Intermarriage, Technological Diffusion, and Boundary Objects in the U.S. Southwest. *Journal of Archaeological Method and Theory*. doi:10.1007/s10816-018-9392-0.

Mokrišová, J. (2016) Minoanisation, Mycenaeanisation, and Mobility: A View from Southwest Anatolia. Oxford: Oxbow Books, 43–57.

Moran, W.L. (1992) *The Amarna Letters*. Baltimore: Johns Hopkins University Press.

Muller, S. 2013. Away From Home: Ancient Greek Colonization Seen As A Migratory Process. *Mediterranean Review* 6, 2, 33–57.

Mustafa, M., Young, A., Galaty, M.L. and Lee, W.E. (2013) Spatial and Temporal Patterns in Kinship Relations: Descent, Marriage, and Feud. In *Light and shadow : isolation and interaction in the Shala Valley of northern Albania*, edited by M.L. Galaty, O. Lafe, W.E. Lee and Z. Tafilica. Monumenta Archaeologica 28. Los Angeles: Cotsen Institute of Archaeology Press, 85–106.

Nafplioti, A. (2009) Mycenae Revisited Part 2. Exploring the Local versus Non-local Geographical Origin of the Individuals from Grave Circle A: Evidence from Strontium Isotope Ratio (87Sr/86Sr) Analysis. *The Annual of the British School at Athens* 104, 279–291.

Nafplioti, A. (2011) Tracing population mobility in the Aegean using isotope geochemisty: A first map of local biologically available 87Sr/86Sr signatures. *Journal of Archaeological Science* 38, 1560–1570.

Nikolakopoulou, I. and Knappett, C. (2016) Mobilities in the Neopalatial Southern Aegean: The Case of Minoanisation. In *Human Mobility and Technological Transfer in the Prehistoric Mediterranean*, edited by E. Kiriatzi and C. Knappett. British School at Athens Studies in Greek Antiquity. Cambridge: Cambridge University Press, 102–115.

Nosch, M.-L.B. (2003) The Women at Work in the Linear B Tablets. In *Gender, Cult, and Culture in the Ancient World from Mycenae to Byzantium*, edited by L.L. Lovén and A. Strömberg. SIMA-PB 166. Sävedalen: Paul Åströms Förlag, 12–27.

Nosch, M.-L.B., Perna, M., Perna, M., Pomponio, F., Schmandt-Besserat, D. and Younger, J.G. (2006) *More Thoughts on the Mycenaean ta-ra-si-ja System. Studi egei e vicinorientali.* Paris: De Boccard, 161–182.

Olsen, B.A. (2014) *Women in Mycenaean Greece: The Linear B tablets from Pylos and Knossos.* London and New York: Routledge.

Overbeck, J.C. (1989) *Ayia Irini: Period IV. Part 1: The Stratigraphy and the Find Deposits.* Keos VIII. Mainz on Rhine: Philipp von Zabern Verlag.

Panagiotopoulos, D. (2012) Encountering the Foreign. (De-)constructing Alterity in the Archaeologies of the Bronze Age Mediterranean. In *Materiality and Social Practice: Transformative Capacities of Intercultural Encounters*, edited by J. Maran and P.W. Stockhammer. Oxford: Oxbow Books, 51–60.

Papadimitriou, N. (2010) Attica in the Middle Helladic Period. In *Mesohelladika. Μεσοελλαδικά: La Grèce continentale au Bronze Moyen. Η ηπειρωτική Ελλάδα στη Μέση εποχή του Χαλκού. The Greek Mainland in the Middle Bronze Age. Actes du colloque international organisé par l'École française d'Athènes, en collaboration avec l'American School of Classical Studies at Athens et le Netherlands Institute in Athens, Athènes, 8–12 mars 2006*, edited by A. Philippa-Touchais, G. Touchais, S. Voutsaki and J. Wright. BCH Supplement 52. Athens: École française d'Athènes, 243–257.

Papazoglou-Manioudaki, L., Nafplioti, A., Musgrave, J.H. and Prag, A.J.N.W. (2010) Mycenae Revisted Part 3. The Human Remains from Grave Circle A at Mycenae. Behind the Masks: A Study of the Bones of Study Graves I–V. *The Annual of the British School at Athens* 105, 157–224.

Quercia, A. and Foxhall, L. (2014) Temporality, Materiality and Women's Networks. The Production and Manufacture of Loom Weights in the Greek and Indigenous Communities of Southern Italy. In *Knowledge Networks and Craft Traditions in the Ancient World. Material Crossovers*, edited by K. Rebay-Salisbury, A. Brysbaert and L. Foxhall. Routledge Studies in Archaeology 13. Oxford: Routledge, 62–82.

Ramírez Erre, M. (1997) *Toy an-Horse*. Wood; wood (plant material). InSite Archive. MSS 707. Special Collections & Archives, UC San Diego. http://marcosramirezerre.com/toy-an-horse/.

Ritzer, G. (2003) The Globalization of Nothing. *SAIS Review: A Journal of International Affairs* 23, 2, 189–200.

Robertson, R. (1995) Glocalization: Time-Space and Homogeneity-Heterogeneity. In *Global Modernities*, edited by M. Featherstone, S. Lash and R. Robertson. London: SAGE Publications Ltd.

Rutter, J.B. (2004) Ceramic Sets in Context: One Dimension of Food Preparation and Consumption in a Minoan Palatial Setting. In *Food, Cuisine and Society in Prehistoric Greece*, edited by P. Halstead and J.C. Barrett. Sheffield Studies in Aegean Archaeology 5. Oxford: Oxbow Books, 63–89.

Rutter, J.B. and Van de Moortel, A. (2006) Chapter 3: Minoan Pottery from the Southern Area. In *Kommos. An Excavation on the South Coast of Crete by the University of Toronto under the auspices of the American School of Classical Studies at Athens. Vol V. The Monumental Minoan Buildings at Kommos*, edited by J.W. Shaw and M.C. Shaw. Princeton and Oxford: Princeton University Press, 261–715.

Schofield, E. (1983) The Minoan Emigrant. In *Minoan Society. Proceedings of the Cambridge Colloquium 1981*, edited by O. Krzyszkowska and L. Nixon. Bristol: Bristol Classical Press, 293–301.

Schofield, E. (1984) Coming to Terms with Minoan Colonists. In *The Minoan Thalassocracy. Myth and Reality. Proceedings of the Third International Symposium at the Swedish Institute in Athens, 31 May–5 June 1982*, edited by R. Hägg and N. Marinatos. SkrAth 4° XXXII. Stockholm: Paul Åströms Förlag, 45–48.

Schofield, E. (1990) Evidence for Household Industries on Thera and Kea. In *Thera and the Aegean World III. Vol. 1: Archaeology. Proceedings of the Third International Congress, Santorini, Greece, 3–9 September 1989*, edited by D.A. Hardy, C.G. Doumas, J.A. Sakellarakis and P.M. Warren. London: The Thera Foundation, 201–211.

Shelmerdine, C.W. (2013) Crafts, Specialists, and Markets in Mycenaean Greece. Economic Interplay Among Households and States. *American Journal of Archaeology* 117, 3, 447–452.

Shelton, K. (2010) Citadel and Settlement: A Developing Economy at Mycenae, the Case of Petsas House. In *Political Economies of the Aegean Bronze Age: Papers from the Langford Conference, Florida State University, Tallahassee, 22–24 February 2007*. Oxford: Oxbow Books, 184–204.

Sherratt, S. (1999) E pur si muove: Pots Markets and Values in the Second Millennium Mediterranean. In *The Complex Past of Pottery: Production, Circulation and Consumption of Mycenaean and Greek Pottery (Sixteenth to Early Fifth Centuries BC). Proceedings of the ARCHON International Conference, Held in Amsterdam, 8–9 November 1996*, edited by J.P. Crielaard, V. Stissi and G.J. van Wijngaarden. Amsterdam: J.C. Gieben, 163–211.

Sherratt, S. (2009) The Aegean and the Wider World: Some Thoughts on a World-Systems Perspective. In *Archaic State Interaction: The Eastern Mediterranean in the Bronze Age*, edited by W.A. Parkinson and M.L. Galaty. Santa Fe: School for Advanced Research Press, 81–106.

Stoler, A.L. (2001) Tense and Tender Ties: The Politics of Comparison in North American History and (Post) Colonial Studies. *The Journal of American History* 88, 3, 829–865.

Stos-Gale, S. (2000) Trade in Metals in the Bronze Age Mediterranean: An Overview of Lead Isotope Data for Provenance Studies. In *Metals Make the World Go Round: The Supply and Circulation of Metals in Bronze Age Europe. Proceedings of a Conference Held at the University of Birmingham in June 1997*, edited by C.F.E. Pare. Oxford: Oxbow Books, 56–69.

Tartaron, T.F. (2013) *Maritime Networks in the Mycenaean*. Cambridge; New York: Cambridge University Press.

Thomas, P.M. (2005) A Deposit of Late Helladic IIIB1 Pottery from Tsoungiza. *Hesperia* 74, 451–573.

Tzachili, I. (1990) All Important Yet Elusive: Looking for Evidence of Cloth-Making at Akrotiri. In *Thera and the Aegean World III. Vol. 1: Archaeology. Proceedings of the Third International Congress, Santorini, Greece, 3–9 September 1989*, edited by D.A. Hardy, C.G. Doumas, J.A. Sakellarakis and P.M. Warren. London: Thera and the Aegean World, 380–389.

Tzachili, I. (1997) *Υφαντική και Υφάντρες στο Προϊστορικό Αιγαίο 2000–1000 π.Χ.* Irakleio: Πανεπιστημιακές Εκδόσεις Κρήτης.

Tzachili, I. (2007) Weaving at Akrotiri, Thera: Defining Cloth Making Activities as Social Process in a Late Bronze Age Town. In *Ancient Textiles: Production, Craft and Society. Proceedings of the First International Conference on Ancient Textiles, held at Lund, Sweden, and Copenhagen, Denmark, on March 19–23, 2003*, edited by C. Gillis and M.-L.B. Nosch. Oxford: Oxbow Books, 190–196.

Versluys, M.J. (2014) Understanding Objects in Motion. An Archaeological Dialogue on Romanization. *Archaeological Dialogues* 21, 1, 1–20.

Versluys, M.J. and Pitts, M. (eds) (2015) *Globalisation and the Roman World: World History, Connectivity and Material Culture*. New York: Cambridge University Press.

Voss, B.L. (2008) Domesticating Imperialism: Sexual Politics and the Archaeology of Empire. *American Anthropologist* 110, 2, 191–203.

Wachsmann, S. (1998) *Seagoing Ships & Seamanship in the Bronze Age Levant*. College Station, Texas: Texas A&M University Press.

Wedde, M. (2000) *Towards a Hermeneutics of Aegean Bronze Age Ship Imagery*. Peleus: Studien zur Archäologie und Geschichte Griechenlands und Zyperns 6. Mannheim und Möhnesee: Bibliopolis.
Whitelaw, T.M. (2005). A Tale of Three Cities: Chronology and Minoanisation at Phylakopi in Melos. In *Autochthon: Papers Presented to O.T.P.K. Dickinson on the Occasion of his Retirement, Institute of Classical Studies, University of London, 9 November 2005*, edited by A. Dakouri-Hild and S. Sherratt. BAR International Series 1432. Oxford: Archaeopress, 37–69.
Wiener, M.H. (2013). 'Minding the Gap': Gaps, Destructions, and Migrations in the Early Bronze Age Aegean. Causes and Consequences. *American Journal of Archaeology* 117, 4, 581–592.
Wright, J.C., Polychronakou-Sqouritsa, N., Papadimitriou, N. and Fachard, S. (eds) (forthcoming) *Athens and Attica in Prehistory International Conference Athens, 27–31 May 2015*. American School of Classical Studies at Athens.

Chapter 4

Globalization Processes and Insularity on the Dalmatian Islands in the Late Iron Age

Charles Barnett and Marina Ugarković

Introduction

In certain scholarly circles, the Archaic, Classical, and, particularly, the Hellenistic Mediterranean world is increasingly understood as one in which globalizing processes affected the socio-cultural and economic lives of communities across the entire region.[1] These processes are largely seen as the result of various trading, colonizing and military activities of Greeks, Phoenicians, and, later, Romans. The cultural implications of the developing social and economic connectivity of these periods are increasingly understood as geographically wide ranging, and not confined to the Aegean region, Magna Graecia and parts of northern Africa.[2] Greek colonization of the Mediterranean and Black Sea region during the Archaic period created a kind of 'decentralized network', a 'small space',[3] in which various forms and styles of material culture were transmitted across thousands of miles between intensively connected communities. The networks that these colonies created shaped cultural practices and beliefs among those who engaged in them, both newcomers and indigenous populations, and those who moved through them, while also concurrently generating sharply defined differences.[4] Many maps in scholarship on ancient Greeks abroad ignore the eastern Adriatic above Epidamnos, yet the political and economic impact of Greek merchants and poleis on local communities from Montenegro to Istria is clear in the material record.[5]

Positioned in the middle of the Adriatic Sea and at the convergence of two major sea current systems,[6] wind systems have facilitated the connection of the Dalmatian islands to Adriatic wide networks since prehistory.[7] Colonization of the Dalmatian islands by Greek poleis was a long-distance migratory process that involved interaction between different types of cultural and social groups – Greek colonial and local – and the island is an interesting unit of analysis for investigating how these cultural processes played out. The sea acts equally as a barrier and means for travel, communication, and exploration, meaning that island societies sit on a constantly altering continuum between isolation and interaction.[8] Cultural decisions as well as geographic position influence degrees of isolation and connectivity on islands,[9] and thus, how their communities react to globalizing processes. The Late Iron Age on the Dalmatian islands is an intriguing case study for investigating comparative reactions to changing levels of isolation due to their strategic location, which exposed them to broader globalizing processes perhaps more so or earlier than the mainland, as well as the founding of Greek colonies on several of these islands.

Importantly, reactions to increasing connectivity and Greek colonization appear somewhat different in certain island communities of Dalmatia, as is discussed in the following sections. Looking at these themes through the lens of globalization has the advantage of explaining local diversity in a broader 'global' context. Globalization of culture includes various homogenizing processes, with connectivity facilitating the spread of cultural features that are in turn incorporated into local political and cultural economies in disparate manners and contexts.[10] Therefore, globalization is an irregular process that emphasizes the local context and agency of socio-cultural changes in relation to globalizing processes, such as increasing connectivity and economic integration.[11] Within this framework, this paper seeks to trace the networks that connected Dalmatia to the Greek world, and understand how increasing connectivity affected local communities and colonies on the islands.[12] The first section outlines the extension of Mediterranean-wide commercial and political networks into the Adriatic during the Iron Age. The second section looks at available evidence and seeks to highlight the heterogeneous nature of the cultural change that occurred due to this increasing connectivity and Greek colonization in the Late Iron Age. In this sense, this case study highlights the seemingly contradictory elements of globalization – the emergence of a shared globalizing cultural *koine*, and the apparent increasing localism resulting from such a clash of cultures.[13]

Connectivity in the Adriatic 5th–1st Century BCE

Modern-day Dalmatia is an area of coastal Croatia which stretches from the Velebit mountain range in the north down to the entrance of the Boka Kotor bay (Rt Oštro), including all the adjacent islands (Fig. 14). The current geological structures are the result of formation processes that occurred after the Holocene transgression.[14] The Dinaric alps run parallel to the coast, and act as a natural barrier between the coast and the hinterland. Communities along the coast and on the islands of Dalmatia would have been, to a certain degree, isolated from the hinterland, as movement over the mountains is difficult, and passes through them are few. Given the geographic particularities of Dalmatia, it is unsurprising that its inhabitants have, since prehistory, been seafaring and outward looking people. This is not to say that interaction with the hinterland did not take place – quite the opposite. Archaeological material points

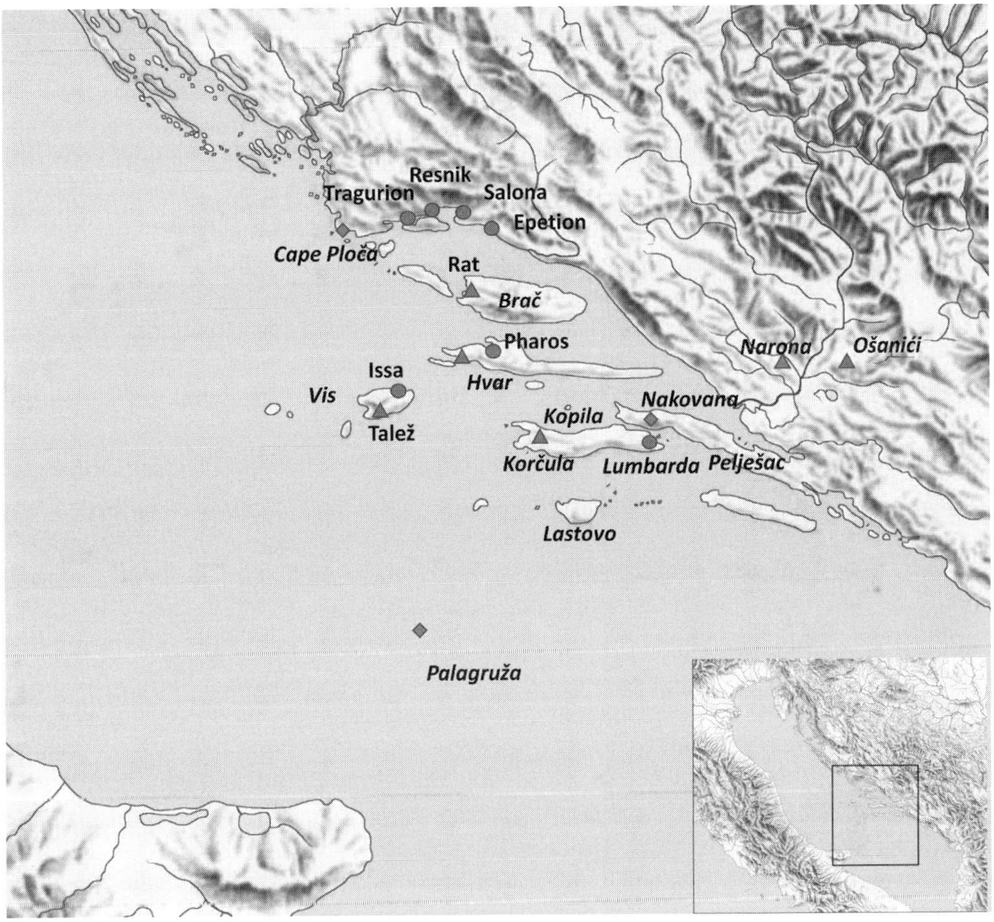

Figure 14: Map of main sites mentioned in text.

to Dalmatia, and particularly its islands, as being something of a 'bridge between the Mediterranean and Balkan cultural zones, and between the ancient cultures of Greece and Italy since prehistory'.[15]

The indigenous Iron Age peoples of the eastern Adriatic left no written sources of their own, but the ethnographic accounts of Greek and Roman authors provide some details about these groups.[16] It is difficult to draw any clear picture of most groups since so many facts are unknown, sources are often contradictory and activities such as wars and migrations must have influenced their settlement patterns and socio-political structures during the last few centuries BCE. Pliny and Florus state that the territory of the Liburni lay within what is modern-day coastal Croatia, from the Raša River to Krka River, including the Kvarner Gulf and Ravni Kotari-Bukovica region (also known as northern Dalmatia, in the modern geo-political sense).[17] Several sources mention the Liburni in various parts of the eastern and western Adriatic coasts,[18] leading to the notion in scholarship of a 'Liburnian thalassocracy' during the Early Iron Age.[19] This notion is problematic due to inconsistencies with the sources, and it is probable that the term 'Liburni' was used in different contexts during the Early Iron Age before the 'Liburnia' of the historical period developed as a socio-political structure sometime during the Late Iron Age.[20] Pseudo-Skylax and pseudo-Skymnus state that the area between the Krka and Cetina rivers (modern-day central Dalmatia) was inhabited by the Hylloi, Bullinoi, and Nestoi.[21] The Delmatae are thought to have originally inhabited the Glamočko, Livanjsko Duvanjsko, Sinjsko, and Imotsko karst fields in the hinterland of central Dalmatia.[22] Pliny also places them between the rivers Krka and Cetina,[23] and it is possible they spread towards the coast in the early 2nd century BCE.[24] This group is not mentioned in the earlier Classical Greek ethnographies, indicating they may have developed as a political or cultural group from the 3rd century BCE.[25]

Most of the information we have about the lives and culture of the local communities from Iron Age Dalmatia comes from archaeological evidence. The Dalmatian Iron Age is considered as dating from approximately the 9th–1st century BCE, and split into the Early Iron Age (9th–5th century BCE) and Late Iron Age (4th–1st century BCE).[26] During the Iron Ages, communities in Dalmatia mostly lived on hills or high-ground in hill fort settlements (known locally as gradina/gradine, they emerged during the Eneolithic and were used throughout the Bronze and Iron Ages), commonly with dry stone walled defences, situated nearby water sources, fertile depressions in the karst landscape and communication routes between pastoral fields.[27] Locally produced pottery from the region was handmade, produced primarily without a potter's wheel from poorly refined clay mixed with varied amounts of fine-grained crystalline limestone (calcite) and quartz sand.[28] Locally produced and imported metal items show links between communities in Dalmatia with the northern Adriatic region, Balkan hinterland and Italic peninsula, and represent the bulk of grave goods in necropolises of local settlements throughout the Iron Ages.[29]

Exchange of material culture between Iron Age communities in Dalmatia and those on the Adriatic coast of Italy, particularly around Apulia and Picenum, took place from the 9th century BCE onwards.[30] The concept of a 'cultural *koine*' for the eastern and western Adriatic during the Early Iron Age, with its roots in the Late Bronze Age, has existed in scholarship for several decades, based primarily on the exchange of metal items and styles between communities in the Balkans and central and southern Italy and the presence of Daunian pottery throughout modern-day Slovenia, Croatia, and parts of Bosnia and Herzegovina.[31] There are few finds of material from the Aegean region in Dalmatia during this period;[32] however, B. Kirigin has argued that the large amounts of coins from Greece and southern Italy held in the Archaeological Museum at Split point to contacts being established as early as the late 6th century BCE.[33] Finds of imported goods on sites in Dalmatia, particularly those of the central Dalmatian islands, suggest that connections with the wider Adriatic and Aegean regions picked up to a certain degree around the late 6th century BCE,[34] with the Hellenistic period,

4th–1st centuries BCE, being a time of intensive connectivity and trans-Mediterranean cultural interaction. These increases in connectivity in Dalmatia are certainly linked to the political and economic arrival of Greek colonists and traders in the Upper and Central Adriatic, and as such, to broader Mediterranean-wide globalizing processes during the Iron Age.

There is no archaeological evidence for any Greek settlements north of Epidamnos-Dyrrachium prior to the 4th century BCE.[35] B. Kirigin argues that the Greeks only became interested in the eastern Adriatic once the potential for trade with communities in the coastal northern Italian region became apparent.[36] Greek traders were becoming increasingly active in the Upper Adriatic, particularly at sites along the Po river delta, Adria, and Spina, during the late 6th and especially 5th century BCE. Epigraphic and archaeological evidence has led archaeologists to argue that both Adria and Spina were Etruscan settlements, trade emporia with mixed Greek, Etruscan, and Venetian populations and culture. They acted as nodes on trans-Mediterranean trade networks that linked the eastern Mediterranean with northern Italy and continental Europe, as evidenced by the vast amounts of Greek imports here.[37]

The penetration of Greeks into the eastern Adriatic sphere has also to be understood in connection with the colonizing and trading activities of Corinth. The city-state had already in the 8th century BCE established Syracuse in Sicily, and Korcyra on Corfu in the eastern Ionian region, and together with the latter continued to diffuse its sphere of influence along the Ionian and southeastern Adriatic coast, which is evident in the foundation of colonies in modern-day Albania (*e.g.* Epidamnos, Apollonia). The earliest Greek material, found on sites in the central eastern Adriatic (*e.g.* ceramic vessels, mostly perfume containers) is of Corinthian provenance, or perhaps indicates their Italic imitation.[38] The strengthening of Korcyra as a naval and trading force that took place from the second half of the 6th and in the 5th century BCE, is attested in central Dalmatia as well, evidenced in amphorae and coin finds of Korcyraean provenance.[39]

While archaeological evidence from both sides of the Adriatic shows that this sea was used as a route of connectivity by indigenous groups, from the 8th century BCE onwards, Greeks slowly started to penetrate the Ionian-Adriatic region.[40] This brought the central Dalmatian islands into contact with Mediterranean-wide networks and globalizing impulses facilitated by the increasingly connected and culturally widespread sphere of the Greek Late Classical and Hellenistic worlds.

The founding of colonies in central Dalmatia was quite late in the context of Greek colonization of the Mediterranean. The timeline for the foundation of these colonies is far from complete, and there are many dates that are still disputed. Pharos and Issa are the two colonies best known through archaeological evidence, and we can argue to a fairly accurate degree that Pharos was founded in 385–384 BCE.[41] The foundation date of Issa is still very much disputed. Some scholars claim that it was founded shortly before Pharos, while others point to the fact that no archaeological evidence for a Greek colony has been found on the island that dates to before the second half of the 4th century BCE.[42] Written sources state that a Cnidian colony existed on the island of Corkyra Melaina, modern day Korčula.[43] It has been suggested that this colony was founded in the early 6th century BCE.[44] An overview of historical and political circumstances in the wider Mediterranean has lead scholars to agree that this should be set within the context of friendly Corcyrean-Cnidian relations, and Corkyraean influence in the region.[45] However, systematic archaeological surveys of the island have found no trace of this colony.[46] An early 3rd-century BCE Issaean colony on Korčula is attested by the famous Lumbarda *psephisma*,[47] as well as Hellenistic period graves.[48] Another supposed Greek colony, Heraclea, might have existed in central Dalmatia contemporarily with these others, though it is only known through a brief mention from Pseudo Sklyax,[49] and a rather large number of coins dated to the 4th century BCE with the name of Heraclea in several variants.[50] While several scholars have made suggestions based on circumstantial evidence, the actual location of the site of Heraclea remains unknown.[51]

Statements of Diodorus Siculus suggest the colonization efforts in Dalmatia during the early 4th century BCE were undertaken under the patronage of Dionysios I of Syracuse.[52] However, other sources on Pharos mention only Paros in connection with the colony's foundation.[53] Pseudo-Skylax refers to Issa as a Greek city around the mid-4th century BCE, while pseudo-Skymnus states that there was a Syracusan colony on the island of Issa (modern-day Vis).[54] However, it is not clear exactly when the colony was founded.[55] The names of Issaeans who set up the colony on Corkyra Melaina, as attested by the Lumbarda *psephisma*, possibly point to Syracusan origins.[56] The foundation of Issa is often attributed to the establishment of colonies in the Adriatic by Dionysios I.[57] However, direct evidence to support this is lacking,[58] and archaeological evidence could suggest that Issa grew into a city in the course of the 4th century, possibly as one of the later ventures of Dionysios I, but perhaps somewhat after his reign.

Two specific sites, one located on an island in the small archipelago of Palagruža, and another on the mainland at Cape Ploča, underline the importance of the location of central Dalmatia in Adriatic seafaring routes. Recent excavations and surveys on the island of Vela Palagruža highlight that the island had a significant role in maritime communications in various periods from as far back as the late 6th millenium BCE, including during the Early Neolithic and Late Copper/Early Bronze Ages.[59] Interestingly, the site has yielded barely any finds from between the Early Bronze Age and the 6th century BCE.[60] Excavations since the early 1990s have been conducted on the main archaeological site on Vela Palagruža, Salamadrija, and have uncovered large amounts of Greco-Roman pottery sherds and some coins. The earliest of that pottery dates to the late 6th century BCE, with the majority coming from the 5th–3rd century BCE, while later Hellenistic and Early Roman pottery is less common.[61] It appears that Attic pottery (black-figure and red-figure ware) is dominant at Palagruža for the late 6th–5th century BCE, and preliminary observations point out that the material here corresponds well with that from Apulia and the Upper Adriatic.[62] This highlights the islands' importance on maritime trade routes linking mainland Greece with the emporia along the Po river delta, as well as the dominant role of Athenian trade in these events during the Late Archaic and Classical periods.[63] The sherds with south Italian origin at the site dating to the Late Classical and Hellenistic periods (Late Apulian red-figure and Gnathia ware) point to at least a partial shift in orientation of trade links and highlight once more the routes between the two Adriatic coasts.[64] Greek and Italic coins found at Palagruža date from the 4th–1st century BCE (with most from the 3rd and transition to the 2nd century BCE), and include issues from cities in southern and central Italy, Sicily, Sardinia, the central Adriatic, Epirus and as far away as Samos in the Aegean.[65] The appearance of coins as possible votive offerings in this period, along with the diversity of origins of finds (coins and pottery), also possibly points to a shift in cultural activity starting from the 4th century BCE.

Among the c. 12,000 sherds found at Palagruža, mostly tableware, especially drinking cups, more than 230 fragments of fine pottery have Greek graffiti inscribed on them.[66] Though few are legible, it is clear they are mostly of a dedicatory nature.[67] For example, a fragment of a late 6th-century black-glazed phiale is marked with ΔΙΟΜΕΔ[...].[68] Through an analysis of the ancient sources, particularly Strabo's account, it slowly became apparent that the Palagruža islands are the Islands of Diomedes.[69] The site on Vela Palagruža is now widely argued to be a cult site to Diomedes, visited by Greek merchants sailing across the Adriatic. Although the sanctuary itself did not survive, due to later building activities and natural degradation of the site, this argument is supported by the large proportion of fine ware here, pointing to them being used in libation and votive offerings,[70] as well as the inscriptions which include references to Diomedes, *anatheke*, 'to dedicate', as well as *soteria*, 'safety', a common word used in sailors' prayers, and *euploia*, a reference to a good voyage.[71]

The site of Cape Ploča (*Punta Planka*) was identified as Pliny's *Promunturium Diomedis*[72] in the 17th century CE by the Dalmatian historian Ivan Lucić. It is situated on the most prominent point of the Hyllus peninsula, on the mainland of central Dalmatia, and as such it is an important milestone for people sailing along the Dalmatian coastline. It is also a spot notorious for sudden changes in winds, and though the site itself offers no shelter, ships and sailors could find safety in the nearby bays of Rogoznica or Stari Trogir.[73] Most of the pottery from the Cape Ploča site is made up of fine tableware that indicates the site was in use from the late 4th century BCE until the 1st century CE, but apparently had its heyday in the 2nd and early 1st century BCE.[74] The earliest fragments, of the late 4th and early 3rd century BCE, are of Apulian Middle and Late Gnathia ware and fragments of North Adriatic Alto Adriatico ware, dating to the late 4th and early 3rd century BCE, while early Roman thin-walled and terra sigillata wares, found here in very small numbers, are the latest.[75] Importantly, much of the pottery comes from local Adriatic production, conceivably from central Dalmatian workshops, while documented imports stem from central and southern Italy, and a smaller portion can be connected with Albania, northwest Greece and Asia Minor.[76] As at Palagruža, inscriptions on the pottery sherds from Cape Ploča point to the site being a cult place to Diomedes, visited by sailors and merchants.[77] Around 15 personal names have been preserved, from which all except Tritos are typical Greek names.[78] The identifiable coins form the site date to between the early 3rd century BCE to the 40s BCE. They include issues from the Greek mints in the Adriatic – Ancona, Issa, Apollonia, Ionian Korcyra, and Leukas, as well as two cities from the Peloponnesus, Aegium and Argos, the island of Cyprus, Carthaginia, Numidia, and the Roman Republic.[79]

Palagruža was first established as a cult site dedicated to Diomedes in the late 6th or 5th century BCE, around the time of the development of the Greek emporia on the western Adriatic coast, and no doubt utilized initially by traders sailing between the Aegean and the emporia on the Po River delta. Situated approximately half way from Ionian Corkyra to Spina, it was a crucial landmark and navigational point on the optimal northwest and southwest open sea route.[80] The sanctuary at Cape Ploča was developed after the founding of the Greek colonies in central Dalmatia during the 4th century BCE, probably by Issaean sailors, and certainly before the end of that century.[81] Its development no doubt reflects the increasing interaction of this region with wider Adriatic and Mediterranean economic and cultural networks and the strengthening of the eastern Adriatic as a maritime route that connected central Europe with the Mediterranean.[82] As N. Čašule has argued, these two sites were involved in a network of trade and communication which spanned the Adriatic Sea, though had broader connections, in which activity increased markedly during the late 4th and 3rd century BCE, and this network seemingly has a link to the Diomedes myth.[83]

As outlined in this first section, increasing connectivity in Dalmatia during the Iron Age was caused by the political and economic penetration of Greeks into the Adriatic, especially from the 6th century BCE. The Late Iron Age was a period of particularly intensive interaction and cultural change in the region. The central Dalmatian islands, particularly those with Greek colonies, acted as nodes which integrated the region into the social and economic sphere of trans-Mediterranean networks, and enhanced the transmission of material culture to and from local communities in Dalmatia. Globalizing influences from around the Adriatic and Mediterranean (*i.e.* the increased connectivity caused by Greek colonization and economic interaction between both coasts of the Adriatic as well as between the Upper Adriatic and the Aegean region) caused this increasing engagement of local communities with wider 'Hellenizing' material culture.

Insular Identities on Dalmatian Islands

Settlement patterns on the central Dalmatian islands began to gradually change during the Early Iron Age, as individual sites began to emerge in positions of pre-eminence. The positioning of several important settlements along shipping lanes, and the presence of significant amounts of imported pottery in them, suggest that connectivity and inclusion in large scale sea trading networks were important to their development.[84]

Prior to Greek colonization, the islands of Dalmatia, similarly with groups along the coast of the mainland, were inhabited by hill fort communities. They had connections with groups on the western coast of the Adriatic, the Dalmatian coastal region and hinterland, and, to a lesser extent, the wider Mediterranean. During the course of the Iron Age, communities here held dominant positions within the region based on their command of agricultural land and trade routes.[85] This section of the paper discusses key sites from the Dalmatian islands, both Greek colonies and local/indigenous communities, that provide further evidence for how these relationships played out, and how material culture and cultural rituals were selectively adopted and adapted in both local and colonial contexts.

Pharos

Pharos is the ancient name for the modern-day island of Hvar, in central Dalmatia, as well as the Greek *polis* that was founded here in 385/384 BCE.[86] While it has been suggested that a colony named Anchiala was founded on Pharos by Parians in the Archaic period,[87] there is no archaeological evidence on the island dating to this period to suggest it existed. The Parian colony of Pharos was founded in the north of Hvar, at the site of modern-day Stari Grad, which is surrounded by a large area of agricultural land known today as the Stari Grad plain. This is the largest fertile zone on any of the Adriatic islands,[88] and it is unsurprising that the Parian colonists chose this location for their settlement.

In terms of studying interaction between colonists and local inhabitants, Pharos is of interest since it was apparently founded initially through an amicable agreement between the two parties.[89] Otherwise, the island of Hvar provides relatively little evidence for such interactions. The current state of research does not allow us to say much about the island during the Iron Age, and it is possible that this hinders our ability to recognize cultural integration on the island. There is evidence for increased settlement activity during this period, and among the known prehistoric hill forts, the Hvar town hill fort, with the nearby Bronze Age barrow necropolis at Vira, appears to be the strongest community during the Iron Age.[90] Other known funerary evidence from several sites (*e.g.* in the locality of Spile, east of Hvar) indicates prehistoric single burials in stone walled tombs (foetal position) under cairns, some perhaps dated to the Iron Age, but none safely confirmed.[91] There is a curious lack of 'Greek' material culture outside of the Pharian *chora*. Despite intensive field surveys, such material has otherwise only so far been found in the town of Hvar, in small quantities, and in Duboka Bay, located at the entrance to Manios Bay (the Neretva Bay), where several fragments of a skyphos were found.[92] The Pharian *chora* and its territory were protected by observatory towers built on prominent sites on the Stari Grad plain, at Maslinovik, and Tor. Greek and presumed indigenous pottery and coins have been found at the site of Tor, possibly pointing to some contact.[93] This situation has led to the argument that the colonists in Pharos did not interact with the indigenous population of the island, or that such interaction is so far not archaeologically visible.[94] This was perhaps due to fighting between the Parian colonists and indigenous population in the earliest phases of the colony. This is confirmed by Diodorus Siculus,[95] and could be reflected in the so-called Pharian *tropaeum*, a damaged Greek inscription that refers to the Parian colonists confiscating weapons from the 'Iadasinoi' and their allies.[96] Evidence for this conflict is possibly found in some recent archaeological discoveries at the site of Stari Grad-Remete that point to a demolition of the settlement.[97]

Evidence for burials is unfortunately lacking at the site of Pharos. Several Hellenistic graves were discovered outside of the urban center of Pharos,[98] including at Čolovica, Garmice,[99] Jurjevac, Knežine,[100] and Kučišće, however, there exists no documentation about the context and circumstances under which these were found. According to an unsigned article from the late 19th century, five graves made of stone slabs and 'other similar and simple graves', some with small statuettes and vessels 'made in the Vis manner', were discovered in the area known as Jurjevac.[101] A group of radially placed tombs that contained Hellenistic jewelry were apparently found on the south slope of St Vid. These would, it was argued, point to a local community appropriating Hellenistic material culture into its burial practices and coexisting with Greek colonists.[102] However, more recent field surveys in the Zahum area near Vrbanj, where these graves were supposedly located, have found no evidence for them.[103]

While the evidence for burials at Pharos is extremely limited, some general characteristics are recognizable. Out of the seven known funerary monuments from Pharos, all but one include names of a single deceased individual, while one includes two names.[104] This suggests that graves in Pharos may have included mostly individual burials. The inscriptions were in Greek and generally simple, including only the name and surname of the deceased on funerary monuments, while the example of one Aristophanes includes a mention to his hometown – ΣΥΡΑΚΟΣΙΟΣ (this latter example could highlight the Syracusan connections in Pharos).[105] While the graves mentioned above are poorly documented, it appears the burial goods were modest and simple.[106] However, due to the lack of proper documentation and the small number of graves, monuments and artifacts available for analysis, we cannot know how representative these are of the various social, political and ethno-cultural groups in Pharos, nor to what specific time-period they relate to.

Pharos had its own production of fine ware pottery and amphorae.[107] There are indications that these products, especially amphorae finds, might reflect wine trade with the indigenous communities (Pharian amphorae were found in the Daorson region, at Ošanjići on the mainland in southern Dalmatia, and at the Kopila hill fort on the island of Korčula).[108] Further studies of Pharian ceramic traits, which are underway, should shed more detailed light on their distribution pattern. Besides pottery manufacture, Pharian economic activity included minting its own coinage. Different denominations of silver and bronze coins depicting on the obverse and reverse Zeus/Capricorn, Dionysion/grapes, Persephora and Demeter/Capricorn or a goat, the head of a man/kantharos, offer clear cultural insight into cults that played an important role in this community, but also its economic activities.[109] For now,

Pharian coins are only known from archaeological contexts from Hvar island (the city of Pharos, including the Škudljivac hoard, and elsewhere on Hvar), Ošanjići, and Palagruža. While there is limited evidence for this case-study, it tentatively reflects a situation in which Greek expansion and domination of the polis of Pharos did not lead to significant interaction with local communities in the first century or so after the colony was founded.[110] This was perhaps a result of conflict between the colonists and local inhabitants during the early stages of Greek settlement.

Issa

Issa is the ancient name for both the island of Vis, the farthest of the bigger inhabited islands off the coast of modern-day central Dalmatia, as well as the ancient Greek settlement on the island (Fig. 15). The site lay on the western side of the northern bay (Sv. Juraj) of the island, a position known as Gradina located in the modern-day town of Vis. This is the largest and best protected natural port on the Dalmatian islands.[111] Surveys have shown that Vis was less inhabited than other Dalmatian islands during the Bronze and Early Iron Ages, with most sites on the island dating to the Hellenistic and Early Roman periods.[112]

Burying the dead under tumuli or cairns was a typical Bronze Age burial custom in central Dalmatia. Though evidence is still scanty, this appears to have changed in the Iron Age, as only inhumation burials in flat necropolises are known from this period. The significantly small amount of funeral evidence from the island of Vis prior to the arrival of the Greeks allows us to suspect that such practices on the island

Figure 15: Map of Vis (Issa), its bay and sites of the Hellenistic necropoleis.

Figure 16: Dressed stone tomb 180 from the eastern necropolis at Vlaško njiva, Issa. Documentation of the Archaeological Museum in Split. Published in Kirigin 1986 (B. Kirigin, Otok Vis v helenizmu, Ljubljana 1986).

Figure 17: Tomb 168, a pit grave with cover of stone slabs from the eastern necropolis at Vlaško njiva, Issa before removal of the slabs. Documentation of the Archaeological Museum in Split (published in Ugarković 2016, 68, fig. 3a).

fit into the regional picture, while exhibiting some local peculiarities as well.[113] Vis has a number of tumuli,[114] and the largest of these, known as Vela Gomila, is located nearby the Iron Age settlement of Talež, across a steep valley running down towards the bay of Taleška.[115] These features are usually interpreted within the region as ritual monuments associated with the control of agricultural land during the Late Bronze Age–Early Iron Age.[116] Sherds of local and imported Iron Age pottery have been found at both Talež and Vela Gomila, including black glazed, light colored, Daunian bichromic wares as well as Corinthian A and B amphorae. Vela Gomila was certainly an important site for the local population, and remained in use after Talež was abandoned following the foundation of Issa in the 4th century.[117] Its long-term use might point to the continuity of local cults. The pottery evidence suggests Talež was at its height during the 5th century BCE, at the same time of the ascendancy of Spina.[118] The evidence from these two sites shows that prior to the Greek colonization

Figure 18: Tomb 168, after removal of the stone slabs. Documentation of the Archaeological Museum in Split (published in Ugarković 2016, 68, fig. 3b).

of Issa in the 4th century BCE, the local population was possibly already engaged in trans-Adriatic and, consequently, Mediterranean wide economic networks.

Issa's cultural history is (at the moment) best highlighted in the material remains of funerary activities. Excavations of two necropolises, Martvilo and Vlaška njiva, situated on the southwestern and eastern outskirts of the city wall, provide good evidence for interaction between colonial and local populations. Importantly, these are, so far, the only known, and partially investigated, necropolises of Greek cities in Dalmatia. All together there are around 200 tombs dated to the Hellenistic period, with a handful that could perhaps be Late Classical.[119] These included a high percentage of tombs with the remains of multiple deceased, but single adult and child burials are present as well (Figs 16–18). Grave finds included mostly ceramic vessels, which can from a functional perspective be grouped into five categories: tableware-drinking sets (*oinochoai*, *skyphoi*, *pelikai*), vessels for solid food (one handler, bowls, saltcellars), ritual vessels (*lebes gamikos*, saucers), small ointment containers (*lekythos*, bottles, unguentaria), and toilet vessels (*e.g. pyxis*) (Fig. 19). Other items, such as lamps and remains of different personal items (*e.g. strigiles*), terracotta, coins, or parts of dress (clothing remains or adornment) are found as well. The finds in these burials are indicative of Issa's connectedness to wide ranging trade networks, as well as the development of local ceramic production, which is supposed to have started at the latest in the

Figure 19: Grave assemblage of tomb 168 from the eastern necropolis at Vlaško njiva, Issa. Documentation of the Archaeological Museum in Split (published in Ugarković 2016, 71, fig. 4).

mid-3rd century BCE.[120] The majority of offerings dated to before this time are made up of imports primarily from the central Mediterranean, chiefly from Apulia (but also the northwest Adriatic, southwest/mainland Greece and Sicily), while after this period they are mostly locally produced fine wares, although deposition of imported vessels in graves continued until the end of the Hellenistic period, most notably in the later period, from the eastern Aegean and even the Levant.[121]

The custom of compound body disposal, with multiple consecutive burials, is typical, although not exclusively, an Issaean trait. It assumes the reuse of the grave architecture, mostly stone cists or dressed stone tombs, although pits as well, designed for individual burials to fit another burial that occurred at a later stage.[122] At the Martvilo necropolis, this practice appears almost exclusively, documented in stone tombs interpreted as family tombs.[123] It is found at the eastern necropolis as well, although single burials appear much more commonly here, and only in the course of the 3rd century BCE does the ratio head in favor of the multiple burials.[124] Some of these graves at Martvilo were accompanied by stone monuments acting as family grave stelae, indicating these were in fact family tombs. Unlike the Hellenistic hypogaea from Rhodes, which included separate loculi and tombstone for each family member, the Issaean tombs include a single tombstone for the entire family, mostly simple shapes with a triangular 'gable'. It seems the funerary *columellae* monuments, commonly found at Dyrrachium and Apollonia, on the southeastern Adriatic, are missing at Issa, and had no influence on the style of funerary monuments here.[125] Certain attributes in several of these show similarities with features known from western Greek contexts, particularly relating to the Corinthian colonies. For example, the use of bounding of names by a raised fillet on the tombstone.[126] However, the names on inscriptions from tombstones at Issa are usually more carefully planned and executed. They display none of the relief-letters, cartouches and vegetal decoration that feature on Hellenistic tombstones from Epirus to Acarnania and Aetolia.[127]

Some aspects of the burials at Issa point to the influence of local burial practices. The deposition of heaps of sea gravel in or around tombs at Issa, can be considered an influence from indigenous communities from both sides of the Adriatic, including in Liburnia and Histria, from the 8th century BCE onwards.[128] The deposition of crushed murex shell, usually next to the graves, on the other hand, has no apparent analogies, and is for now considered a local Issaean trait. The practice of multiple successive burials is far from unique to Issa. We can currently not confirm if such a practice was adopted from the locals on Vis, although this looks plausible since the custom was recorded on the nearly island of Brač.[129] Furthermore, the practice is known from different indigenous communities on both the eastern and western Adriatic coasts.[130] Chronologically speaking, and taking into account the entire Adriatic region, the current state of research suggests that the earliest occurrence of such a practice came from the central Dalmatian hinterland, where it is common from the 10th–1st century BCE, and can be traced even back into the Late Bronze Age.[131] This points to indigenous influences on important patterns of cultural behavior in a Greek Dalmatian city. This is not to say that such a custom was unknown to Greeks per se, as evidenced in different cities in the Peloponnesus and northwestern Greece, Macedonia or Cyprus, but it seems not to have been practiced in the Greek west.[132]

Typical Issaean grave architecture includes stone tombs, enclosed with vertical slabs, or dressed stone, although there are numerous varieties that appear as well. Some forms of 4th–3rd century BCE grave architecture at Issa, despite finding no analogies in the documented contemporary tombs in the eastern Adriatic, can be found at several local sites on the island of Sicily and in Daunia.[133] Like graves from northern Dalmatia in this period, the Issaean graves include pottery and items of attire, and usually no weapons. However, sometimes weapons do appear, like a find from a pre-Roman pilum in grave 243/237 from Vlaška njiva, which might point to interactions with foreigners or immigration. Analogies of both the form of the weapon, dated to the 4th century BCE, as well as the practice of depositing such weapons in graves with the deceased, which can be traced to the other side of the Adriatic, especially on the middle and southern part of the Italian peninsula, point to links with the western Adriatic indigenous communities.[134] Some other graves from associated nuclei offer more interesting evidence, as the position of the body of the deceased person was in semi-foetal position on one side, a practice again associated with the indigenous cultural groups.[135]

At several indigenous sites from central Dalmatia, including on the islands of Korčula and Brač, discussed below, graves from this period include weapons, items of attire, and pottery.[136] It is probable that the Issaean tombs provided an example that was emulated at many local sites, particularly in northern Dalmatia, where large tombs made of worked stone blocks, including multiple deceased and large amounts of imported Hellenistic pottery along with some locally made (increasingly under Hellenistic influence) and imported metal items, appear from the 4th century BCE.[137] It has been suggested that large amounts of pottery found as grave offerings here indicate local communities adopted burial practices and material culture from the Hellenistic world.[138] A certain amount of cultural exchange and communication plausibly resulted from Issa's interactions with indigenous groups, and it appears that the Issaeans picked up some aspects of local burial practices. These were then mixed with practices that drew upon broader Hellenistic, globalizing cultural templates, resulting in unique burials rites on the island. These are also potent indicators of the existence of several cultural groups in Issa that mutually contributed to shaping and reinforcing aspects of cultural identities and practices creating a unique Issaean culture.

Issa's prosperity in the production and exportation of wine and pottery, particularly following Rome's victory in the first and second 'Illyrian Wars', is certainly highlighted by the large amounts of ceramics and amphorae found both on the island and in underwater contexts. The importance of the wine trade is also reflected in the images of volute craters and grape clusters on Issaean coins minted in the late 3rd century.[139] As in many Hellenistic centers, wine played an important role in Issaean social and cultural life, as attested by the large amounts of wine drinking vessels in tombs, the popularity of the cult of Dionysus, and frequency of the name Dionysios on Issaean tombstones.[140] Wine from Issa was no doubt well known across the Mediterranean, as the superiority of Issaean wine is mentioned in a statement of Agatharchides, related through Athenaeus.[141] Archaeological evidence suggests wine-filled amphorae were exported from Issa to other islands and mainland sites in central Dalmatia, to Liburnia, Istria, Adria, perhaps some other western Adriatic sites, and potentially as far away as Alexandria.[142] The colonizing activities of Issa appear to point at efforts to control trade between Cape Ploča and the Neretva valley, as it founded settlements at Lumbarda on the island of Korčula, and made alliances with Tragurion, Epetium,[143] and perhaps also Salona and Aspalathos on the nearby coastal area.[144] A significant presence at these sites gave them access to important communication routes, including the pass of Klis and the eastern entrance to the Pelješac Channel towards the Narona river, as well as some of the most fertile agricultural land in central Dalmatia (the bay of Kaštela).[145]

Clearly Issa was a significant production and export center in the Hellenistic period, both regionally and perhaps broadly in the Adriatic – a topic that is subject to further enquiry. It had a strong influence on indigenous populations throughout Dalmatia, acting as a node linking them to Mediterranean-wide Hellenistic cultural templates, but precisely how interactions between Issa and local communities played out in economic and political terms is difficult to determine at this stage. In the later Hellenistic period (2nd–1st century BCE), incorporation of Issa into broader Mediterranean networks is highlighted by the presence of finds here from Asia Minor and the Levant. This was most probably a result of their close relationship with the expanding Roman Republic, whose influence in the eastern Adriatic, as well as the

Aegean region, greatly increased during this period.[146] As opposed to Pharos, the evidence from Issa and nearby communities indicates more interaction occurred between Greek colonists and local inhabitants soon after the establishment of this settlement. Material culture and perhaps aspects of burial ritual were shared between these groups, and Issa appears to have acted as a major entrepôt in the region, helping to expose local communities to globalizing Greek culture.

Corkyra Melaina

The island of Korčula is marked by its position between the southern Adriatic indigenous communities and the central Adriatic Hellenistic cities. Based on the island having considerable arable land, Korčula had the necessary requirements for self-preservation and socio-economic progress, as evidenced in more than 20 strategically placed Iron Age settlements.[147] These communities were at the peak of their power during the 4th–1st century BCE, at which point they played an important role in cultural-historical events of the immediate area.[148] This is also reflected in the fact that they were able to influence the activities of Issaean colonists on the island. The Lumbarda *psephisma* is a Greek inscription found in 1877 by a local villager nearby the modern-day town of Lumbarda, on the eastern part of the island. The inscription details an agreement between Issaean colonists and a local community about the distribution of land to the colonists. Thus, the agreement on the *psephisma* implies the colony, although short-lived, was established under peaceful conditions,[149] suggesting the local community had enough power to negotiate with Issa.

Ceramic evidence from hill forts indicates that local communities on the island interacted with trade networks linking them with the Aegean and southern Italy from as early as the 7th/6th century BCE.[150] The willingness of locals to engage in dynamic interaction in the context of trade/exchange of goods no doubt facilitated the development of identity and prosperity in these communities. The evidence for imports on Iron Age Korčula matches with that of the other Dalmatian islands mentioned here in that imported ceramics initially came from Aegean and south Italian production centers, while in the Hellenistic period trade with southern Italy, particularly Apulia, intensified. During the latter part of this period, local production centers, particularly at Issa, began manufacturing ceramics and exporting to local communities throughout Dalmatia, including Kopila on Korčula, as evidenced from grave goods documented in its necropolis.[151] Glass material found in tombs also attests to links with all of the important Hellenistic glass making regions, including in the Aegean, eastern Mediterranean, Alexandria, Carthage, and northern Italian centers.[152] Metal items here, particularly fibulae, are characteristic of items from the northern Adriatic and Alpine regions.[153]

Most of these interactions no doubt took place independently from the Greek colonies on the island. As Borzić notes, the Greek settlements on Korčula were obviously short lived, despite the strategic position of Korčula in relation to trade and communication networks – at the entrance to the Pelješac canal and the Neretva valley on the mainland in southern Dalmatia, and its proximity to the Greek colonies on Hvar and

Vis.[154] However, connection to these networks no doubt, as well as adoption of newly acquired goods into their cultural repertoire, encouraged the exchange of material culture. The only indication of the adoption of 'Hellenistic' style fortifications on the island is a limestone tower with a dry-stone quadratic shape made of roughly dressed stones at the hill fort site of Velo Gračišće.[155] However, the necropolis at the major hill fort of Kopila has provided important evidence for cultural interaction.

Several aspects of the necropolis at Kopila, particularly the manner of construction and specific spatial organization of tombs, highlight its unique character within the region. The westernmost section of the Kopila necropolis includes a structure consisting of at least twelve interrelated round monumental grave parcels with concentric stone rings, spread over an area of at least 500 m^2.[156] Similarities are noticeable between the burials at Kopila and those at Issa. Both include multiple burials, and while those at Issa are confirmed as family tombs through their accompanying inscriptions, we can only presume the same at Kopila. The use of sea gravel as paving at the bottom of the tombs is known from both sites, and is a practice known from earlier Iron Age Dalmatian graves. Various jewelry items and a large amount of ceramic Hellenistic tableware have been found in the graves at Kopila, and unlike in those at Issa, they also contain offensive weapons, primarily spears.[157] There is a striking resemblance of so-called symposiatic types of wares both at the Issa and Kopila necropolises, and yet the latter community formed their assemblages to contain slightly different sets of particular forms.[158] Clearly, the community at Kopila drew selectively on influences from local and broader Hellenistic cultural templates, adopting them to fit the needs of their own expressions of identity, in the development of funerary rites in the Late Iron Age.

Brač

Field surveys have recorded numerous sites on the island of Brač, mostly dating to the Bronze and Iron Ages.[159] While Greek and Italian imported ceramics and coins found at several sites point to indirect contacts, not a single Greek settlement is known to have existed on the island.[160] In the Iron Age layers excavated at the hill fort site of Rat, on the hillside which overlooks the village of Ložišća (western Brač) from 2007–2010, 4% of sherds are thought to have been imported from southern Italy (Daunian 8th–6th century BCE) and the Greek world (black-figured and red-figured vessels, including some of probable Attic production), while the rest is local pottery.[161] Local farmers have found a variety of metal helmets, greaves, sherds of ceramics, rings, and glass and amber beads around the nearby site of Vičja luka, located near Ložišća, since the 19th century,[162] and in 1908 four graves were discovered here and their contents entered into an inventory by the Archaeological Museum in Split.[163] Their contents provide evidence for a flat necropolis and a variety of contacts local communities had during the Late Iron Age. These graves, three of which include multiple burials (graves 2, 3, and 4), are dated between the 5th and 3rd century BCE.[164] The grave goods speak to broad and numerous contacts with Adriatic-wide and Balkan cultural *koines*. Finds of whorls and spools are unusual for central Dalmatian burial contexts.[165] Spools are found frequently as grave goods in Iron Age female burials in Venetia, Etruria, Picenum, and Salento. In Etruria during the 7th and 6th century, these types of artifacts were important grave goods for females of high status, and the role of weaver was related to the familias-domina mater in Etruscan society.[166] Since this custom of depositing weaving items in graves is not found elsewhere in central Dalmatia it is interpreted as presumably the result of direct connections with Italy.[167]

Other items, such as the pseudo-certosa type fibulae with a zoomorphic termination of the foot, point to more broad eastern Adriatic relations.[168] These items are found in the territory of the Delmatae, in the central Dalmatian hinterland, among the Iapodi in the Lika area, and in the *Caput Adriae* area.[169] In Italy, where animal fibulae were favored, this type is found in relatively small numbers of local variations, yet it is still considered a guiding form of fibulae for the Adriatic *koine*, dispersed through maritime communications.[170] A range of items, including belt buckles, fibulae, and tweezer types point to interaction with groups in northern Dalmatia. As mentioned above, three of these graves have multiple burials. It is possible that this was a shared custom of family burials in tombs, as is confirmed in Issa, but, as with multiple burials in northern Dalmatia, it is not possible here to determine whether the individuals buried were in fact related. As with some tombs from northern Dalmatia and Issa, some of the grave goods appear to have been intentionally broken before deposition. M. Blečić-Kavur and B. Kavur have suggested that this practice relates to a symbolic demonstration of the termination of the status of the deceased in this world and creation of his status in the next.[171] This was, perhaps, a cultural habit shared among communities in central and northern Dalmatia, as it was with others further abroad.

There are several items from Vičja luka that are considered in scholarship as related to status in other socio-cultural settings. For example, a belt hook with a palmette from grave 4, is also known from limited examples on the eastern Adriatic – found in Otišić, in the central Dalmatian hinterland, and from Dragišić and Asseria in northern Dalmatia.[172] These are Italic belt hooks, imported from central or southern Italy,[173] and are a result of the constant cultural contacts between Italian communities and those in northern and central Dalmatia, also emphasized by the presence of Apulian pottery in grave 4 at Vičja luka.[174] These items were, in Italic funerary contexts, status symbols associated with warriors, high ranking citizens, and in children's graves where they are considered as a metaphorical symbol of the transition into adulthood and full membership of their community.[175] In graves 2, 3, and 4 at Vičja luka are examples of the so-called Greco-Illyrian helmets, well known from grave contexts in the western Balkan peninsula.[176] Babić has identified the emergence of the practice of deposition of these types of helmets in funerary contexts in the central Balkans from the 5th century BCE as part of a shift in ideological ordering, reflecting the development of a subversive strategy whereby the hereditary status of the elite was challenged.[177]

Several glass objects from graves 3 and 4 also point to Vičja luka being something of a redistribution center on a trade route linking the Macedonian world with the Adriatic Sea and western Balkans. Two glass seals, one depicting Herakles holding a winged lion/lioness and another two goats rearing, reflect similar objects mass manufactured in Macedonia, particularly during the 4th century BCE.[178] These items were used for stamping and as jewelry, often associated with gifts of the Macedonian aristocracy,[179] and thus represented status symbols and a means for social identification. Transparent yellow amphoriskos-shaped glass beads, found in graves 3 and 4, were also the products of Macedonian workshops. These are considered luxurious emblematic items associated with female elites and are found distributed widely northwards through the Balkans and across the Adriatic.[180]

The impact of Greek colonization of the central Dalmatian islands on the local communities on Brač is, for the time being, unknown due to a lack of investigation of Late Iron Age sites on the island. The material so far discovered at the site of Vičja luka reflects interaction with Italic and local communities in northern and central Dalmatia, as well as wider cultural networks linking Macedonia with the Adriatic and the broader Balkan region, at least during the 5th–3rd century BCE. Whether the community at Vičja luka considered the items found in graves here as status symbols is hard to say for certain. However, it is certainly significant that the grave assemblages include a wide range of imported objects considered status symbols in the communities from which they came. Blečić-Kavur and Kavur interpret the status of the deceased at Vičja luka as reflected through the diversity of their grave goods, representing a community that controlled and stimulated long-distance trade to become important cultural mediators linking Mediterranean culture with that of 'prehistoric' European societies.[181] The community at Vičja luka seemingly represents a meeting point between Dalmatian, Italic and broader Balkan cultural networks. Its proximity to the mainland perhaps ensured its connectivity to networks linked to the hinterland, while being an island made it an ideal node through which cultural goods were exchanged along the Adriatic. Hopefully more data will come to light during future excavations that will provide further clues about the impact of globalizing processes on local communities on Brač over time during the Iron Age.

Conclusion

This paper has sought to trace the development of economic and political networks in the Late Iron Age linking the central Dalmatian islands to the wider Adriatic and Mediterranean worlds. Socio-economic factors certainly drove Greek political penetration of the Adriatic from the 6th century. Evidence from the Dalmatian islands allows us to trace these networks in time and space. Though rather late in terms of Greek colonizing efforts, the incorporation of the Adriatic into the realm of the Hellenizing cultural *koine* certainly relates to similar globalizing processes seen throughout the Mediterranean world during the Iron Age, as Greek colonies established social and economic networks linking communities from Spain to the Black Sea. The examples from the Dalmatian islands provided here show the variation in cultural experiences that resulted from such connectivity, the effects of which went both ways, affecting both immigrant and indigenous communities. The Greek cities, or at least Issa, accepted various aspects of material culture and burial rituals, resulting in a unique community. No doubt, important aspects of its identity were Greek, for instance its political organization, but funeral rituals can say a lot about other types of identities that make up this community. It is possible that it was in fact this intensive mixture of different cultural traits – this melting pot of cultures driven by socio-economic interests – in combination with some clever political maneuvers and its strategic position that made Issa one of the most important players in the region.

All the central Dalmatian islands developed their own specific traits that drew from globalizing styles and cultural practices, adopting them according to local preferences in a way that incorporated both global and local sets in processes that were driven by contemporary geostrategic, cultural, economic, and political contexts. That Greek colonies were primarily focused on the Dalmatian islands, as opposed to the mainland, is unsurprising given that the islands were strategically close to trans-Adriatic Sea lanes. Yet, their location also facilitated trade with communities on the coast and in the hinterland. Local communities on the islands were also potentially more susceptible to globalizing processes, and some conceivably acted as nodes connecting Balkan and Adriatic cultural circles. Incorporation into Mediterranean-wide networks opened local communities up to new sets of symbols and material cultures with which to engage in their own socio-cultural lives. It is difficult to determine to what extent their understanding of these new objects and styles was reflective of their original meaning, since consumption is always culturally specific and socially constructed.[182] However, the evidence discussed above suggests that they regarded much of their newly acquired material fondly, as the context of their acquisition (import) and deposition (funerary) would imply. It is possible that imported Greek and Italian material culture, and possibly certain aspects of burial architecture and rituals, were adopted as luxury items and high status practices to legitimize and strengthen the position of those who utilized them within their society.[183] It is hoped that through future excavation and research on the Dalmatian islands we may understand further how such material was utilized in expressions of status and identity within their specific social and cultural setting.

Notes

1 For example, Hodos 2009; 2010a; 2016; Jennings 2011; Vlassopoulos 2013, 226–319; Pitts and Versluys 2014; Thonemann 2015, 3–42; Mazurek in this volume.
2 Prag and Quinn 2013.
3 Malkin 2011, 5–8.
4 Hodos 2014, 25–26.
5 See papers in Cambi, Čače and Kirigin 2002; Poklečki Stošić 2010.
6 Surić *et al.* 2005; Korbar 2009.
7 See papers in Forenbaher 2009.
8 Erlandson 2008, 2.
9 Fitzpatrick 2004, 6.

10 Appadurai 1996, 42.
11 Pitts 2008, 494.
12 Here we define 'local' communities as those existing since before the colonization of the islands by Greeks from the 4th century BCE.
13 Hodos 2010b, 23.
14 Blašković 1998; Bognar 2006.
15 Gaffney *et al.* 2001, 139.
16 For overviews and critiques of historical sources relating to the inhabitants of pre-Roman Dalmatia see Čače 2002; Šašel Kos 2005; Dzino 2014; Barnett 2017. According to these sources, groups associated with the coastal region from northern to southern Dalmatia include the Liburni, Iapodes, Hylleis, Bullinoi, Nestoi, Manoi, Delmatae, Ardiaei, Plearei, and Daorsi.
17 Plin. *NH*. 3.139; Flor. *Epit*. 1.21.
18 Str. 6.2.4; App. *Bell. Civ*. 2.39; Theopomp. *FGrHist* 115 F 131, Steph. Byz. s.v. Λάδεστα ἤ Λάδεστον; Skymn. *FGrHist* 2047 F 2 Steph. Byz. *s.v.* Πάρος; Apoll. *Arg*. 4.562–66; Pomp. Mel. 2.57; Plin. *NH*. 3.110, 112.
19 See sources in Barnett 2017, n. 71.
20 Čače 2002; Dzino 2014; Barnett 2017.
21 Ps-Skyl. 22; Ps-Skymn. 403–411.
22 On the Delmatae, see Zaninović 1967; Šašel Kos 2005, 292.
23 Plin. *NH*. 3.142.
24 Čače and Milivojević 2017, 148–149.
25 Dzino 2013, 148.
26 On the Late Iron Age in Dalmatia, see Čović 1987 (central Dalmatia); Batović 2005 (Liburnia).
27 On hill forts from Liburnia, see Čelhar 2014; from central Dalmatia, see Kirigin *et al.* 2006 (Vis island); Barbarić 2010; Katić 2010; Miletić 2014 (Hvar island); Babić 2016, 57–58; Šuta 2016, 147–156; Radić and Borzić 2017a, especially pp. 32 with a map of all hill forts on the island of Korčula. On the various interpretations of hill fort sites from the Iron Age in temperate Europe, see Woolf 1993; Thurston 2009, 362.
28 Barbarić 2011a; Šašelj and Vuković 2013; Čelhar and Borzić 2016, 70–72.
29 Čović 1987; Batović 2005, 30–39; Čelhar and Vujević 2014.
30 Batović 1976; Blečić 2007. Pliny mentions that the Liburni, whom he says elsewhere stretched from the river Raša to river Krka (Plin. *NH*. 3.139; see also Flor. *Epit*. 1.21), inhabited parts of Italy, including Picenum, Plin. *NH*. 3.110, 112.
31 For discussion and bibliography on the Adriatic *koiné*, see Blečić Kavur 2009; 2015.
32 Kirigin 2006a, 19.
33 Kirigin 1990, 320.
34 In contrast with the Italian coast of the Adriatic, finds of Archaic and Classical Greek artifacts in Dalmatia are limited, and spread over indigenous sites of strategic and geographic importance. Nicolanci 1973; Kirigin 2006a, 21; Šešelj 2010, 411–439.
35 Written sources possibly indicate earlier Greek settlements in central Dalmatia; see below.
36 Kirigin 2006a, 19; 2006b.
37 Lomas 2006, 178.
38 Šešelj 2009, 411–439; Borzić 2017a, 61–63.
39 Borzić 2017b. For distribution of amphorae types A and B, see Šešelj 2010, 431, map 23. See also Čače for sources and discussion.
40 Čače 2002; Radić and Borzić 2017a, 23.
41 See Kirigin 2006, 64–67.
42 See Kirigin 1999, 158–159.
43 Ps-Skymn. 427–428; Str. 7.5.5; Plin. *NH*. 3.152; see Radić and Bass 2002.
44 Beaumont 1936, 187.

45 Kirigin 2010; Radić and Borzić 2017a, 20–23.
46 Radić and Bass 2002.
47 Lombardo 1993; Solarić and Solarić 2009.
48 Kirigin 1990, 311.
49 Ps-Skyl. 22.
50 Kirigin 1990, 295; for bibliography, see Visonà 2005, 29–30.
51 Kirigin 1999, 148–150.
52 See Diod. Sic. 15.13.4, 14.2.
53 Ephor. Fr. 89; Ps-Skym. 426–427; Str. 7.5.5.
54 Ps-Skyl. 23; Ps-Skym. 413–414.
55 Kirigin 1990, 310.
56 Wilkes and Fischer-Hansen 2004, 331–332; Marohnić 2012, 168–169.
57 Braccesi 1977, 230–232; Stylianou 1998, 196.
58 Beaumont 1936, 202; Wilkes and Fischer-Hansen 2004, 331–332.
59 Forenbaher 1999; 2018; Kaiser and Forenbaher 1999; Kirigin, Miše and Barbarić 2009, 104–105.
60 Kirigin *et al.* 2009, 139.
61 Kirigin, Miše and Barbarić 2009, 106; Kirigin 2012.
62 Kirigin and Čače 1998, 65; Kirigin *et al.* 2009, 141; Semeraro and Kirigin 2017.
63 Čašule 2012, 215.
64 Miše 2017.
65 Bonačić Mandinić 2012/13.
66 Kirigin 2012, 62.
67 Kirigin *et al.* 2009, 141.
68 Kirigin and Čače 1998, 64, fig. 3, 85; Kirigin 2012, 41–42, fig. 26.
69 Forenbaher *et al.* 1994, 45; Kirigin and Čače 1998, 66, particularly 76–77.
70 Čašule 2012, 209–210.
71 Kirigin *et al.* 2009, 141; Kirigin 2012, 60–63.
72 Plin. *NH.* 3.141.
73 Kirigin 2006a, 22.
74 Čače and Šešelj 2005, 165, 167; Šešelj 2010, 636, 638.
75 Kirigin 2004, 142–143; Šešelj 2010, 39–45, 55–57.
76 Miše and Šešelj 2007; Šešelj 2010, 301.
77 More than 500 graffiti inscriptions, Čače and Šešelj 2005, 166–167; Šešelj 2010, 543–544.
78 Šešelj 2010, 543.
79 Banačić Mandinić 2004.
80 Kirigin *et al.* 2009.
81 Bilić Dujmušić 2004; Čače and Šešelj 2005.
82 Šešelj 2010, 636–638.
83 Čašule 2012.
84 Gaffney *et al.* 2002, 36.
85 Kirigin *et al.* 2009, 140.
86 Ps-Skyl. 23; Ephoros in *FGrH* 70 F 89; Eratosth. *ap*. School. in Ap. Rhod. *Argon.* 4.1215.
87 Steph. Byz. s.v. Ἀγχιάλη; Nikolanci 1989; Schilardi 2002.
88 Slapšak and Kirigin 2001, 561.
89 Kirigin 2006b.
90 Gaffney and Stanšić 1992, 115; Miletić 2014.
91 Gaffney *et al.* 1997; Miletić 2014, with earlier bibliography.
92 Kirigin 2006b, 28.
93 Kirigin and Slapšak 2010, 137.

94 Kirigin 2006a, 21.
95 Diod. Sic. 15.14.2.
96 *CIG* 2, 1837c; Kuntić-Makvić and Mahronić 2010.
97 Popović 2010, 139; Jeličić-Radonić and Katić 2015, 169–170, 180.
98 On Hellenistic pottery from Pharos, acquired by the Archaeological Museum in Split from the late 19th to the mid-20th century, see Miše 2005. Of this pottery, examples from Garmice and Knežine are confirmed from grave contexts, though those from other sites are also conceivably from burials due to their preservation.
99 Gaffney *et al.* 1997, 194.
100 Gaffney *et al.* 1997, 179.
101 Anonymous, 1985, cited in Kirigin 2006b, 139.
102 Kirigin 1990, 300.
103 Kirigin 2006b, 140.
104 Mahronić 2012, 36–41.
105 Kirigin 1990, 301, fig. 5.
106 Miše 2005; Kirigin 2006b, 139–140.
107 Katić 1999/2000; Kirigin, Hayes and Leach 2002.
108 Marić 2004; Borzić 2017b.
109 On the coinage of Pharos, see Jelčić-Radonić and Katić 2015, 117–130; Visonà 2017, 201–203, with earlier literature.
110 Later historical circumstances indicate this might have changed in the course of the late 3rd century BCE and later (Matijašić 2009, 83), but the archaeological evidence does not allow more in-depth discussion at this point.
111 Kirigin 1990, 305.
112 For these sites, see Kirigin *et al.* 2006.
113 Barbarić 2011b.
114 Kirigin *et al.* 2006, 11, VS 1017.00; VS 1216.00; VS 1116.01; VS 1103.00; VS 1158.00; VS 1181.00; VS 1009.10; VS 1118.00. See also Kirigin 1985, 100, n. 38.
115 Kirigin *et al.* 2006, VS 1096.00.
116 Kirigin 1999, 157.
117 Kirigin 1999, 156–158; *cf.* Katić 2009, 45.
118 Kirigin 2006a, 21.
119 Ugarković 2015, 48. For earlier bibliography on both necropolises, see Ugarković 2016, 67.
120 Miše 2015.
121 Kirigin 1990, 308–309; Ugarković 2015; Miše and Touloumtzidou 2016.
122 Ugarković 2016, 85–88.
123 Kirigin 1985.
124 Ugarković 2016, 86.
125 Fraser 1991, 252, 259.
126 Fraser 1991, 254.
127 Fraser 1991, 262–263.
128 Ugarković 2015, 656, n. 474.
129 For insights into 5th–3rd century BCE stone tombs from Vičja Luka see Barbarić 2006, with older literature. For late 7th- and 6th-century BCE tombs from Žaganj dolac, see Marović 1971, especially tomb 3, a stone cist, with 5 individuals, conceivably deposited in a flexed position.
130 Ugarković 2016, 86–88, with bibliography.
131 Ugarković 2016, 87, n. 124.
132 Ugarković 2016, 87, with literature.
133 Ugarković 2016, 85, with literature.
134 Ugarković 2017.

135 Ugarković 2017, 163.
136 Kirigin 1985, 102–103 (English summary); Kirigin 1990, 309.
137 Batović 2005; Kukoć 2011b.
138 Brusić 1993; 1999;.
139 Visonà 1996, 155–156; Bonašić Mandinić and Visonà 2002, 361.
140 Kirigin, Katunarić and Šešelj 2006, 193.
141 Athen. I, 28 (51).
142 Kirigin, Katunarić and Šešelj 2006, 197.
143 Polyb. 32.9; see Šašel Kos 2005, 296; Dzino 2010, 62–63.
144 Radić and Borzić 2017a, 25.
145 Dzino argues that the Dalmatian wars of the 2nd–1st century BCE were related to this indigenous group attempting to take control of these exchange networks. See Dzino 2013, 155.
146 Eckstein 2008; Dzino 2010.
147 Radić and Borzić 2017a.
148 Borzić 2010, 28-29; Radić and Borzić 2017a.
149 Solarić and Solarić 2009, 82.
150 Borzić 2017a.
151 Kirigin, Katunarić and Šešelj 2006; Borzić 2017a.
152 Eterović Borzić 2017.
153 Radić 2017.
154 It was perhaps its position between two opposing regional powers, the Roman Republic (allied to the Issaean commonwealth) and the Illyrian kingdom, that brought the short life of the Issaean colony to an end; see Borzić 2010, 32.
155 Possibly a replication of the kind of Greek tower known from Hvar at Maslinovik, Radić, and Bass 2002, 294–295; Borzić 2010, 33.
156 Radić and Borzić 2017b, 49-50, fig. 15, 20.
157 Radić and Borzić 2017b, 57.
158 Borzić 2017a.
159 Stančić *et al.* 1999.
160 Kirigin 1999, 161; Bonačić Mandinić 2003.
161 Gaastra *et al.* 2014, 11.
162 Bulić 1900.
163 Marović and Nikolanci 1969.
164 Barbarić 2006, 58; 2010, 159–162. For earlier evidence indicating multiple burials on Brač, *e.g.* 7th- and 6th-century BCE graves from Žaganj Dolac, particularly stone cist grave n. 3, where 5 individuals were documented fit into a crouched position, Marović 1971.
165 These types of items are, however, found in grave 53 from Nin, in northern Dalmatia, Batović 1968, T. XV.
166 Barbarić 2006, 48; Meyers 2016.
167 Barbarić 2006, 48–49.
168 For certain fibulae and tweezers from these finds that show similarities with finds from the Liburnian region, as well as grave type, omega pins and helmets, which show connections to the Dalmatian region, see Barbarić 2006, 56.
169 Blečić Kavur and Podrug 2014.
170 Blečić Kavur and Kavur 2016, 241.
171 Blečić Kavur and Kavur 2016, 251.
172 Otišić and Marović 1984, 56, fig. 23:12; Dragišić and Brusić 2000, 8–9, T. IV, 9; Asseria and Kukoć 2011a, 16–17, 20–27, fig. 2–4; Kukoć 2011a, fig. 21.
173 Kukoć 2011a, 12, 40–45.

174 Barbarić 2006, 51–54.
175 Blečić Kavur and Kavur 2016, 242–244.
176 Barbarić 2006, 48–55.
177 Babić 2005, 79–82.
178 Blečić Kavur and Kavur 2017, 99–100, fig. 1.16–17, with extensive bibliography.
179 Ignatiadou 2013; Blečić Kavur and Kavur 2016, 248; Blečić Kavur and Kavur 2017, 100.
180 Blečić Kavur and Kavur 2017, 103–105, fig. 1.15, 3, 4, see 100–103 for bibliography on these items.
181 Blečić Kavur and Kavur 2017, 106.
182 Appadurai 1986, 29–31; Dietler 1998, 299–300.
183 Dzino 2013, 153.

Ancient Sources

Appian *Roman History*, trans. H. White, *The Loeb Classical Library*. Cambridge: Harvard University Press, 1988.
Apollonius Rhodius, *Argonautica*, trans. W.H. Race, *The Loeb Classical Library*. Cambridge: Harvard University Press, 2009.
Athenaeus, *The Deipnosophists*, trans. C.B. Gulick, *The Loeb Classical Library*. Cambridge: Cambridge University Press, 1969.
Corpus Inscriptionum Graecarum. Berlin: 1869–.
Diodorus Siculus, *Library of History*, Vol. 5 & 6, trans. C.H. Oldfather, *The Loeb Classical Library*. Cambridge: Harvard University Press, 1935–1953.
Florus, *Epitome of Roman History*, trans. E.S. Forster, *The Loeb Classical Library*. Cambridge: Harvard University Press, 1929.
Fragmente der griechischen Historiker, ed. F. Jacoby. Leiden, 1958.
Pliny the Elder, *Natural History*, Vol. 2, 3, 10, trans. H. Rackham, *The Loeb Classical Library*. Cambridge: Harvard University Press, 1989, 1997, 2014.
Polybius, *The Histories*, trans. W.R. Paton, *The Loeb Classical Library*. Cambridge: Harvard University Press, 1922–1927.
Pomponius Mela, *Chorography*, trans. F.E. Romer, *Pomponius Mela's Description of the World*, Ann Arbor: University of Michigan Press, 1998.
Pseudo-Skylax, *Periplous*, trans. G. Shipley, Exeter: Bristol Phoenix Press, 2011.
Pseudo-Skymnos, ΠΕΡΙΗΓΗΣΙΣ, in *Geographi Graeci Minores*, vol. 1, edited by K. Müller, Paris, 1855.
Strabo, *Geography*, trans. H.L. Jones, *The Loeb Classical Library*. Cambridge: Harvard University Press, 1917–1932.

Bibliography

Appadurai, A. (1986) Introduction: Commodities and the Politics of Value. In *The Social Life of Things: Commodities in Cultural Perspective*, edited by A. Appadurai. Cambridge: Cambridge University Press, 3–63.
Appadurai, A. (1996) *Modernity at Large: Cultural Dimensions of Globalization*. Minneapolis: University of Minneapolis Press.
Babić, I. (2016) *Trogir - Grad i spomenici*, Split: Književni krug Split and Muzej hrvatskih arheoloških spomenika Split.
Babić, S. (2005) Status Identity and Archaeology. In *The Archaeology of Identity: Approaches to Gender, Age, Status, Ethnicity and Religion*, edited by S. Lucy, M. Díaz-Andreu, S Babić and D.N. Edwards. London; New York: Routledge, 67–85.

Barbarić, V. (2006) Nekropola u Vičjoj luci i gradina Rat na otoku Braču – nova razmatranja. *Vjesnik za arheologiju i povijest dalmatinsku* 99, 43–62.

Barbarić, V. (2010) Gradina Rat kod Ložišća, otok Brač, 2007–2008. In *Arheološka istraživanja na srednjem Jadranu*, edited by S. Ivčević. Zagreb-Split: Hrvatsko arheološko društvo i Arheološki muzej u Splitu, 157–173.

Barbarić, V. (2011a) *Tipologija lončarije iz kasnoga brončanoga i željeznoga doba s područja Dalmacije.* Sveučilište u Zagrebu: Unpublished Doctoral Thesis.

Barbarić, V. (2011b) Tumulus or Cairn? A Case of the Central Dalmatian Islands. In *Ancestral Landscapes: Burial Mounds in the Copper and Bronze Ages (Central and Eastern Europe-Balkans- Adriatic-Aegean 4th-2nd millenium)*, edited by E. Borgna and S. Muller Celka. Lyon: Maison de l'Orient e de la Méditerrenée, 145–152.

Barnett, C. (2017) Rethinking Identity, Ethnicity and 'Hellenization' in pre-Roman Liburnia. *Miscellanea Hadriatica et Mediterranea* 3, 63–98.

Batović, Š. (1968) *Nin – Problems of Archaeological Excavations.* Zadar: Arheološki muzej u Zadru.

Batović, Š. (1976) Le relazioni culturali tra le sponde adriatiche nell'età dell ferro. In *Jadranska obala u protohistoriji, Kulturni i etnički problemi*, edited by B. Čečuk, N. Majnarić-Pandžić, V. Mirosavljević and M. Suić. Zagreb: Liber, 11–94.

Batović, Š. (2005) *Liburnska kultura.* Zadar: Matica Hrvatska.

Beaumont, R.L. (1936) Greek Influence in the Adriatic Sea before the Fourth Century BC. *The Journal of Hellenic Studies* 56(2), 159–204.

Bilić-Dujmušić, S. (2004) Excavations at Cape Ploča near Šibenik. In *I Greci in Adriatico, 2. Hesperia: Studi sulla grecita di Occidente* 18, edited by L. Braccesi and M. Luni. Roma: L'Erma di Bretschneider, 123–140.

Blašković, I. (1998) The Two Stages of Structural Formation of the Coastal Belt of the External Dinarides. *Geologia Croatica* 51(1), 75–89.

Blečić, M. (2007) Reflections of Picens Impact in the Kvarner Bay. In *Piceni ed Europa: atti del convegno*, edited by M. Guštin, P. Ettel and N. Buora. Archaeologia di frontiera 6. Udine: Società friulana di archeologia onlus, 109–122.

Blečić Kavur, M. (2009) Japodian Forearm Bracelets: The Symbolism of the Female principle in the Circulation of Ideas and Creations of the Adriatic Cultural *Koiné. Vjesnik Arheološkog muzeja u Zagrebu* 3.s. XLII, 231–258.

Blečić Kavur, M. (2015) *A Coherence of Perspective: Osor in Cultural Contacts during the Late Iron Age.* Koper-Lošinj: University of Primorska Press-Lošinjski muzej.

Blečić Kavur, M. and Kavur, B. (2016) *Pars Pro Toto*: A World in a Small Place – The Example of Iron Age Grave Goods from Vičja luka. In *Funerary Practices During the Bronze and Iron Ages in Central and Southeast Europe: Proceedings of the 14th International Colloquium of Funerary Archaeology in Čačak, Serbia, 24th-27th September 2015*, edited by V. Sîrbu, M. Jevtić, K. Dmitrović and M. Ljuština. Beograd-Čačak: University of Belgrad, Faculty of Philosophy-Čačak Nationam Museum, 237–56.

Blečić Kavur, M. and Kavur. B. (2017) Many Shades of Translucent: amphoriskos-shaped Glass Beads from Vičja luka. *Vjesnik za arheologiju i historiju dalmatinsku* 110–1, 93–112.

Blečić Kavur, M. and Podrug, E. (2014) The Necropolis at the Velika Mrdakovica Hill fort – Early Iron Age Graves*. *Vjesnik za arheologiju i povijest dalmatinsku* 107(1), 31–112.

Bognar, A. (2006) The Geomorphological Evolution of Dinarides. In *Adria 2006: International Geological Congress on the Adriatic Area, Field Trip Guide*, edited by M. Menichetti and D. Mencucci. Urbino: Universita di Urbino, 23–26.

Bonačić Mandinić, M. (2003) Nekoliko primjerka novca 2. i 1. st. prije Krista s Brača. *Opuscula Archaeological* 27, 435–441.

Bonačić Mandinić, M. (2004) The Coin Finds at Ploča Promonotory. In *I Greci in Adriatico 2*, edited by M. Luni and L. Braccesi. Roma: L'Erma di Bretschneider, 151–161.

Bonačić Mandinić, M. (2012/13) Greek and Italic Coinage from Palagruža. *Diadora* 26/27, 351–380.
Bonačić Mandinić, M. and Visonà, P. (2002) Monetary Circulation on the Island of Vis (Issa), c. 350 BC–AD 600. In *Greek Influence Along the East Adriatic Coast: Proceedings of the International Conference held in Split from September 24th to 26th 1998*, edited by N. Cambi, S. Čače and B. Kirigin. Split: Književni krug, 319–374.
Borzić, I. (2010) Značajke naseljenosti otoka Korčule u antičko doba. *Arheološka istraživanja na srednjem Jadranu, Izdanja Hrvatskog arheološkog društva* 26, 27–42.
Borzić, I. (2017a) Ceramic Finds. In *The City of the Dead on the Field of Life: The Necropolis of the Kopila Hill fort on the Island of Korčula*, edited by I. Fadić and A. Eterović Borzić. Zadar: Museum of Ancient Glass in Zadar, 61–85.
Borzić, I. (2017b) Korint B i srodne amfore s istočnojadranskih gradinskih lokaliteta. In *AdriAmphorae: Amphorae as a Resource for the Reconstruction of Economic Development in the Adriatic Region in Antiquity: Local Production*. Zagreb: Institut za arheologiju Zagreb, 5–13.
Braccesi, L. (1977) *Grecità adriatica: un capitolo della colonizzazione greca in Occidente*. 2nd edn. Bologna: Pàtron.
Brusić, Z. (1993) Vrste importa helenističke i rimske keramike u Liburniju. In *Umjetnost na istočnoj obali Jadrana u kontekstu europske tradicije*. Rijeka: Zbornik pedagoškog fakulteta, 81–90.
Brusić, Z. (1999) *Hellenistic and Roman relief Pottery in Liburnia, British Archaeological Reports International Series*. Oxford: Archaeopress.
Brusić, Z. (2000) Nekropola gradine kod Dragišića. *Radovi Filozofskog fakulteta u Zadru* 38(25), 1–15.
Bulić, F. (1900) Ritrovamenti antichi a Bobovišće dell'Isola Brazza. *Bullettino di archeologia e storia dalmata* XXIII, 23–30.
Čače, S. (2002) Corcira e la tradizione greca dell'espansione dei Liburni nell'Adriatico orientale. In *Greek Influence along the East Adriatic Coast*, edited by N. Cambi, S. Čače and B. Kirigin. Split: Književni Krug, 83–100.
Čače, S. and Milivojević, F. (2017) Rimski Ilirik u 1. st. pr. Kr: nekoliko zapažanja. *Vjesnik za arheologiju I historiju dalmatinsku* 110–2, 425–450.
Čače, S. and Šešelj, L. (2005) Finds from the sanctuary of Diomedes on Cape Ploča: new contributions to the discussion of Hellenistic period on the east Adriatic. In *Illyrica antiqua, Ob honorem Duje Rendić-Miočević. Radovi s međunarodnog skupa o problemima antičke arheologije*, Zagreb, 6.–8. XI. 2003., edited by M. Sanader. Zagreb: Odsjek za arheologiju, Filozofski fakultet, Sveučilište u Zagrebu, 163–186.
Cambi, N., Čače, S. and Kirigin, B. (eds) (2002) *Greek Influence Along the Eastern Adriatic Coast*. Split: Književni Krug.
Čašule, N. (2012) 'In Part a Roman Sea': Rome and the Adriatic in the Third Century BC. In *Imperialism, Cultural Politics and Polybius*, edited by C. Smith and L. Yarrom. Oxford: Oxford University Press, 205–229.
Čelhar, M. (2014) *Naselja južne Liburnije u željezno doba*. Sveučilište u Zadru: Unpublished Ph.D. Thesis.
Čelhar, M. and Borzić, I. (2016) Gradina u Zemuniku Donjem- nalazi željeznog i rimskog doba. In *Zemunik u prostoru i vremenu*, edited by J. Faričić and Z. Dundović. Zadar: Sveučilište u Zadru, 68–117.
Čelhar, M. and Vujević, D. (2014) A Contribution to Understanding Metallurgic Activities of the Liburnians. *Archaeologica Adriatica* VII (2013), 113–132.
Čović, B. (1987) Srednjodalmatinska grupa. In *Praistorija jugoslavenskih zemalja V: Željezno doba*, edited by A. Benac. Sarajevo: 'Svjetlost', & Akademija nauka I umjetnosti Bosne I Hercegovine, 442–80.
Dietler, M. (1998) Consumption, Agency, and Cultural Entanglement: Theoretical Implications of a Mediterranean Colonial Encounter. In *Studies in Culture Contact: Interaction, Culture Change, and Archaeology*, edited by J.G. Cusick. Carbondale: Southern Illinois University, 288–315.
Dzino, D. (2010) *Illyricum in Roman Politics 229 BC–AD 68*. Cambridge: Cambridge University Press.
Dzino, D. (2013) The Impact of Roman Imperialism on the Formation of Group Identities in Some Indigenous Societies from the Eastern Adriatic Hinterland. In *Armées Grecques et romaines dans*

le Nord des Balkans, edited by A. Rufin Solas. Gdańsk & Toruń: Foundation Traditio Europeae, 145–169.

Dzino, D. (2014) 'Illyrians' in Ancient Ethnographic Discourse. *Dialogues d'histoire ancienne* 40, 45–65.

Eckstein, A.M. (2008) *Rome Enters the Greek East: From Anarchy to Hierarchy in the Hellenistic Mediterranean, 230–170 BC.* Malden, Oxford and Carlton: Blackwell.

Erlandson, J.M. (2008) Isolation, Interaction, and Island Archaeology. *Journal of Island & Coastal Archaeology* 3, 1–4.

Eterović Borzić, A. (2017) Glass Finds. In *The City of Dead Above the Field of Life: Necropolis of Kopila Hill fort on the Island of Korčula*, edited by I. Fadić and A. Eterović Borzić. Zadar: Museum of Ancient Glass in Zadar, 99–117.

Fitzpatrick, S.M. (2004) Synthesizing Island Archaeology. In *Voyages of Discovery: The Archaeology of Islands*, edited by S.M. Fitzpatrick. Westport; London: Praeger, 3–20.

Forenbaher, S. (1999) The Earliest Islanders of the Eastern Adriatic. *Collegium Antropologicum* 23, 521–530.

Forenbaher, S. (ed.) (2009) *A Connecting Sea: Maritime Interaction in Adriatic Prehistory.* Oxford: Archaeopress.

Forenbaher, S. (2018) *Special Place, Interesting Times: The Island of Palagruža and Transitional Periods in Adriatic Prehistory.* Oxford: Archaeopress.

Forenbaher, S., Gaffney, V., Hayes, J.W., Kaiser, T., Kirigin, B., Leach, P. and Vujnović, N. (1994) *Hvar-Vis- Palagruža 1992–1993. A Preliminary Report of the Adriatic Island Project (Contact, Commerce and Colonisation 6000BC–600 AD), Vjesnik za arheologiju I historiju dalmatinsku* 86, 13–52.

Fraser, P. (1991) The Family Tombstones of Issa. *Vjesnik za arheologiju i historiju dalmatinsku* 84, 247–274.

Gaastra, J.S., Cristiani, E. and Barbarić, V. (2014) Herding and Hillforts in the Bronze and Iron Age Eastern Adriatic: Results of the 2007–2010 Excavations at Gradina Rat. *Vjesnik za arheologiju i historiju dalamatinsku* 107, 9–30.

Gaffney, V. and Stančić, Z. (1992) Diodorus Siculus and the Island of Hvar, Dalmatia: Testing the Text with GIS. In *Computer Applications and Quantitative Methods in Archaeology 1991*, edited by G. Lock and J. Moffett. BAR International Series S577. Oxford: BAR Publishing, 113–125.

Gaffney, V., Kirigin, B., Petrić, M., Vujnović, N. and Čače, S. (1997) *Archaeological Heritage of the Island of Hvar, Croatia, British Archaeological Reports International Series 660.* Oxford: Archaeopress.

Gaffney, V., Čače, S., Hayes, J., Kirigin, B., Leach, P. and Vujnović, N. (2002) Secret Histories: The Pre-colonial Archaeological Context for Greek Settlement of the Central Adriatic Islands. In *Greek Influence Along the East Adriatic Coast*, edited by N. Cambi, S. Čače and B. Kirigin. Split: Književni Krug, 25–50.

Gaffney, V., Čače, S., Kirigin, B., Leach, P., Vujnović, N., Wardle, K. and Wardle, D. (2001) Enclosure and Defence: the Context of Mycenaean Contact within Central Dalmatia. In *Defensive Settlements of the Aegean and Eastern Mediterranean after c. 1200 BC: Procesdings of an International Workshop held at Trinity College Dublin, 7th–9th May, 1999*, edited by V. Karageorghis and C.E. Morris. Nicosia; Dublin: Anastasios G. Leventis Foundation; Trinity College, 137–156.

Hodos, T. (2009) Colonial Engagements in the Global Mediterranean Iron Age. *Cambridge Archaeological Journal* 19(2), 221–241.

Hodos, T. (2010a) Globalization and Colonization: A View from Iron Age Sicily. *Journal of Mediterranean Archaeology* 23(1), 81–106.

Hodos, T. (2010b) Local and Global Perspectives in the Study of Social and Cultural Identities. In *Material Culture and Social identities in the Ancient World*, edited by S. Hales and T. Hodos. Cambridge: Cambridge University Press, 3–31.

Hodos, T. (2014) Stage Settings for a Connected Scene: Globalization and Material-Culture Studies in the Early First-Millenium BCE Mediterranean. *Archaeological Dialogues* 21(1), 24–30.

Hodos, T. (eds) (2016) *The Routledge Handbook of Archaeology and Globalization.* London: Routledge.

Ignatiadou, D. (2013) *Colourless Glass for the Elite in Ancient Macedonia*. Thessaloniki: Archaiologikó Institoúto Makedonikō̃n kai Thrakikō̃n Spoudō̃n.
Jeličić-Radonić, J. and Katić, M. (2015) *Faros osnivanje antičkog grada*. Split: Književni krug.
Jennings, J. (2011) *Globalizations and the Ancient World*. Cambridge: Cambridge University Press.
Kaiser, T. and Forenbaher, S. (1999) Adriatic Sailors and Stone Knappers: Palagruža in the 3rd Millenium BC. *Antiquity* 73, 313–324.
Katić, M. (1999/2000) Uvod u proučavanje keramičkih radionica Farosa. *Opuscula Archaeologica* 23–24, 49–58.
Katić, M. (2009) *Urbanistički i kulturni profil Isse*. Sveučilište u Zadru: Unpublished Ph.D. Thesis.
Katić, M. (2010) Prethistorijske gradine solinskoga i kliškoga područja. *Tusculum* 3, 7–19.
Kirigin, B. (1985) Zapažanja o helenističkoj nekropoli Isse. In *Sahranjivanje pokojnika sa aspekta ekonomskih i društvenih kretanja u praistoriji i antici*, edited by N. Tasić and B. Brukner. Beograd: Savez arheoloških društava Jugoslavije: Arheološko društvo Bosne i Hercegovine, 91–110.
Kirigin, B. (1990) The Greeks in Central Dalmatia: Some New Evidence. In *Greeks Colonists and Native Populations: Proceedings of the First Australian Congress of Classical Archaeology Held in Honour of Emeritus Professor AD. Trendall, Sydney 9–14 July 1989*, edited by J-P. Descoeudres. Canberra: Humanities Research Centre, 291–321.
Kirigin, B. (1999) The Greeks in Central Dalmatia. In *La Dalmazia e l'altra sponda. Problemi di archaeologhia Adriatica*, edited by L. Bracessi and S. Graciotti. Firenze: Leo S. Olschki.
Kirigin, B. (2004) The Beginning of Promunturium Diomedis: Preliminary Pottery Report. *Hesperia* 18, 141–150.
Kirigin, B. (2006a) The Greek Background. In *Dalmatia: Research in the Roman Province 1970–2001. Papers in Honour of J.J. Wilkes*, edited by D. Davison, V. Gaffney and E. Marin. Oxford: Archaeopress, 17–26.
Kirigin, B. (2006b) *Pharos: the Pharian Settlement in Dalmatia, BAR International Series 1561*. Oxford: Archaeopress.
Kirigin, B. (2010) Otok Korčula. In *Antički Grci na tlu Hrvatske*, edited by J. Poklečki Stošić. Zagreb: Galerija Klovićevi dvori, 113–117.
Kirigin, B. (2012) *Palagruža: Diomedov otok*. Split: Književni krug.
Kirigin, B. and Čače, S. (1998) Archaeological Evidence for the Cult of Diomedes in the Adriatic. *Hesperia* 9, 63–110.
Kirigin, B. and Slapšak, B. (2010) Farska hora. In *Antički Grci na tlu Hrvatske*, edited by J. Poklečki Stošić. Zagreb: Galerija Klovićevi dvori, 135–137.
Kirigin, B., Hayes, J. and Leach, P. (2002) Local Pottery Production at Pharos. In *Greek Influence Along the Eastern Adriatic Coast*, edited by N. Cambi, S. Čače and B. Kirigin. Split: Književni Krug, 241–254.
Kirigin, B., Katunarić, T. and Šešelj, L. (2006) Preliminary Notes on Some Economic and Social Aspects of Amphorae and Fine Ware Pottery from Central Dalmatia, 4th–1st BC. In *Rimini e l'Adriatico nell'età delle guerre puniche: atti del Convegno internazionale di studi Rimini, Musei Comunali, 25–27 marzo 2004*, edited by F. Lenzi. Bologna: Ante Quem, 191–226.
Kirigin, B., Miše, M. and Barbarić, V. (2009) Palagruža – The Island of Diomedes. Summary Excavation Report 2002–2008. *Hesperia* 25, 87–113.
Kirigin, B., Johnston, A., Vučetić, M. and Lušić, Z. (2009) Palagruža – The Island of Diomedes – and Notes on Ancient Greek Navigation in the Adriatic. In *A Connecting Sea: Maritime Interaction in Adriatic Prehistory*, edited by S. Forenbaher. Oxford: Archaeopress, 137–155.
Kirigin, B., Vujnović, N., Burmaz, J., Čače, S., Gaffney, V. and Podobnikar, T. (2006) *The Archaeological Heritage of Vis, Biševo, Svetac, Palagruža and Šolta*, BAR International Series 1492. Oxford: Archaeopress.
Korbar, T. (2009) Orogenic Evolution of the External Dinarides in the NE Adriatic Region: a Model Constrained by Tectonostratigraphy of Upper Cretaceous to Paleogene Carbonates. *Earth-Science Reviews* 96(4), 296–312.
Kukoč, S. (2011a) Pojasne kopče italskog tipa na istočnom Jadranu. *Asseria* 9, 11–74.

Kukoč, S. (2011b) Liburnska nekropola u prirodnom i kulturnom okolišu. *Histria Antiqua* 20, 189–221.

Kuntić-Makvić, B. and Marohnić, J. (2010) Natpisi. In *Kataolg izložbe Antički Grci na tlu Hrvatske*, edited by J. Poklečki Stošić. Zagreb: Galerija Klovićevi Dvori, 73–89.

Lomas, K. (2006) Beyond Magna Graecia: Greeks and Non-Greeks in France, Spain and Italy. In *A Companion to the Classical Greek World*, edited by K.H. Kinzl. Malden: Blackwell, 174–196.

Lombardo, M. (1993) Lo *psephisma* di Lumbarda: note critiche e questioni esegetiche. *Hesperia* 3, 161–188.

Malkin, I. (2011) *A Small Greek World: Networks in the Ancient Mediterranean*. Oxford: Oxford University Press.

Marić, Z. (2004) Grafiti sa grčkih posuda iz razorenog ilirskog grada Daorsona iznad sela Ošanići kod Stoca u Hercegovini. *Godišnjak centra za balkanološka ispitivanja* 33/31, 185–216.

Marohnić, J. (2012) *Stanovnici polisa srednjeg Jadrana od 4.–1. st. pr. K.* University of Zagreb: Unpublished Ph.D. Thesis.

Marović, I. (1971) Željezdodobni grobovi u Žaganj docu kod Sumatrina (o. Brač). *Vjesnik za arheologiju i historiju dalmatinsku* 65–67, 5–25.

Marović, I. (1984) Sinjska regija u prahistoriji. *Izdanja Hrvatskog arheološkog društva* 8, 27–63.

Marović, I. and Nikolanci, M. (1969) Četiri groba iz nekropole u Vičoj luci (o. Brač) pronađena u 1908. god. *Vjesnik za arheologiju i historiju dalmatinsku* 70–71, 5–51.

Meyers, G.E. (2016) Tanaquil: The Conception and Construction of an Etruscan Matron. In *A Companion to the Etruscans*, edited by S. Bell and A.A. Carpino. Malden, MA: Wiley Blackwell, 305–320.

Miletić, A. (2014) Contributions to an Understanding of Human Settlement in the Island of Hvar in Prehistory. *Vjesnik za arheologiju i historiju dalmatinsku* 107, 113–128.

Miše, M. (2005) Grčka i helenistička keramika iz Farosa u Arheološkom muzeju u Splitu (stari fond). *Vjesnik za arheologiju i povijest dalmatinsku* 98, 25–48.

Miše, M. (2015) *Gnathia and Related Hellenistic Ware on the East Adriatic Coast*. Oxford: Archaeopress.

Miše, M. (2017) Banquet Among the Stars: Gnathia and West Slope Ware from the Diomedes Sanctuary on the Island of Palagruža. *Vjesnik za arheologiju i historiju dalmatinsku* 110–1, 233–255.

Miše, M. and Šešelj, L. (2007) The Late Hellenistic and Early Roman Fine Pottery from the Sanctuaries of Diomedes in Dalmatia. *Rei Cretariae Romanae Fautores Acta* 40, 113–119.

Miše, M. and Touloumtzidou, A. (2016) Hellenistic Tomb in Stonca Bay near Issa on the Island of Vis, Croatia: New Evidence on Imports from Sicily and Mainland Greece. *Hesperia* 32, Studi sulla Grecità di occidente, 273–322.

Nikolanci, M. (1989) Paros, Pityeia i Anchiale u Jadranskoj Iliridi. *Vjesnik za arheologiju i historiju dalmatinsku* 82, 35–62.

Nikolanci, N. (1973) Arhajski import u Dalmaciji. *Vjesnik za arheologiju i historiju dalmatinsku* 68, 89–118.

Pitts, M. (2008) Globalizing the Local in Roman Britain. *Journal of Anthropological Archaeology* 27, 493–506.

Pitts, M. and Versluys, M.J. (eds) (2014) *Globalisation and the Roman World: World History, Connectivity and Material Culture*. Cambridge: Cambridge University Press.

Poklečki Stošić, J. (ed.) (2010) *Antički Grci na tlu Hrvatske*. Zagreb: Galerija Klovićevi dvori.

Popović, S. (2010) Rezultati novih zaštitnih istraživanja u Starom gradu na otoku Hvaru. *Izdanja Hrvatskog arheološkog društva* 26, 137–149.

Prag, J.R.W. and Crawley Quinn, J. (eds) (2013) *The Hellenistic West: Rethinking the Ancient Mediterranean*. Cambridge: Cambridge University Press.

Radić, D. (2017) Metal Finds. In *The City of Dead Above the Field of Life: Necropolis of Kopila Hill fort on the Island of Korčula*, edited by A. Eterović Borzić and I. Fadić. Zadar: Museum of Ancient Glass in Zadar, 85–99.

Radić, D. and Bass, B. (2002) Back to the Current Greek Reality on Korčula: the Ground Situation Reviewed, New Evidence, and Future Investigations. In *Greek Influence Along the East Adriatic Coast*, edited by N. Cambi, S. Čače and B. Kirigin. Split: Književni krug, 289–302.

Radić, D. and Borzić, I. (2017a) The Island of Korčula on the Crossroad from Prehistory to Antiquity. In *The City of the Dead on the Field of Life: The Necropolis of the Kopila Hill fort on the Island of Korčula*, edited by I. Fadić and A. Eterović Borzić. Zadar: Museum of Glass in Zadar, 19–35.

Radić, D. and Borzić, I. (2017b) Kopila Hill fort. In *The City of the Dead on the Field of Life: The Necropolis of the Kopila Hill fort on the Island of Korčula*, edited by I. Fadić and A. Eterović Borzić. Zadar: Museum of Glass in Zadar, 36–61.

Šašel Kos, M. (2005) *Appian and Illyricum*. Ljubljana: Narodni Muzej Slovenije.

Schilardi, D. (2002) Notes on Paros and the Colonies Anchiale and Pharos on the Dalmatian Coast. In *Greek Influence Along the Eastern Adriatic Coast*, edited by N. Cambi, S. Čače and B. Kirigin. Split: Književni Krug, 159–194.

Semeraro, G. and Kirigin, B. (2017) Black-figured vases from Palagruža. *Studi di antichità* 15, 5–34.

Šešelj, L. (2009) *Promunturium Diomedes: Svetište na rtu Ploča i jadranska pomorska trgovina u helenističkom razdoblju*. Sveučilište u Zadru: Unpublished Ph.D. Thesis.

Šešelj, L. and Vuković, M. (2014) Thoughts on Liburnian Pottery found in Archaeological Trench 63 at the Beretin Hillfort in Radovin. *Diadora* 28, 21–52.

Slapšak, S. and Kirigin, B. (2001) Pharos and its Chora. In *Problemi della Chora coloniale dall'occidente al Mare Nero: Atti del quarantesimo convegno di studi sulla Magna Grecia, Taranto, 29 settembre–3 ottobre 2000*, edited by A. Stazio. Taranto: Istituto per la storia e l'archeologia della Magna Grecia, 567–591.

Solarić, M. and Solarić, N. (2009) Lumbarda Psephisma, the Oldest Document about the Division of Land Parcels in Croatia from the Beginning of the 4th or 3rd Century BC. *Kartografija i geoinformacije* 8(12), 78–88.

Stančić, Z., Vujnocić, N., Kirigin, B., Čače, S., Podobnikar, T. and Burmaz, J. (1999) *The Adriatic Island Project. The Archaeological Heritage of the Island of Brač, Croatia*. Oxford: Archaeopress.

Stylianou, J. (1998) *A Historical Commentary of Diodorus Siculus Book 15*. Oxford: Clarendon Press.

Suić, M. (1953) Prilog poznavanju odnosa Liburnije i Picenuma u starije željezno doba. *Vjesnik za arheologiju i historiju dalmatinsku* 55, 71–97.

Surić, M., Juračić, M., Horvatinčić, N. and Krajcar Bronić, I. (2005) Late Pleistocene-Holocene Sea-level Rise and the Pattern of Coastal Karst Inundation: Records from Submerged Speleothems along the Eastern Adriatic Coast (Croatia). *Marine Geology* 214(1–3), 163–175.

Šuta, I. (2016) *Prapovijest Kozjaka-Prehistory of Kozjak, Exhibition Catalogue*. Kaštela: Muzej grada Kaštela.

Thonemann, P. (2015) *The Hellenistic World: Using Coins as Sources*. Cambridge: Cambridge University Press.

Thurston, T. (2009) Unity and Diversity in the European Iron Age: Out of the Mists, Some Clarity? *Journal of Archaeoogical Research* 17, 347–423.

Ugarković, M. (2015) *Pogrebni običaji grčke Ise na temelju arheoloških iskopavanja nekropole na položaju Vlaška njiva u Visu*. Sveučilište u Zagrebu: Unpublished Ph.D. Thesis.

Ugarković, M. (2016) Trouble in Paradise? Among the last Comedy Scene in Red-figure: An Oinochoe from Issa and its Cultural Context. *Vjesnik za arheologiju i historiju dalmatinsku* 109, 57–97.

Ugarković, M. (2017) On Funerary Rites of Hellenistic Issa – an Early Pilum Find and its Cultural significance. *Vjesnik za arheologiju i historiju dalmatinsku* 110–1, 135–172.

Visonà, P. (1996) The Chronology of Issa's Early Hellenistic Coinage. In *Zbornik Radova, I.Međunarodni Numizmatički Kongres u Hrvatskoj*. Opatija: Numizmatički studio Dobrinić & Dobrinić, 149–160.

Visonà, P. (2005) Greek-Illyrian Coins in Trade 1904–2005. *Schweizerische numismatische Rundschau* 84, 27–41.

Visonà, P. (2017) Rethinking the Coinage of Issa, a Greek Island Polity. *Vjesnik za arheologiju i historiju dalmatinsku* 110–1, 193–232.

Vlassopoulos, K. (2013) *Greeks and Barbarians*. Cambridge: Cambridge University Press.

Woolf, G. (1993) Rethinking the Oppida. *Oxford Journal of Archaeology* 12(2), 223–234.
Wilkes, J. and Fischer-Hansen, T. (2004) The Adriatic. In *An Inventory of Archaic and Classical Poleis*, edited by M. Herman Hansen and T. Heine Nielsen. Oxford: Oxford University Press, 321–337.
Zaninović, M. (1967) Ilirsko pleme Delmati II. *Godišnjak Centra za balkanološka ispitivanja* V-3, 5–101.

Chapter 5

Apollo Archegetes as a Globalizing Divinity: Numismatic Iconography and the Memory of Sicilian Naxos[1]

Leigh Anne Lieberman

Introduction

A wide range of catalysts, including overpopulation, resource strain, political tension, state-sponsored economic ventures, and private commercial opportunities encouraged the Greeks to leave their familiar coasts and establish apoikies along Sicily's eastern shore in the 8th century BCE.[2] At this time, because of its strategic location, Sicily simultaneously marked both a boundary and a crossroads. On the one hand, the island served as a peripheral gateway for the Greeks to the west; on the other hand, it stood as the central node of a quickly developing global network that put Greeks in constant contact, for the first time, with the people and material assets of North Africa, the Iberian peninsula, and Italy's Tyrrhenian coast (Fig. 20).[3] In this way, the island and its colonies were ideally situated from the 8th century to be isolated and connected at the same time.

From the late 6th century, the settlements of Sicily saw the rise of powerful tyrants, assaults by foreign forces, and both hostile and friendly relationships with immediate neighbors and more distant populations. The Sicilian Greeks fought amongst themselves and with Carthaginian settlers to gain the allegiance of indigenous communities across the island. They prioritized strengthening their holdings on the coasts so that they could easily access not only Sicily's agriculturally rich interior but also the not-so-distant shores to the north and west of the island. Caught in this dangerous crossfire, Sicilian cities were regularly destroyed and subsequently refounded. Entire populations were frequently relocated and sometimes enslaved. Settlements were often repopulated with free citizens and hired mercenaries from diverse cultural backgrounds, and the mixed communities that came to occupy these settlements were well-positioned to participate in what Tamar Hodos described as 'a global culture that is comprised of a set of practices, or bodies of knowledge that transgress national or cultural ideas'.[4]

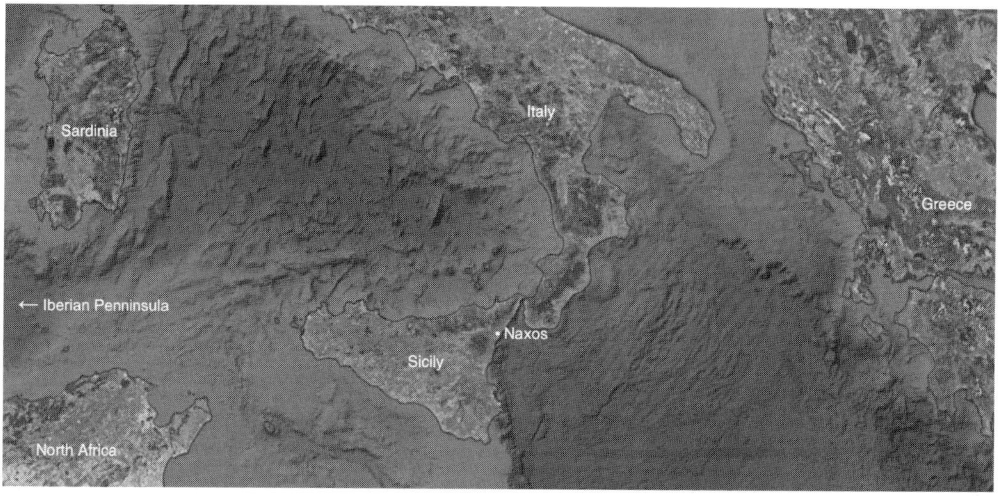

Figure 20: Map of the western Mediterranean with Naxos indicated (author, adapted from maps.google.com).

Following Justin Jennings, I understand global cultures to be those 'created through the dynamic tension between the global and the local'.[5] The processes which created these cultures are characterized by eight complementary trends (time-space compression, deterritorialization, standardization, unevenness, homogenization, cultural heterogeneity, re-embedding of local culture, and vulnerability) which not only dismantled 'local social structures and behavioral norms that maintain[ed] group identities' but also, in contrast, led 'to the strengthening or invention of local traditions'.[6] These processes were complex and, in many ways, contradictory. For this reason, the global cultures that were born out of these circumstances were resilient in the face of belligerent challengers but negotiable among allies.

In this chapter, I examine the impact that these processes had on the Sicilian Naxians and their settlement (Fig. 21). Founded by Chalkidians in the third quarter of the 8th century (Thuc. 6.3.1; *FGrHist* 4 F 82; *FGrHist* 70 F 137a), Naxos, like the island itself, marked both periphery and center. Physically, as the first Greek colony in Sicily, Naxos was located at the westernmost perimeter of the Greek world. Strategically sited both at the northern edge of the fertile plain of Catania and on the coast commanding a large, natural harbor, Naxos served as an ideal gateway, one that was perfectly situated not only to take advantage of Sicily's vast natural resources but also to regulate access to the island and Italy's Tyrrhenian coast from the sea, and back to the Greek mainland from the western Mediterranean. Ideologically, Naxos represented the Hellenic world's first permanent point of contact in the West.[7] As the first Sicilian Greeks, the Naxians would have held pride of place among their Greek neighbors, and this sense of cultural capital made Naxos one of the most important cultural centers on the island.[8]

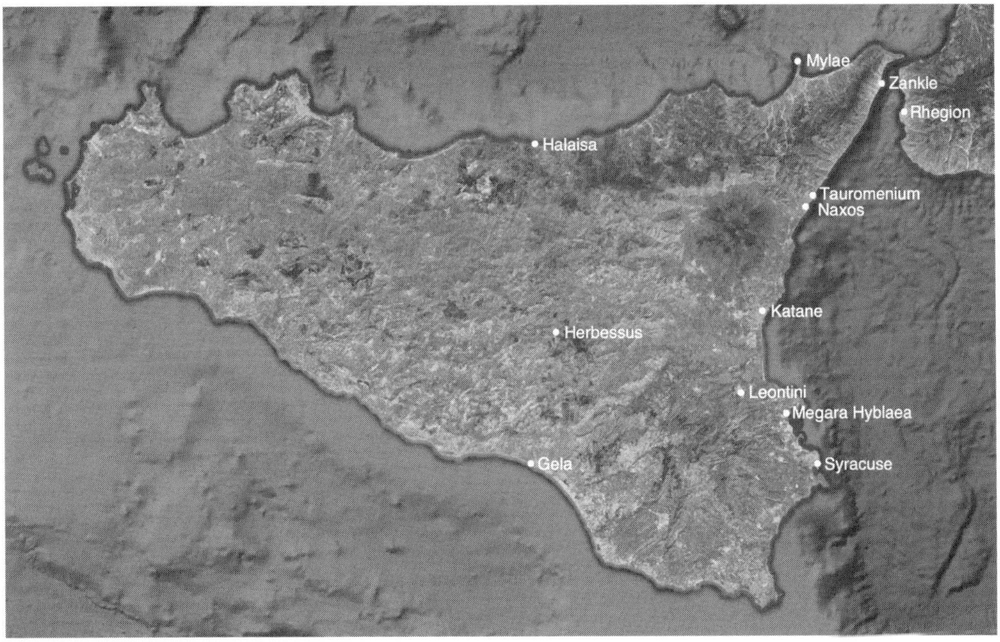

Figure 21: Map of Sicily with major settlements discussed in this chapter indicated (author, adapted from maps.google.com).

While the settlement prospered from its foundation in the late 8th century, Naxos was depopulated by Hieron I of Syracuse in the early 5th century (Diod. Sic. 11.49.1–2; 76.3) and, after a period of recovery, ultimately destroyed by Dionysius I of Syracuse at the end of the 5th century (Diod. Sic. 14.14.1–2; 15.2).[9] At this time, the territory of the Naxians was occupied by the neighboring indigenous Sikels, but the site of their settlement was never formally revived (Diod. Sic. 14.15.3). Scholars have largely relied on this historical framework to understand the fate of Naxos and its citizens, but have been less concerned with understanding how the Naxians and their neighbors coped with these pivotal transitions. I target precisely this question by examining how, why, and by whom the iconographies of specific divinities, namely Dionysus and Apollo, were exploited in response to the depopulation and destruction of Naxos. These cults, I demonstrate, served different yet parallel roles in the strategic construction, appropriation, and perpetuation of Naxian identity.[10] The former was an internal point of reference, a divine patron to whom the Naxians themselves would repeatedly return following periods of social turbulence. The latter was a sacred fixture to whom other communities were able to anchor themselves during periods of political unrest.

I investigate the roles played by these important cults by focusing in particular on the representation of these divinities and their attributes on coins. I argue that the Naxians and those claiming Naxian heritage creatively manipulated numismatic iconography in three ways. First, Naxian issues regularly featured Dionysus and

Dionysiac themes, drawing upon an internally important iconographic vocabulary. Second, coins minted by Katane and Leontini following the interventions of Hieron I employed both Apolline and Dionysiac imagery, on the one hand staking a claim in a religious landscape that Naxos had commanded, while on the other hand demonstrating familiarity with specifically Naxian references. Third, issues of Tauromenium and Halaisa, both founded after the destruction of Naxos, adopted the image and epithet of Apollo Archegetes, directly referencing the sacred landscape of their Naxian predecessors.

I examine these carefully constructed iconographical programs chronologically. I begin by outlining some of the important scholarship concerning how the Greeks designed and interpreted the images and legends on their coins. In doing so, I both describe the methodological apparatus that informs my study of these coins and establish the important role that standardized icons played in numismatic contexts. I then turn to the sacred landscape and coinage of archaic Naxos; the impact of the campaigns of Hippokrates of Gela and Hieron I in the first half of the 5th century;[11] and the destruction of Naxos and the fate of the Naxians at the end of the 5th century. Finally, I consider the Nachleben of Naxos, describing how a cult particular to a single settlement came to transcend the specificity of its original context and become a truly pan-Sicilian symbol. I conclude that by deliberately choosing specific icons for their respective issues, each responsible settlement was keenly invested in directly referencing a particular aspect of the Naxian past in order to claim a share of the settlement's important legacy.

Methodology

It has been widely accepted that the minting of coins in the ancient world, used as a standard and repository for value as well as a means of exchange and payment,[12] must also be examined within 'the framework of the development of social relations and the definitions of values'.[13] It is not necessary to review here the extensive bibliography concerning the economic consequences of the development of coinage in the ancient world.[14] However, it will be worthwhile to review recent work on how the Greeks designed and interpreted the images and legends that decorated their coins, thus describing the methodological apparatus that informs my analysis in this chapter.

A city's decision to issue coins was not only economically driven but also politically dictated and socially determined.[15] The images and legends struck on coins thus served first and foremost as recognizable icons of the issuing authorities.[16] In other words, these images, collectively chosen by the community – or rather, by the politically enfranchised members of the community – for the community, were embedded with cultural meanings. While we must necessarily be cautious when trying to understand the relationship between these images and the groups that they came to represent, 'the repeated act of conceptualising a community by means of a specific blazon or device, representing values and attributes held in common, was arguably constitutive of a shared sense of identity'.[17]

The images and legends consequently conveyed an intentional message, one that 'reflect[ed] some component of the identity of the polis as represented to itself and to others'.[18] This identity, as we'll see in the discussion that follows, was often directly tied to a settlement's religious landscape. However, 'the successful reception of that image and its correct interpretation relies upon shared backgrounds, experiences, and cultural similarities'.[19] Joseph Skinner argued that because coins were intended to circulate, they were not designed to function in isolation, but were rather part of a complex system of exchange of knowledge.[20] This system both contributes to and develops from globalizing processes, especially those that are characterized by standardization (*i.e.* the development of a common visual vocabulary), deterritorialization (*i.e.* the reliance on emblems that were disconnected from their immediate spatial context), and the re-embedding of local culture (*i.e.* the adaptation of old symbols to fit new cultural contexts).[21]

Within this globalized knowledge network, these carefully chosen images and legends also had the potential not simply to reflect but moreover to define the collective personality of a community. John Papadopoulos successfully illustrated this agency in action. In his examination of coins minted by the Achaian colonies of southern Italy, he prioritized numismatic iconography, demonstrating that the colonists creatively manipulated culturally relevant images in order to appropriate a fictive birthright and consequently justify territorial expansion. In this way, the settlements he considered had employed culturally potent symbols to develop and internally reinforce their collective identity while simultaneously communicating this identity to a wider audience.[22]

Coins could thus serve as a visual index for how communities thought about, constructed, and advertised their collective identities. Moreover, the successful interpretation of the messages conveyed by the images and legends on any given issue relied considerably on collective participation in a globalized knowledge network. In what follows, I demonstrate that the Naxians and others selectively adopted and adapted Naxian-inspired images and legends following periods of social and political unrest in order to engage with the past; the different yet parallel roles played by Dionysus and Apollo in this numismatic corpus were able to develop precisely as a result of the fact that Naxos was at once a spatial gateway and cultural center. In taking advantage of this meaningful iconographic repertoire, these communities necessarily stressed divinely-sanctioned, long-established privilege in a turbulent present.

The Religious Landscape and Coinage of Archaic Naxos

Thucydides reports that, when they arrived in Sicily, the colonists who settled at Naxos constructed an altar to Apollo Archegetes (Apollo the Founder). Upon this altar, the sacred ambassadors for the Panhellenic games, the theoroi, would offer sacrifice before sailing from Sicily (Thuc. 6.3.1), a regular practice that confirmed Naxos' complementary roles as both gateway to the west and central to Sicilian collective identity. Although no physical traces of the cult of the Archegetes have been definitively identified in the Sicilian landscape, much ink has been spilled attempting to locate it[23] and to understand the origin of the divinity.[24] While the results of these debates are inconclusive and unsatisfying, it is nevertheless imperative to highlight the complementary roles that the god and his altar performed in this context.

As the first Greeks to settle on the island, the Naxians immediately constructed this visible and recognizable manifestation of their divinely sanctioned presence in this new and unfamiliar landscape. The Naxians deliberately chose Apollo Archegetes as their personal defender and patron, and there are no known parallels for this cult in other western settlements. Commitment to maintaining the altar of the Archegetes therefore defined membership to the Naxian collective. In other words, Apollo Archegetes, his altar, and those who sponsored its construction were principally Naxian.

At the same time, the sanctuary of the Archegetes represented the Hellenic world's first permanent point of contact in the West, 'a sacred spot whose symbolism radiated to all the Greeks living in Sicily'.[25] Ritual practice honoring Apollo Archegetes, undertaken regularly by Sicilian theoroi before returning to the Greek mainland for the games, constituted nomima, long-standing customs by which diverse groups were able to confirm their membership to a wider Sicilian community and define common cultural standards while simultaneously announcing what it meant to be Sicilian to a global audience.[26] The altar of Apollo Archegetes, therefore, was an important religious node which not only created but also advertised a pan-Sicilian collective internally and externally.

To summarize, like Naxos, which stood as both a peripheral gateway and a cultural center, Apollo Archegetes and his now lost altar served two complementary roles. On the one hand, as the first divinity honored by the Naxians, the Archegetes served as a focal point to which the community was able to secure itself. On the other hand, Apollo's monument both received new arrivals to the island and briefly hosted sacred ambassadors immediately before their departure to the Greek mainland. A liminal space, this monument, and Apollo Archegetes himself, symbolically marked one of the core characteristics of Sicilian identity. In this way, while the monument was particular to a single settlement, the cult ultimately transcended the specificity of its original context, and worship of the Archegetes more generally commemorated the historical circumstances by which the Greeks came to dominate Sicily.

The monumentalization of the urban center at Sicilian Naxos during the Archaic period suggests that the settlement flourished immediately after its foundation.[27] Of particular interest, an extra-urban sanctuary was sited in the first half of the 6th century in an area referred to today as Scalia-Maloprovvido.[28] The figural and inscribed artifacts from Scalia-Maloprovvido document the variety of divinities worshiped at the extra-urban sanctuary.[29] Overall, however, Dionysiac themes prevailed. Painted terracotta antefixes that decorated the sanctuary featured satyrs, gorgons, and sphinxes, suggesting the important role that the god, his attributes, and his associates played in the early colony.[30]

Dionysiac motifs were also prominently featured on the colony's earliest coin types, two series of silver drachms and litras, the first minted from 550 to 530 (Table 7, cat. 1–2; Fig. 22) and the second minted from 530 to 490 (Table 7, cat. 3–4; Fig. 23). These issues exclusively paired an ivy-crowned and bearded Dionysus on the obverse with a grape cluster that hung between stylized tendrils and leaves above the legend NAXION on the reverse. These symbols necessarily served as recognizable and deliberately selected icons of the city and its community. Although literary sources advertised Apollo as the Naxian divinity par excellence, Dionysus conspicuously dominated the archaic settlement's numismatic iconography and likewise occupied a prominent position in the settlement's sacred landscape. In this way, Dionysus not only maintained an important position in the Naxian pantheon but also served as an important symbol by which the Naxians constructed their identity and communicated it to their island neighbors.

Naxos and Naxian Identity in the 5th Century

Despite their success in the Archaic period, the Naxians suffered two substantial losses during the first half of the 5th century that resulted in significant changes for their community. First, at the beginning of the century, Hippokrates besieged Naxos and several other, namely Chalkidian, cities. The tyrant deprived their populations of freedom in his attempt to extend his influence over the northeastern portion of the island (Hdt. 7.154). Second, in 476, Hieron I aimed to subjugate and enslave the Chalkidian and Sikel populations of Sicily in order to strengthen and consolidate his power in Syracuse. Diodorus reported that the tyrant forcibly removed the Naxians and Katanians from their respective homes and drove them to live at Leontini. In their place, Hieron I installed 5,000 of his own settlers from Syracuse and 5,000 from the Peloponnese (Diod. Sic. 11.49.1–2). In 461, following the death of Hieron I in 467, the Katanians, together with Sikels who had also been displaced by Hieron I, took arms against the tyrant's mercenaries and recovered their ancestral homes (Diod. Sic. 11.76.3). Although

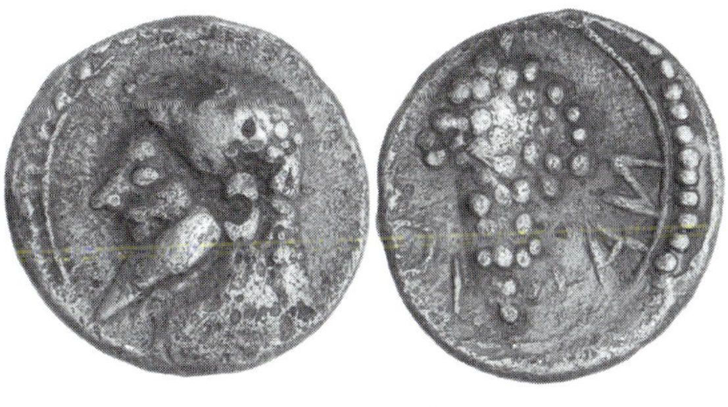

Figure 22: AR drachm; Naxos (ANS 1944.100.10046).

Figure 23: AR drachm; Naxos (ANS 1944.100.10047).

Table 7: Naxian Coins

Cat.	*Start date*	*End date*	*Denomination*	*Obverse type*	*Obverse legend*	*Reverse type*	*Reverse legend*	*Reference*	*Figure*
1	550	530	AR Drachm	Head of Dionysus, crowned with ivy, in profile		Grape cluster between vines and leaves	NAX ION	Cahn 1944, Group 1a	
2	550	530	AR Litra	Head of Dionysus, crowned with ivy, in profile		Grape cluster between vines and leaves	NAX ION	Cahn, Group 1b	Fig. 22 – ANS 1944.100.10046
3	530	490	AR Drachm	Head of Dionysus, crowned with ivy, in profile		Grape cluster between vines and leaves	NAX ION	Cahn 1944, Group 2a	Fig. 23 – ANS 1944.100.10047
4	530	490	AR Litra	Head of Dionysus, crowned with ivy, in profile		Grape cluster between vines and leaves	NAX ION	Cahn 1944, Group 2b	
5	461	430	AR Tetradrachm	Head of Dionysus, crowned with ivy, in profile		Crouching, ithyphallic satyr. Kantharos high over right shoulder. Thyrsus in left hand	NAXI ON	Cahn 1944, Group 3a	Fig. 24 – ANS 1997.9.87
6	461	430	AR Drachm	Head of Dionysus, crowned with ivy, in profile		Crouching, ithyphallic satyr. Kantharos high over right shoulder. Thyrsus in left hand	NA XI ON	Cahn 1944, Group 3b	
7	461	430	AR Litra	Head of Dionysus, crowned with ivy, in profile		Grape cluster. Sometimes leaves		Cahn 1944, Group 3c	
8	461	430	AR Hemilitron	Head of Dionysus, crowned with ivy, in profile		Kantharos. Six pellets		Cahn 1944, Group 3d	

(Continued)

Table 7: (Continued)

Cat.	Start date	End date	Denomination	Obverse type	Obverse legend	Reverse type	Reverse legend	Reference	Figure
9	430	420	AR Tetradrachm	Head of Dionysus, crowned with ivy, in profile		Crouching, ithyphallic satyr in landscape. Kantharos high over right shoulder. Thyrsus over left shoulder	ΝΑΞΙΟΝ	Cahn 1944, Group 4a	Fig. 25 – ANS 1967.152.149
10	430	420	AR Litra	Head of Dionysus, crowned with ivy, in profile	ΝΑΞΙΟΝ	Grape cluster between two leaves		Cahn 1944, Group 4b	
11	420	403	AR Tetradrachm	Head of young Dionysus in profile	ΝΑΞΙΩΝ	Nude satyr leaning on wine sack. Kantharos high over right shoulder		Cahn 1944, Group 5a	
12	420	403	AR Didrachm	Head of a wreathed youth (Apollo?) in profile	ΝΑΞΙΟΝ	Nude, crouching satyr leaning on herm or herm/stele at left. Kantharos high over right shoulder. Thyrsus in left hand	ΠΡΟΚΛΗΣ	Cahn 1944, Group 5b	
13	420	403	AR Hemidrachm	Head of Assinos, wreathed, in profile. Small horn on forehead	ΑΣΣΙΝΟΣ	Nude satyr. Kantharos high over right shoulder	ΝΑΞΙ ΩΝ, Π	Cahn 1944, Group 5c	Fig. 26 – ANS 1944.100.10057
14	420	403	AR Litra	Head of young Dionysus in profile	ΝΑΞΙΩΝ	Grape cluster between two leaves		Cahn 1944, Group 5d	
15	420	403	AR Trias	Head of a youth in profile		Grape cluster between two leaves		Cahn 1944, Group 5e	
16	420	403	AR Onkia	Head of a youth in profile		Ivy leaf. One pellet	Ν Α	Cahn 1944, Group 5e	

not mentioned in the historical sources, it is likely that the exiles from Naxos likewise returned home at this time.[31] While these historical circumstances have been clearly outlined by the written sources, they are also well-illustrated, but nevertheless complicated, by the material remains.

Following the interventions of Hippokrates, the settlement's urban fabric was substantially altered.[32] Diagnostic artifacts associated with this phase of urban development are not dated precisely enough to enable us to connect it with any specific historic event; nevertheless, two scenarios may be proposed concerning the agents responsible for these changes. On the one hand, this radical transformation has generally been attributed to the initiative of Hieron I, the Syracusan tyrant responsible for transferring both the Naxians and the Katanians to Leontini in 476. On the other hand, the city may have been transformed by the Naxians themselves when they returned to their home shortly after Hieron I's death in 467.

But, while the archaeological evidence is ambivalent regarding these alterations, the numismatic record clarifies the experience of the oppressed Chalkidians in three ways. First, at the beginning of the 5th century, the Naxians stopped minting coins. This ceasura has often been associated with the fall of the city to Hippokrates in 494 (Hdt. 7.154). Although the Geloan tyrant and his forces may have left little, if any, recognizable traces in the settlement's physical infrastructure, the suspension of mint activity suggests that the Naxians surrendered their political autonomy at this time. Second, coins minted by the Naxians after their return from exile embraced the iconographic vocabulary of earlier issues. Finally, coins issued by Leontini and Katane after the death of Hieron I engaged in a similarly sophisticated iconographic program that selectively drew upon Naxian images and institutions.

Following the interruption in mint activity, from the time of their homecoming in 461 until 430, the Naxians minted a range of coin types that prioritized Dionysiac imagery. Silver tetradrachms (Table 7, cat. 5; Fig. 24) and drachms (Table 7, cat. 6) paired an ivy crowned and bearded Dionysus on the obverse with an ithyphallic satyr on the reverse. The satyr squats among vines holding two Dionysiac attributes: a kantharos high on his right shoulder and a thyrsus in his left hand. The legend on the reverse, NAXION, clearly indicates the issuing authority. Dionysus was likewise featured on the obverse of contemporary silver litras (Table 7, cat. 7) and hemilitrons (Table 7, cat. 8), here paired with two Dionysiac attributes: a grape cluster on the reverse of the former and a kantharos on the reverse of the latter.

The attention paid to earlier prototypes and themes suggests that the Naxians were interested in evoking the iconography of coins that their community had issued before the campaigns of Hippokrates and Hieron I and the forced deportations that followed. The persistence of Dionysiac motifs, an explicit instance of the re-embedding of local culture that is a hallmark of globalization processes, illustrates that the recently repatriated Naxians were keen to maintain a link to their past. In this way, the Naxians would have been able to reestablish the connections – cultural, economic, and social – that had been associated with their earlier issues, and essentially

Figure 24: AR tetradrachm; Naxos (ANS 1997.9.87).

Figure 25: AR tetradrachm; Naxos (ANS 1967.152.149).

pick up where their predecessors had left off. The resettlement of Naxos was, then, not a fresh start but rather a continuation; by means of these conspicuous icons, the Naxians reclaimed and reaffirmed their antique heritage.

The Naxians issued two additional series in the final three decades of the 5th century. The first series, produced between 430 and 420, consisted of silver tetradrachms (Table 7, cat. 9; Fig. 25) and litras (Table 7, cat. 10). The tetradrachms were typologically identical to coins minted in the mid-5th century, featuring Dionysus on the obverse with the satyr on the reverse, now accompanied by the legend ΝΑΞΙΟΝ. The silver litras adapted the iconography of the colony's archaic issues, pairing the divinity and the legend ΝΑΞΙΟΝ on the obverse with a grape cluster hanging between two leaves on the reverse.

The second series, produced between 420 and 403, consisted of a variety of silver types that drew upon a familiar visual vocabulary. On the tetradrachms, a young Dionysus with the legend ΝΑΞΙΩΝ on the obverse joined a satyr leaning on a wine sack and holding a kantharos over his right shoulder on the reverse (Table 7, cat. 11). The city's didrachms featured the wreathed head of a youthful male, often identified as Apollo, on the obverse and a nude satyr, now leaning on a herm, holding a kantharos over his right shoulder and a thyrsus in his left hand on the reverse (Table 7, cat. 12). While the legend ΝΑΞΙΟΝ persisted on the obverse, ΠΡΟΚΛΗΣ[33] on the reverse may have referred either to the artist or the issuer, perhaps the infamous Naxian commander who would, at the end of the 5th century, betray his settlement to Dionysius I. On the hemidrachms, another wreathed youth on the obverse was paired with the legend ΝΑΞΙΩΝ, a Π (likely short for ΠΡΟΚΛΗΣ), and a nude satyr, kantharos slung high over his right shoulder, on the reverse (Table 7, cat. 13; Fig. 26). The youth on these issues has been identified as Assinos, the personification of a local river, not only on account of the legend ΑΣΣΙΝΟΣ but also because of the small horn that protrudes from his forehead.[34] Finally, Naxian litras were typologically similar to those of the earlier series, once again adopting the symbols that had characterized the coins issued by the community during the Archaic period (Table 7, cat. 14).

Figure 26: AR hemidrachm; Naxos (ANS 1944.100. 10057).

The Naxians similarly preferred Dionysiac motifs for their contemporary bronze issues. On the trias denominations, the head of an unidentified youth on the obverse was paired with a grape cluster between two leaves on the reverse (Table 7, cat. 15). The same youth on the obverse of the city's onkiai joined an ivy leaf and the legend NA on the reverse (Table 7, cat. 16).

Thus, although the community issued a variety of types in the late 5th century, all of these coins faithfully maintained Dionysiac allusions. In contrast, contemporary coins issued by other Sicilian settlements exhibited a much broader iconographic range.[35] The iconographic consistency of these Naxian issues illustrates the community's desire to sustain the memory of the past, both in light and in spite of recent demographic interventions. In other words, by demonstrating knowledge of the images and symbols employed by their predecessors, the Naxians emphasized their link to the past.

While the Naxians prioritized Dionysus, the settlement's Chalkidian neighbors more frequently chose other meaningful symbols. Leontini's first coins were produced as early as 476, before Hieron I's death, when Leontini served as a refuge for the Naxians and Katanians exiled by the tyrant. This series of silver tetradrachms paired a quadriga and rider crowned by Nike on the obverse with a lion's head surrounded by barley grains and the legend ΛΕΟΝΤΙΝΟΝ on the reverse (Table 8, cat. 17). While the legend and lion, a pun on the settlement's name, on the reverse communicated the issuing authority, both the type of the obverse and the Syracusan lambda employed in the legend on the reverse betrayed a striking allegiance to Syracusan prototypes.[36] These choices clearly conveyed the historical circumstances: Leontini at this time was a satellite of Syracuse.

Coins issued by the Leontinoi after the tyrant's death in 467 partially broke from the iconographic precedent set by the settlement's first series. A second series of silver tetradrachms, minted in 466, featured a similar obverse type with the addition of a lion running in exergue and the head of a goddess (usually identified as Artemis or Demeter) or Apollo on the reverse with the legend ΛΕΟΝ or ΛΕΟΝΤΙΝΟΝ (Table 8, cat. 18). A third series, issued in 450, paired laureate Apollo on the obverse with a lion surrounded by barley on the reverse; the accompanying legend, ΛΕΟΝ, ΛΕΟΝΤΙΝΟΝ, or ΛΕΟΝΤΙΝΟΣ, employed a Chalkidian lambda (Table 8, cat. 19; Fig. 27).

Because these new coins featured symbols that specifically referenced the Leontinoi and the divine patron of the Naxians, they not only visually emphasized the weakening of Syracuse's control over her Chalkidian neighbors but also

Table 8: Leontinine Coins

Cat.	*Start date*	*End date*	*Denomination*	*Obverse type*	*Obverse legend*	*Reverse type*	*Reverse legend*	*Reference*	*Figure*
17	476		AR Tetradrachm	Quadriga and Nike		Head of a lion in profile, surrounded by four barley grains	ΛΕΟΝΤΙΝΟΝ	Boehringer 1998, cat. 1–5, 7–10	
18	466		AR Tetradrachm	Quadriga and Nike; running lion in exergue		Head of a goddess (Artemis or Demeter) or laureate head of Apollo	ΛΕΟΝ, ΛΕΟΝΤΙΝΟΝ	Boehringer 1998, cat. 14–19, 30–32	
19	450		AR Tetradrachm	Laureate head of Apollo in profile		Head of a lion in profile, surrounded by three barley grains	ΛΕΟΝ, ΛΕΟΝΤΙΝΟΝ, LEONTINOΣ	Boehringer 1998, cat. 33–37	Fig. 27 – ANS 1983.51.28

Figure 27: AR tetradrachm; Leontini (ANS 1983.51.28).

Figure 28: AR tetradrachm; Katane (ANS 1967.152.120).

illustrated a dramatic shift in the cultural priorities of the Leontinoi. After the interventions of Syracuse, the Leontinoi were necessarily keen to rearticulate their political autonomy and distance from Syracuse. In choosing to use Apollo on the coins they minted immediately following this turbulent period, the Leontinoi made two claims. First, although the Naxians did not prefer to use Apollo on their own coinage, the cult of Apollo Archegetes had clear connections to Naxos. By adopting the divinity, even without his evocative epithet, the Leontinoi illustrated not only their friendship with the Naxians, the first Greeks in Sicily, but also their allegiance to inclusive Sicilian values at the expense of rather narrow Syracusan standards. Second, because Apollo Archegetes also served pan-Sicilian interests, the divinity featured on Leontini's issues highlighted their divinely sanctioned right to freedom from the imperial ambitions of Syracuse. By including the legend and the lion, the Leontinoi emphasized the originally Naxian deity's new cultural context; in this way, Apollo could serve not only as the guardian of the Naxians specifically but also as a patron to other Sicilian communities more generally.

This claim is further substantiated by contemporary issues from Katane. The settlement's earliest coin types, silver tetradrachms minted after the Katanians took back their ancestral home in 461, featured a man-headed bull, the personification of the Amenanos River, crowned by Nike on the obverse, and a running Nike holding a wreath or fillet on the reverse (Table 9, cat. 20). The legend KATANE, KATANAION, or KATANAIOS on the reverse proudly identified the issuing authority. On some of these issues, a long-tailed satyr rode the bull; while this Dionysiac addition may have discreetly referenced contemporary Naxian coins, the Katanians more emphatically advertised their relationship with their Chalkidian neighbors with their second series of coins. These were silver tetradrachms, issued after the mid-5th century, that paired a quadriga on the obverse with laureate Apollo and the legend KATANAION or KATANAΩN on the reverse (Table 9, cat. 21; Fig. 28). While the quadriga drew inspiration from other Sicilian, particularly Syracusan, models,[37] the divinity served once again as a deliberate reference to the well-known cult of the Naxians with the accompanying legend confirming the divinity's new cultural context. Most contemporary smaller denominations featured related types; additionally, the introduction of an image of a satyr, crowned with ivy, on some types may have been a more direct reference to an image type that the Naxians themselves would have employed.

Like the Leontinoi, after the severe restrictions imposed by Hieron I, the Katanians strategically chose Apollo as one of their numismatic icons, distinguishing themselves from the Syracusans and emphasizing their kinship with the Naxians. Moreover, the satyr featured on many Katanian issues further advertised the relationship between the two settlements, suggesting that the Katanians actively embraced the visual vocabulary that the Naxians themselves preferred. Once again, the legends on these coins assured the new cultural context of these potent and recognizable symbols.

The minting habits of the Naxians, Leontinoi, and Katanians after the death of Hieron I thus illustrate how the cults of Dionysus and Apollo served complementary roles in the expression and marshaling of Naxian identity. While the Naxians consistently favored Dionysus, the Leontinoi and Katanians creatively demonstrated their kinship with the Naxians by selectively employing a recognizably Naxian visual vocabulary. In this way, Dionysus remained an internal referent by which the Naxians were able to stay connected to their past and the Katanians were able to advertise their intimate relationship with the Naxians. At the same time, Apollo had become a pan-Sicilian institution to which the Leontinoi and Katanians may have been able to anchor themselves not only to evoke the Naxians in their role as the first Greeks in Sicily but also to communicate their own antiquity and independence in the face of Syracusan aggressions and divisions.

Table 9: Katanian Coins

Cat.	*Start date*	*End date*	*Denomination*	*Obverse type*	*Obverse legend*	*Reverse type*	*Reverse legend*	*Reference*	*Figure*
20	461		AR Tetradrachm	Man-headed bull crowned by Nike; sometimes features satyr riding bull		Running Nike holding wreath or fillet	KATANE, KATANAION, or KATANAIOS	Manganaro 1996, 307–308	
21	450		AR Tetradrachm	Quadriga		Laureate head of Apollo	KATANAION or KATANAΩN	Manganaro 1996, 309	Fig. 28 – ANS 1967.152.120

The Physical Destruction of Naxos and the Cultural Resilience of Naxian Identity

Any stability that Naxos had gained during the second half of the 5th century was suddenly extinguished at the end of the century.[38] In 403, Dionysius I, seeking to expand his empire, moved against the Chalkidian colonies of northeast Sicily (Diod. Sic. 14.14.1–2). Both Katane and Naxos were betrayed by their commanders to the Syracusan general and his forces; Dionysius I reduced the citizens of Naxos to slavery, allowed his mercenaries to seize their property, utterly razed the city, and gave their territory to the neighboring Sikels (Diod. Sic. 14.15.1–3).[39] The historicity of Diodorus' account is corroborated by a substantial layer of destruction debris from the late 5th century at the site and the abandonment of nearby sanctuaries.[40] In her discussion concerning the impact of demographic changes upon identity, Kathryn Lomas asserted that, because the Naxians were enslaved and scattered at this time, they '[lost] the ability to be a part of any polis'.[41] However, a close examination of the fate of Naxos and the consequences for the Naxians suggests that the destruction of the settlement marked neither the eradication of the site nor the dissolution of the community.

While the urban center was not extensively reoccupied during the following century, the settlement was also not entirely abandoned at this time. Limited activity following the destruction of Naxos demonstrates that parts of the site were selectively rehabilitated and occupied by a small group of squatters.[42] While activity at the site persisted, so too did the community of Naxians, although they had no permanent home to call their own. Diodorus proposed no details beyond his mention that the Naxians had been enslaved, but he did report that in 396 the Rhegians settled the Chalkidian exiles at Mylae (Diod. Sic. 14.87.1). His detail presumed that several years after the destruction of their settlement, wherever they had wandered in the meantime, the Naxians still considered themselves and were still considered by others to be a collective. Although their actions were certainly motivated by a need to strengthen their own forces against Syracusan aggressions, the Rhegians must have also realized the potential cultural advantage of their magnanimous gesture. As the first Sicilian Greeks, the Naxians maintained pride of place among their peers; for this reason, having Naxians in your population must have cultivated a certain sense of symbolic capital. It was a particularly powerful move on the part of Dionysius I to raze the first Greek settlement in Sicily, but it was equally as powerful to extend refuge and friendship to the Naxians in their time of need.

In this way, although they lost their home and were likely dispersed and perhaps enslaved, the Naxians lost neither their sense of community nor their sense of what it meant to be Naxian. This is further suggested by the iconography of two silver dilitras, stylistically dated to the early 4th century (Table 10, cat. 22). The provenance of the coins is unknown; it is likewise unknown where or by whom they were produced. On these issues, a youth crowned with laurel on the obverse is paired with a satyr, draped with vines, crouching next to a herm of Dionysus. The legend ΝΕΟΠΟΛΙ, short for

Neopoliton, marks the reverse. Both the iconographical resonances and the formal rendering of the satyr and the youth on these issues draw upon earlier Naxian prototypes, suggesting that whatever community was responsible for issuing these coins boasted a strong connection to the Naxian exiles. At the same time, the provocative legend implies novelty and youth, contrasting sharply with the familiar, venerable images.

Several scholars have offered creative suggestions as to who these new citizens were and where they might have lived. Arthur Evans attributed these coins to an unidentified settlement referred to as the neapolis, located in close proximity to the Naxos, which in its ruined state had come to be identified as the palaiopolis.[43] Alternatively, Adolf Holm suggested that these coins were minted by the Naxian and Katanian exiles during their stay at Mylae.[44] Salvatore Calderone argued that these issues were minted by the Tauromenitans between 367 and 358, after the death of Dionysius I and during the reign of his son, Dionysius II;[45] his hypothesis has been followed by several more recent studies, and the historical circumstances that guided Calderone's suggestion will be discussed later.[46] Based on the limited evidence that we have, none of these proposals can be definitively confirmed; nevertheless, Herbert Cahn's assertion in his comprehensive study of Naxos' mint carries weight: 'Die Ähnlichkeit mit den naxischen Münztypen ist so offensichtlich, daß ein Zusammenhang bestehen muß.'[47]

It is likely that exiled Naxians had some influence over the production of these distinctive, portable objects. As the Naxians of the 5th century had chosen to re-embed Dionysiac symbols on their coins in order to connect to their archaic past, so too would we expect the Naxians of the 4th century to employ Dionysiac symbols in order to sustain that link as they wandered. Although the city of Naxos, both geographical gateway and cultural center, was not resettled, Naxian identity persisted as a cultural characteristic that could and should be advertised, and the authority responsible for issuing these coins deliberately established a striking iconographic link to the Naxian past. The iconography of these coins suggests that the Naxians, albeit dispersed, may have continued to be recognized by others and 'to identify themselves as citizens of their original polis ... a polis [that] remained intact so long as there were citizens to identify themselves with it, irrespective of whether it existed in a fixed location';[48] in other words, wherever they found themselves, the collective was still at its core Naxian.

The Nachleben of Naxos

After the death of Hieron I in 467 and the subsequent repatriation of the Chalkidian exiles, the communities that had been directly affected by the Syracusan tyrant employed strikingly sophisticated iconographic programs. When the Naxians began minting coins again, their issues frequently featured Dionysus or Dionysiac attributes, drawing directly from the iconographic precedents that the Naxians themselves had established in the Archaic period. In this way, the Naxians of the mid-5th century

Table 10: Unidentified Coins

Cat.	Start date	End date	Denomination	Obverse type	Obverse legend	Reverse type	Reverse legend	Reference	Figure
22	403		AR Dilitron	Laureate head of Apollo(?) in profile		Nude, crouching satyr with vines on shoulder. Herm to the right	ΝΕΟΠΟΛΙ[ΤΩΝ]	Cahn 1944, Group 6	

forged a tangible connection to their past. At the same time, Leontini and Katane had likewise suffered under the Syracusan tyrant. The Katanians sometimes employed Dionysiac attributes on their coins; by adopting these images, this community demonstrated kinship with the Naxians. Furthermore, Leontini and Katane regularly produced coins that featured Apollo, a characteristically Naxian divinity that had certainly evolved by this time to simultaneously represent pan-Sicilian interests. While the Naxians consistently returned to Dionysus in order to establish a link to their predecessors, other communities more frequently chose Apollo in order to establish a link to the first Sicilian Greeks.

Whereas the destruction of Naxos is well-documented historically and archaeologically, it is less clear what happened to the Naxians after they were initially removed from their settlement at the end of the 5th century. Although the settlement itself was never fully revived and the Naxians were likely dispersed and in part enslaved, Naxian identity transformed in the 4th century, persisting perhaps independent of the Naxians themselves in the adaptation and adoption of Apollo. In other words, after the destruction of Naxos, the characteristics that defined Naxian identity had shifted away from the specific settlement and its people. In this way, building on precedents established by Leontini and Katane, Naxian identity was appropriated by other communities wanting to express both distance from Syracuse's hegemonic behavior and a connection, justified or fictive but nevertheless constructed, to the Naxians and their respected past. The standardization of Naxian motifs, those that came to be recognized as the hallmarks of Sicilian culture, enabled other communities, namely those heterogenous collectives that developed on the island as a direct result of globalizing processes, to claim the Naxian past as part of their own. In the following section, I will discuss how two communities, Tauromenium and Halaisa (Fig. 21), thus manipulated this powerful image and legacy in order to project a more broadly defined Naxian heritage in a profound way.

As noted earlier in this chapter, Diodorus reported that after Dionysius I razed Naxos, he offered the territory of the Naxians to the neighboring Sikels. Although they did not reoccupy the site of Naxos itself, the indigenous population took control of the nearby Taurus Hill and called their settlement Tauromenium (Diod. Sic. 14.59.2). No archaeological traces of this early settlement have been identified; nevertheless, according to Diodorus, this was the first of Tauromenium's three foundations: an informal indigenous endeavor, perhaps originally encouraged by Dionysius I or the Carthaginians. Tauromenium's second foundation came in 392, when Dionysius I banished most of the indigenous population that had settled there and replaced them with his own mercenary entourage (Diod. Sic. 14.96.4). Tauromenium at this time was formally under Syracusan control.

In 358, Tauromenium was founded for a third time by the Greek general Andromachos. Although little is known about Andromachos' life, Plutarch called him the leader of the city (δυναστεύων, Plut. *Tim.* 10.4) and it is likely that, if not directly appointed by Dionysius II, he was acting under the auspices of the Syracusan tyrant. Upon taking control of Tauromenium, Andromachos formally invited the Naxian exiles to return to the fortified slopes near their former coastal colony (Diod. Sic. 16.7.1).

While the first two foundations at Tauromenium may have involved Naxians, Diodorus definitively articulated that Naxians were involved in the settlement's third foundation. We might assume then that under Andromachos, Tauromenium was populated primarily by Syracusan mercenaries and formerly exiled Naxians. However, it is here necessary to try to understand the intentions behind Andromachos' invitation; nearly fifty years after their exile, the Naxians addressed by the Tauromenitan general were surely not the same Naxians who had witnessed the destruction of their home. Rather, because this community likely consisted of their descendants who had perhaps wandered for over a generation, the symbolic strength of the offer, the importance of the *idea* of old Naxians in the young, strategically sited settlement, enabled the Tauromenitans to justify their claim to the recently disputed territory. Because no archaeological evidence has survived from 4th-century Tauromenium, it is difficult to know much about how the settlement's mixed community may have characterized itself. However, four series of coins minted by the Tauromenitans conspicuously and consistently employed traditionally Naxian symbols and legends, suggesting that the community had a vested interest in evoking a very specific past.

The first series, produced between 357 and 345, consisted of bronze litras (Table 11, cat. 23; Fig. 29) and hemilitrons (Table 11, cat. 24) that paired laureate Apollo and the legend ΑΡΧΑΓΕΤΑΣ or ΑΡΧΑΓΕΤΑ on the obverse with a bull, a pun on the settlement's name, a grape cluster, and some form of the legend ΤΑΥΡΟΜΕΝΙΤΑΝ on the reverse. Contemporary bronze trias featured laureate Apollo on the obverse and a bull with the legend ΤΑΥ on the reverse (Table 11, cat. 25). On coins of the second series, bronze hemilitrons (Table 11, cat. 26) and sextants (Table 11, cat. 27) minted from 345 to 338, laureate Apollo, accompanied by the legend ΑΡΧΑΓΕΤΑΣ or ΑΡΧΑΓΕΤΑ on the obverse was joined by a lyre and grape cluster on the reverse of the former and a grape cluster with vines on the reverse of the latter. The legend ΤΑΥΡΟΜΕΝΙΤΑΝ on both reverses once again confirmed the issuing authority. Produced between 338 and 320, two types of bronze hemilitrons made up the third series (Table 11, cat. 28–29; Fig. 30). On one, laureate Apollo with the legend ΑΡΧΑΓΕΤΑΣ or ΑΡΧΑΓΕΤΑ was paired with a tripod and the legend ΤΑΥΡΟΜΕΝΙΤΑΝ on the reverse. On the other,

Table 11: Tauromenitan Coins

Cat.	*Start date*	*End date*	*Denomination*	*Obverse type*	*Obverse legend*	*Reverse type*	*Reverse legend*	*Reference*	*Figure*
23	357	345	AE Litra	Laureate head of Apol-lo in profile	ΑΡΧΑΓΕΤΑΣ or ΑΡΧΑΓΕΤΑ	Bull with wild or human face. Grape cluster	ΤΑΥΡΟΜΕΝΙΤΑΝ; or ΤΑΥΡΟΜ, ΤΑΥΡΟΜΕ, ΤΑΥΡΟΜΕΝ with EN-ΙΤΑΝ, ΝΙΤΑΝ ΙΤΑΝ in exergue	Consolo Langher 1967, Series 1, Group A	Fig. 29 – ANS 1957.172.1949
24	357	345	AE Hemilitron	Laureate head of Apol-lo in profile	ΑΡΧΑΓΕΤΑΣ or ΑΡΧΑΓΕΤΑ	Charging bull. Grape cluster. Half moon	ΤΑΥΡΟΜΕΝΙΤΑΝ; or ΤΑΥΡΟΜΕ with ΝΙΤΑΝ in exergue	Consolo Langher 1967, Series 1, Group B	
25	357	345	AE Trias	Laureate head of Apol-lo in profile		Protome of charging bull. Half moon	ΤΑΥ	Consolo Langher 1967, Series 1, Group C	
26	345	338	AE Hemilitron	Laureate head of Apol-lo in profile	ΑΡΧΑΓΕΤΑΣ or ΑΡΧΑΓΕΤΑ	Lyre. Grape cluster	ΤΑΥΡΟ ΜΕΝΙΤΑΝ	Consolo Langher 1967, Series 2, Group A	
27	345	338	AE Sextant	Laureate head of Apol-lo in profile	ΑΡΧΑΓΕΤΑ	Grape cluster with vines	ΤΑΥΡΟ ΜΕΝΙΤΑΝ	Consolo Langher 1967, Series 2, Group C	
28	338	320	AE Hemilitron	Laureate head of Apol-lo in profile	ΑΡΧΑΓΕΤΑΣ or ΑΡΧΑΓΕΤΑ	Tripod lebes	ΤΑΥΡΟΜ/ΕΝΙΤΑΝ	Consolo Langher 1967, Series 4, Group A	Fig. 30 – ANS 1986.77.55
29	338	320	AE Hemilitron	Ivy crowned head of Dionysus in profile	ΤΑΥΡΟΜΕΝΙ-ΤΑΝ	Tripod lebes	ΑΠΟΛ/ΛΩΝΟΣ	Consolo Langher 1967, Series 4, Group B	

(Continued)

Table 11: (Continued)

Cat.	*Start date*	*End date*	*Denomination*	*Obverse type*	*Obverse legend*	*Reverse type*	*Reverse legend*	*Reference*	*Figure*
30	320	306	AE Hemilitron	Laureate head of Apollo in profile		Charging bull	ΤΑΥΡΟ with MENITAN in exergue	Consolo Langher 1967, Series 5, Group A	
31	320	306	AE Hemilitron	Laureate head of Apollo in profile	ΑΡΧΑΓΕΤΑΣ or ΑΡΧΑΓΕΤΑ	Charging bull	ΤΑΥΡΟΜΕΝΙΤΑΝ	Consolo Langher 1967, Series 5, Group B	

the same reverse, this time accompanied by the legend ΑΠΟΛΛΩΝΟΣ, was joined by ivy-crowned Dionysus and the legend ΤΑΥΡΟΜΕΝΙΤΑΝ on the obverse. Coins of the final series, two more types of bronze hemilitrons produced from 320 to 306, featured laureate Apollo, with or without the legend ΑΡΧΑΓΕΤΑΣ or ΑΡΧΑΓΕΤΑ, on the obverse and a charging bull with the legend ΤΑΥΡΟΜΕΝΙΤΑΝ on the reverse (Table 11, cat. 30–31).

While these images conspicuously referenced an iconographic vocabulary associated with the sacred landscape of the Naxians, the accompanying legends placed them firmly within their new cultural context. By means of their coinage, the mixed community at Tauromenium was able both to adapt the well-known Dionysian iconography of the original coastal colony and use Apollo Archegetes in the way that the Naxians themselves never had. Moreover, these choices clearly demonstrated that the residents of this young settlement, wherever they may have originally come from, actively strove to define themselves by means of these recognizable Naxian emblems.

Tauromenium, however, was not the only settlement to adopt and adapt these potent Naxian symbols. Halaisa, identified with modern Castel di Tusa on the northeast coast of the island also issued coins in the mid-4th century that prominently featured the well-known Naxian divinity. Halaisa was established by Archonides in 403, shortly after the destruction of Naxos. Archonides was the leader of Herbessus, an indigenous center likely located at modern Montagna di Marzo. Diodorus reported that after the citizens of Herbessus had concluded peace with Dionysius I, Archonides removed a portion of the population in order to found a new city (Diod. Sic. 14.16.1).

Antonino Facella argued that Archonides' decision to establish a new colony was in part motivated by his desire to maintain stability in the socially unbalanced metropolis.[49] According to Diodorus, the Archonidean foundation was made up of the poorest residents of Herbessus, an overtly heterogenous group that included both mercenary soldiers and Greek refugees.[50] Facella went on to argue that Halaisa was strategically

Figure 29: AE litra; Tauromenium (ANS 1957.172.1949).

Figure 30: AE hemilitron; Tauromenium (ANS 1986.77.55).

and deliberately sited near Kale Akte, a primarily indigenous settlement founded by Duketios in 440 (Diod. Sic. 12.29.1). For this reason, Archonides must have expected the Halaisans both to thwart the political ambitions of Syracuse and to reinforce an already strong Sikel community on the Tyrrhenian coast of the island.[51]

It is in the context of this ambitious political plan that we should consider the earliest numismatic evidence from Halaisa. Between 343 and 341, the settlement briefly issued two series of coins that featured a familiar range of iconographic elements. The first series of bronze litras paired laureate Apollo and the legend ΑΡΧΑΓΕΤΑΣ on the obverse with a flaming torch between two stalks of barley and the legend ΣΥΜΜΑΧΙΚΟΝ on the reverse (Table 12, cat. 32).[52] Coins of the second series, bronze litras (Table 12, cat. 33) and hemilitrons (Table 12, cat. 34), maintained the same obverse but favored a lightning bolt and grape cluster with the ΣΥΜΜΑΧΙΚΟΝ legend on the reverse.[53] As at Tauromenium, the employment of both the image and well-known epithet of the Naxian divinity and the appropriation of the Naxian grape cluster suggests that the young, mixed community at Halaisa deliberately attempted to define itself by means of these well-known, culturally compelling symbols.

Conclusion

The Naxians and those claiming Naxian heritage creatively manipulated numismatic iconography in order to create and maintain a link to their well-established roots in spite of the political and social turbulence throughout the 5th and 4th centuries. By consistently returning to Dionysus on their coins, the Naxians firmly connected themselves to their ancestors, the first Greeks to call Sicily home. Similarly, by sometimes referencing Dionysiac imagery on their own coins, the Katanians advertised their friendship with the Naxians. Moreover, by regularly featuring the image of Apollo, the Leontinoi and Katanians may have been cleverly referencing the sacred landscape of the Naxians, the important cult of Apollo Archegetes. Thus, these other communities used and presented Apollo in a new way. The cult of Apollo had truly become a pan-Sicilian cult, and although his important sanctuary had been maintained by and associated with the Naxians themselves, this cult inherently represented broader collective values.

The attention paid to Naxos by neighboring and younger communities after the destruction of the coastal colony in 403 is noteworthy. Despite the absence of Apollo Archegetes from the Naxian iconographic program, by adopting and adapting certain Naxian motifs, the young, culturally aggregate communities at Tauromenium and Halaisa manipulated the memory both of Naxos and of its iconic cult in order to lend themselves a degree of historical legitimacy in a socially turbulent environment.

After the destruction of their settlement, the Naxians came to represent a pan-Sicilian ideal. The Naxians were the first Sicilian Greeks. The establishment of their settlement, divinely sanctioned by Apollo Archegetes, gave this community pride of place in the Greek west. At the same time, the cult of the Archegetes belonged not only to the Naxians, but to all the Greeks in Sicily. These later settlements' emphasis on Apollo Archegetes above all affirmed the citizens' identity. As Tauromenium had recently been occupied by indigenous Sikels, the new Greek colonists had a definite need to show their rightful claim to the land, a claim that had been sanctioned by the foremost Sicilian divinity. Similarly, Halaisa was intentionally organized by Archonides as a culturally diverse endeavor. The symbolic strength of the image of the Archegetes on the settlement's coinage allowed the new colony to position itself on a pan-Sicilian and Mediterranean socio-political stage. Furthermore, the focus on Apollo Archegetes places these later settlements in line as the true heirs to the Naxian legacy. Naxian identity in the 4th century was therefore predicated not necessarily upon the presence of Naxians but rather upon the adoption and adaptation of this symbolically potent cult. These newly founded settlements were thus able to construct their identity on the solid foundations of the past, engaging with Apollo Archegetes in a way that the original Sicilian Greeks themselves never had.

Table 12: Halaisan Coins

Cat.	*Start date*	*End date*	*Denomination*	*Obverse type*	*Obverse legend*	*Reverse type*	*Reverse legend*	*Reference*	*Figure*
32	343	341	AE Litra	Laureate head of Apollo in profile	ΑΡΧΑΓΕΤΑΣ	Torch between two stalks of barley	ΣΥΜΜΑΧΙΚΟΝ	Calciati 1986, cat. 14	
33	343	341	AE Litra	Laureate head of Apollo in profile	ΑΡΧΑΓΕΤΑΣ	Winged thunderbolt. Grape cluster	ΣΥΜΜΑΧΙΚΟΝ	Calciati 1986, cat. 15	
34	343	341	AE Hemilitron	Laureate head of Apollo in profile	ΑΡΧΑΓΕΤΑΣ	Winged thunderbolt. Grape cluster	ΣΥΜΜΑΧΙΚΟΝ	Calciati 1986, cat. 15a	

Notes

1 I would like to thank Anna Kouremenos and Jody Michael Gordon for their guidance and patience and many other colleagues who have encouraged these ideas to develop over the years, especially Nathan Arrington, Nino Luraghi, and D. Alex Walthall.
2 Osborne 1998. All dates presented in this chapter are BCE.
3 Malkin 2011, 98–118.
4 Hodos 2010, 82.
5 Jennings 2011, 29.
6 In identifying these trends, Jennings draws substantially on studies of the cultural impact of globalization. See Jennings 2011, 31–32.
7 According to various sources, the Sicilian Naxians were responsible for the foundation of many other colonies in Sicily, including Leontini (Thuc. 6.3.3; Ps-Skymn. 284; Str. 6.2.7), Zankle (Ps-Skymn. 284; Str. 6.2.3), Katane (Ps-Skymn. 284; Str. 6.2.3), and Kallipolis (as yet unidentified; Ps-Skymn. 284; Str. 6.2.6). These acts would have allowed the Naxians to serve simultaneously as colonists and colonizers.
8 For a discussion of cultural capital in another insular context, see Francis in this volume.
9 These political leaders will be referred to as Hieron I and Dionysius I throughout the rest of this chapter.
10 For a discussion of the important role that representations of divinities played in the development of global identities, see Mazurek in this volume.
11 Hippokrates of Gela will be referred to as Hippokrates throughout the rest of the chapter.
12 Schaps 2004, 12–13.
13 Austin and Vidal-Naquet 1977, 56. See also, for example, the discussion of ML 45, an Athenian decree that restricted the minting of coins by other polities in the empire, necessarily calling their autonomy into question, in Finley 1985, 168–169.
14 For recent discussion and bibliography, see Kroll 2012 and Meadows 2014.
15 Austin and Vidal-Naquet 1977, 57–58. See also, a 2nd-century inscription from Sestos in Thrace (OGIS I, no. 339, lines 43–51): τοῦ τε δήμου προελομ̣έ̣νου νομίσματι χαλκίνῳ χρῆσθαι ἰδίωι χάριν τοῦ νομειτεύεσθαι μὲν τὸν τῆς π[όλ]εως χαρακτῆρα, τὸ δὲ λυσιτελὲς τὸ περιγεινόμενον ἐκ τῆς τοιαύτης προσόδου̣λαμβάνειν τὸν δῆμον, καὶ προχειρισαμένου τοὺς τὴν πίστιν εὐσεβῶς τε καὶδ̣ικαίως τηρήσοντας, νν Μηνᾶς αἱρεθεὶς μετὰ τοῦ συναποδειχθέντος τὴν καθ̣ήκουσαν εἰσηνέγκατο ἐπιμέλειαν, ἐξ ὧν ὁ δῆμος διὰ τὴν τῶν ἀνδρῶν δικ̣αιοσύνην τε καὶ φιλοτιμίαν χρῆται τῶι ἰδίωι νομίσματι, ἔν τε ταῖς ἄλλαις ἀ[ρ]χαῖς καὶ λειτουργίαις. ('And when the people decided to use its own bronze coinage, so that the city's coin type should be used as a current type/and the people should receive the profit resulting from this source of revenue, and appointed men who would safeguard this position of trust piously and justly, Menas was appointed and together with his colleague in office showed suitable care, as a result of which the people thanks to the justice and emulation of these men has the use of its own coinage.' Trans. Austin 2006, no. 252). For additional commentary, see Howgego 1990, 20–21. For a counter argument, see Martin 1996, 261–265.
16 Arist. *Pol.* 1.1257a.
17 Skinner 2010, 146.
18 Martin 1996, 265.
19 Krmnicek and Elkins 2014, 8.
20 Skinner 2010, 145–146.
21 Jennings 2011, 30–31.
22 Papadopoulos 2002.
23 See Magnelli 1991.

24 For an emphasis on Delian Apollo, see Brugnone 1980. For an emphasis on Delphic Apollo, see Malkin 1986.
25 Malkin 2011, 103.
26 Malkin 2011, 103–104.
27 For a discussion of Naxos' early road network, see Pelagatti 1981, 295–304 and Lentini 2006. For the settlement's early domestic spaces, see Lentini 2004. For the so-called Sanctuary of Aphrodite, see Mele 1977, 504–507; Pelagatti 1977, 281–282; Lentini 2005, 339.
28 Many of the terracotta revetments from the buildings that made up the Scalia-Maloprovvido Sanctuary were discovered in a nearby secondary deposit; for this reason, it is difficult to reconstruct the buildings that stood in the precinct during the Archaic period. For an attempted reconstruction, see Lentini and Pakkanen 2011.
29 Ciurcina 1985, 66–72; Guarducci 1985.
30 It must be noted that Dionysus was an important divinity in the pantheon of the Cycladic Naxians, a community that may well have played a role in the foundation of the Sicilian settlement. Known in antiquity as the spot where the god stumbled upon his consort, Ariadne, Cycladic Naxos maintained an important cult to Dionysus that is reflected on several of the island's own coin types. Lentini 1995; 2011.
31 Asheri 1980, 151–152.
32 In the second quarter of the 5th century, the archaic settlement was thoroughly razed, and an extensive orthogonal grid was superimposed upon the area. At the same time, the extra-urban sanctuary at Scalia-Maloprovvido was destroyed and subsequently rebuilt.
33 For Prokles as the name of the artist, see Cahn 1944, 70–72. For the possibility of the Prokles responsible for minting being the same leader (ἀφηγούμενος) who betrayed Naxos to Dionysius I, see Rossi 2005, 432–433.
34 Today this river is likely to be identified with the modern Alcantara.
35 For a glimpse of this range, see Rutter 1997.
36 Contemporary Syracusan silver drachms featured a quadriga and rider crowned by Nike on the obverse and the head of Arethusa encircled by dolphins, a visual reference to the city's mythic history and connection to the sea, on the reverse. For an example of this type, see ANS 1967.152.506. For a discussion of the Syracusan lambda, see Johnston 2010.
37 Once again, for an example of this type, see ANS 1967.152.506.
38 For Naxos' role in the Peloponnesian War, see Thuc. 4.25.7–9; 4.65.1–2.
39 Polyaenus 5.2.5 describes these same historical circumstances albeit in less detail.
40 Lentini 2002, 224–226.
41 Lomas 2006, 110.
42 Although it is impossible to discern who was responsible for reviving these few spaces, this activity nevertheless demonstrates that the site of Naxos itself was still frequented following the destruction of the settlement and the formal expulsion of the Naxians. For details concerning the reoccupation of houses in the city center, see Pelagatti 1976, 544 and Lentini 1993, 1007. For a discussion of bronze coins of Dionysius I identified in the city and near its port, see Lentini 2002, 231–240. For the rehabilitation of the extra-urban sanctuary at Scalia-Maloporvvido, see Pelagatti 1980, 703 and Lentini 2002, 231–240.
43 Freeman 1891, 37, n. 1.
44 Holm 1901, 234, n. 3.
45 Calderone 1956 stressed that Dionysius I would not have permitted a city within the political sphere of Syracuse to mint coins during his reign. For this reason, these issues could not have been the product of the indigenous, pre-mercenary community in the area of Tauromenium and must post-date the tyrant's death. This attribution will be discussed in the next section.
46 For example, Rossi 2005 and Arena 2008, 97–98.

47 Cahn 1944, 72 does not exclude the possibility that these coins are forgeries and should be discounted entirely.
48 Garland 2014, 58–59.
49 Facella 2006, 80–115.
50 While it cannot be excluded that some Naxian exiles may have been included in this group, it is likely that the majority of those Greeks enrolled by Archonides were those who had taken refuge in and were subsequently displaced from the chora of Leontini by Dionysius I in 405, likely citizens from Akragas, Selinunte, Gela, and Kamarina who had taken refuge there in the preceding years. See Diod. Sic. 14.15.4.
51 In a sense, Archonides followed the path first paved by the Sikel general Duketios. Diodorus reported that Archonides was in some way involved in the Duketian foundation. While it is unlikely that Archonides served as the leader of the citizens of Herbessus when he participated in the foundation of Kale Akte in the mid-5th century, he was likely keenly aware of the ambitious political and social efforts of Duketios. See Diod. Sic. 12.8.2.
52 Calciati 1986, 446–447, cat. 14.
53 Calciati 1986, 448, cat. 15, 15a.

Ancient Sources

Aristotle, *Politics*, trans. H. Rackham, *The Loeb Classical Library*. Cambridge: Harvard University Press, 1932.

Diodorus Siculus, *Library of History*, Vol. 4 & 6, trans. C.H. Oldfather, *The Loeb Classical Library*. Cambridge: Harvard University Press, 1946–1954.

Diodorus Siculus, *Library of History*, Vol. 7, trans. C.L. Sherman, *The Loeb Classical Library*. Cambridge: Harvard University Press, 1952.

Fragmente der griechischen Historiker, ed. F. Jacoby. Leiden, 1958.

Herodotus, *The Persian Wars*, Vol. 3, trans. A.D. Godley, *The Loeb Classical Library*. Cambridge: Harvard University Press, 1922.

Plutarch, *Lives*, Vol. 6, trans. B. Perrin, *The Loeb Classical Library*. Cambridge: Harvard University Press, 1918.

Polyaenus, *Stratagems of War*, trans. F.R.S. Shepherd. London: G. Nicol, 1793.

Pseudo-Skymnos, ΠΕΡΙΗΓΗΣΙΣ, in *Geographi Graeci Minores*, Vol. 1, edited by K. Müller, Paris, 1855.

Strabo, *Geography*, Vol. 3, trans. H.L. Jones, *The Loeb Classical Library*. Cambridge: Harvard University Press, 1924.

Thucydides, *History of the Peloponnesian War*, Vol. 2 & 3, trans. C.F. Smith, *The Loeb Classical Library*, Cambridge: Harvard University Press, 1920–1921.

Bibliography

Arena, E. (2008) La Fondazione di Tauromenion Fra i Dionisi Ed Andromaco. *Scienze dell'antichita: Storia, archeologia, antropologia* 5, 93–114.

Asheri, D. (1980) Rimpatrio di Esuli e Ridistribuzione di Terre Nelle Città Siciliote, ca. 466–461 a.C. In *φιλίας χάριν: Miscellanea di Studi Classici in Onore di Eugenio Manni*, 1, edited by E. Manni. Rome: G. Bretschneider, 143–157.

Austin, M. (2006) *The Hellenistic World from Alexander to the Roman Conquest: A Selection of Ancient Sources in Translation*. 2nd edn. Cambridge: Cambridge University Press.

Austin, M., and Vidal-Naquet, P. (1977) *Economic and Social History of Ancient Greece: An Introduction*. Berkeley, CA: University of California Press.

Boehringer, C. (1998) Zur Müngzgeschichte von Leontinoi in Klassischer Zeit. In *Studies in Greek Numismatics in Memory of Martin Jessop Price*, edited by R. Ashton and S. Hurter. London: Spink, 43–54.

Brugnone, E. (1980) Annotazioni sull'Apollo Archegetes di Nasso. In *Miscellanea di Studi Classici in Onore di Eugenio Manni*, edited by E. Manni. Rome: G. Bretschneider, 279–291.

Cahn, H.A. (1944) *Die Münzen der sizilischen Stadt Naxos; ein Beitrag zur Kunstgeschichte des griechischen Westens*. Basler Studien zur Kunstgeschichte Bd. 2. Basel: Birkhäuser.

Calciati, R. (1986) *Corpus nummorum siculorum: la Monetazione di Bronzo*. Milan: Edizioni G.M.

Calderone, S. (1956) I Neopolitai di Tauromenion. In *Studi in Onore di Aristide Calderini e Roberto Paribeni*, edited by A. Calderini and R. Paribeni. Milan: Casa Editrice Ceschina, 71–78.

Ciurcina, C. (1985) Nuovi Rivestimenti Fittili da Naxos e da Altri Centri della Sicilia Orientale. In *Il Tempio Greco in Sicilia: Architettura e Culti*, edited by G. Pugliese Carratelli. Cron. Arch. Catania: Università di Catania, Istituto di Archeologia, XVI, 66–81.

Consolo Langher, S.N. (1967) *Ricerche di Numismatica*. Messina: Universita degli studi di Messina, 63–165.

Facella, A. (2006) *Alesa Arconidea: Ricerche su un'Antica Città della Sicilia Tirrenica*. Pisa: Scuola normale superiore di Pisa.

Finley, M.I. (1985) *The Ancient Economy*. Sather Classical Lectures v. 43. Berkeley, CA: University of California Press.

Frederiksen, M.W. (1976) Archaeology in South Italy and Sicily, 1973–76. *Archaeological Reports* 23, 43–76.

Freeman, E.A. (1891) *The History of Sicily from the Earliest Times*. 4 vols. Oxford: Clarendon Press.

Garland, R. (2014) *Wandering Greeks: The Ancient Greek Diaspora From the Age of Homer to the Death of Alexander the Great*. Princeton, NJ: Princeton University Press.

Guarducci, M. (1985) Una Nuova dea a Naxos in Sicilia e gli Antichi Legami fra la Naxos Siceliota e l'Omonima Isola delle Cicladi. *Mélanges de l'École française de Rome, Antiquité* 97, 7–34.

Hodos, T. (2010) Globalization and Colonization: A View from Iron Age Sicily. *Journal of Mediterranean Archaeology* 23, 1, 81–106.

Holm, A. (1901) *Storia della Sicilia nell'Antichità*. Translated by G.B. dal Lago and V. Graziadei. Vol. *II*. Torino: Forni.

Howgego, C.J. (1990) Why did Ancient States Strike Coins? *Numismatic Chronicle* 150, 1–25.

Jennings, J. (2011) *Globalizations and the Ancient World*. Cambridge: Cambridge University Press.

Johnston, A. (2010) Leontini – Some Remarks on Epichoric Texts. *Zeitschrift für Papyrologie und Epigraphik* 175, 150–152.

Krmnicek, S. and Elkins, N.T. (2014) Dinosaurs, Cocks, and Coins: An Introduction to 'Art in the Round'. In *'Art in the Round': New Approaches to Ancient Coin Iconography*, edited by S. Krmnicek and N.T. Elkins. Tübinger archäologische Forschungen 16. Rahden: Verlag Marie Leidorf, 7–22.

Kroll, J.H. (2012) The Monetary Background of Early Coinage. In *The Oxford Handbook of Greek and Roman Coinage*, edited by W.E. Metcalf. New York City, NY: Oxford University Press, 33–42.

Lentini, M.C. (1993) Nuove Esplorazioni a Naxos (scavi 1989–1994). *Kokalos* XXXIX–XL, 1001–1025.

Lentini, M.C. (1995) Il Culto di Dioniso a Naxos: due Antefisse Dipinte con Figure di Sileni. *Bollettino d'arte* XCII, 49–56.

Lentini, M.C. (2002) Testimonianze della Prima Metà del IV Secolo a.C. a Naxos. In *La Sicilia dei due Dionisî*, edited by N. Bonacasa, L. Braccesi and E. De Miro. Progetto Akragas. Rome: L'Erma di Bretschneider, 223–242.

Lentini, M.C. (2004) L'Abitato Proto-arcaico di Naxos di Sicilia (scavi 1998–1999). In *Le due Città di Naxos. Atti del Seminario di Studi, Giardini Naxos 29–31 Ottobre 2000*, edited by M.C. Lentini. Florence: Giunti, 28–39.

Lentini, M.C. (2005) Naxos di Sicilia. In *Lo Stretto di Messina nell'Antichità*, edited by F. Ghedini. Rome: Società Stretto di Messina, 333–348.

Lentini, M.C. (2006) Naxos of Sicily: The First Colonial Settlement. *Annuario della Scuola archeologica di Atene e delle Missioni italiane in Oriente*, 493–508.

Lentini, M.C. (2011) Un'Antefissa con Sileno Danzante e il Mondo Dionisiaco a Naxos di Sicilia. *Bollettino d'arte* 10, 1–8.

Lentini, M.C. and Pakkanen, J. (2011) The Sanctuary to the West of Santa Venera: A Review. In *Deliciae Fictiles IV*, edited by P.S. Lulof and C. Rescigno. Oxford: Oxbow Books, 417–425.

Lomas, K. (2006) Tyrants and the Polis: Migration, Identity, and Urban Development in Sicily. In *Ancient Tyranny*, edited by S. Lewis. Edinburgh: Edinburgh University Press, 95–118.

Magnelli, A. (1991) Naxos, Apollo Archegetes, e la Composizione delle Storie di Tucidide. *Sileno* 17, 281–286.

Malkin, I. (1986) Apollo Archeghetes and Sicily. *Annuario della Scuola archeologica di Atene e delle Missioni italiane in Oriente* 16, 4, 3, 959–972.

Malkin, I. (2011) *A Small Greek World: Networks in the Ancient Mediterranean*. Greeks overseas. New York City, NY: Oxford University Press.

Manganaro, G. (1996) La monetazione di Katane dal V al I sec. a.C., In *Catania Anticia*, edited by B. Gentili. Pisa: Istituti editoriali e poligrafici internazionali, 303–321.

Martin, T.R. (1996) Why Did the Greek 'Polis' Originally Need Coins? *Historia* 45, 3, 257–283.

Meadows, A. (2014) The Spread of Coins in the Hellenistic World. In *Explaining Monetary and Financial Innovation*. Financial and Monetary Policy Studies 39, edited by P. Bernholz and R. Vaubel. Basel, Switzerland: Springer, 169–195.

Mele, N. (1977) Hera ed Apollo nella Colonizzazione Euboica d'Occidente. *Mélanges de l'École française de Rome, Antiquité* 89, 2, 493–524.

Osborne, R. (1998) Early Greek colonization? The Nature of Greek Settlement in the West. In *Archaic Greece: New Approaches and New Evidence*, edited by H. Van Wees and N.R.E. Fisher. London: Duckworth.

Papadopoulos, J. (2002) Minting Identity: Coinage, Ideology, and the Economics of Colonization in Akhaian Magna Graecia. *Cambridge Archaeological Journal* 12, 1, 21–55.

Pelagatti, P. (1976) L'Attività della Soprintendenza alle Antichità della Sicilia Orientale. *Kokalos* XXII–XXIII.

Pelagatti, P. (1977) Naxos. In *Bibliografia topografica della colonizzazione greca in Italia e nelle isole tirreniche,* edited by G. Nenci, G. Vallet, and G. Panessa, XII. Pisa and Rome: Scuola normale superiore and École française de Rome.

Pelagatti, P. (1980) L'Attività della Soprintendenza alle Antichità della Sicilia Orientale. *Kokalos* XXVI–XXVII, 694–736.

Pelagatti, P. (1981) Bilancio degli Scavi di Naxos per l'VIII e il VII sec. a.C. *Annuario della Scuola archeologica di Atene e delle Missioni italiane in Oriente* 43, 291–311.

Rossi, M. (2005) Naxos di Sicilia: Due Monete Posteriori alla Distruzione della Città. *RItNum* 106, 431–434.

Rutter, N.K. (1997) *The Greek Coinages of Southern Italy and Sicily*. London: Spink.

Schaps, D.M. (2004) *The Invention of Coinage and the Monetization of Ancient Greece*. Ann Arbor, MI: University of Michigan Press.

Skinner, J. (2010) Fish Heads and Mussel-Shells: Visualizing Greek Identity. In *Intentional History: Spinning Time in Ancient Greece*, edited by L. Foxhall, H.-J. Gehrke and N. Luraghi. Alte Geschichte. Stuttgart: Franz Steiner Verlag, 137–160.

Chapter 6

Balearic Indigeneity in a Global Mediterranean: Considering Circular Domestic Structures of Late Iron Age Menorca

Alexander Smith

Menorca, Mallorca, Cabrera, Ibiza, and Formentera constitute the modern autonomous region of the Balearic Islands (Fig. 31). As the Mediterranean's westernmost island chain, the islands are often considered by scholars in isolation from other cultures of the Classical world. The islands were divided into two pairs in antiquity by Classical authors. The southern two islands, Ibiza and Formentera, were called the Pityuses or Pine Islands, and were sometimes referred to as the Punic Islands owing to the established Phoenician-then-Carthaginian colony of *Iboshim.* The northern two islands of Mallorca and Menorca, along with the small Cabrera, were known to the Roman and Greek worlds as the Balearic Islands. The term 'Balearic' stems from the Greek verb *βαλλω*, translated to the infinitive 'to throw' after the Balearic slingers who were recruited as Carthaginian and Roman mercenaries.

There are only small bits of text from Roman and Greek historians informing modern researchers of the indigenous history of the Balearics. Despite the piecemeal nature of these historical texts, the colonial vantage point is often privileged when discussing the islands. In older scholarship, the nature of indigenous life on Mallorca and Menorca is generally left out of the discussion of the 6th century BCE to the 1st century CE, or roughly the Classical Greek to the Imperial Roman periods of the Mediterranean. In the past twenty years, scholars have begun critically addressing the cultures of this period in what is known as the Late Talayotic era, by focusing on funerary, domestic, and military archaeological evidence. Nevertheless, the lack of discussion prior to the past two decades is a problem symptomatic of a historical or even Classical perception of the islands as provincial or unimportant.[1] Such a historical focus detracts from the dynamic, flourishing indigenous life that can be seen in the archaeological record on Menorca and Mallorca from the 6th/5th century BCE into the 1st century CE. The inherent differences in cultural manifestations, biogeography, geology, and

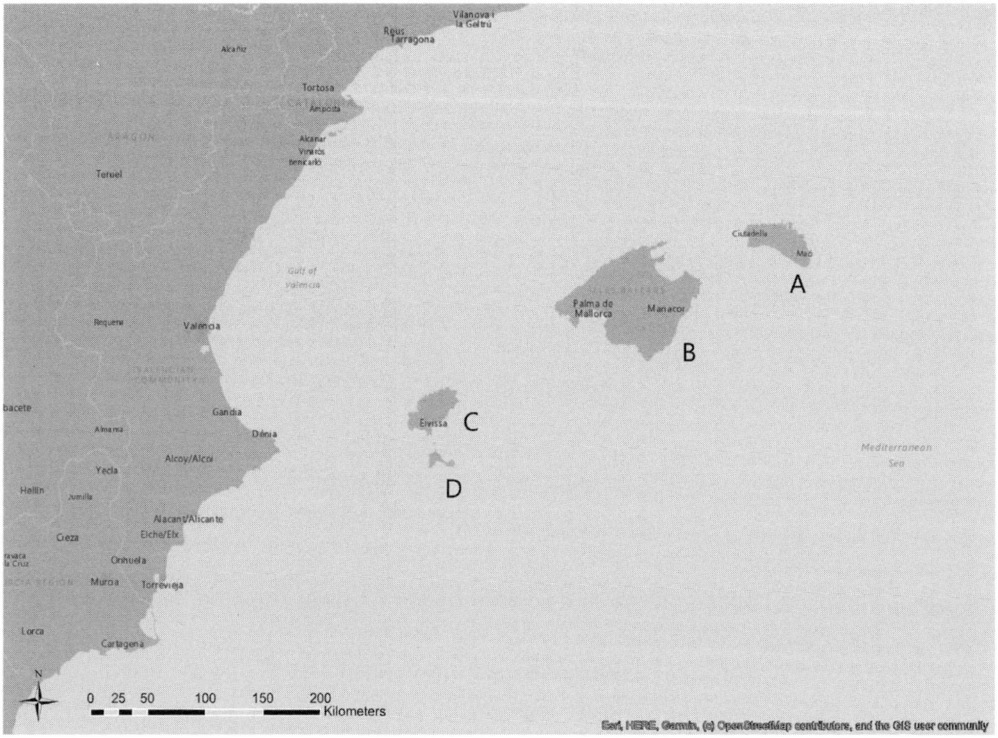

Figure 31: A satellite image of the Balearic Islands. A is Menorca, B is Mallorca, C is Ibiza and D is Formentera. Cabrera is too small to display on this map (map generated by the author).

chronological sequences on both islands are often lumped together due to proximity and some shared trading relations. This is particularly evident in modern Anglophone scholarship, despite the fact that Spanish or Catalan studies of the islands today mostly focus on a single island or consider the two islands separately.[2] Mallorca and Menorca were very different, at times remarkably so. From an outsider's perspective however, the complexities of these two islands and subtle intricacies of their differences are lost.

The islands' differences are also obscured by colonial labels that have and continue to be used to describe their indigenous cultures. To borrow from Edward Said's notions of orientalism and the creation of an Eastern 'other',[3] the Balearic Islands have always been viewed from the vantage point of the colonizer, conqueror, or outsider. For example, the names Mallorca and Menorca, come from the Latin *maiorica* and *minorca*, denoting the larger and smaller island. The indigenous people most likely did not name their islands 'the big one' and 'the small one', but indeed the modern name for the islands comes from the eventual conquerors. The name Balearic stems from a Greek verb, as mentioned above, but the other lesser-known term for the islands, Gymnasiae, is also derived from the Greek noun *γυμνός* or naked, owing to the perceived nakedness and barbarity of the indigenous inhabitants. Histories created by outsiders have constructed a powerful colonial narrative about the ancient islanders, so much that even the famous megalithic talayots that are found throughout the landscape owe their name to the Arabic term for watch tower. Although some scholars have attempted to identify indigenous languages in modern place names,[4] few connections can be firmly established. As a result, the islands remain subject to colonial names and histories, which in turn influence the way scholars approach them. The shift to post-colonial understandings of western Mediterranean indigenous groups, spurred by work in Sardinia, Spain, and North Africa, has helped fuel a critical reevaluation of this era and these people. In response to these trends, scholars of the Balearic Islands have begun reexamining the nature of this Late Talayotic culture on both islands in great detail by stepping away from the colonial or imperial gaze and attempting to approach the local, indigenous perspective. Continuing in this vein, this study focuses exclusively on Menorcan domestic evidence, isolating the small, yet prolific island (Fig. 32) as a source of information on colonialism, contact, and understandings of indigenous life in the Classical Era Mediterranean.[5]

The following study begins with a brief historical narrative and is then split into two sections: the first focusing on circular house architecture on Menorca and the second on the delineation and control of domestic space within these indigenous households.

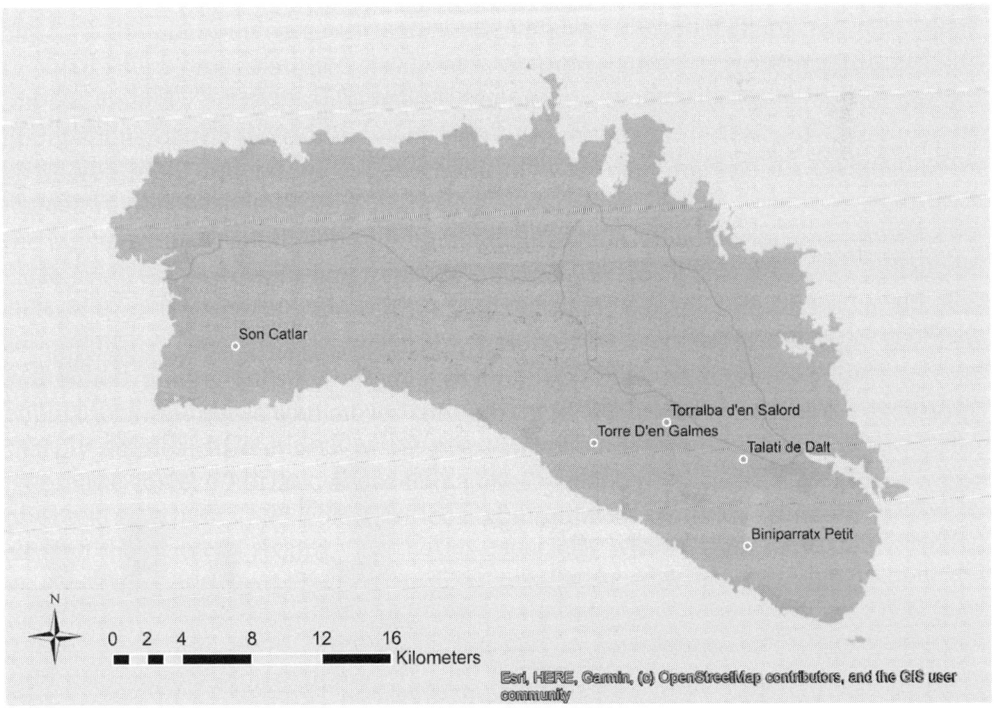

Figure 32: The island of Menorca with the major sites mentioned in the text (map generated by the author).

The study concludes with a discussion of the terms indigenous and indigeneity in the Mediterranean, responding to the data from Menorca. Domestic archaeology can provide a glimpse into the lifeways of a community and the many different social, economic, and stratified groups within it. The following case studies are important, well-documented indigenous sites of the Late Talayotic on Menorca. These are sites that display domestic habits reflecting expressions of indigenous identity in a world slowly being subsumed by 'global' powers of the western Mediterranean, such as Rome and Carthage. This study by no means represents an encyclopedic attempt at concentrating all known information on Late Talayotic indigenous households. Instead, the intention is to provide a didactic account of better-known or better-published sites in order to isolate general trends observed on the islands during this period and to relate them to larger processes of interaction, colonization, and imperialism in the western Mediterranean.

This case study presents a culture that responds to globalization through self-reflection and an emphasis on indigenous customs, despite a lack of a colonial population on the island. In other words, there was no one to impress besides themselves. Practices for domestic architecture emerge that do not reflect hybrid or even glocal manifestations.[6] Instead the circular houses provide a means of reinforcing local identity among the elite of Menorcan society. Indigenous forms are a source of prestige and social weight for Menorcans. Yet, as this study argues through the lens of indigeneity, the turn to a local identity is not so much resistance, as they were not really resisting anyone, but persistence and internal change. Similar to what Jennings calls the cultural consequence of the 're-embedding of local culture',[7] the emphasis on the local was arguably the result of increased exposure to extra-island culture and globalizing forces, as the social construction of difference led many Menorcans to emphasize local-ness in domestic architecture over external elements that were inundating other facets of society, such as ceramic and metallic material culture. In this manner, hybridity or glocality[8] are not the entire story of globalization. Indigeneity, as a self-conscious understanding of indigenousness and a reaction to global forces, should also be considered part of this dynamic. This study is intended to illustrate how that might appear in a prehistoric archaeological context through the domestic remains of Menorca's Late Iron Age.

A Brief Historical Context

As Balearic prehistory is not necessarily common knowledge, it is important to outline a few key elements to the Bronze and Iron Age that help inform this study. The islands were first colonized by humans notoriously late, as conservative estimates place permanent settlement on Mallorca in the 3rd millennium BCE, and as late as the 2nd millennium BCE on Menorca.[9] Bronze Age monuments in the Balearic Islands were constructed similarly late, dating to the middle and end of the 2nd millennium BCE.[10] Around 900 to 850 BCE, the islands saw a dramatic shift in both settlement and internal economic functions. This period is considered the beginning of the Talayotic period, named for the large, tower-like edifices that were constructed out of megalithic blocks and placed at strategic locations throughout both islands. Hundreds of talayots were built from the 9th century to the 7th century, potentially reflecting growing communities, elite social structures, or even the territorial fragmentation of both islands. Until the late 1990s and early 2000s,[11] these monuments were considered to be Bronze Age sites, similar to structures located on Sardinia and Corsica.[12] Today, however, these monuments are widely accepted as 1st millennium BCE structures, constituting the islands' Iron Age, though some recent excavations at Cornia Nou have revealed potentially 10th or 11th century inhabitation of talayots and surrounding structures.[13]

Talayotic culture persisted into the 1st millennium when Phoenician, Greek, and eventually Carthaginian colonies began interacting with the islands more heavily beginning in the 7th century. While artifacts from the eastern Mediterranean as well as the Iberian world attest to interaction before this century, the amount of interaction began to increase with the Phoenician and Carthaginian presence on the Pityuses. The Phoenician colony of *Iboshim* was founded in 654 BCE[14] on Ibiza.[15] When Carthage became autonomous in the 6th century BCE, the Phoenician communities on Ibiza and Formentera became part of Carthage's economic network, providing a convenient trade connection for Mallorca and Menorca. Not only did the colonial presence on the Pityuses seemingly expand trading possibilities to and from Mallorca and Menorca, but the creation of Punic ceramic factories on Ibiza shortly thereafter changed the nature of trade among the islands, facilitating connections throughout the western Mediterranean.[16] Menorcan and Mallorcan mercenary slingers were used by Carthaginian and Roman armies during this era.[17] There are also some small Punic emporia sites located on the southern coast of Mallorca.[18] Despite evidence of increased connections to the world outside of the islands, Menorca and arguably Mallorca[19] remain free of colonial infrastructure or territorial control by foreigners until after the Roman conquest. Archaeologists have noted the dramatic increase in imports from the 4th century BCE on, as well as the incorporation of Punic material culture, ceremonial objects, and some practices into the island cultures.[20] Although Menorca sits in what appears to be an advantageous position in the western Mediterranean, the seasonally tumultuous Gulf of Leon and Balearic Sea may have prevented easy travel at certain times of the year in antiquity, save to and from Mallorca. Mallorca may be more accessible, but it is also quite large with a lack of easily harvestable natural resources, a seasonally difficult sea, and the potential for resistance along with Menorca. Carthage may have thought that anything beyond trade with the islands was unnecessary. In other words, the islands were certainly in contact with the outside world but were not controlled by it.[21]

Rome's victories in the First and Second Punic Wars dismantled Carthage's power in the western Mediterranean, but Menorca, Mallorca, Ibiza, and Formentera remained independent. In 201 BCE, the two southern islands entered into a *foedus* with Rome as a result of an unprompted, unconditional surrender, resulting in the islands retaining a relative degree of autonomy, yet pledging their fealty to the Roman Republic.[22] Mallorca and Menorca remained independent throughout the Third Punic War, despite Rome's growing control of the Mediterranean coastline surrounding the islands. However, in 123 BCE the northern two islands were accused of piracy and were conquered by Quintus Metellus, later Balearicus. Over the course of the 1st centuries BCE and CE, Rome begins to change the islands dramatically. Two major colonies were established on Mallorca after conquest – Palma and Pollentia – alongside other sites mentioned by Pliny the Elder which are not archaeologically attested.[23] On Menorca, new Roman colonies were placed at modern day Mahón, Ciutadella, and Sanisera, known in antiquity as Magon, Iamnon, and Sanisera.[24] The islands were folded into Hispania Citerior and other infrastructure was introduced to facilitate trade and commerce on Menorca and Mallorca. Contact with the Mediterranean world seems to increase, as attested on Menorca by a sharp increase in shipwrecks off the northern coast of the island.[25] The island populations gradually shifted away from indigenous population centers, adopted an increasing amount of Roman material culture, began using Roman currency, and by the beginning of the 2nd century CE, the indigenous customs of the islanders had mostly disappeared.

With the Roman conquest, the indigenous chronology ends, ushering in a Roman period of the islands' history. The Late Talayotic period is understood as the last era of indigenous autonomy and has traditionally been defined as the 6th century to the 2nd century BCE, ending precisely at the Roman conquest in 123 BCE. Recently, particularly in Menorca, the period has been reestablished from the 5th century BCE to the 1st century BCE, after the Roman conquest. It has also been renamed the Final Talayotic period, reinforcing notions that this was the last era of indigenous autonomy. Institutions like the Museu de Menorca now utilize the revised Final Talayotic periodization.[26] By extending the final era of observable indigenous culture beyond the Roman conquest, archaeologists on Menorca are conceding that indigenous lifeways persisted after the conquest, something that many lines of evidence regarding life in the Balearics support. Considering this new understanding of the later chronology, this study uses the term Late Talayotic, but defines the period as roughly 6th/5th century BCE to the 1st century CE, acknowledging that in the 2nd century BCE, there does appear to be a shift in indigenous lifeways. This shift is perhaps related to the Second Punic War, Carthaginian trade network collapse, or Roman conquest, though internal, indigenous factors must be considered as well. These trends are all reflected in the domestic data of Menorca's circular houses, which can provide further insight into the changing nature of indigenous life during the Late Talayotic period.

The Circular Houses of the Late Talayotic

One of the most overt or hyper-representative indigenous features of the Late Talayotic culture of Menorca is the circular, megalithic house form. Dozens of these large houses

(Fig. 33) are found throughout the island, starting in the 6th century and continuing into the 2nd century BCE.[27] The circular house was standard for the Late Talayotic on Menorca, and although some similarities can be drawn between sites like El Turó or S'Illot on Mallorca,[28] the complex structure of Menorcan houses clearly differentiates the architectural style from all other neighboring traditions – a process which continues with the additions of hypostyle halls and megalithic architectural elements, a point which this study will return to later.

There are no architectural precursors of the circular form on the island. Houses from the previous Talayotic period on Menorca have largely gone unexcavated or are unknown. The closest architectural form related to a domestic function or place of production in the Talayotic period comes from monumental redistribution centers like Cornia Nou,[29] yet houses largely remain a mystery.[30] Still, a formal indigenous tradition might be assumed by the consistency of the circular domestic form throughout the Late Talayotic period. On Mallorca, for instance, evidence for the maintenance and use of indigenous cult areas persists into the Late Talayotic and Roman periods, yet their domestic forms change significantly to reflect external influences. Menorca sees both the persistence of cult areas and domestic forms,

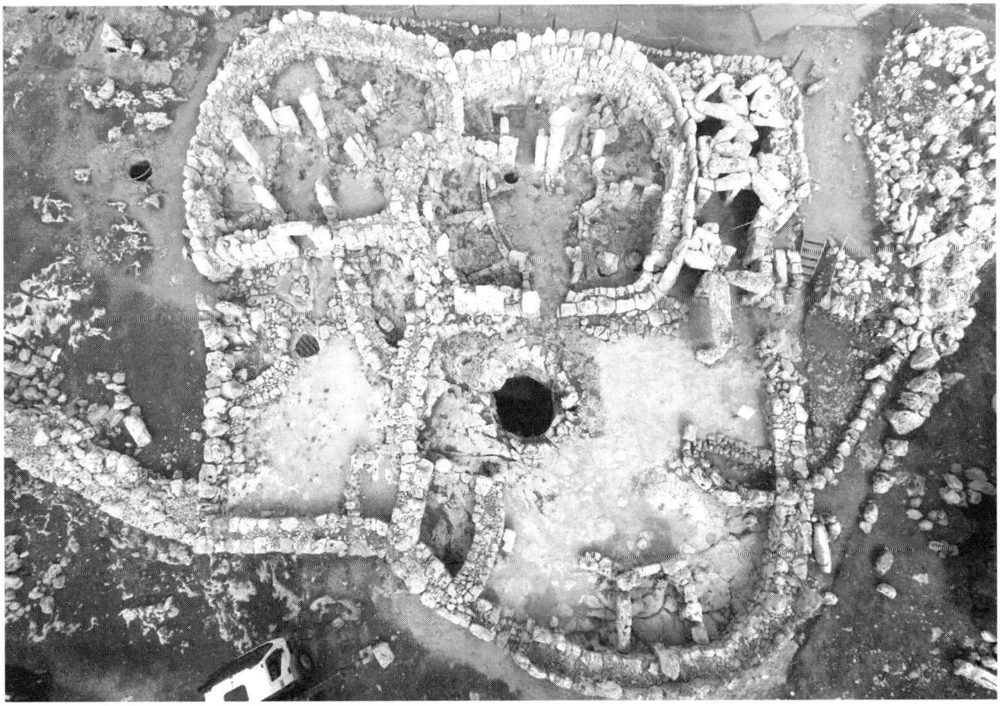

Figure 33: Aerial view of House 6 (right) and House 7 (left) precincts at Torre d'en Galmés. Notice the circular architectural syntax and large external delineated spaces, along with the covered hypostyle hall attached to the right wall of House 6 (open source photo provided by Wikimedia Commons).

exhibiting a clear domestic building tradition during the Late Talayotic that is quite different from Mallorca.

Menorcan household architecture appears in a non-orthogonal, circular plan at the end of the Talayotic and the beginning of the Late Talayotic, around the 6th to 5th centuries BCE (see Fig. 33).[31] The construction of circular households appears to intensify over the course of the 4th and into the 3rd centuries BCE, followed by progressive abandonment by the 2nd century BCE.[32] The Late Talayotic period appears to be a time of cultural change and potential prosperity on the island, as sites like Torre d'en Galmés increase in size with the construction of numerous dwellings.[33] In terms of demography, Diodorus provides a population estimate of 30,000 individuals for Menorca in pre-Roman times.[34] While it is difficult to come up with an estimate for earlier periods on the island, archaeological evidence points to an increasing emphasis on domestic architecture during the Late Talayotic. With settlement intensification, the circular Menorcan architectural style becomes consistent. Domestic architecture is not entirely circular on Menorca, as some houses are more rectangular, like a select few at Torre d'en Galmés. These houses are built roughly in the fourth and 3rd centuries BCE, but occupied into the Roman period and the 1st century CE.[35] Nevertheless, these quasi-orthogonal buildings are still very irregular and usually the smaller dwellings on the site of Torre d'en Galmés,[36] with the larger, more impressive dwellings exhibiting circular form, and contemporary dates of construction.[37] For this reason, particularly at Torre d'en Galmés, the smaller, quasi-orthogonal buildings have, for the most part, not been excavated.[38]

The megalithic circular house type is evident across the island, particularly for freestanding houses. A modest example of this style of architecture can be seen at the site of Biniparratx Petit, with houses excavated in association with the elongation of Menorca's airport runway in the 1990s and subsequent excavations in the early 2000s.[39] Archaeologists Victor Guerrero and Jordi Hernández-Gasch led excavations of House 1 at the site from 2000–2003,[40] which consists of a series of compartmentalized spaces surrounding an open-air courtyard (for an example of such a house, see Fig. 35). The house is relatively modest in size (79 square meters of interior space), yet has large, square columns defining the indoor space.[41] Cisterns, raised platforms for hearths or ovens, as well as work areas were all typical of such houses and were clearly identified by the excavators.[42] House 1 provides a blueprint for the Late Talayotic house, complete with megalithic stone building materials and an outdoor courtyard (H6 in Fig. 35).

The walls of said houses were dry-stone masonry and double-faced, constructed on a first course of long, horizontal rectangular stones, on which cyclopean, rectangular stones were erected upright to face the exterior of the home wall (see Fig. 35 and Fig. 38). A matrix of gravel, small stones, and earth constitutes the wall's fill, and a second, interior wall surface layer of quasi-rectangular, medium sized stones arranged in irregular patterns.[43] The walls were also likely faced with waddle and daub, in some instances. While this construction style is common for other western

Figure 34: Aerial view of the Carthailac precinct from Torre d'en Galmés (photo courtesy of Amalia Pérez-Juez).

Figure 35: Image of Carthailhac displaying the prototypical house structure. H1 is a storage magazine, while H2 and H3 are supposedly bedrooms. H6 is a work area and H5 represents the kitchen (room designations after Hernández-Gasch 2007, fig. 1, open source photo provided by Wikimedia Commons).

Mediterranean cultures in previous periods, its use on Menorca during this later period is noteworthy. The internal workspace was small but shows an early interest in shifting work areas to indoor or private spaces.

One of the most noteworthy circular dwellings on the island is the Cartailhac domestic structure and precinct at Torre d'en Galmés. At 375 square meters, Cartailhac is one of the largest domestic areas at Torre d'en Galmés and possibly the largest domestic space on Menorca (see Fig. 34). It exhibits a large boundary wall, which surrounds the house and outdoor area for domestic production activities. The house structure, not including the workspace, is 145 square meters, roughly twice the size of Biniparratx Petit House 1.[44] It is also one of the latest constructions at Torre d'en Galmés, dating to the 3rd century BCE and occupied into the 2nd century BCE.[45]

The circular structures throughout Menorca do not conform to expectations of a society in contact with a 'global' entity, in this case the Punic world. One of the arguments for Menorcan houses retaining their circular form is a lack of contact with the outside world. While evidence for external contact should not be the only lens for understanding cultural change on the island, it is important to remember that Menorca was exposed to Punic, Roman, and Iberian trading networks. There is evidence from sites like Torre d'en Galmés that there was quite a bit of Punic-based trade occurring, as demonstrated by large quantities of Ibizan Punic amphorae littered across the surface of the site and within excavated contexts. For example, House 7, excavated by the Museu de Menorca in the late 2000s (see Fig. 33), was occupied from the 4th until the 2nd century BCE, and of the ceramics recovered, Ibizan Ebusitano wares made up 15% of the total ceramic assemblage, whereas other Punic ceramics made up 3%, and non-Punic imports 1% or less.[46] House 1, also excavated by the Museu de Menorca in the early 2000s, had approximately 30% Ebusitano ceramics.[47] It could be suggested that perhaps the large amount of Punic pottery found at Torre d'en Galmés was the result of some sort of redistributive area for commercial goods located on the site. All the same, almost all other sites on the island of Menorca appear to exhibit the same approximate proportions of Punic wares and amphora sherds. There are no sites on Menorca that are conclusively redistribution centers, including Torre d'en Galmés, as the sites seem relatively homogenous in the presence and prevalence of Punic, Ebusitano wares. Some arguments have been put forth regarding the degree of interaction with Iberian and Greek traders,[48] though material evidence relating to this trend tends to be scarce, unlike the relatively ubiquitous Ebuistano wares. All this evidence for interaction and trade shows that Menorca was not by any means isolated from the Punic world and would have probably known about orthogonal building styles. Despite this probable knowledge, they nevertheless built large-scale circular constructions that necessitated a significant amount of human capital, such as House 1 of Biniparratx Petit and Cartailhac.

Domestic structures are consistently a focus of new excavations on the island. There has been a sizeable surge in domestic data over the past two decades and we now understand much more about the daily life of native Menorcans. Nevertheless, while an analysis of domestic spaces is important for understanding how people lived on a basic level, it does not necessarily represent all individuals in a society equally. For instance, Menorca offers a glimpse into the domestic architecture of perhaps a handful of sites and elite houses therein, almost exclusively located within larger, quasi-urban settlements. Temporary structures, farmhouses, or smaller dwellings outside of major sites are poorly known, primarily due to a lack of pedestrian survey carried out on the islands and limited resources for excavation. Still, the fact that these houses represent the elite structures of Menorca is important as a marker of indigenous identity and cultural persistence. Standard acculturation models, such as Romanization, expect the elite to adopt the foreign trends they may have had contact with.[49] The opposite is seen on Menorca. Late Talayotic Menorcan houses represent a mobilization of large amounts of human labor and natural resources to perpetuate their traditions, indicating the elite status and wealth of the homeowners along with the continued use of an indigenous form.

The trend of large-scale, megalithic and elite representations of indigenous forms continues with other architectural embellishments specific to Menorca. Some of these circular houses during the Late Talayotic also employ additional megalithic architectural features, including hypostyle halls and megalithic, t-shaped supporting stones within the house structures. Both of these features will be highlighted here to further showcase Menorca's traditional architectural repertoire. The hypostyle halls and the internal, t-shaped supporting blocks represent mobilization of human labor at a large-scale in addition to the efforts made to build the circular house in the first place. They are architectural embellishments that also represent possible connections to the monumental and ritual heritage of Menorca.

Settlements across Menorca developed hypostyle halls, which were attached to an outer wall of the circular house. The shape of these structures was generally an elongated, skinny U, with an apsidal or quasi-apsidal back wall. Despite the fact that most houses in Menorca were likely covered by waddle and daub or adobe-like materials, these hypostyle halls were roofed with large megalithic blocks and supported by a central row of megalithic columns (Fig. 36). While hypostyle halls are not on every circular house and their exact function remains unclear, they may have been used as a relatively extravagant animal pen or storage area. It is quite a pronounced domestic feature, and notable examples include those found at Torre d'en Galmés, Torralba d'en Salord, and Talatí de Dalt, though many other, large examples exist around the island.[50]

Along with hypostyle halls, many houses often exhibit megalithic stones that act as support beams, ranging in shape from circular drums to large rectangular blocks. These columns can extend to the height of the house with just one megalithic stone (sometimes more than 3 m in height). Menorcan circular houses usually contain multiple columns positioned in a circular pattern in the center of the dwelling and were perhaps used as support beams. Houses of all sizes have these megalithic columns, including the quasi-rectangular House 2 at Torre d'en Galmés, which has one large extant column. In comparison, the circular House 7 at Torre d'en Galmés has evidence of at least four columns in the center of the house.[51] As discussed in Smith and van Dommelen 2018, the similarities between the supporting, internal columns of the house and the shape of a taula megalith are striking. A taula is a large t-shaped megalith (Fig. 37a),

Figure 36: Hypostyle hall of House 6 at Torre d'en Galmés. The hall is actually roofed with megalithic limestone blocks and was most likely used as a storage facility (photo by the author).

located in what are known as taula precincts, which are thought to be gathering areas for ritual feasting. Crucially, taula structures and their surrounding precincts are also specific to Menorca. Although the columns within these houses were most likely not serving a ritual purpose, perhaps these stones were more than functional, even referential to the taula itself as a kind of decorative motif. Taula sanctuaries were in fact heavily used during the Late Talayotic period. The Menorcan house was possibly utilizing domestic architectural forms that drew inspiration from the ritualized monumental landscape characterized by buildings such as taulas, as the taula sanctuaries seem to date to just before the construction of many of these houses in the 7th and 6th centuries BCE.[52] One of the most remarkable of these megalithic arrangements can be seen at the Cartailhac domestic structure, where we also have one of our latest (3rd century BCE) and largest examples (Fig. 37b).

Given these distinctive architectural features and the increase in size of domestic structures, it appears the indigenous communities around the island may have been enacting a sort of obvious and overt representation of indigenous forms. The hyper-iteration of local culture may have been an expression of indigenous identity in response to increasing and consistent contact with global cultures, objects, and economic networks. Given the lack of evidence for the presence of foreign populations

Figure 37: The internal columns of the Cartailhac precinct at Torre D'en Galmés (A), reminiscent of the taula form which is (B) seen here from Torre Blanca (photos by the author).

on the island, these architectural forms may have not been intended for display to extra-island cultures, but instead served to reinforce indigenous identity or act as a form of prestige within the island culture. Such an expression of difference can be seen in Mediterranean island contexts with the work of John Robb in Neolithic Malta,[53] but also in examples from Native American archaeology of the Southwest during Spanish colonization, which will be discussed below. Couched in these terms, perhaps interpreting some of the t-shaped supporting columns as a reference to the taula is not preposterous, though still must be considered tenuous. It may also be possible to interpret the U-shaped hypostyle halls as referencing something akin to a naveta, or a Bronze Age funerary structure again specific to Menorca.[54] The islanders may have been actively referencing Menorca's unique megalithic ritual architecture in their domestic embellishments.[55] These structures are used and reused into the 1st century CE in many cases, hinting at a society that is both aware of an indigenous island identity and thought of themselves as a coherent community.

Menorcan houses offer a fascinating case study in hyper-indigenous forms. They are not similar to Mallorca, nor are they reminiscent of contemporary Punic, Roman, Greek, or Iberian houses. One could make connections to the circular structures of Sardinia or Corsica, yet those were built in the Bronze Age, as much as a thousand years removed from the structures of Menorca. The large scale and ubiquity of the circular house across the island indicates that the communities who shared this custom were probably aware of its difference from other foreign customs, including orthogonal domestic structures adopted on Mallorca, and continued to invest in its display as a symbol of a Menorcan culture or identity.

Private Space, Elite Status, and Indigenous Architecture in the Late Talayotic

During the Late Talayotic, production spaces change from public areas to private domestic settings across Menorca. This section will discuss how over the course of the 6th to 2nd centuries BCE, Menorcan houses began gradually incorporating public space into private domestic units as the result of elite consolidation of production. Following the 2nd century BCE, production spaces become communal again in what appears to be a collapse of the island's elite. The discussion of private versus public space has been featured in a few works concerning Balearic households.[56] Of course, the terms private and public should be seen as artifacts of modernism and western culture.[57] In the Menorcan context, they might be understood as representing communal behavior (public) or elite control (private) rather than direct ownership. The circular courtyard houses on Menorca (such as House 7 and Cartailhac at Torre d'en Galmés) have parallels in both Iberia[58] from the 6th to 2nd centuries BCE and in southern France[59] from the 3rd to 1st centuries BCE. In both regions, we encounter walled indigenous settlements that employ courtyard architecture, just as Menorca seems to do during the Late Talayotic period.

Although the houses on the mainland are much more orthogonal than the examples mentioned on Menorca, the social and elite motivations for the construction of these houses seem similar.

Given a lack of evidence for traditional house forms from the earlier Talayotic period on Menorca, it is worthwhile to compare the evidence from Southern France when assessing circular courtyard houses. Appearing around the 3rd century BCE, the French examples incorporate a number of rooms surrounding an open-air courtyard, even expanding into public spaces, such as predefined streets or walkways within settlements. This is apparent at the site of Lattes, in which houses during the 3rd century incorporated part of the street in a process of expanding the household precinct to incorporate activities that were once outdoors.[60] This is exactly what some authors have proposed for Menorca.[61] At Lattes, Belarte suggests that not all members of the community opted to build these larger houses, as smaller free-standing houses and connected houses are also evident, often with a communal courtyard.[62] This is seen, for example, at the site of Talatí de Dalt on Menorca.[63] Large courtyard houses may indicate elite dwellings with the capability of controlling production space, while smaller houses with communal courtyards or an accessible outdoor space may be both a remnant of previous practices and a mark of the non-elite. Evidence exists for other smaller houses functioning into the 1st or even 2nd centuries CE.

To further contextualize the examples from Menorca, during the 6th and 5th centuries BCE, circular houses contain an internal patio area for domestic and craft production that seems to expand to a large outdoor courtyard over time. Salvá and Hernández-Gasch[64] see the emerging circular domestic form and control of space as a societal shift through architectural form and function that is not shared with Mallorca, at least during this era. Nevertheless, during the earlier Talayotic period on Mallorca, there is indeed evidence of increased control of activities that would have been external to the household. The shift can be seen in examples from Ses Païsses and other sites on Mallorca that show an increased emphasis on delineated production spaces.[65] This trend appears later in Menorca, showing a separate cultural trajectory and hinting at a Late Talayotic emergence of Menorcan elites. The smaller, irregular houses on Menorca from the Late Talayotic rely more heavily on external spaces between houses, with only modest areas for craft production located within the dwelling itself.

To understand the growth of private space and elite control in the Late Talayotic period, one can return to the village of Biniparratx Petit. Biniparratx Petit is smaller than the large regional centers of Torre d'en Galmés and Son Catlar, but provides a chronology that is important for understanding the control of domestic space. House 1 mentioned above has two hypothesized bedrooms, a series of work spaces, a cistern, a hearth, and a food production area (Fig. 35). House 1 is mentioned again here as it has two main phases of occupation representing two different periods in the history of circular houses on Menorca. The excavators describe an initial phase of occupation from the 6th century until the second half of the 3rd century BCE when the house is abandoned.[66] Overall, the domestic area conforms to a standard model of a delineated space for the control of household activities. As previously mentioned, House 1 is a modest size, at 79 square meters of internal space, with only a small portion of that constituting the indoor work space, meaning some activity must have taken place outside the house structure. House 1 is an early example of domestic production activities within private space in the Late Talayotic period, a trend which continues in earnest until the 2nd century BCE.

The second phase of House 1 dates to the 1st century BCE until the second half of the 1st century CE based on the presence of later imported pottery.[67] The reoccupation of the house sees the function change to a communal space, perhaps owing to shifting economic networks or the loss of elite control. Hernández-Gasch attributes its use in this later period to some sort of shepherd activity, as multiple spaces or rooms in the house's original ground plan are consolidated to form a large animal pen area.[68] There is some new construction, including the creation of a paved area in the central portion of the house, though its function remains uncertain. Despite the ambiguity of later occupation, the shift in the use of the house represents a change seen around the island by the 2nd century BCE, as large private spaces are converted to communal spaces.

Another example of privatized domestic space with a similar chronology of abandonment can be seen with the precinct of Cartailhac at Torre d'en Galmés (see Fig. 34). The house structure shows a similar layout of domestic usage to Biniparratx Petit. But the chronology and the expansive domestic production area is striking. In many ways, Cartailhac is a great example of private control, incorporating a large outer wall to fully encompass the entire intended production space, complete with a large patio and outdoor oven. Cartailhac is a courtyard house to begin with, but like Houses 6 and 7 at the same site, the structure delineates this courtyard with a megalithic boundary wall (see Fig. 38). The external space accounts for over 150 square meters doubling the size of the domestic precinct. Cartailhac is constructed in the 3rd century BCE, three centuries after the circular houses first appear, showcasing the growing emphasis on the control of space surrounding a domestic structure. The walls delineating space were clearly built to control movement and were directly associated with individual domestic structures.[69] As Hernández-Gasch rightly points out, the foci of these circular houses are the workspaces, exemplified by Biniparratx Petit House 1 and later by Cartailhac, and while these private areas start at a modest size, they grow dramatically in the Late Talayotic period.

The persistence of circular dwellings into the 3rd or even 2nd centuries BCE reflects a continuing traditional trajectory that emphasizes the control of domestic and associated production space within the precinct. From about the 6th to 2nd centuries BCE, the archaeology shows a delineation of private space, potentially indicating a shift to elite control of goods resulting in a privatization of household production.[70] Menorca appears to maintain a system of local elite families that control space through circular house complexes and perimeter walls. In the 2nd century BCE, there seems to

Figure 38: The megalithic precinct wall surrounding the courtyard at Cartailhac (photo by the author).

be a sort of shift in practices after a lengthy period of circular house construction and occupation. Circular houses are reoccupied, restructured, or reorganized to reflect more communal living via pastoralism, and shared production spaces. The earlier attempts at controlling public space show us that there was an indigenous elite who grew in influence and power in the Late Talayotic period. This power is expressed through both the control of space and megalithic constructions around the island. While there appears to have been a loss of elite status by the 2nd century BCE and an accompanying change in the use of these large structures, the evidence of a Menorcan elite that emphasized an island-specific architecture attests to a society that understood the potential of an island-based identity and celebrated their indigenous culture. Instead of conforming to external influences, the wealthy chose to focus on maintaining tradition.

Approaching Indigeneity on Menorca

The concept of the indigenous in the western Mediterranean is not new, nor is it uncommon, yet it is rarely critically commented upon. The term 'indigenous' is often used in theoretical works regarding the Iberian Peninsula,[71] Southern France,[72] Sardinia,[73] and even mainland Italy.[74] The indigenous peoples of these studies are the inhabitants that first interacted with Phoenician, Greek, Punic, or even Roman traders in the central and western Mediterranean. Interestingly, indigenous does not appear as often as an operative term in the eastern Mediterranean, owing largely to colonial histories and protohistoric cultures framing our understanding of the western Mediterranean as well as different historical and cultural trajectories of the eastern Mediterranean islands.

When the Romans conquered the Balearic Islands in 123 BCE a transformation took place. This was not simply a colonization episode, but the transition from the modern conceptualization of a protohistoric culture to a historic culture on the islands. A similar transformation takes place in the Late Talayotic period with the establishment of the Phoenician colony of *Iboshim* on Ibiza, as both Mallorca and Menorca transition in modern academia from prehistoric to protohistoric cultures. Of course it is only with hindsight that scholars can recognize this shift, as ancient populations could have had no way of knowing that the script and histories of the Carthaginian and

Roman peoples would have such long afterlives. Nor can a responsible scholar assume that everything changed in the northern two Balearic Islands after the 7th century, or even 123 BCE, on account of a 'historical' culture coming into contact with an area where an indigenous script did not exist or is not known. Periodization is the result of extant evidence, be it archaeological or historical. Yet the perception of the Classical culture as somehow either superior or corrupting, creating a one-way, diffusionist notion of cultural exchange often dominates our perception of an indigenous cultures in the Mediterranean in contact with a colonial or global entity.

Depending on the period, different theoretical lenses are used to approach the archaeological data. These lenses can ultimately undermine the study of the indigenous Balearics during their historical or protohistoric time periods. For example, as a general trend, the indigenous cultures that precede Carthaginian and Roman interaction on Mallorca and Menorca are approached with a high level of theoretical engagement. This includes notions of initial colonization, ecological theory, insularity, as well as other theoretical approaches to the data.[75] In the Late Talayotic period of the islands, theoretical engagements regarding insularity, post-colonialism, or other post-processual ideas are largely ceded to issues of acculturation, at least until recently.[76] Meanwhile, the Romans are treated as a historical culture with a historical record, which is relied upon to frame archaeological data.[77] Because of this, a term like Romanization, stemming from the vantage point of the Romans as the dominant cultural system, is regularly used to describe these interactions without theoretical disentanglement. Even the term protohistory implies an inferior version of the previous indigenous inhabitants rendered impure by cultural contact. It also assumes an inevitable progression toward literacy, that unavoidably changes non-literate cultures. It is impossible to deny that change occurred during the Late Talayotic period, yet the way cultural change is perceived remains part of a colonial dynamic, privileging external stimulus rather than internal modification. The culture of Menorca remained indigenous, did not develop its own script, and exhibited many connections to their past customs during the Late Talayotic and into the Roman Period. This leads to two important discussions regarding the archaeological data at hand: the idea of indigeneity on the Balearic Islands, and the perception of colonialism as the loss of a 'pure' indigeneity with exposure to global Mediterranean societies.

Indigeneity is not quite the same as indigenous or indigenousness, but perhaps useful in discussing Menorca. As Jace Weaver notes, indigenousness is a term often used to imply the social status or place of indigenous groups in larger cultural frameworks, while indigeneity is a heuristic term that encapsulates the multi-faceted nature of an indigenous identity in a post-colonial framework.[78] Many post-colonial scholars have further defined indigeneity as a cultural self-awareness that results from an acting colonial control or affecting force that threatens the way of life of inhabitants who consider themselves autochthonous.[79] In other words, if there were no territorial or cultural threats in the world, self-identified autochthonous cultures would still exist, but ideas of indigeneity would not. Indigeneity is community, an identity couched in landscape, and the social construction of difference from a colonial force.[80] Despite these ideas being primarily modern constructs of nation-state colonialism, the concept of indigenous self-identification and the binding force of indigeneity may be extended into antiquity. Colonial or imperial encroachment in antiquity was martial, territorial, political, and even economic. It also created a growing awareness of foreignness and cultural difference through the interaction and exchange inherent to the colonial experience.

In other words, foreign interactions result in self-reflection by both the foreigner and the inhabitant. In both cases, this self-reflection can be creative; it can lead to further differentiation of indigenous cultural traits, it can spur hybridization, or it can result in both of these processes simultaneously. Contact is an important factor in cultural change or solidification. Neither culture is static nor is it entirely changed by contact. Although indigeneity may be seen as a product or response to colonialism, it is just as cohesive and culturally creative as the act of colonizing. Colonies and colonists have been the focus of archaeological attention, particularly for the Greek, Roman, and even Punic worlds, for understanding the coherence of colonial, Classical communities in the western Mediterranean. In this context, indigenous groups are seen only within the framing mechanism of colonial dynamics. But indigenous cultures are not static or monolithic, and when faced with a foreign community, they can change internally as well, not necessarily through cultural adoption or explicit resistance, but through changing perceptions of themselves, their cultural memory, and their connections to the landscape.

This study has considered the circular courtyard houses of Menorca in the context of an indigenous culture expressing traditional lifeways during a time of intensified interaction with global Mediterranean cultures. In this capacity, the unique shape of these houses begs further, anthropological comparison with cultures in transition. As many archaeologists and anthropologists have discussed, the spatial syntax of the house can be interpreted as a reproduction of the inhabitant's worldview.[81] Having a megalithic circular dwelling, coupled with an obvious control of domestic and productive space – when elite household constructions outside of Menorca are utilizing orthogonal or quasi-orthogonal ground plans – is telling of a significant difference in worldview. In fact, it may be an assertion of indigenous identity among Menorcans, not necessarily to external forces, but internally as a sign of prestige or wealth despite increasing contacts with globalizing forces and cultures. The islands may not have been very important from a political or geographic, but they were connected to other cultures throughout the western Mediterranean via trade. Their autonomy, due to resistance or a lack of external interest, as well as their cultural persistence allowed these elite practices to persist in the Late Iron Age, long after many other cultures in the western Mediterranean abandoned such traditions.

Robert Preucel's work concerning Native American communities during the 17th-century Pueblo Revolt may be of some use in understanding these processes.

In his works, Preucel describes a series of indigenous communities fragmented by Spanish colonialism in the American Southwest, yet during the two decades of the Pueblo Revolt, they create new mesa-top settlements with central plaza areas that assert tradition through architectural elements.[82] This tradition does not stem from a particular village, but is a fabricated landscape, incorporating elements of multiple villages in a display of communal ethnogenesis as a rhetoric of resistance.[83] Menorca did not see formal colonization until the Roman conquest in 123 BCE and only really in the subsequent 1st centuries BCE and CE do we see the establishment of colonies and colonial infrastructure. In this capacity resistance is maybe not the best word to use in describing why these houses remain circular or traditional. But perhaps the circular houses represent a conscious assertion of shared origins, or even a shared island identity in the face of increasing outside pressures from the 6th to the 2nd centuries BCE.[84] In other words, like the mesa-top villages of the Pueblo Revolt, architecture is potentially serving as an ethnogenetic force, emphasizing distinction and tradition among Menorcan elites in a newly fabricated domestic form. External pressures throughout the Late Talayotic period – such as increasing ties to Ibiza, trade networks opening across the western Mediterranean, mercenary recruitment by the Carthaginian and Roman armies, as well as the Punic Wars – may have spurred the creation of a particularly Menorcan circular architectural form or even the conversion of previous domestic structures into a megalithic form, along with creating a delineated domestic space not previously seen on Menorca, Mallorca, or any nearby cultures in the western Mediterranean.[85] This form, perpetuated and expanded by elite households, may have served as a symbol of island identity. In this manner, as opposed to the elites of hellenizing or romanizing areas around the Mediterranean that tend to foster the incorporation or even hybridization of incoming customs, the elites of Menorca cultivated indigenous, traditional spaces.

The evidence in this study has outlined how Late Talayotic Menorcans literally constructed difference from outsiders through their household architecture. Their use of space reflects a growing change in wealth differentiation and a growing sense of private or elite control. Yet the people of Late Talayotic Menorca remained true to their idiosyncratic architectural forms. The emphasis on self-referential architecture coupled with local status appears to be an expression of indigenous identity within the island culture itself. A Roman who visited the island might see the culture as impressive to some extent, but they would have no cultural understanding of what the large houses or taula precinct meant. It is clear, however, that despite discussions of globalization,[86] hybridity,[87] and post-colonialism more generally in the Mediterranean, particularly in the western Mediterranean, more discussions need to revolve around the conception of the indigenous, particularly as they relate to an era of increased contact in the second half of the 1st millennium BCE. This includes the potential of a term like indigeneity in understanding the change, persistence, and metamorphosis of indigenous cultures in the Late Iron Age or Classical Periods. Menorca is a useful starting place to begin discussion, and as excavations and evidence continue to be published on Late Talayotic dwellings, this picture will only become clearer. For now, a trait as simple as a circular domestic wall hints at an entirely different worldview of the communities of Menorca, including their perception of themselves and their perception of those outside of the island.

Notes

1 For a discussion of this perception, see Broodbank 2000, 13–15.
2 For a convincing exception to this regarding Bronze Age naviform culture, see Anglada *et al.* 2014a.
3 Said 1978.
4 Grinsell 1984.
5 This study presents information that is similar in many ways to Torres Gomariz 2017a, but arrives at different conclusions regarding the nature of circular dwellings in the Late Talayotic era. This confluence of information is pure coincidence and largely based on the evidence available, as much of the data presented in this study was originally part of Smith 2015. For a further discussion of islands as useful places for the interpretation of colonial dynamics, see Broodbank 2000, 13–15.
6 '...the ways in which broadly shared ideas, goods, and practices are modified and adapted locally to accord with local practice, customs, habits, and beliefs,' from Hodos 2017, 6–7.
7 Jennings 2017, 15.
8 Also grobality, or the active expansion of producers to find new markets and new places; see Hodos 2017, 7.
9 For a discussion of this, see Cherry and Leppard 2018.
10 For more discussion of the chronological sequence of naviform houses and structures, see Guerrero *et al.* 2006, as well as García 2006 for a discussion of Son Mercer de Baix, a Bronze Age naviform house from Menorca. Recent work has also been carried out at multiple sites on Menorca and Mallorca, particularly at Sa Ferradura on Mallorca and Cala Morell on Menorca (Anglada *et al.* 2014a).
11 This changed with Guerrero *et al.* 2002.
12 Kolb 2005.
13 Anglada *et al.* 2014b.
14 Diodorus Siculus *Historical Library* V.
15 Aubet 1994, 338.
16 Costa Ribas 2007.
17 Contreras *et al.* 2006.
18 Guerrero 1997.
19 While Menorca shows no evidence of colonies during the Late Talayotic, some scholars, such as Guerrero 1997, have argued that the Punic emporia on the south coast of Mallorca were formal colonies.
20 For an introductory resource, see Guerrero 1997.
21 This remains contentious, as the lack of colonization is much more obvious on Menorca than Mallorca.
22 Costa Ribas 2007, 88.
23 Pliny the Elder *Natural History* III. These other sites included Bocchorus, Cinium and Tucis.
24 Pliny the Elder *Natural History* III. It is likely that in the case of Magon and Iamnon, the Roman ports were placed over indigenous sites.
25 See Smith 2015.
26 See Anglada *et al.* 2017.

27 For a list of known excavations at such houses, see Torres Gomariz 2016.
28 Camps and Vallespir 1998. Also, Torres Gomariz 2017a has pointed to certain building techniques in the house reflecting Punic traditions, as well as the importance of a central patio, but the circular shape remains unique to Menorca.
29 Anglada *et al.* 2014b.
30 For more information, see Plantalamor 1991 and Guerrero *et al.* 2006.
31 The most prolific author commenting on the phenomenon of circular houses is Jordi Hernández-Gasch. Examples include an overall synthesis of domestic space construction in Salvá and Hernández-Gasch 2009; a specifically iron age synthesis found in Hernández-Gasch 2011; as well as the description of Biniparratx Petit, Hernández-Gasch 2007; Guerrero *et al.* 2007b.
32 For an example of this, see the late 3rd-century precinct of Cartailhac in Torre d'en Galmés, described by Sintes and Isbert 2009.
33 Pérez-Juez *et al.* 2007, 53.
34 Diodorus Siculus, *Historical Library* V.
35 Based on excavations carried out by the Boston University team of House 2 (Pérez-Juez *et al.* 2007).
36 Pérez-Juez *et al.* 2007; Pérez-Juez 2011.
37 Sintes and Isbert 2009, 256.
38 With the exception of House 2, excavated by the Boston University team from 2001-2010 (Pérez-Juez *et al.* 2007).
39 Nicolás 1997; Guerrero *et al.* 2007b; Hernández-Gasch 2007.
40 Guerrero *et al.* 2007b; Hernández-Gasch 2007.
41 Salvá and Hernández-Gasch 2009, 309.
42 Hernández-Gasch 2007, 18.
43 This description largely comes from Torres Gomariz 2017c, 47.
44 See Fig. 34; Sintes and Isbert 2009, 254.
45 Sintes and Isbert 2009, 256.
46 Ferrer *et al.* 2011, 113.
47 Juan and Pons 2011, 98.
48 Hernández-Gasch 2007, 13.
49 Obviously this is a debated topic, particularly concerning Romanization. For basic references see Gosden 2004, 104, 106, but also Dietler 2010. Elite members of a community both adopt colonial ideas to emphasize distinction or privilege, but have also been known to adapt incoming traits to internal customs, creating hybrid, approachable, and ultimately popular forms of traditional culture.
50 Although 'hypostyle halls' exist on Mallorca, and the term is used to denote Building 6 at Ses Païsses, this example is far smaller and less megalithic in nature (Guerrero *et al.* 2006, 55).
51 Ferrer *et al.* 2011.
52 For the dating of these sanctuaries, see Micó 2005a; Guerrero *et al.* 2006; Anglada *et al.* 2017.
53 Robb 2001.
54 Though naviform structures are found on both Mallorca and Menorca in the Bronze Age. The naveta, however, is a funerary form specific to Menorca. Anglada *et al.* 2014a.
55 Smith and van Dommelen 2018.
56 Salvá and Hernández-Gasch 2009; Hernández-Gasch 2011.
57 Kent 1990; Nevett 2010, 6.
58 Belarte Franco 2008.
59 Dietler 1997; 2010; Belarte 2009.
60 Belarte Franco 2009, 240–241.
61 Salvá and Hernández-Gasch 2009; Hernández-Gasch 2011.
62 Belarte Franco 2009, 254.

63 Juan Benejam *et al.* 2002.
64 Salvá and Hernández-Gasch 2009, 311.
65 For a brief yet fascinating article comparing the delineation of space between Menorcan houses and Ses Païsses in particular, see Torres Gomariz 2017b.
66 Hernández-Gasch 2007, 10–12.
67 Ibid., 11.
68 Ibid., 12.
69 The control of space and resources is also represented with House 6 at Torre d'en Galmés, where the external wall controls movement around a large cistern. Communal water collection areas are evident to the west of the house, differentiating a private and public control of water at the site.
70 Salvá and Hernández-Gasch 2009.
71 Jiménez 2008.
72 Dietler 2010.
73 van Dommelen 1998.
74 Attema and Van Leusen 2010.
75 Castro-Martínez *et al.* 2003; Micó 2005b; Alcover 2008; Calvo *et al.* 2011.
76 Fernández-Miranda 1997; Guerrero *et al.* 2007a.
77 Contreras 1998; Zucca 1998; Contreras *et al.* 2006.
78 Weaver 2005, 221.
79 Echoed in Verdesio 2008.
80 Similar to Wilk 1995's notion of 'learning to be local'.
81 Broadbent *et al.* 1980; Preucel 2000, 69.
82 Preucel 2000, 70; Liebmann *et al.* 2005.
83 Preucel 2000, 73.
84 One could also cite El Turó de Ses Baies as another example of this happening on Mallorca during the 3rd to 1st centuries BCE, though in this case it was just part of the Mallorcan landscape, nearby the larger, earlier settlement of Puig de Sa Morisca. In that sense, it may simply represent a small-scale village community asserting its cultural independence amidst the growing forces and colonial ventures of the Romans in nearby Palma.
85 Though Torres Gomariz 2016 argues for broad similarities between the internal patios of Punic and Late Talayotic Circular houses.
86 Hodos 2009.
87 van Dommelen 1998.

Bibliography

Alcover, J.A. (2008) The First Mallorcans: Prehistoric Colonization in the Western Mediterranean. *Journal of World Prehistory* 21, 19–84.

Anglada, M., Ferrer, A. and Ramis, D. (2017) Actividad Humana en el Litoral de Menorca Durante la Prehistoria. In *Geomorgologia Litoral de Menorca: Dinámica, Evolución y Practices de Gestion*, edited by L. Gómez-Pujol and G.X. Pons. Palma de Mallorca: Societat d'Història Natural de Balears, 213–233.

Anglada, M., Ferrer, A., Ramis, D. and Salas, M. (2014a) Resultas Preliminars del Projecte Entre Illes: El Cas dels Jaciments de Sa Ferradura (Manacor) I Cala Morell (Ciutadella). In *V Jornades d'Arqueologia de les Illes Balears (Palma, 28 A 30 De Setembre, 2012)*, edited by M. Riera Rullan and J. Cardell. Palma de Mallorca: Edicions Documenta Balear.

Anglada, M., Ferrer, A., Plantalamo, L., Ramis, D., Van Strydonck, M. and De Mulder, G. (2014b) Chronological Framework For the Early Talayotic Period in Menorca: The Settlement of Cornianou. *Radiocarbon* 56.2, 411–424.

Attema, P., Burgers, J. and Van Leusen, M. (2010) *Regional Pathways to Complexity*. Chicago, IL: University of Chicago Press.

Aubet, M.E. (1994) *The Phoenicians and the West: Politics, Colonies, and Trade*. New York: Cambridge University Press.

Belarte Franco, M.C. (2008) Domestic Architecture and Social Differences in North-Eastern Iberia During the Iron Age (c. 525–200 BC). *Oxford Journal of Archaeology* 27.2, 175–199.

Belarte Franco, M.C. (2009) Courtyard Houses and Other Complex Buildings in the Protohistory of Southern Gaul: From Architectural to Social Change. *Journal of Mediterranean Archaeology* 22.2, 235–259.

Broadbent, G., Bunt, R. and Llorens, T. (1980) *Meaning and Behaviour in the Built Environment*. Chichester: Wiley.

Broodbank, C. (2000) *An Island Archaeology of the Early Cylcades*. Cambridge: Cambridge University Press.

Calvo Trias, M., Javaloyas, D., Albero Santacreu, D., Garcia-Rosello, J. and Guerrero Ayuso, V.M. (2011) The Ways People Move: Mobility and Seascapes in the Balearic Islands during the Late Bronze Age (c. 1400–850/800 bc). *World Archaeology* 43.3, 345–363.

Camps, J. and Vallespir, A. (1998) *Excavacions a Santa Ponça. Mallorca. El turó de les Abelles*. Palma de Mallorca: Consell de Mallorca.

Castro-Martínez, P., Escoriza Mateu, T. and Sanahuja, M.E. (2003) *Mujeres y Hombres en Espacios Domésticos: Trabajo y Vida Social en la Prehistoria de Mallorca (c. 700–500 cal ANE): el Edificio Alfa del Puig Morter de Son Ferragut (Sineu, Mallorca)*. BAR International Series No. 1162. Oxford: Archaeopress.

Cherry, J. and Leppard, T. (2018) The Balearic Paradox: Why Were the Islands Colonized So Late? La Paradoja Balear: ¿Por qué las Islas fueron Colonizadas tan Tarde? *Pyrenae* 49.1, 49–70.

Contreras Rodrigo, F. (1998) Sanisera, Ciudad Romana de Menorca. Su Origen. In *La Mirada del Pasado. Edicions de Turisme Cultural*. Fornells, Menorca: Ecomuseu de Sanisera, 303–305.

Contreras Rodrigo, F., Müller, R. and Valle de Tarzaga, F.J. (2006) El Asentamiento military Romano de Sanitja (123–45 a.C.): Una Aproximación a su Contexto Histórico. *Mayurqa* 31, 231–250.

Costa Ribas, B (2007) Punic Ibiza Under the Roman Republic. In *Articulating Local Cultures: Power and Identity Under the Expanding Roman Republic*, edited by P. van Dommelen and N. Terrenato. *Journal of Roman Archaeology Supplementary Series* 63 . Portsmouth, RI: Journal of Roman Archaeology, 85–102.

Dietler, M. (1997) The Iron Age in Mediterranean France: Colonial Encounters, Entanglements, and Transformations. *Journal of World Prehistory* 11, 269–357.

Dietler, M. (2010) *Archaeologies of Colonialism: Consumption, Entanglement, and Violence in Ancient Mediterranean France*. Berkeley: University of California Press.

Diodorus Siculus (1989) *Diodorus of Sicily in Twelve Volumes*. Translated by C.H. Oldfather. Cambridge, MA: Harvard University Press.

Fernández-Miranda, M. (1997) Aspects of Talayotic Culture. In *Encounters and Transformations: The Archaeology of Iberia in Transition*, edited by M. Balmuth, A. Gilman and L. Prados-Torreira. Sheffield: Sheffield Academic Press, 59–68.

Ferrer Rotger, A., Juan Benejam, G., Lara Astiz, C. and Pons Machado, J. (2001) El Jaciment de Torre d'en Galmés (Alaior, Menorca). Les Intervencions d'Amics del Museu de Menorca: Cercle 7. In *III Jornades d'Arqueologia de les Illes Balears (Maó, 3 I 4 d'Octubre, 2008)*, edited by J. Gual Cerdó. Mahón, Menorca: Consell Insular, 109–117.

García Amengual, E. (2006) El Proceso Constructivo de un Edificio de la Edad del Bronce de Menorca: El Caso de Son Mercer de Baix (Ferreries, Menorca). *Mayurqa* 31, 113–136.

Gosden, C. (2004) *Archaeology and Colonialism*. Cambridge: Cambridge University Press.

Grinsell, L.V. (1984) The Popular Names and Folklore of Prehistoric Sites in Menorca. *Folklore* 95.1, 90–99.

Guerrero Ayuso, V.M. (1997) *Colonización Púnica de Mallorca: La Documentación Arqueológica y el Contexto Histórico.* Palma de Mallorca: Universitat de les Illes Balears.

Guerrero Ayuso, V.M., Calvo Trias, M. and Salvá Simonet, B. (2002) La Cultura Talayótica: Una Sociedad de la Edad del Hierro en la Periferia de la Colonización Fenicia. *Complutum* 13, 221–258.

Guerrero Ayuso, V.M., Calvo Trias, M. and Salvá Simonet, B. (2006) *Historica de las Islas Baleares 2: Mallorca y Menorca en la Edad del Hierro.* Palma de Mallorca: El Mundo.

Guerrero Ayuso, V.M., Calvo Trias, M. and Salvá Simonet, B. (2007a) Insularity and the Indigenous World on the Periphery of the System: The Balearic islands (Mallorca and Menorca) between the 6th and 1st c. BC. In *Articulating Local Cultures: Power and Identity Under the Expanding Roman Republic*, edited by P. van Dommelen and N. Terrenato. *Journal of Roman Archaeology Supplementary Series* 63. Portsmouth, RI: Journal of Roman Archaeology, 71–84.

Guerrero Ayuso, V.M., Gornés, S., Hernández, J., de Nicolàs, J., Morales, J.V., Morales, A. and Pino, B. (2007b) Avanç de les Investigacions Argueològiques Realitzades a l'Assentament de Biniparratx Petit (Sant Lluís). In *L'Arqueologia a Menorca: Eina per al Coneixement del Passat.* Mahón, Menorca: Consell Insular, 9–51.

Hernández-Gasch, J. (2007) *Les Cases de Planta Circular i Pati Central de la Segona Edat del Ferro a Menorca: L'Exemple de la Casa 1 del Poblat Talaiòtic de Biniparratx Petit (Sant Lluís).* Unpublished Field Report.

Hernández-Gasch, J., Ramis, D. and Rosselló, J.A. (2011) Económia, Societat i Canvi Cultural a les Gimnèsies. La Interprectació de les Dades Bioarqueològiques a les Illes Balears en el Primer Millenni A.N.E. In *Economia Agropecuària i Canvi Social a Partir de les Restes Bioarqueològiques. El Primer Millennia Ac a la Mediterrània Occidental: Actes de la V Reunió Internacional d'Arqueologia de Calafell (Calafell, 16 al 18 d'Abril de 2009)*, edited by S. Valenzuela-Lamas, N. Padrós, M.C. Belarte and J. Sanmartí. Barcelona: Universitat de Barcelona, 123–138.

Hodos, T. (2009) Colonial Encounters in the Global Mediterranean Iron Age. *Cambridge Archaeological Journal* 19.2, 221–241.

Hodos, T. (2017) Globalization: Some Basics. An Introduction to *The Routledge Handbook of Archaeology and Globalization*. In *The Routledge Handbook of Archaeology and Globalization*, edited by T. Hodos. New York: Routledge, 3–11.

Jennings, J. (2017) Distinguishing Past Globalizations. In *The Routledge Handbook of Archaeology and Globalization*, edited by T. Hodos. New York: Routledge, 12–28.

Jiménez, A. (2008) *Imagines Hibridae: Una Aproximación Postcolonialista al Estudio de las Necrópolis de la Bética.* Madrid: Consejo Superior de Inestigaciones Científicas.

Juan Benejam, G. and Pons Machado, J. (2011) El Jaciment de Torre d'en Galmés (Alaior, Menorca). Les Intervencions d'Amics del Museu de Menorca: Edifici 1. In *III Jornades d'Arqueologia de les Illes Balears (Maó, 3 I 4 d'Octubre, 2008)*, edited by J. Gual Cerdó. Mahón, Menorca: Consell Insular, 97–107.

Juan Benejam, G., Pons Machado, J., Pons, O., Lara, C., Marques, J. and Isbert, F. (2002) Talatí de Dalt (Maó – Menorca) Avenç dels Resultats del les Excavacions Fetes Entre 1997 i 2000. *Bolleti de la Societat Arqueológica Lulliana* 58, 371–378.

Kent, S. (1990) A Cross-Cultural Study of Segmentation, Architecture, and the Use of Space. In *Domestic Architecture and Use of Space*, edited by S. Kent. Cambridge: Cambridge University Press, 127–152.

Kolb, M. (2005) The Genesis of Monuments among the Mediterranean Islands. In *The Archaeology of Mediterranean Prehistory*, edited by E. Blake and A.B. Knapp. Malden, MA: Blackwell Publishing, 156–179.

Liebmann, M., Ferguson, T.J. and Preucel, R.W. (2005) Pueblo Settlement, Architecture, and Social Change in the Pueblo Revolt Era, A.A. 1680 to 1696. *Journal of Field Archaeology* 30.1, 45–60.

Micó Pérez, R. (2005a) *Cronología Absoluta y Periodización de la Prehistoria de las Islas Baleares.* BAR International Series No. 1373. Oxford: Archaeopress.

Micó Pérez, R. (2005b) Towards a Definition of Politico-Ideological Practices in the Prehistory of Minorca (the Balearic Islands): The Wood Carvings from Mussol Cave. *Journal of Social Archaeology* 5.2, 276–299.

Nevett, L. (2010) *Domestic Space in Classical Antiquity*. Cambridge: Cambridge University Press.

Nicolás Mascaró, J.C. de (1997) Casa Prehistórica en el Aeropuerto de Menorca. *Aena Arte* 3, 46–49.

Pérez-Juez, A. (2011) Excavaciones en la Casa 2 del Yacimiento de Torre d'en Galmés, Alaior: Propuestas para el Hábitat Talayótico. In *III Jornades d'Arqueologia de les Illes Balears (Maó, 3 I 4 d'Octubre, 2008)*, edited by J. Gual Cerdó. Mahón, Menorca: Consell Insular, 119–130.

Pérez-Juez, A., Wiseman, J., Goldberg, P., Hansen, J., Mullen, K., Ostovich, M., Payne, C., Gornés, S., Cabanes, D., Euba, I., Morales, J.V., Morín, J. and López Fraile, F.J. (2007) El Uso del Espacio Doméstico de una Estructura del Talayótico Final: Excavación de la Casa 2 del Yacimiento de Torre d'en Galmés, Alayor 2003–2006. In *L'Arqueologia a Menorca: Eina per al Coneixement del Passat*. Mahón, Menorca: Consell Insular, 53–74.

Plantalamor Massanet, L. (1991) La Arquitectura Prehistòrica i Protohistòrica de Menorca i el seu Marc Cultural. In *Treballs del Museu de Menorca* 12. Mahón, Menorca: Museu de Menorca.

Pliny the Elder (1945) *Natural History*. Translated by Harris Rackham. Cambridge, MA: Harvard University Press.

Preucel, R.W. (2000) Making Pueblo Communities: Archaeological Discourse at Kotyiti, New Mexico. In *Archaeology of Communities: A New World Perspective*, edited by M.A. Canuto and J. Yeager. New York: Routledge, 58–77.

Robb, J.E. (2001) Island Identities: Ritual, Travel and the Creation of Difference in Neolithic Malta. *European Journal of Archaeology* 4, 175–202.

Said, E. (1978) *Orientalism*. New York: Pantheon Books.

Salvá Simonet, B. and Hernández-Gasch, J. (2009) Los Espacios Domésticos en las Islas Baleares Durante las Edades del Bronce y del Hierro. De la Sociedad Naviforme a la Talayótica. In *Actes de la IV Reunió Internacional d'Arqueologia de Calafell (Calafell - Tarragona, 6 al 9 de Març de 2007)*, edited by M.C. Belarte. Barcelona: Universitat de Barcelona, 299–321.

Sintes Olives, E. and Isbert Vaquer, F. (2009) Investigación Arqueológica y Puesta en Valor del Recinto Cartailhac. *Patrimonio Cultural de España* 1, 251–260.

Smith, A. (2015) *Indigeneity and Colonial Response: The Metamorphoses of Balearic Culture in the Late Iron Age*. Unpublished Dissertation.

Smith, A. and van Dommelen, P. (2018) Monumental Engagements: Cultural Interaction and Island Traditions in the West Mediterranean. In *Regional Approaches to Society and Complexity: Studies in Honor of John F. Cherry*, edited by A. Knodell and T. Leppard. Sheffield: Equinox Publishing, 158–181.

Torres Gomariz, O. (2016) Viviendas Postalayóticas: Una Aproximación a los Espacios Domésticos en el Archipiélago Balear (550–123 ANE). *Documentos de Arqueología y Patrimonio Histórico* 1, 41–53.

Torres Gomariz, O. (2017a) Cercles Menorquins: Aproximación a la Influencia de la Arquitectura Púnica en las Viviendas Postalayóticas de Menorca. In *Menorca Entre Fenicis I Púnics*, edited by F. Prados Martínez, H. Jiménez Vialás and J.J. Martínez García. Murcia: Centra del Estudios del Próximo Oriente y al Antigüedad Tardía, 231–243.

Torres Gomariz, O. (2017b) Aplicacions de Sintaxi Espacial En Espais Domèstics Balears en el Marc del Projecte Modular. In *VII Jornades d'Arqueologia de les Illes Balears (Maó, 30 de setembre i 1 i 2 d'octubre, 2016)*, edited by M. Anglada Fontestad, M. Riera Rulla, A. Martinez Ortega. Mahón, Menorca: Consell Insular, 133–138.

van Dommelen, P. (1998) *On Colonial Grounds: A Comparative Study of Colonialism and Rural Settlement in First Millenium BC West Central Sardinia (Archaeological Studies Leiden University, 2)*. Leiden: Faculty of Archaeology, University of Leiden.

Verdesio, G. (2008) Indigeneity. In *A Historical Companion to Postcolonial Literatures: Continental Europe and its Empires*, edited by P. Poddar and R. Patke. Edinburgh: Edinburgh University Press.
Weaver, J. (2005) Indigeneity and Indigenousness. In *A Companion to Post-Colonial Studies*, edited by H. Shwartz and S. Ray. Malden, MA: Blackwell Publishing, 221–235.
Wilk, R. (1995) Learning to be Local in Belize: Global Systems of Common Difference. In *Worlds Apart. Modernity through the Prism of the Local*, edited by D. Miller. New York: Routledge, 110–133.
Zucca, R. (1998) *Insulae Bailares: Le Isole Baleari sotto il Dominio Romano*. Rome: Carocci editore.

Chapter 7

Fashioning a Global Goddess: The Representation of Isis across Hellenistic Seascapes*

Lindsey A. Mazurek

In this paper, I take a seascape-oriented approach to the study of island and mainland port relations in the Hellenistic Mediterranean. In order to study these relationships, I focus on the distribution of sculptures of Isis in the Hellenistic Mediterranean. When Greek devotees began to worship the Egyptian goddess Isis in the late 4th century BCE, they chose to develop new ways to represent her. While some of the earliest examples of Isis statuettes, which date to the mid-Hellenistic period, come from the islands of Delos and Rhodes, another roughly contemporary example of this type was found at Amphipolis and published in 2013 (Fig. 39). Integrating Amphipolis, a key port during the Hellenistic period, into this network offers a new way to consider how cults and their material culture could be transformed through island-mainland interactions during eras of increasing, or globalizing, connectivity. By tracing the early spread of this cult-specific image, I argue that mainland ports were integrated into island-based social and religious networks, which complicates the assumption that regions were primarily land-based.

In order to explore these questions of globalization and region, I focus on the 2nd–1st centuries BCE distribution of a particular sculptural type: the statue of Isis in the *Knotenpalla*, a costume distinguished by a fringed mantle knotted over the chest. The knot produces a characteristic set of dress folds that cascade in a chevron pattern over the lower half of the body. Though derived from earlier images of pharaonic Egyptian deities, the costume becomes associated with Isis and Ptolemaic queens in the Hellenistic period and, by the 2nd century BCE, is used to depict the Egyptian goddess Isis for a primarily Greek audience.[1] By the end of the 1st century CE, *Knotenpalla* statues appeared in many variants throughout the Mediterranean, a shift that gestures towards the broader globalization of Isiac cult.[2] Though the mid-to-late Hellenistic examples are few, I argue here that the examples found at Rhodes, Delos,

Figure 39: Map of the Aegean Sea (Ancient World Mapping Center © 2019 (awmc.unc.edu). Used by permission).

and Amphipolis display certain stylistic similarities that may suggest they belonged to a highly connected and perhaps even unified community of Isis devotees that existed across geographic space (Fig. 39). The type, then, highlights an instance of artistic and religious connectivity across insular and mainland communities. Through an examination of how the *Knotenpalla* moves between islands, ports, and hinterlands, we can begin to theorize how these areas saw themselves in relation to each other in the Hellenistic period.

This chapter begins with a theoretical reconsideration of the port city as a vector of globalization. Though many scholars focus on ports as facilitators of connectivity, literary and epigraphic evidence indicates that ports could halt connectivity just as easily, which suggests that these cities should be considered through the metaphor of the valve, open to the dissemination of desired phenomena and closed to others. In order to evaluate this claim, I turn next to the case of Isis statuettes and their distribution in the early Hellenistic Mediterranean. The distribution of the *Knotenpalla* indicates that islands functioned imagined communities that included ports as part of their common culture.[3] I then turn to an Isis *Knotenpalla* statuette from Amphipolis, whose presence complicates the association between this type and island sites. Setting the Amphipolis statuette in its regional context, formal differences between this image and another roughly contemporaneous example from Beroia indicates a sharp distinction in Macedonian sculptural types. This suggests that Amphipolis looked outward into the Mediterranean Sea for its version of Isis. In this case, then, Amphipolis served as a valve, allowing the Macedonian hinterland to develop its own version of Isiac representation around the same time that the port city engaged in island-based networks of religious material culture.

Theorizing Port and Island Networks

Egyptian cults relied on a history and memory of travel across the Mediterranean.[4] We need to contextualize Egyptian religion within its physical and conceptual landscape in order to understand its mobility. One of the Mediterranean's defining features is its closely connected network of islands. Despite their prevalence, islands are difficult to define as a theoretical concept. Ostensibly, islands should be a small-scale piece of land surrounded on all sides by water, but such a basic description does not explain their historical and cultural significance.[5] Fernand Braudel saw islands as surrounded by sea, fundamentally cut off from other lands and thus critically independent from larger trends.[6] His islands, however, formed part of the sea itself, and became part of the unified Mediterranean space. Islands are thus a paradox in Braudelian thought: connected yet isolated, separating while unifying.[7] In examining the relationship between these two disparate functions, we can see how islands both organized and bounded the conceptual and physical Mediterranean for those who sailed it while simultaneously facilitating safe passage through that seascape. Because these islands divided the Mediterranean into a network of smaller seas defined by the lands surrounding them, travelers who transgressed these spaces experienced the sea in small parts.[8] In sailing the Mediterranean, then, the sailor really traveled across many micro-Mediterraneans, each separated from the next by the islands, rocks, and sandbars that bounded its edges.[9] Rather than a single sea, ancient peoples experienced the Mediterranean as a series of localities resistant to 'homogeneity, order, and control'.[10]

If travels through these interconnected seas were linear processes, port cities would mark beginnings and endings. Travelers and merchants would start out from one port, visit a series of intermediate ports along their route, and reach the end of their journey at some point, even if the terminus is the same place from which the journey began. Rather than clustering within the networks of Mediterranean insularity, ports should stand at the edges and provide a moment of transition, a way of marking an exit from the Mediterranean and an entrance into the landed littoral.[11] The material culture of these sites, however, often suggests otherwise. Port cities frequently act as sites of cross-cultural contact and diaspora capitals, intensifying transcultural connectivity and eroding cultural and other symbolic boundaries with frequency and fervor.[12] Mediterranean networks require ports to act as loci of exchange, connecting mainland and hinterland settlements with the island seascape as part of a broader interconnected experience of globalization.

For many scholars, particularly those outside the disciplines of classics and ancient history, the Hellenistic period and its cosmopolitan culture represents the beginnings of globalization.[13] Many of Justin Jennings' key tenets of globalization (particularly time-space compression, standardization, simultaneous homogeneity/heterogeneity, and unevenness) can be identified in Hellenistic history and archaeology.[14] As this volume demonstrates, globalization and globalizations occur in earlier periods, and the Hellenistic period's experience of globalization has its own peculiar texture. Alexander's conquests and the development of rival, large-scale Greek empires enveloped diverse groups within the same political boundaries, results in a shared set of cultural symbols and meanings often referred to as the *oikoumene*.[15] These developments were supported by intensifications of trade and travel, including increasing integration of long-distance trade routes between the western and eastern Mediterranean, that made far-off places feel closer and more immediate, an example of space-time compression.[16] As part of this expansion, the social worlds of Mediterranean cities, including port cities, grew smaller and more enmeshed with those of other regions. Though connectivity increased, the Hellenistic period is marked by a form of subordinate cosmopolitanism, in which imperial political power and dominance was inscribed onto local features. In turn, local elites engage themselves in the expression of that power at the local level, resulting in a dynamic interrelationship between heterogeneity and homogeneity.[17] That is, local elites promote a sense of local identity at the same time that their involvement in trans-Mediterranean power structures promote increased adoption of shared cultural elements, and these two phenomena are closely intertwined. Because of the importance of local reception and interpretation, and perhaps even appropriation,[18] in these phenomena, we might also describe these patterns as examples of the uneven experience of Hellenistic globalization at the local level.

Because of the constant movement and people and goods through them, port cities necessarily operate with different sets of priorities than hinterland sites. I focus on port cities as a way to examine the rhythms and flows of Hellenistic globalization. Many ports stood apart from the cities they served,[19] and customs houses and port officials stopped sailors and their ships from landing and interacting with port and hinterland communities. As early as the 5th century BCE, Xenophon discusses the role of the port and collection of customs and taxes on metics as part of a broader inquiry into methods for alleviating poverty in Athens,[20] linking economic protectionism with the betterment of the Athenian population. In the Hellenistic period, these port taxes and duties were one of the city's few reliable sources of income, which rendered their collection of the highest importance.[21] In the process of collecting these taxes, civic officials often had the right to refuse landing on many criteria. In Philostratus' *Life of Apollonius of Tyre* 6.12, Apollonios and Thespesion debate the value of teaching Indian wisdom through the metaphor of testing and rejecting merchandise. While arguing in favor, Thespesion says 'But if you were a merchant or a seafarer, and you brought to us some cargo or other from over there, would you claim, merely because it came from India, to dispose of it untested and unexamined, refusing us either the liberty of looking at it or tasting it?'[22] Though metaphorical, this passage suggests a form of customs practice supported by literary and epigraphic evidence,[23] in which local officials have the ability to deny entry based on the quality of goods upon inspection or perhaps even their point of origin. Ports and the administrative entities that monitored them could use their actions to create barriers or boundaries by determining whose goods and ideas would enter a city, and whose would be left outside their community.[24]

This evidence, often overlooked in studies of ancient connectivity, suggests a new way of thinking through ports in the ancient Mediterranean. Though often seen as drivers of connectivity, ports also acted as boundaries. I propose here that we think of them through the metaphor of the valve, able to be opened and closed, selective in their ability to facilitate mobility and connectivity. In addition to their role as conduits and points of dissemination, ports could also block circulations of goods and ideas. Local officials were able to choose who and what they allowed into their cities and regions, and this selection process must have been informed by a matrix of economic, social, cultural, and political factors. Though we cannot always reconstruct the ideologies and processes underlying this matrix, we should not overlook its existence. Second: that the opportunity to accept or reject must reshape how we locate ports in global networks of connectivity. In sum, ports are valves in networks of insular connectivity, a point of contact and restraint between exterior and interior and a catalyst for engagement between the two.[25] Ports define here and there, separating terrestrial and oceanic connectivity into discrete networks. These arguments gesture towards a sea-based form of regionality, in which inhabitants determine which cities and peoples are close and part of the same group not based solely on land-based proximity. Rather, as I will argue in the conclusion, proximity could have been reckoned by time and difficulty of journey between two cities, a metric that would have privileged port-to-port connectivity over port-to-hinterland connectivity.

Isis' Cult and the Knotenpalla *in the Mediterranean World*

Isis and her cult were a global phenomenon, one that extended beyond the physical borders and endured past the temporal limits of the Hellenistic and Roman Mediterranean. Her worship began in Old Kingdom Egypt, and she grew increasingly central within the Egyptian pantheon throughout the pharaonic and later periods. Isiac worship spread beyond Egypt and Nubia during the 4th century BCE through the 4th century CE, and the cult of Isis (and those of her companions Sarapis, Anubis, and Harpokrates) became especially popular through the Greek world. [26] Some of the earliest communities were founded in major Hellenistic ports, and epigraphic evidence attests to Egyptian priests of Isis active in 4th and 3rd centuries BCE Delos, Rhodes, Demetrios, and Argos, and possibly Amphipolis.[27] Often on the outskirts of major cities, temples to Isis and Sarapis tended to mix prevailing trends in Hellenistic and Roman sanctuary architecture with the cult's peculiar needs for secluded meeting spaces and processional routes.[28] Many sanctuaries served a large, ethnically diverse devotee population that included Italian merchants, Greeks from the surrounding regions, and other groups from around the Mediterranean basin, and these groups reconfigured Egyptian deities in manners that made them appropriate for local use.[29] By the early Roman period (the mid-1st century BCE) the cults had become a Mediterranean-wide phenomenon, an example of successful globalization in the ancient world.

In most areas, the cult followed what scholars commonly call a 'mystery' format. Devotees underwent a series of initiation rituals in which specific texts, objects, and myths were revealed to them. Many of these rituals may have been performances of myths in which the devotee acted the part of divine and semi-divine mythological figures.[30] As part of their religious practice, these initiates wore cult costumes and participated in processions and ritual dramas that performed the cult's otherness.[31]

One example of the cult's unusual material culture includes the *Knotenpalla* costume. The outfit consists of a mantle, usually knotted between the breasts, over a simple chiton (Fig. 40). The knot, which forms the key element in the composition, can be large or small, realistic or not. Many variants exist. Some examples have a simpler, one-sided knot that sits between the breasts, creating a triangular rather than X shape across the chest. In most statuettes, however, the knot produces an unusual set of chevron folds over the bottom half of the body, which permits identification as a *Knotenpalla* even in examples where the knot itself is not preserved. Though most examples are too fragmentary to restore attributes, several more complete examples hold a *situla* (a breast-shaped vessel for ritual libations), a *sistrum* (a ritual rattle, found frequently in Egyptian cultic contexts, used for creating music), or both. Headdresses are also common. In some cases, Isis' *basileion*, a crown that combines a solar disc with other Egyptian iconography like feathers, sheaves of wheat, or a cobra, is attached and made in marble or in metal.

The overall effect is designed to incorporate earlier forms of Egyptian dress and iconography within traditional Greek styles and materials, producing a new version of the goddess that is neither fully Greek nor fully Egyptian. [32] Viewers in the eastern

Figure 40: Statue of Isis Capitolina, *preserving most of the relevant iconography of the* Knotenpalla *type. Palazzo Nuovo, Musei Capitolini (© Vanni Archive/Art Resource, NY).*

Mediterranean would be familiar with the costume primarily from portraits of the Ptolemaic queens, but those portraits often incorporate similar forms of dress meant to elide the queen with Isis as part of establishing the queens' legitimacy within Egypt.[33] In cultural terms, then, the image is liminal. The *Knotenpalla* does not invert completely the Greco-Roman paradigms of ideal sculpture, but this invented costume certainly played a key role in constructing Isis' difference from other deities. While other Greek goddesses often wear identifiable costumes, these costumes are usually variations on the *chitons* and mantles worn by mortal women. The point of the *Knotenpalla*, then, is to remove Isis from the realm of the everyday and to place her and her unusual dress in the realm of cultural imagination.[34]

Many of the physical and artistic markers of the cult's Otherness may have served to build a sense of group identity for devotees. In his book *Ethnicity without Groups*, sociologist Rogers Brubaker argues that groups are events, created through relational and dynamic processes of identification.[35] Using and wearing costumes like the *Knotenpalla*, then, may have been part of a practice of creating commonality, an intra-group process aimed at setting devotees apart from the rest of Mediterranean society and framing these practices as essential to devotee's self-understanding.[36] In a passage from Book XI of Apuleius' *Metamorphoses*, the protagonist Lucius dresses up in the guise of Isis and receives veneration on a wooden dais as part of his initiation into the cult: *Namque in ipso aedis sacrae meditullio ante deae simulacrum constitutum tribunal ligneum iussus superstiti, byssina quidem, sed floride depicta vesta conspicuus* ('Following instructions I stood on a wooden platform set up in the very center of the holy shrine in front of the statue of the goddess, the focus of attention because of my garment, which was only linen, but elaborately embroidered').[37] The passage goes on to describe Lucius' costume in great detail: the colorfully embroidered Indian dragons and Hyperborean gryphons, the torch, the crown with palm leaves arranged like rays of the sun. Thus attired, Lucius becomes the object of ritual gaze: *Sic ad instar Solis exornato me et in vicem simulacri constituto, repente velis reductis in aspectum populus errabat* ('After I had thus been decorated in the likeness of the Sun and set up in the guise of a statue, the curtains were suddenly opened and the people wandered round to view me').[38]

Though Apuleius cannot be considered an unquestionably trustworthy source for ritual knowledge, two key aspects of this passage may provide useful ways to understand the role of dress in the cult. First, Lucius repeatedly connects himself to the *cult image*. Apuleius' language here repeats the term *simulacrum*, indicating that Lucius stands in front of it (presumably obscuring it from view) and stands in the guise of the image (*in vicem simulacri*). Though Lucius is dressed as Sol, not Isis, in this case, it demonstrates the importance of costume to cult practice.[39] In this passage, his human body *elides* with divine sculptural representation. In this account, then, devotees are using the cult image and its costume in tandem with their own bodies as part of the process of joining the cult community. Second, the ritual relies on both othering and the performance of that othering. Lucius' dress is consciously othered by including fantastical beasts, an unusual palm frond hat, and put on display for all to see. The theomorphic costume created a sense of belonging within the group and marked devotees as outside the norm in Greco-Roman society.[40] Though Apuleius' text was produced in the 2nd century CE, long after the *Knotenpalla* type had been adopted across the Mediterranean, this passage reflects the key role that costume played in both the cult's rituals and identification processes. Alongside their ritual functions, these costumes 'pick out Isiac attachments as crucial attributes' for devotees and their families.[41] There is evidence from the mid-to-late Hellenistic period that costumes did form a part of the cult's ritual practice and self-identification. Funerary reliefs depict women in the costume as early as the mid-2nd century BCE in Smyrna, and the well-known corpus of grave reliefs from Athens uses the costume as early as the 1st century BCE.[42] Images using these types of cult-specific dress may have argued for a consistent set of visual identifiers that mark out shared forms of self-identification and understanding, across geographic boundaries. For the Isiac communities of the Hellenistic period, including Isiac dress in their portraiture and

Isis' statues defined and bounded their group and thus contributed to processes of identification and connectedness.

The Early Examples as Evidence of Hellenistic Connectivity

By the end of the Hellenistic period the *Knotenpalla* (as used for Isis) appears in free-standing marble statuettes at three sites in the Mediterranean: the islands of Delos and Rhodes, and the port site of Amphipolis.[43] These examples seem to follow similar precedents, which I argue suggests a close relationship between the cultic communities at all three sites. On Rhodes, two examples of this type have been published. In recent excavations of an Egyptian sanctuary just outside of the city walls of ancient Rhodes Town, a white marble statuette of Isis was found (Fig. 41).[44] Most of the statuette (Rhodes Archaeological Museum Γ2765) is preserved, though the head, shoulders,

Figure 41: Rhodes Archaeological Museum Γ2765. Statuette of Isis in Knotenpalla *costume found in the Egyptian Sanctuary in Rhodes Town (© Ministry of Culture and Sports – Ephorate of Antiquities of the Dodecanese).*

Figure 42: Rhodes Archaeological Museum E 425. Fragmentary statuette of Isis in Knotenpalla *costume (© Ministry of Culture and Sports – Ephorate of Antiquities of the Dodecanese).*

and arms are missing. This type closely follows examples from Delos. The goddess is positioned frontally and stands in a light *contrapposto*, with the weight on the left leg. She wears a chiton with a mantle knotted over the right breast in a variant of the *Knotenpalla* type. The missing arms would have been held free from the body and, based on comparisons with other statuettes from this period, the missing face may have taken a Greek format.[45]

Fantaoutsaki compares this example with another poorly preserved example found in Rhodes, Rhodes Archaeological Museum E 425, that Giorgio Gualandi describes as a liberal interpretation of the same type (Fig. 42).[46] Preserving the torso, hips, and upper legs, the statue depicts a female figure. Her mantle is knotted at the center of her chest, creating an X-pattern, and falls behind the body like a cape. The drapery is rendered carefully, with deep channels cut to create the ruching around the waist. The mantle falls realistically over the hips and thighs to produce not the schematic chevrons seen in many *Knotenpalla* examples, but more naturalistic rendering of the

Figure 43: Delos Archaeological Museum A 2255. Statuette of Isis Fortuna *in* Knotenpalla *costume (École française d'Athènes/Jean Marcadé).*

same drapery folds. Based on artistic style and sculptural technique and comparison with examples from Delos, discussed below, Gualandi dated it to the second half of the 2nd century BCE. Gualandi links the statue stylistically and formally with Delos Archaeological Museum A 2255 and A378 (Figs 43 and 44).[47] All three examples wear similar costumes, featuring a mantle knotted between the breasts over a thin chiton. Most importantly, all exhibit a similar freedom of movement, with a raised right arm and a realistic, vivacious rendering of the upper torso. Another example in white marble, found without context on Rhodes (Rhodes Palace of the Grand Master Γ58) depicts Isis in a variant of the *Knotenpalla*, which indicates further the popularity of this type in Hellenistic Rhodes.[48]

On Delos, the *Knotenpalla* examples can be grouped into three types. The first group includes two examples derived from the Classical Aphrodite of Dafni by Phidias (the Isis *du Cynthe* cult statue on display in the Iseion of Sarapieion C and Delos Museum A2399, a torso of Isis-Aphrodite found in the cistern of the Grand Palestra).[49] The second group consists of three marble *Knotenpalla* statues with a pronounced central fold and gentle chevron folds rendered in an archaicizing style

Figure 44: Delos Archaeological Museum A 378. Statuette of Isis in Knotenpalla *costume (École française d'Athènes).*

(Delos Museum A 5370, A 5302, A5373).[50] The third group consists of two statuettes of Isis-Tyche wearing a *Knotenpalla* variant (Delos Museum A 378, A 2255, which preserves a cornucopia in the right hand).[51] The earliest among these seems to be the statue of Isis *du Cynthe*, which Marcadé dates to the 2nd century BCE based on an epigraphic mention of a stone statue described as κυπαρίττινον in the Iseion in 128/127 BCE,[52] as well as stylistic and technical details (Fig. 45). The statue is carved at an over-life-sized scale and stands inside the Temple to Isis on a statue base at the sanctuary's rear, two factors that suggest it served as a cult image.[53] Though the knot itself is not preserved, indications of chevron folds are preserved above the hip mantle. The rest of the statues, which are produced on a much smaller scale, have been dated on the same evidence more generally to the Hellenistic period or in some cases to the mid-2nd century BCE. There are also terracotta figurines that use this costume. C. Barrett identifies the figurine A 2191 as an example of a *Knotenpalla* type. The partial figurine preserves the hips and torso of Isis or one of her devotees in a knotted, fringed mantle with a black sash running from the left shoulder to

Figure 45: Statue of Isis du Cynthe *in Sarapieion C, Delos (École française d'Athènes/Jean Marcadé).*

the waist.[54] The left leg appears to advance and the right arm may have been lifted, possibly to hold a cult instrument like a sistrum or a torch.[55] The body's position may indicate a more dynamic posture than the stone examples, aligning it more closely with Rhodes Archaeological Museum E 425.

Until Dimitris Damaskos' publication of the sculpture from Amphipolis, now in the Archaeological Museum of Kavala, these island statuettes were the earliest known examples of the type in stone. This example, however, opens up a broader horizon for considering how islands and port cities engaged with each other. Discovered by Dimitris Lazarides in 1957, the white marble statuette preserves only the bottom half of the body (Fig. 46).[56] Broken at the natural waist, the head, arms, feet, and plinth are missing. The statuette stands about 35 cm tall and depicts a female standing in a *contrapposto*, with her weight on the left leg and right leg bent. She wears three distinct pieces of draped clothing. Closest to the skin, the figure wears a thin chiton that flows to the plinth, with delicate drapery folds whose fine texture has been abraded. Over the chiton, she also wears a light mantle that ends just around the ankles. Completing the ensemble is a heavy hip mantle, rolled at the top and draped across her thighs,

Figure 46: Kavala Archaeological Museum Λ 195. Statuette of Isis from Amphipolis (photo by Stefanos Stournaras, © Ephorate of Kavala and Thasos).

that hangs down the left side. Based on stylistic comparison, Damaskos dates the statuette generally to the Hellenistic period.[57]

The Amphipolis Isis statuette is not the only Hellenistic period example of the *Knotenpalla* in Macedonia. A terracotta statuette from the hinterland site of Beroia, which has been dated stylistically to the 1st century CE and, more convincingly, to the 2nd century BCE, also depicts the goddess in the *Knotenpalla* costume (Fig. 47a and b).[58] The statuette is well preserved, and only the left arm is missing. On her head, she wears a large plain diadem over a simple classicizing hairstyle. She wears a heavy mantle, knotted between the breasts, over a chiton that is barely indicated. The drapery folds cascade in a series of chevrons arranged around a central vertical fold that characterize the *Knotenpalla* type.

Figure 47: Archaeological Museum of Veria Π4069. Terracotta figurine of Isis with a diadem and in the Knotenpalla *(© Greek Ministry of Culture and Sports/Ephorate of Antiquities of Imathia).*

Stylistically, the Amphipolis and Beroia examples have little in common. Since the Amphipolis statuette is broken at the waist, it is impossible to determine whether the arms, head, and hair had any connections with the Beroia example. Still, the two statuettes wear distinctly different versions of the Isis costume. The Amphipolis statuette wears a second mantle draped over the hips, while the Beroia example wears only one. Admittedly, some of these differences may result from its medium. While coroplasts and sculptors shared in a mutual artistic tradition, their materials required different techniques and often produced different forms. Still, the connections between the Amphipolis and Beroia statuettes are minimal and largely superficial. If we compare the Beroia statuette with another terracotta figurine, however, the division persists. Delos Museum A 2191, which preserves part of a *Knotenpalla* figure, renders the body in a much more dynamic fashion and seems to have included several attributes that are missing from the Beroia statuette. Notably, the statuette also preserves a black sash, which may refer to a particular priesthood called the *melanophor* known from Isiac epigraphy and connected with the wearing of black garments.[59] Again, any connections between the Delian and Beroia figurines seem to be general, referring to basic participation in the same cult, rather than connections to any specific group or strain of that religious practice.

Instead of grouping the Amphipolis statuette with the Beroia statuette by virtue of geographic distance, I argue that stylistic and iconographic issues would have been more relevant to ancient devotees because these images operated as a method of creating and identifying with a trans-Mediterranean community of Isis devotees. As Damaskos noted, the best comparanda for the Amphipolis statuette comes from Hellenistic Delos: the cult image of Isis *du Cynthe* from Sarapieion C on Delos, dated on stylistic and technical grounds to the 2nd century BCE. The Isis *du Cynthe* and the Amphipolis Isis statuette wear a highly unusual third garment (a hip mantle), which highlights the importance of this connection.[60] There are further similarities. Like the Amphipolis statuette, the Delian example depicts the goddess standing in a *contrapposto* stance, with a thin, knotted mantle underneath a heavier one draped across the hips and thighs.[61] Despite the Isis *du Cynthe*'s abraded surface, we can still observe the remains of a thick, vertical center fold and flanking chevron folds, suggesting a similar knotted mantle pattern once characterized this image.

The iconographic, formal, and stylistic similarities between these two statues suggest that the Hellenistic-period Amphipolitan Isis community looked outward to the Aegean for its Isiac prototypes. Unlike the Beroia figurine, whose *Knotenpalla* costume displays significant differences from that of the Amphipolis example, the Delian statue and the Amphipolis statuette wear the same format of Isis' *Knotenpalla* costume. Similarly, the connections between the Rhodian statues, particularly Rhodes Archaeological Museum E 425 (Fig. 42) and Delos A 378 (Fig. 44), suggest a similar form of artistic connection between those two Isiac communities.[62] This commonality may suggest knowledge of a similar prototype or a shared group of artisans operating in these cities,[63] which gives some indication of an interest in creating a common version of Isis. More importantly, it may allude to the existence of a shared social and possibly religious community that spanned large geographic distances.

A Migrating Image? The Hellenistic Knotenpalla *in its Historical Context*

There are social and historical factors that suggest a further connection between Isiac communities in island and mainland port cities, particularly between Delos and Macedonia. Several scholars have suggested that Mithradates IV's 88 BCE sack of the island and Athenodorus the pirate's sack in 69 BCE prompted most Delians to abandon the island in the early to mid-1st century BCE.[64] As Rebecca Sweetman discusses in her contribution to this volume, these upheavals caused a Delian diaspora across the Mediterranean in the late Hellenistic and early Roman periods. Italian families and communities appear in Macedonia's epigraphy as early as the mid-2nd century BCE, though they do not appear in significant numbers until the 1st century BCE.[65] Based on his survey of epigraphy in the region, Athanasios Rizakis demonstrated that most *negotiatores*, a frequent term used to refer to Italian merchants on Delos and around the Mediterranean, immigrated to Amphipolis and Thessaloniki, the region's two largest port cities, and may have been responsible for introducing Isiac cult to the region.[66]

Tracing this diffusion, Paraskevi Martzavou has argued that several Delian families involved in Isiac cult made their way to Thessaloniki and other Macedonian cities from the 1st century BCE onwards.[67] Most relevant among these are two inscriptions that provide clear socio-historical and ritual links between Amphipolis and Delos. These are primarily references to the *Anthestii*, a large family attested throughout the empire, including at Rome, Pompeii, the Aegean islands, and much of imperial-period Greece, whose Macedonian branch has been identified as *negotiatores*.[68] The first is a marble stele commemorating a crown awarded in 67/66 BCE to Aulus Anthestius for his excellence as a trierarch.[69] R. Veymiers has argued that Aulus Anthestius must be a member of the Anthestii. An epigraph of one Markia Anthestia, believed to be a member of the Anthestii clan, was found in Delos' Sarapieion C, the same sanctuary where the cult image of Isis *du Cynthe* stood, and dates to the end of the 2nd century BCE.[70] Later, a series of inscriptions at the Roman colony of Dion names many generations of this same clan that suggest the family arrived in Macedonia, perhaps as freedmen, as early as the Late Republican period. Several of these inscriptions were found in the 2nd–3rd-century CE Iseum.[71] A second inscription from Amphipolis (on a small marble column of the 1st to 2nd centuries CE) includes dedications to the *synnaoi theoi* and *synbomoi theoi*. These terms are not exclusive to Egyptian cults, but they do appear in Isiac epigraphy at Delos and in cultic communities that Martzavou has linked with the Isiac diaspora, particularly Thessaloniki and Eretria, with some frequency.[72]

We can thus hypothesize the movement of at least a small number of Isiac devotees from Delos to Amphipolis during the mid-1st century BCE. While many traders lived mobile lives in the Hellenistic and Roman Mediterranean, generally following the expansion of the empire and its growing trade networks, migration across cultures tends to move in patterns. Scholars of migration often speak of 'push' and 'pull' factors that help shape migration. In many cases, migrants forced from their homes move to regions where they have familial or social ties. Indeed, the presence of other members of an ethnic or social group tends to 'pull' other members towards that region in a phenomenon that David Anthony has described as chain migration.[73] In a recent book, Laurens Tacoma remarks on the supposed 'permanence' of these Italian merchant communities, suggesting that they moved together and saw themselves as a group even when moving across the empire.[74] In the case of the Anthestii, who are our best link between Delos and the cult's early history in Amphipolis, they may have been drawn not only by their familial ties to Macedonia, but also by the mass migration of their Delian community to the region.

These Delian emigrants may have brought their versions of Isiac material culture with them as part of their cult practice. The close stylistic connections between the Amphipolis statuette and the Delian examples, particularly the Isis *du Cynthe* displayed in Sarapieion C, reconcile well with the broader historical connectivity between the two sites. The Amphipolis statuette cannot be an import. Made in local marble and carved with local techniques, the statuette must be a Macedonian product.[75] The stylistic and formal similarities may be indicative of an allusion to the cult community's origins. Perhaps the city's Isis devotees, including those who emigrated from Delos and other island communities, asked sculptors to reproduce an image of their beloved cult statue for a new locale.[76]

It would be too simplistic to assume a neat, uni-directional form of transmission from Delos to Amphipolis. First, because all of the statues described above can only be dated based on relative stylistic criteria, it has been difficult for scholars to date them more precisely than to the later 2nd century BCE.[77] Most of the Delian examples are dated to the end of the 2nd century in no small part because that period marks the apogee of Delian sculptural activity. Most of the Rhodian examples are dated to the same period based on comparison with the Delian sculptures. Recognizing this pattern, Damaskos dates the Amphipolis statuette to the Hellenistic period more generally. It is possible that these dates are correct, but it is also plausible that these types were used on Delos into the mid-1st century BCE as the cults continued to flourish. For example, the *sphinxallée* and most of the South Terrace of Sarapieion C, the same sanctuary where the Isis *du Cynthe* statue stood, was not constructed until about 90 BCE. This late date indicates the cult was still actively engaged in construction and sculptural dedication and that the sanctuary's cult sculpture continued to be used into the 1st century BCE.[78]

Second, the variegated aesthetic, historical, and religious connections between the three sites gesture to a complex, multi-faceted form of community. The statuettes produced on Delos and Rhodes and at Amphipolis as well might have been a general format available for use and reinterpretation across the eastern Mediterranean, part of a religious community that became increasingly deracinated as historical and economic factors forced its spread across the region. Using this statue type to depict Isis, I argue, was part of a broader identification process, a way to claim membership in a cultic community that crisscrossed the eastern Mediterranean and followed broader patterns of insular connectivity and movement in the Hellenistic world. Thus, while it is tempting to see the Amphipolis statuette as an adaptation of a popular Delian cult image, I would argue that the connections instead demonstrate the possibility of shared innovation and religious movement in a period of increasing mobility and space-time compression that characterizes Hellenistic globalization.

Conclusions: Statues, Ports, and Globalization

What, then, do these stylistic connections have to tell us about insular networks of connectivity in the age of globalization? The close connection between the Amphipolitan and Delian examples may indicate some important aspects of how port cities like Amphipolis interacted with and participated in island networks. As globalization intensified, certain groups of people moved further abroad at more rapid paces, finding new homes and bringing aspects of religion and culture from their previous homes. In the case of Hellenistic-period Isis devotees, these groups seemed to cluster in islands and port cities, but the connection with hinterlands is more complex. In the case of the early *Knotenpalla* examples in Macedonia, the distinction between the Amphipolis and Beroia examples clarifies this issue. While the Amphipolis example demonstrates a clear engagement with island models and communities, the Beroia example, produced during the height of Isiac cult practice on Delos, diverges. Epigraphically, there is no connection to Delos. Though the earliest evidence for Roman communities in Macedonia does come from Beroia,[79] there is no evidence that would link the Isis community of Beroia with that of an island community. Rather, it seems that the port community of Amphipolis and the inland community of Beroia used two different forms of cult image. Based on the material and epigraphic evidence, then, I argue that these communities participated in different social and geographic networks.

In later periods, land-based regional connections are easier to see in the historical record.[80] The Anthestii, for example, dedicate frequently in sites around Macedonia, particularly the Iseum at the Roman colony of Dion, located at the foot of Mount Olympus.[81] A 2nd-century CE dedication to the Egyptian sphinx god Tutu was found at Amphipolis and echoes a small imported statuette of the same god found in the Sarapeum at Thessaloniki, a pattern that suggests a regional preference for particular Egyptian deities not seen elsewhere.[82] If we look at the distribution of this type by the end of the 1st century CE, the *Knotenpalla* appears in a variety of forms all across the Mediterranean, a veritable explosion of popularity that makes it nearly impossible to tease out the strands of discrete Isiac cult communities, networks, and material cultures from sculpture alone. These differences gesture towards a more intensive form of globalization in the Roman period, one in which cultural forms are deeply deterritorialized and universalized, and penetrate deeper into the Mediterranean's hinterlands, but also promote a different kind of regionalism.[83]

For the Hellenistic period, however, the stylistic contrast between Amphipolis and Beroia suggests that geographic space is not always experienced objectively. Even though ports like Amphipolis and islands like Rhodes and Delos are far apart in the ways that we measure distance today, premodern people experienced maritime connectivity in a different way. Sailing collapsed the human experience of time and distance, making islands seem closer than they were.[84] In contrast, the mountainous and heavily wooded topography of Macedonia would have made east–west travel more challenging, difficult, and expensive, especially prior to the construction of the Via Egnatia in the 2nd century BCE. Even after the road was constructed, Beroia still lies about 46 km to the south of this major Roman artery. If we use Walter Scheidel's ORBIS database, we can calculate the relative speed of traveling between Amphipolis and Pella, the Macedonian city in the ORBIS database closest to Beroia.[85] Using the Via Egnatia, the journey would take 4.6 days. If they traveled by sea, sailing around the Chacidike peninsula, travelers could complete their journey in only 3.9 days. On the other hand, a sea journey from Amphipolis to Delos would take only 5 days, including stops in Selinous and Thessaloniki, and a journey to Rhodes would take 5.1 days and include stops at Hephaistia, Mytiline, Chios, and Ephesus. Amphipolitans thus experienced no significant difference in travel time between sites like Rhodes and Beroia.[86] Sea travel made islands seem not as far off and challenges recent scholarly emphasis on the importance of studying land-based regionality as a major part of identity. In the case of Isiac material culture of the Hellenistic period, Amphipolitans may have sought to identify themselves as part of a trans-Mediterranean network rather than (or perhaps in addition to) a Macedonian one.

Though its insistence on self-othering as part of community identity formation makes Isis devotee groups easier to spot in the epigraphic and archaeological record, Egyptian cult was just one part of this movement. This case study helps us reposition ports as parts of island networks and see the shores of the Mediterranean more clearly as part of seascapes. There may be many different ways in which ports embed themselves in material and social networks that span large geographic areas. As we continue our study of Mediterranean globalization, it is imperative that we turn off our own perceptions of geographic space. Though modern mapping and GIS feels objective, it can also obscure our understanding of how ancient peoples experienced time and space. Rather, future research should attempt to reconstruct ancient perceptions of both landscapes and seascapes in order to better access key questions of identity and self-location.

Notes

* Research in support of this chapter was funded by the Faculty of Humanities and Social Sciences at the Memorial University of Newfoundland. Thanks to Richard Veymiers and Laurent Bricault who inspired me to begin this project, and to Dimitri Damaskos, Noah Eber-Schmid, Vicky Hioureas, Alicia Hayashi Lazzarini, and Stephanie Pearson for their help in preparing the manuscript. Special thanks to the editors and reviewers for including me in the volume and providing helpful and incisive suggestions that improved the manuscript.

1 The costume has its roots in pharaonic Egyptian art and in earlier periods could be used to represent other goddesses, including Hathor. By the Hellenistic period, however, it came to be used primarily by Isis and is deeply associated with her in Greek sculpture. It is not clear if Greek audiences would have associated the costume with earlier pharaonic precedents or if they saw the costume as Isis' alone, though scholarly opinion in recent years has tended towards the latter. See Bianchi 1980; Eingartner 1991, 8–32; Malaise 1992; Nagel 2015; Albersmeier 2018.

2 Several scholars have argued that Isiac cult exemplifies globalization under the Roman Empire, and as such I will not treat this issue in detail here. See Woolf 2014; Versluys 2015.

3 Here, I rely on Benedict Anderson's idea of the imagined community, which refers to the connection of peoples across broad spans of time and space without direct or daily contact: Anderson 1991, 6.

4 Mazurek 2016.

5 Scholars of insularity have defined islands in many ways, a topic discussed in this volume's introduction.

6 Braudel 1972, 149; Constantakopoulou 2007, 3; Knapp 2007.

7 Braudel 1972, 161; Horden and Purcell 2000, 22–25; Bresson 2005, 99–100; Constantakopoulou 2007, 2–6, 12–25; Rainbird 2007, 1–25; Broodbank 2013, 67.

8 On the network approach to Mediterranean connectivity, especially regarding religion, see Rutherford 2007; Malkin 2011; Collar 2013; Woolf 2016.

9 Braudel 1972, 108.

10 Purcell 2005, 13–16.

11 The port, in my reckoning, has some characteristics in common with the gateway city, particularly in its role as a facilitator and restrictor of relationships and its reliance on transportation for its character. The port, however, need not be separated from its hinterland. For some discussion of the gateway, see Burghardt 1971. On sailor and port cultures, see Reger 2016.

12 Butler 2001, 211. For case studies of this phenomenon from multiple periods, see Constable 2003, 2–39; Bresson 2005; Kravaritou 2016, 128–151; Reger 2016, 20–22.

13 See, for example, Van Pelt Campbell 2007, 287–89; Beck and Sznaider 2015, 577.

14 Jennings 2011, 129–141.

15 Versluys 2015, 142–144. This attitude plays a prominent role in general handbooks on the material culture of the era, appearing in the introductions of works like Pollitt 1986; Smith 1991.

16 For example, shipwrecks off the coast of Massalia, most of which carried cargoes of over 10,000 amphorae, significantly increased during the 2nd and 1st centuries BCE: Geraghty 2007, 1046; Dietler 2010, 134–38; Rauh, Dillon and McClain 2008, 223.

17 See the essays in Payne, Levan and Weisweiler 2016. In particular, the models of local relationships with cosmopolitan imperial power are best described in Fischer-Bouvet 2016, 106–109.

18 See the definition and discussion in MacDonald *et al.* 2017.

19 Rainbird 2007, 51.

20 Xen. *Ways and Means*, Book III. Interestingly, Xenophon argues to the Council of 500 that his approaches could relieve the need for a large Athenian empire.

21 Billows 2008, 212.

22 Phil. *Life of Apoll.* 6.12.3. I thank Emilia Mataix Ferrandiz for highlighting this point and sharing these citations with me.

23 Morely 2007, 59–77. See further Arist. *Pol.* 7.5.4–5, Plato, *Leg.* 705a. On attempts to restrict sailors to specific areas of ports and prevent their entry into cities, see Reger 2016, 19–23.

24 In a study of the itinerant maritime class of the Hellenistic period, Rauh, Dillon, and McClain have argued that sailors on Delos would have been restricted to specific neighborhoods and brothels around the island's northern shore: Rauh *et al.*, 197–208.

25 We might consider here the cognate concept of *peraiai*, in which island states control a small part of land on the mainland. Though most of Constantakopoulou's examples date to the Classical period, Samos continued to possess a *peraia* into the Hellenistic and Roman period (*IG* XII.1 694 = *Syll*[3] 339). See, with bibliography, Constantakopoulou 2007, 243–245.

26 Isis and Sarapis are frequently worshipped as a triad. According to epigraphic evidence, the third member is Anubis and Harpokrates most frequently, but in a few examples the third can be Bubastis, Osiris, Thermouthis, Tutu, or Bes. On the worship of Isis and Sarapis in Egypt during the Hellenistic and Roman period, see the essays in Bricault and Versluys 2010.

27 It is unclear whether these priests were acting as missionaries, migrated for religious or political reasons, or if they knew about each other. On the spread and transmission of the cults, see Dunand 2000, 67–70; Bricault 2004; Woolf 2014, 51–52; Moyer 2017.

28 Regarding the architecture of Egyptian sanctuaries in the Greco-Roman world, see Kleibl 2009.

29 On the ethnic makeup of Hellenistic Isiac devotee communities, see Martzavou 2010; 2011; Price 2012, 9–12; *contra* Baslez 1977, 35–49.

30 Nielson 2002, 212–236.

31 Our best evidence for these practices comes from Apuleius' descriptions in the *Metamorphoses*, though scholars are divided on the appropriateness of Apuleius as a source for religious rituals. Some scholars have argued that the novel, and in particular Book XI, which describes Lucius' encounters with Isiac cults, is entirely fictional or metaphorical: Winkler 1985, 219–227; Harrison 2012; Tilg 2014, 84–130. I side with those who think the book represents a more serious, but still literary, attempt to represent Isiac cults: Merkelbach 1962; Griffiths 1975; Martzavou 2012.

Ultimately, since there is no comparable source, Apuleius' veracity is a matter of scholarly opinion: Pfeiffer 2018.

32 Nagel 2015; Mylonopoulos 2016, 164–166.

33 Plantzos 2011, 392–396.

34 Nagel 2015.

35 Brubaker 2004, 28–63.

36 Ibid. Though he uses the language of the modern concept of 'self', Brubaker's concept does not rely explicitly on the idea of an individualized self (34). Instead, he proposes a flexible version of the self that can extend beyond the individual to the communal.

37 *Met.* XI.24, trans. Hanson 1989.

38 Ibid.

39 Theomorphic dress plays a key role in rituals in many religious rites, including other 'mystery' cults. See Connelly 2007, 85–115; Gawlinski 2008, 150–61; Platt 2011, 13–14.

40 Isiac rituals often included processions of devotees in strange dress and holding unusual ritual objects, including the *Navigium Isidis* (perhaps described in Apul. *Met.* XI, 5–6) and the *Isea*. See Alvar 2008, 296–303. On the creation of commonality, see Brubaker 2004, 47–50.

41 Beard, North and Price 1998, 309.

42 Based on the ideas of group formation and symbolism outlined in Brubaker 2004. The examples from Smyrna are Ashmolean Museum inv. G 1171, dated to the end of the 2nd–beginning of the 1st century BCE, Pfuhl and Möbius 1977, cat. 878, pl. 131; Walters 1988, pl. 1c. The second is British Museum inv. SC. 639, dated to the beginning of the 2nd century BCE, Pfuhl and Möbius 1977, no. 376, pl. 61; Walters 1988, pl. 1b; Eingartner 1991, no. 98, pl. LXII, 98. The Athenian reliefs have been published in Walters 1988. Malaise and Veymiers (2018, 470–508) have recently reassessed the Athenian corpus in terms of identification.

43 No Hellenistic marble statuette in the *Knotenpalla* costume has been found elsewhere in mainland Greece. In Egypt, this costume does not belong to Isis alone. Knotted costumes are used in representations of other Egyptian deities, particularly Hathor, and in representations of Ptolemaic queens. This material is outside the scope of my inquiry, but see Albersmaier 2002; Ashton 2010, 970–990.

44 Rhodes Museum Γ2765. Fantaoutsaki 2011, 56, fig. 13.

45 Tran Tam Tinh 1990, 791. Fantaoutsaki also compares this example to one from Cyrene: Cyrene Inv. 14.274, published in Paribeni 1959, 143, no. 412, pl. 180. Paribeni does not date the statue, but stylistically it seems to have much in common with Delian images produced during the mid to late Hellenistic period.

46 Rhodes Archaeological Museum E425. 18.5 cm tall. Gualandi 1976, no. 160, fig. 199.

47 Ibid., 166.

48 This piece has not been published, but I viewed it on display in the Palace of the Grand Master in April 2014. The statue depicts a female figure dressed in a chiton, a mantle knotted over the right breast, and another mantle draped diagonally over the hips and follows the triangular knot shape seen in the Cyrene example. Museum displays date this object to the 2nd century BCE, though I believe the high level of finish and fine details in the carving of the drapery makes a later date, perhaps into the early 1st century BCE, possible.

49 Preserved height of A 2399: 28 cm. Findspot reconstructed from ephoreia records. Marcadé 1969, 228 n. 4.

50 Ibid., 432, pl. 57.

51 Discussed as a typological group in Marcadé 1969.

52 *ID* 1442, A, 52 and 56.

53 In addition to its findspot, there is an indication of the *Knotenpalla*'s characteristic chevron folds visible just above the hip mantle in the Isis *du Cynthe*. On common features of Hellenistic cult statues, see Mylonopoulos 2016, 119–126.

54 Barrett 2011, 143–146.
55 Laumonier 1956, 14; Barrett 2011, 146. Barrett also describes an unpublished fragmentary figurine depicting a female torso with a knot from the 2008 excavations of the Aphrodision on Delos.
56 Damaskos 2013, cat. 95. The precise location of the Konstantinides plot, where the statuette was found, is not known: Damaskos, pers. comm. 6/17.
57 It is not clear how any of these statues were used, though it is not unlikely that they served as votives or cult images in sanctuaries. None of the Delian examples has a good archaeological context, and the same is true for the Amphipolis statuette, the Beroia figurine, and most of the Rhodian statuettes. One of the Rhodian statuettes, Rhodes Archaeological Museum Γ2765, was found in a water-crypt along with several other pieces of Egyptian and Egyptianizing sculpture in the Sanctuary of the Egyptian Gods outside of Rhodes Town (Fantaoutsaki 2011). It is unclear, however, if that deposit represents a primary use context or a later secondary deposition.
58 Tzanavari 1993, 1671–1676, fig. 2. Tzanavari ultimately concludes that the 2nd century BCE date is more convincing based on stylistic parallels with Delian marble statuettes, particularly Delos Archaeological Museum inv. A 2255 (fig. 5). Terracotta figurines appear much more frequently in Hellenistic sanctuaries of Egyptian deities (*cf.* the large corpus defined in Barrett 2011), though that prevalence could stem from postdepositional processes or the increased scholarly attention to coroplastic material in the Hellenistic period.
59 The figurine may depict a *melanophor* priest. These priests are epigraphically and visually attested back to the mid-2nd century BCE. On the melanophor costume, see Eingartner 1991, 60–80. A mid-2nd-century BCE relief from Thessaloniki, dedicated to Osiris μύστει by Demetrios in honor of his parents depicts a man in *melanophor* costume. *IG* X, 2, 107; Despinis, Stefanidou-Tiveriou and Voutiras 1997–2010, cat. 67. Figurines are not frequently associated with portraiture, however, and Barrett's study of Egyptianizing figurines on Delos only features one category associated with mortals (the generalized representations of Nubians that serve as part of the goddess' entourage): Barrett 2011, 262–274.
60 The statuette's iconography and drapery also have much in common with the statuette Delos Museum A2399. Because that object was found in a secondary deposition context, I will focus on the Isis *du Cynthe*.
61 Statue of Isis *du Cynthe*, standing *in situ* in Sarapieion C. About 2.5 m tall. See Marcadé 1969, pl. LVII; 1996, cat. no. 30. Marcadé dates the statue on the basis of its dedicatory inscription (*ID* 2044) to 128/127 BCE, but Damaskos argues for a date of 129/128 BCE: Damaskos 1999, 99 n. 157.
62 These connections are solidified further by the statue of Sarapis found in Rhodes' Egyptian Sanctuary (Rhodes Archaeological Museum Γ2772) and a similar statue found in Delos' Sarapieion B (Delos Archaeological Museum A 1990+ A 2003; Marcadé 1969, 427–428, pl. LVIII). See Fantaoutsaki 2011, 56–57.
63 Marcadé 1969, 429–430.
64 There is some evidence that Romans continued to inhabit the island after these wars, but the archaeological evidence makes it difficult to argue against a significant population contraction in this period. See Bruneau 1968, 633–708; Ferrary 1980.
65 Rizakis 2002, 110–114. Italian communities appear earlier in Thessaly and Epiros.
66 Ibid., 109–112.
67 Martzavou 2010, 184–190, relying particularly on *IG* X 2 1, 32; Bricault 2005, cat. 113/0538. On the contested dating of *IG* 2 1, 32, which seems to be roughly around the early years of the Principate, see ibid., n. 24. See also *SEG* 46, 812, published more extensively in Velenis 1996. Based on onomastic evidence, it seems that most of these Delians were of Italian origin and included mostly tradesmen and freedmen.

68 The family is quite large. They are attested at many sites throughout Greece, usually in small quantities (at Dion, Beroia, Thessaloniki, Heraclea Lyncestis, Styberra, Delos, Corinth, Lakonia, the Argolid, Arcadia, and Eleia). There are 164 mentions of *Anthestii* at Rome, 29 mentions in southern Italy, and a total of more than 240 mentions around the Mediterranean. For these references, see Demaille 2008, 193–198.

69 Amphipolis Archaeological Museum L 1165. Veymiers 2009, 485–487, fig. 8. Rizakis has argued that the Anthestii of Dion were descendents of Italian merchants that settled in the region during the Republican era, and it is possible their relatives included Anthestii at other Macedonian cities. See Rizakis 2003, 120 n. 44; Bricault and Versluys 2014, 20–21.

70 *EAD* XXX, no. 64.

71 Bricault 2005, cat. 113/0207–0212. The dating of these inscriptions, particularly those in the Iseum, is problematic, though, based on the archaeology of the site, it seems most likely to me that those inscriptions would have been carved in final form after the sanctuary's renovation c. 200 CE. See Demaille 2008, 198–201. Others have argued for a 1st-century BCE–1st-century CE date for these inscriptions, including Rizakis 1998, 604. This earlier date would support a stronger link between the movement of *negotiatores* from Delos into Macedonia during the 1st century BCE.

72 Amphipolis Museum 1070, Veymiers 2009, 497. From Delos: *IG* 11 4, no. 1223 (196 BCE), *ID* 2146 (127/126 BCE), *ID* 2128 (105/104 BCE), *ID* 2157 (105/104 BCE?), *ID* 2131 (after 140 BCE), *ID* 2387 (a little after 166 BCE). From Eretria: *IG* 12 Suppl., no. 565 (1st century BCE). From Thessaloniki: *IG* 10 2, no. 85 (15/14 BCE), *IG* 10 2, no. 88 (1st century CE). On *synnaoi theoi* in other cults as early as the 5th century BCE, see Lamont 2015, 37–50.

73 Anthony 1997, 26–27.

74 Tacoma 2016, 43–45. See also the discussion of mariner communities in Rainbird 2007, 49–53.

75 Damaskos 2013, cat. 95.

76 Based on the local stone and style of carving, it is unlikely but not impossible that the Amphipolis statuette was made by a migrant sculptor.

77 I date the statuette to the mid-2nd through 1st century BCE in Mazurek 2020.

78 Siard 2003, 193–197; 2009, 155–161.

79 A group of ἐγκεκτημένοι Ῥωμαῖοι, along with the rest of the city, honored the Roman governor L. Calpurnius Piso in 57–55 BCE. See Rizakis 2002, 116, n. 26, with accompanying bibliography. The Anthestii are attested in an unpublished inscription from Beroia dated to the 2nd–3rd centuries CE. The inscription was found in the sanctuary of Leukopetra and names a priest of the sanctuary of *Mater Deorum Autochthonous* with the *nomen* of Athestios. See Demaille 2008, 193, n. 41. The Anthestii are also attested in Thessaloniki two inscriptions: *IG* 10 2, 1.545 and *IG* 10 2, 1.170, both of which date to the 2nd or 3rd century CE.

80 Veymiers 2009, 510–511.

81 Demaille 2008.

82 Veymiers 2009, 498–501, with accompanying bibliography. The Amphipolis relief now stands in the Museum of Fine Arts in Budapest (inv. 50.958), and the Thessaloniki statuette is in the Thessaloniki Archaeological Museum: Despinis, Stefanidou-Tiveriou and Voutiras 1997–2010, cat. 46.

83 Versluys 2015, 152–165; Pitts and Versluys 2015.

84 Rainbird 2007, 57–62; Jennings 2011, 123. See also Francis' chapter in this volume.

85 Meeks and Scheidel 2012. I use Pella as a stand-in, assuming that travelers along the Via Egnatia would have roughly traveled an additional 46 km along a minor road, as defined and described by Talbert 2000, map 50. It is worth noting that the ORBIS database relies primarily on evidence from later periods of ancient history, particularly late Roman price edicts.

86 Jennings 2011, 123–125.

Ancient Sources

Apuleius, *Metamorphoses*
Philostratus, *Life of Apollonius of Tyre*
Xenophon, *Ways and Means*

Bibliography

Albersmaier, S. (2002) *Untersuchungen zu den Frauenstatuen des ptolemäischen Ägypten*, Aegyptiaca Treversnia. Mainz: von Zabern.

Albersmeier, S. (2018) The Garments of the Devotees of Isis. In *Individuals and Materials in the Greco-Roman Cult of Isis. Agents, Images, and Practices*, edited by V. Gasparini and R. Veymiers. Leiden: Brill, 448–469.

Alvar, J. (2008) *Romanising Oriental Gods: Myth, Salvation and Ethics in the Cults of Cybele, Isis and Mithras.* Translated by R. Gordon. Leiden: Brill.

Anderson, B. (1991) *Imagined Communities: Reflections on the Origin and Spread of Nationalism.* Verso: New York.

Anthony, D. (1997) Prehistoric Migration as Social Process. In *Migrations and Invasions in Archaeological Explanation* (British Archaeological Reports S664), edited by J. Chapman and H. Hamerow. Oxford: Archaeopress, 21–32.

Ashton, S.A. (2010) Ptolemaic and Romano-Egyptian Sculpture. In *A Companion to Ancient Egypt*, edited by A.B. Lloyd. Malden, MA: Blackwell, 970–990.

Barrett, C. (2011) *Egyptianizing Figurines from Delos*, Columbia Studies in the Classical Tradition 36. Leiden: Brill.

Baslez, M.F. (1977) *Recherches sur les conditions de pénétration et de diffusion des religions orientales à délos, IIe-Ier s. avant notre ère.* Paris: De Boccard.

Beard, M., North, J. and Price, S. (1998) *Religions of Rome. Volume I: A History.* Cambridge: Cambridge University Press.

Beck, U. and Sznaider, N. (2015) New Cosmopolitanism in the Social Sciences. In *The Routledge International Handbook of Globalization Studies*, edited by R.J. Holton and B.S. Turner. New York: Routledge, 572–588.

Bianchi, R.S. (1980) Not the Isis Knot. *Bulletin of the Egyptological Seminar* 2, 9–31.

Billows, R. (2008) Cities. In *A Companion to the Hellenistic World*, edited by A. Erskine. Malden, MA: Blackwell, 196–215.

Braudel, F. (1972) *The Mediterranean and the Mediterranean World in the Age of Philip II.* Translated by S. Reynolds. New York: Harper & Row.

Bresson, A. (2005) Ecology and Beyond: the Mediterranean Paradigm. In *Rethinking the Mediterranean*, edited by W.V. Harris. Oxford: Oxford University Press, 94–114.

Bricault, L. (2004) La diffusion isiaque: une esquisse. In *Fremdheit-Eigenheit: Ägypten, Griechenland und Röm, Austausch und Verständnis*, Städel-Jahrbuch, edited by G. Kaminski, P.C. Bol and C. Maderna. Munich: Prestel, 548–556.

Bricault, L. (2005) *Recueil des inscriptions concernant les cultes isiaques: RICIS.* Mémoires de l'Académie des inscriptions et belles-lettres. 3 vols. Paris: De Boccard.

Bricault, L. and Versluys, M.J. (2014) Isis and Empires. In *Power, Politics and the Cults of Isis. Proceedings of the Vth International Conference of Isis Studies, Boulogne-Sur-Mer, October 13–15, 2011*, edited by L. Bricault and M.J. Versluys. Leiden: Brill, 3–35.

Bricault, L. and Versluys, M.J. (eds) (2014) *Power, Politics and the Cults of Isis. Proceedings of the Vth International Conference of Isis Studies, Boulogne-sur-Mer, October 13–15, 2011.* Leiden: Brill.

Broodbank, C. (2013) *The Making of the Middle Sea: A History of the Mediterranean from the Beginning to the Emergence of the Classical World.* London: Thames & Hudson.

Brubaker, R. (2004) *Ethnicity without Groups.* Cambridge, MA: Harvard University Press.

Bruneau, P. (1968) Contribution à l'histoire urbaine de Délos à l'époque hellénistique et à l'époque impériale. *Bulletin de Correspondance Hellénique*, 92(2), 633–708.

Burghardt, A.F. (1971) A Hypothesis About Gateway Cities. *Annals of the Association of American Geographers* 61(2), 269–285.

Butler, K.D. (2001) Defining Diaspora, Refining a Discourse. *Diaspora* 10(2), 189–219.

Collar, A. (2013) *Religious Networks in the Roman Empire: the Spread of New Ideas.* Cambridge: Cambridge University Press.

Connelly, J.B. (2007) *Portrait of a Priestess: Women and Ritual in Ancient Greece.* Princeton, NJ: Princeton University Press.

Constable, O.R. (2003) *Housing the Stranger in the Mediterranean World. Lodging, Trade, and Travel in Late Antiquity and the Middle Ages.* Cambridge: Cambridge University Press.

Constantakopoulou, C. (2007) *The Dance of the Islands: Insularity, Networks, the Athenian Empire and the Aegean World*, Oxford Classical Monographs. Oxford: Oxford University Press.

Damaskos, D. (1999) *Untersuchungen zu hellenistichen Kultbildern.* Stuttgart: Franz Steiner Verlag.

Damaskos, D. (2013) *Κατάλογος γλυπτών του Αρχαιολογικού Μουσείου Καβάλας.* Thessaloniki: Archaeological Institute of Macedonian and Thracian Studies.

Decourt, J.-C. and Tziafalis, A. (2007) Cultes et divinités isiaques en Thessalie: identité et urbanisation. In *Nile into Tiber: Egypt in the Roman World*, edited by L. Bricault, M.J. Versluys and P.G.P Meybook. Leiden: Brill, 329–363.

Demaille, J. (2008) Les *P. Anthestii*: une famille d'affranchis dans l'élite municipale de la colonie romaine de Dion. In *La fin du statut servile? Affranchissement, libération, abolition. Volume I. Besançon 15–17 Décembre 2005*, Actes des colloques du Groupe de recherche sur l'esclavage dans l'antiquité 30-1, edited by J. Annequin and M. Garrido-Hory. Besançon: Presses Universitaires de Franche-Comté, 285–302.

Despinis, G., Stefanidou-Tiveriou, T. and Voutiras, E. (1997–2010) *Catalogue of Sculpture in the Archaeological Museum of Thessaloniki*, 3 vols. Thessaloniki: National Bank Cultural Foundation.

Dietler, M. (2010) *Archaeologies of Colonialism: Consumption, Entanglement, and Violence in Ancient Mediterranean France.* Berkeley: University of California Press.

Dunand, F. (2000) *Isis, mère des dieux.* Paris: Errance.

Egelhaaf-Gaiser, U. (2000) *Kulträume im römischen Alltag: Das Isisbuch des Apuleius und der Ort von Religion im kaiserzeitlichen Rom.* Stuttgart: Franz Steiner Verlag.

Eingartner, J. (1991) *Isis und ihre Dienerinnen in der Kunst der römischen Kaiserzeit.* Mnemosyne Supplement 115. Leiden: Brill.

Fantaoutsaki, C. (2011) Preliminary Report on the Excavation of the Sanctuary of Isis in Ancient Rhodes: Identification, Topography, and Finds. In *Bibliotheca Isiaca II*, edited by L. Bricault and R. Veymiers. Bordeaux: Éditions Ausonius, 47–64.

Ferrary, J.-L. (1980) Délos vers 58 a.C. In *Insula Sacra: la loi Gabinia-Calpurnia de Délos (58 a.C.)*, Collection de l'École française de Rome 45, edited by C. Nicolet. Rome: École française de Rome, 35–44.

Finkelpearl, E. (1998) *Metamorphosis of Language in Apuleius: a Study of Allusion in the Novel.* Ann Arbor, MI: University of Michigan Press.

Fischer-Bouvet, C. (2016) Toward a Translocal Elite Culture in the Ptolemaic Empire. In *Cosmopolitanism and Empire: Universal Rulers, Local Elites, and Cultural Integration in the Ancient near East and Mediterranean*, edited by R.E. Payne, M. Levan and J. Weisweiler. Oxford: Oxford University Press, 103–129.

Gawlinski, L. (2008) 'Fashioning' Initiates: Dress at the Mysteries. In *Reading a Dynamic Canvas: Adornment in the Ancient Mediterranean World*, edited by C. Colburn and M.C Heyn. Newcastle: Cambridge Scholars Publishing, 149–169.

Geraghty, R.M. (2007) The Impact of Globalization on the Roman Empire 200 BC–AD 100. *Journal of Economic History* 67, 1036–1061.

Griffiths, J.G. (1975) *The Isis-Book (Metamorphoses, Book XI)*. Leiden: Brill.

Gualandi, G. (1976) Sculture di Rodi. *Annuario della Scuola Archeologica di Atene* LIV, 7–260.

Harrison, S.J. (2012) Narrative Subversion and Religious Satire in *Metamorphoses* 11. In *Aspects of Apuleius' Golden Ass III: The Isis-Book*, edited by W. Keulen and U. Egelhaaf-Gaiser. Leiden: Brill, 73–85.

Horden, P. and Purcell, N. (2000) *The Corrupting Sea: a Study of Mediterranean History*. Malden, MA: Blackwell.

Jennings, J. (2011) *Globalizations and the Ancient World*. Cambridge: Cambridge University Press.

Kleibl, K. (2009) *Iseion: Raumgestaltung und Kultpraxis in den Heiligtümern gräco-ägyptischer Götter im Mittelmeerraum*. Worms am Rhein: Wernersche Verlagsgesellschaft.

Knapp, A.B. (2007) Insularity and Island Identity in the Prehistoric Mediterranean. In *Mediterranean Crossroads*, edited by S. Antoniadou and A. Pace. Athens: Pierides Foundation, 37–62.

Kravaritou, S. (2016) Sacred Space and the Politics of Multiculturalism in Demetrias (Thessaly). In *Hellenistic Sanctuaries between Greece and Rome*, edited by M. Melfi and O. Bobou. Oxford: Oxford University Press, 128–151.

Lamont, J. (2015) Asklepios in the Piraeus and the Mechanisms of Cult Appropriation. In *Autopsy in Athens: Recent Archaeological Research on Athens and Attica*, edited by M. Miles. Oxford: Oxbow Books, 37–50.

Levan, M., Payne, R.E. and Weisweiler, J. (eds) (2016) *Cosmopolitanism and Empire: Universal Rulers, Local Elites, and Cultural Integration in the Ancient near East and Mediterranean*. Oxford: Oxford University Press.

Loar, M.P., MacDonald, C. and Padilla Peralta, D. (2017) Introduction. In *Rome, Empire of Plunder. The Dynamics of Cultural Appropriation*, edited by C. MacDonald, M.P. Loar and D. Padilla Peralta. Cambridge: Cambridge University Press, 1–11.

Malaise, M. (1972) *Les conditions de pénétration et de diffusion des cultes égyptiens en Italie*. Études préliminaires aux religions orientales dans l'Empire romain 22. Leiden: Brill.

Malaise, M. (1992) À propos de l'iconographie 'canonique' d'Isis et des femmes vouées à son culte. *Kernos* 5, 329–361.

Malaise, M. and Veymiers, R. (2018) Les dévotes isiaques et les atours de leur déesse. In *Individuals and Materials in the Greco-Roman Cults of Isis: Agents, Images, and Practices*. Religions in the Graeco-Roman World 187, edited by V. Gasparini and R. Veymiers. Leiden: Brill, 470–508.

Malkin, I. (2011) *A Small Greek World: Networks in the Ancient Mediterranean*. Greeks Overseas. Oxford: Oxford University Press.

Marcadé, J. (1969) *Au musée de Délos. Étude sur la sculpture hellénistique en ronde bosse découverted dans l'île*. Paris: De Boccard.

Marcadé, J. (1996) *Sculptures déliennes*. Athens and Paris: École française d'Athènes and de Boccard.

Martzavou, P. (2010) Les cultes isiaques et les italiens entre Délos, Thessalonique, et l'Eubée. *Pallas* 84, 181–205.

Martzavou, P. (2011) Priests and Priestly Roles in the Isiac Cults: Women as Agents in Religious Change in Late Hellenistic and Roman Athens. In *Ritual Dynamics in the Ancient Mediterranean; Agency, Emotion, Gender, Representation*, edited by A. Chaniotis. Stuttgart: F. Steiner, 61–84.

Martzavou, P. (2012) Isis Aretalogies, Initiations, and Emotions. The Isis Aretalogies as a Source for the Study of Emotions. In *Unveiling Emotions: Sources and Methods for the Study of Emotions in the Greek World*, edited by A. Chaniotis. Stuttgart: Franz Steiner Verlag, 267–291.

Mazurek, L. (2016) Material and Textual Narratives of Authenticity? Creating Cabotage and Memory in the Hellenistic Eastern Mediterranean. In *Across the Corrupting Sea: Post-Braudelian Approaches to the Ancient Eastern Mediterranean*, edited by C. Concannon and L. Mazurek. London: Routledge, 39–61.

Mazurek, L. (2020) An Isis Statuette from Amphipolis in Context. In *Bibliotheca Isiaca IV*, edited by L. Bricault and R. Veymiers. Bordeaux: Éditions Ausonius, 85–93.

Meeks, E. and Scheidel, W. (2012) *ORBIS*. (21 November 2014). Orbis.stanford.edu. Accessed 25 March, 2020.
Merkelbach, R. (1962) *Roman und Mysterium in der Antike*. München-Berlin: C.H. Beck.
Morely, N. (2007) *Trade in Classical Antiquity*. Cambridge: Cambridge University Press.
Moyer, I. (2017) The Memphite Self-revelations of Isis and Egyptian Religion in the Hellenistic and Roman Aegean. *Religion in the Roman Empire* 3 (3), 318–343.
Mylonopoulos, I. (2016) Hellenistic Divine Images and the Power of Tradition. In *Hellenistic Sanctuaries between Greece and Rome*, edited by M. Melfi and O. Bobou. Oxford: Oxford University Press, 106–127.
Nagel, S. (2015) The Goddess's New Clothes. Conceptualising an 'Eastern' Goddess for a 'Western' Audience. In *The Dynamics of Transculturality: Concepts and Institutions in Motion*, edited by A. Flüchter and J. Schlöttli. New York: Springer Publishing, 187–217.
Nielson, I. (2002) *Cultic Theatres and Ritual Drama*. Aarhus Studies in Mediterranean Antiquity IV. Aarhaus: Aarhaus University Press.
Paribeni, E. (1959) *Catalogo delle sculture di Cirene. Statue e rilevi di carattere religioso*. Roma: di Bretschneider.
Pfeiffer, S. (2018) Comments on the Egyptian Background of the Priests' Procession During the *Navigium Isidis*. In *Individuals and Materials in the Greco-Roman Cults of Isis: Agents, Images, and Materials*, Religions in the Graeco-Roman World 187, edited by V. Gasparini and R. Veymiers. Leiden: Brill, 672–689.
Pfuhl, E. and Möbius, H. (1977) *Die ostgriechischen Grabreliefs*. 2 vols. Mainz am Rhein: von Zabern.
Pitts, M. and Versluys, M.J. (2015) Globalisation and the Roman World: Perspectives and Opportunities. In *Globalisation and the Roman World: World History, Connectivity, and Material Culture*, edited by M. Pitts and M.J. Versluys. Cambridge: Cambridge University Press, 3–31.
Plantzos, D. (2011) The Iconography of Assimilation. Isis and Royal Imagery on Ptolemaic Seal Impressions. In *More than Men, Less than Gods: Studies on Royal Cult and Imperial Worship. Proceedings of the International Colloquium Organized by the Belgian School at Athens (November 1-2, 2007)*, edited by A. Chankowski, P. Ioassif and C. Lorber. Leuven: Peeters, 389–416.
Platt, V. (2011) *Facing the Gods: Epiphany and Representation in Graeco-Roman Art, Literature, and Religion*. Cambridge: Cambridge University Press.
Price, S.R.F. (2012) Religious Mobility in the Roman Empire. *Journal of Roman Studies* 102, 1–19.
Pollitt, J.J. (1986) *Art in the Hellenistic Age*. Cambridge: Cambridge University Press.
Purcell, N. (2005) The Boundless Sea of Unlikeness? On Defining the Mediterranean. In *Mediterranean Paradigms in Classical Antiquity*, edited by I. Malkin. London: Routledge, 9–29.
Rauh, N.K., Dillon, M.J. and McClain, T.D. (2008) *Ochlos Nautikos*: Leisure Culture and Underclass Discontent in the Roman Maritime World. In *The Maritime World of Ancient Rome*. Memoirs of the American Academy in Rome, Supplementary Volume, edited by R. Hohlfelder. Ann Arbor, MI: University of Michigan Press, 197–242.
Rainbird, P. (2007) *The Archaeology of Islands*. Cambridge: Cambridge University Press.
Reger, G. (2016) Nodes of Sea and Sand. Ports, Human Geography, and Networks of Trade. In *Ancient Ports: The Geography of Connections. Proceedings of an International Conference at the Department of Archaeology and Ancient History, Uppsala University, 23-25 September 2010*, Boreas, edited by B. Alroth, K. Höghammar and A. Lindhagen. Uppsala: Uppsala Universitet, 9–36.
Rizakis, A. (1998) *Incolae-Paroikoi*: Populations et communautés dépendantes dans les cités et les colonies romaines de l'Orient. *Revue des Études Anciennes* 100(3–4), 599–617.
Rizakis, A. (2002) L'Émigration romaine en Macédoine et la communauté marchande de Thessalonique: perspectives économiques et sociales. In *Les italiens dans le monde grec. IIe siècle av. J. C. - Ier siècle ap. J. C. Circulation, activités, intégration. Actes de la Table Ronde, École Normale Supérieure.*

Paris 14–16 Mai 1998, edited by C. Müller and C. Hasenohr. Paris: Bulletin de Correspondance Hellénique.

Rizakis, A. (2003) Recrutement et formation des élites dans les colonies romaines de la province de Macédoine. In *Les élites et leur facettes. Les élites locales dans le monde hellénistique et romain.* Collection de l'École française de Rome, edited by M. Cébeillac-Gervasoni and L. Lamoine. Rome: École française de Rome, 107–130.

Rutherford, I. (2007) Network Theory and Theoric Networks. *Mediterranean Historical Review* 22(1), 23–37.

Siard, H. (2003) Nouvelles recherches sur le Sarapieion C de Délos. *Revue Archeologique*, 193–197.

Siard, H. (2009) Le Sarapieion C de Délos. Architecture et cultes. *Revue Archeologique*, 155–161.

Smith, R.R.R. (1991) *Hellenistic Sculpture: A Handbook.* London: Thames and Hudson.

Tacoma, L.E. (2016) *Moving Romans: Migration to Rome in the Principate.* Oxford: Oxford University Press.

Talbert, R.A. (ed.) (2000) *Barrington Atlas of the Greek and Roman World.* Princeton, NJ: Princeton University Press.

Tilg, S. (2014) *Apuleius' Metamorphoses: A Study in Roman Fiction.* Oxford: Oxford University Press.

Tran tam Tinh, V. (1990) Isis. *Lexicon Iconographicum Mythologiae Classicae* VII. Zürich: Artemis Verlag, 761–795.

Tzanavari, K. (1993) Η Λατρεία των αιγυπτίων θεών στη Βέροια. *ΑΡΧΑΙΑ ΜΑΚΕΔΟΝΙΑ V: Ανακοινώσεις κατά το πέμπτο διεθνές συμπόσιο Θεσσαλονίκη, 10–15 Οκτωβρίου 1989.* Thessaloniki: Institute for Balkan Studies, 1671–1682.

Van Pelt Campbell, G. (2007) Religion and Phases of Globalization. In *Religion, Globalization, and Culture*, edited by L.G. Beaman and P. Beyer. Leiden: Brill, 281–304.

Velenis, G. (1996) Sympagmateumenoi Romaioi se mia nea Epigraphi tis Thessalonikis. *Tekmeria* 2, 8–15.

Versluys, M.J. (2010) Understanding Egypt in Egypt and Beyond. In *Isis on the Nile: Egyptian Gods in Hellenistic and Roman Egypt. Proceedings of the IVth International Conference of Isis Studies, Liège, November 27–29 2008*, edited by L. Bricault and M.J. Versluys. Leiden: Brill, 7–38.

Versluys, M.J. (2015) Roman Visual Material Culture as Globalising Koine. In *Globalisation and the Roman World*, edited by M. Pitts and M.J. Versluys. Cambridge: Cambridge University Press, 141–174.

Veymiers, R. (2009) Les cultes isiaques à Amphipolis. *Membra disjecta* (IIIe s. av. J.-C.-IIIe s. apr. J.-C.). *Bulletin de Correspondances Hellénique* 133(1), 471–520.

Walters, E.J. (1988) *Attic Grave Reliefs That Represent Women in the Dress of Isis.* Hesperia Supplement 22. Princeton, NJ: ASCSA.

Winkler, J.J. (1985) *Auctor & Actor: A Narratological Reading of Apuleius' Golden Ass.* Berkeley, CA: University of California Press.

Woolf, G. (2014) Isis and the Evolution of Religions. In *Power, Politics, and the Cults of Isis. Proceedings of the Vth International Conference of Isis Studies, Boulogne-sur-Mer, October 13–15, 2011*, edited by L. Bricault and M.J. Versluys. Leiden: Brill, 62–92.

Woolf, G. (2016) Only Connect? Network Analysis and Religious Change in the Roman World. *Hélade* 2(2), 43–58.

Chapter 8

Globalization and Insularity in (Dis)Connected Crete[1]

Jane E. Francis

Introduction

The Romans conquered the island of Crete by 67 BCE after a contentious series of battles between Caecilius Metellus and Gnaeus Pompeius Magnus that re-defined Hellenistic alliances and pitted major cities against each other.[2] At some point in the next four decades, Crete was joined with Cyrene to form the senatorial province of *Creta et Cyrenaica*.[3] In 27 BCE, Augustus established the *Colonia Julia Nobilis Cnossus*, and around the same time Gortyn was assigned administrative status within the new province.[4] Crete remained in this political union until Diocletian dissolved the province in the late 3rd/early 4th century and attached it to Moesia; it was later joined to Macedonia.[5] After centuries of peace that sustained no active rebellions against Imperial rule, much of Crete was devastated by the massive earthquake of 365 CE, survived the decline of paganism and the rise of Christianity, and suffered various invasions and attacks until the inevitable end of Roman rule, culture, and influence in the 9th century.[6]

The Roman presence on Crete is well attested through abundant archaeological remains that include pottery, architecture of various types and materials, inscriptions, coins, and a vast array of other artifact classes.[7] Recovery of primary data from excavation, survey projects, and underwater explorations as well as intensive research is now adding significantly to knowledge about specific sites and regions (Fig. 48). This increased data and more detailed interpretations have allowed Crete in recent years to contribute to discussions to larger issues like Romanization and acculturation, cultural memory, globalization, and issues of trade and economy.[8] Many gaps still remain; some sites are largely unexplored or unpublished, while others have been investigated through rescue excavations and results are thus variable, but there has

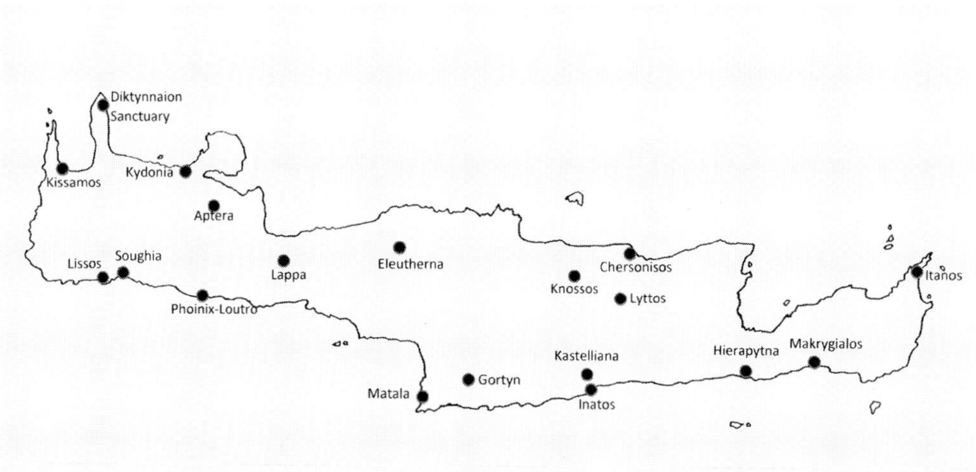

Figure 48: Map of Crete with major cities (Jane Francis).

recently been an overall increase in the efforts devoted to the study of Roman Crete as well as an ongoing integration of this research into the broader Roman world.[9]

This paper explores the archaeological evidence available so far on Crete for the island's involvement with the Romans. Its political orientation as a bi-part province is not in doubt, but the degree to which, and manner in which, its inhabitants participated in Roman cultural and societal 'norms', remains largely unknown. An issue with this study is the island's regionalism and lack of observed unity among sites: one site or areas may be more 'Roman' than its neighbor or express its 'Romanness' in a variety of ways. A tabulated account of 'Roman' elements across Crete is based on available remains and is thus a faulty methodology, but such evidence can at least, as here, provide insights into the value that the Cretans placed upon different aspects of Roman life as they encountered them.

Crete after Conquest

The *Pax Romana* brought an end to centuries of internal war and conflict on Crete and annulled longstanding alliances and disagreements. The ensuing political shift occurred quickly with the establishment of the new government at Gortyn, but the cultural shift took much longer.[10]

The earliest archaeological evidence dated to the first decades after the Roman conquest is ceramic. Beginning in the second half of the 1st century BCE, pottery in typically Roman shapes and wares produced in workshops under Roman control and shipped by Roman merchants around the Mediterranean, begin to trickle into Crete. Fine tablewares are the clearest evidence of this external contact, with Eastern Sigillata A documented at many sites across Crete.[11] This ware had been present in small amounts in the period after its initial manufacture and circulation, but few of these early forms have been identified on Crete, in contrast to the later Augustan and later Roman periods.[12] Imported amphorae from major centers like Rhodes and Kos, as well as forms from Italy occur on Crete as part of lingering Hellenistic trade routes.[13] These small numbers of foreign vessels appear alongside ongoing production and use of local Hellenistic pottery, and there seems to have been no sudden interruption in trade in the years around Crete's conquest.[14]

By the end of the 1st century BCE, in the Augustan age, the influx of imported pottery to Crete is both more sustained and substantial. Local Hellenistic trends die out and are replaced by Cretan pottery imitating or influenced by major imported Roman wares.[15] The last decades of the millennium document Roman pottery flowing into Crete from centers in the east and Italy; these include Eastern Sigillata B, Italian Sigillata, Cypriot Sigillata vessels, lead glaze, thin-walled wares, and Pompeian Red Ware.[16] Amphora-borne commodities from areas like Campania and southern Italy, the eastern Aegean, and Spain, as well as the imitation-Koan amphorae from a variety of workshops began to replace products circulating through the old Hellenistic distribution system.[17] It is clear that by the early Empire, Crete was well within the mainstream circulation of Roman Mediterranean pottery imports, which are found where expected, at large urban centers: western wares like Italian Sigillata are prevalent at Knossos, the Italian colony, and at Gortyn, the capital city.[18] These imports arrived at Crete's many ports, which must have served as distribution points both to the larger coastal cities and towns and to the smaller inland settlements that have been largely explored through survey projects.[19]

Accompanying this flood of Roman imported pottery in the last decades of the 1st century BCE is ... not much of anything, aside from the Roman control of coinage, although coin inscriptions continue to be written in Greek, with the exception of the issues from Knossos, which carry inscriptions in Latin.[20] There is no commensurate surge in public or private architecture in distinctly Roman style or materials on Crete, with the exception of Gortyn, which undergoes a significant building boom.[21] While it is tempting to ascribe this construction to the city's new administrative status and undoubted Roman largesse, Gortyn had been engaged in urban refurbishment from the late Hellenistic period, and the construction in the 1st century BCE seems to be a continuation of this project rather than a separate initiative. Moreover, the activity at Gortyn may have been the result of benefits accrued from the city's long-standing relationship in the 3rd century BCE with the Ptolemies, who sponsored at least some of its architectural renewal, rather than from Roman munificence or incentive.[22]

Outside of Gortyn, sites show no evidence for obvious and well-dated new constructions in this period, and most architectural projects were necessary renovations using traditional techniques and materials: dry-set walls made from local stone.[23] The introduction of an Italian population of veterans from Capua to Knossos similarly leaves no clear architectural mark, and the city remains substantially in its Hellenistic form for some time.[24] Future research at sites like Lyttos, Chersonisos, Lappa, or Sougia may alter this interpretation, but even fairly well excavated sites like Eleutherna preserve no buildings constructed in the century or so after the Roman conquest.[25] In general, no 'markers' of Roman architecture such as concrete, brick, apsidal rooms, or imported stone are evident.[26]

Instead, the Cretans of the early Roman era continue well-established traditions, with only an occasional acknowledgement or acceptance of Roman trends. Commemorative portrait sculpture, for instance, is nearly invisible, aside from two examples: a statue of Agrippa at Lappa, and a portrait of Metellus at Polyrrhenia, both lost and known only from inscribed bases.[27] These monuments indicate more a desire for reciprocal favor and largess to the donor rather than the beginning of a cultural practice. Gortyn, alone in Crete and in a completely expected action, begins to erect images of local grandees and, in the Augustan era, portraits of imperial family members, but the small numbers of preserved examples reinforce the very slow adoption of portraiture as a means to commemorate public activities or private dynastic succession.[28] Other types of early Imperial sculpture are similarly rare. One fragment from a marble table support carved with reliefs is dated to the second half of the 1st century BCE, and a Neo-Attic relief krater is early Augustan.[29]

Crete's participation in the Roman economy also displays a lacuna following conquest, and trade was largely one-sided. The island's ceramic workshops produced amphorae from the late Classical period and more intensively in the Hellenistic era, but few of these vessels were destined for markets off the island, according to their findspots.[30] Most pottery made on the island instead moved only regionally along trade routes perhaps established and maintained according to alliances during the Hellenistic Wars; for example, the East Cretan Cream Ware vessels produced in the Hierapytna area and attested at sites in the east have yet to be found in west Crete.[31] At least some of the Cretan-made transport amphorae probably contained the *passum* wine famous in the later empire, but neither the early Roman settlers on Crete nor the locals engaged in wine and pottery production seem to have recognized the economic potential of this industry until the Augustan period, when Crete standardized its amphora shapes, perhaps under Roman influence, and began to export *passum*, along with other commodities like olive oil and honey, to foreign markets.[32] Before this date, the market for Cretan amphora-borne products was minimal; whether this was also the case for other items packaged in perishable materials – or without containers at all – cannot be known. Certainly literary sources testify to a knowledge off the island of Cretan products like medicinal herbs and timber as early as the Classical period.[33]

A Roman and 'Globalized' Crete

By the second half of the 1st century CE, elements of Roman lifestyle, culture, and economy had become commonplace on Crete. Buildings of a particularly Roman function like baths, amphitheaters, an odeion, and Roman-style theatres were erected throughout the 2nd and 3rd centuries.[34] Infrastructure in the form of water systems with aqueducts, cisterns, and nymphaea were installed.[35] Roads were paved – colonnades bordered some streets at Gortyn – and distance markers erected.[36] Buildings were constructed with brick and concrete, and hydraulic concrete was employed for harbor installations.[37] To decorate these public and private structures, Crete imported colored marbles from a variety of sources.[38] The imperial cult was installed in the early Julio-Claudian period, supplementing the renewed popularity of indigenous Cretan cults like Britomartis, Diktynna, and the Cretan-born Zeus.[39]

Wealthy Cretans – or perhaps Roman immigrants – lived in lavish villas decorated in *au courant* Roman style and many built peristyle houses. The Villa Dionysos at Knossos, constructed in the 1st century CE, flourishing in the 2nd, and finally destroyed c. 160/80 CE, featured a large peristyle garden and an *oecus*, and was decorated with a marble wall veneer.[40] The House of the Diamond Frescoes at the same city has plastered walls painted with elaborate motifs imitating various imported and expensive stone.[41] The House of Phidias at Kissamos also featured a peristyle, an *oecus*, and lavish decor with mosaics, including the only example on Crete with the homeowner's name.[42] The Roman villa at Makrygiallos, in east Crete, included a private bath.[43] Mosaic floors become common; Sweetman's intensive study has demonstrated that the earliest examples occur at south coast cities like Gortyn and Hierapytna in the late 1st century and instances then intensify up towards the north coast in the 2nd century.[44] Other private luxuries include carved marble furniture.[45]

Statues in Greek style and subject are more prevalent and stood in both public and private spaces.[46] The findspots of this sculpture indicate that much of this activity was focused at wealthy urban centers, like Chersonisos, Kydonia, Kissamos, Gortyn, and Lyttos, where the Roman presence seems to have been strong and is attested by accompanying architecture and cultural practices. Some cult centers preserve statuary erected in the Roman era; the Diktynnaion sanctuary, whose refurbishment is thought to have been sponsored by Hadrian, not unexpectedly contained a statue of the emperor. Private villas, such as the villa at Inatos and the House of Phidias at Kissamos, demonstrate the practice for sculpted interior decor.[47]

A Still-Greek Crete

Despite all this palpably Roman evidence, in many areas Crete does not entirely acquiesce to Roman norms and practices established in earlier periods continue. Rome, as elsewhere, adopted a laissez-faire attitude towards the island once it was clear that its rule would be unopposed and thus peaceful, and the administration allowed traditional activities to continue alongside definably Roman intrusions and institutions. Greek remained the primary language, as attested by inscriptions, and surviving Latin texts are well in the minority.[48]

The discovery and study of inscriptions from Crete is ongoing and much can now be added to the early 20th-century four-volume corpus of *Inscriptiones Creticae* edited by Guarducci, which reveals Greek to be the linguistic preference of the island.

Subsequent finds have not changed this picture.[49] While Crete, as part of the Greek world and the eastern Roman empire might be expected to retain a certain amount of Greek, this was neither expected nor required. Even in Cretan cities with documented Roman influence, Greek remained in force, at least for the language of public inscriptions. At Knossos, the Italian colony, 14 inscriptions from *Inscriptiones Creticae* date to the Roman period, plus a further four assigned broadly to the 1st century BCE and thus either late Hellenistic or Roman; only four of these are written in Latin.[50] Gortyn preserves 260 legible inscriptions dating from the 1st century BCE through the Roman era. Two-hundred-and-thirty-four of these texts are in Greek, against only 25 in Latin, despite the city's status as the island's Roman administrative capital.[51] Other cities reflect this pattern. Lyttos, one of the Cretan members of Hadrian's Panhellenic League, preserves 158 potential Roman inscriptions, only two of which are in Latin, while the thriving and wealthy port city of Hierapytna has 47 possible Roman inscriptions, all of which are written in Greek.[52]

Not all Cretan architecture used Roman methods and materials, as has become clear from the abundant survey projects on Crete.[53] Many rural sites, at least into late antiquity, continue traditional methods of dry-set, local stone.[54] Small farmsteads and houses, shelters, and field walls do not always incorporate brick or mortar, although these materials are often the best manner for identifying Roman phases in preserved architecture alone.[55] Roman concrete or mortar, combined with stone facings or brick and especially until the 2nd century, seems to be reserved for buildings of typically Roman style and functions – baths, vaulted structures, cisterns, amphitheaters – which employ materials developed in Italy and trickling into Crete from the late 1st century onwards.[56] Not only form, but also material follows function, and there is often a sharp separation between monumental Roman architecture and the more utilitarian constructions of the modest Cretans, which betray generations of consistency throughout the Imperial era at least in modest private architecture.

Cretan cemeteries and burials of the Roman era similarly retain ties to the past and continue Hellenistic practices of cist graves, shaft graves, chamber tombs, and tile graves into the Roman period.[57] Gortyn preserves a monumental hypogeum constructed in the mid-1st century BCE that continues Hellenistic eastern trends.[58] Regional patterns cannot yet be identified. Vaulted tombs appear in the late antique period at, for example, Phoinix-Loutro and Lissos, and arcosolium tombs were used at Matala, but these types of architectural burials are rare and do not indicate island-wide customs.[59] Commemoration with funerary reliefs is uncommon and few examples have been identified.[60] Italian fashions, such as portraits in tomb monuments, are similarly rare; an example comes from Aptera and dates to the Trajanic era.[61] The trend for decorated marble sarcophagi that swept the Roman world late in the reign of Trajan had a limited impact on Crete, although this situation may be due to fragmentary archaeological evidence.[62]

The public erection of portraits also does not seem to have been widely practiced on Crete, at least for members of the imperial families. A few images of Augustus and

Livia are known, and Tiberius and Caligula represent the Julio-Claudian dynasty.[63] There is a gap in the Flavian period with no identified examples. Several portraits commemorated Trajan, including one from Lyttos, but only Hadrian was particularly celebrated on Crete. While this preference is true of many cities in Roman Greece, Crete's connection may also have been fostered by the emperor's inclusion of its cities into his Panhellenion.[64] Of the later emperors, statues are known of Marcus Aurelius, and Caracalla, both from Gortyn, a statue base at Itanos confirms a dedication to Septimius Severus, and two re-worked portraits represent Constantine the Great, from Kydonia and Gortyn.[65]

More common on Crete are portraits of local grandees and worthies, now mostly anonymous, but these tend to cluster at cities with strong evidence for Roman institutions and cultural practices like baths and theaters.[66] The much higher proportion of local subjects for portraiture as opposed to imperial family members is noteworthy. Public commemoration by portraiture on Crete may constitute a continuation of Hellenistic trends, and the Cretans' physical and possibly even ideological distance from Rome may have resulted in a general disinterest in imperial images that did not play a meaningful role in their urban landscapes, except perhaps at Gortyn.[67] Once again, older practices may have trumped the new, at least in themes.

Less evidence is available for other aspects of the Roman lifestyle on Crete, but archaeological data does not, at present, indicate that the Cretans adopted Roman dietary practices. No studies of cooking and food-related pottery show changes in the manner in which foods were prepared or cooked, or in the types of foods consumed from the Hellenistic into the Roman era. We also lack evidence – and thus identification – from Roman-period sewers on the island or evidence from flotation. The imported fine tablewares do not indicate precise use, and none of the cooking shapes from Crete, aside from occasional use of Roman mortaria, show deviation from earlier culinary practices.[68] In particular, there does not seem to have been much of a market for the fish sauces ubiquitous in other parts of the Roman empire, despite the existence of numerous rock-cut fish tanks around the Cretan coastline, which must have been used for fish farming, and fish consumption is well documented.[69] The number of confirmed imported *garum* amphorae on Crete is about five, and even these might have arrived on the island through re-use; their contents upon arrival were not necessarily fish sauce.[70] Crete preserves no production centers, and no ancient *testimonia* refer to the importation or consumption of these products, which must have played a very limited role in the Cretan diet.[71] The cities with significant Italian populations, Knossos and Gortyn, might be expected to preserve greater evidence, but this does not occur in numbers that confirm widespread use.[72]

Crete: Insular or Globalized?

It is apparent that the impact of the Roman presence on Crete was neither immediate nor uniform across the island, but the implications of this evidence for modern interpretations of the island's history are far from straightforward. There is a significant lacuna between the Roman conquest and the Cretan adoption of the Roman way of life, and while in the 2nd century Crete catches up with the rest of the Roman world, the island in many ways maintains some of its traditional practices. Explanations for this duality are numerous and complex, but it is possible to consider these patterns in terms of modern concepts like globalization and insularity.

The century after the Roman conquest can be understood as a period of cultural and economic conservatism for the Cretans. Rome acquired a strategically located island with good natural resources, and Crete obtained a new master, yet neither side seems to have acted on this change for approximately 40 years. The Romans installed governors, most famously Brutus from 44–42 BCE, but no standing army was established. Some cities, like Knossos, continued to mint their own coins until after the Battle of Actium and the Unexplored Mansion excavations have revealed small numbers of Hellenistic coins in 1st- and 2nd-century CE deposits.[73] Although existing remains are difficult to interpret, no significant architecture is securely datable to this period, and it is only historical documents, some coinage, and the influx of Roman pottery that marks Crete as a Roman holding.

The early Roman pottery imports to Crete, however, do not so much indicate an intention to adopt Roman household objects as they document an important shift in the Cretan economy. By the time of the conquest, Crete's existing maritime trade networks had been usurped by Roman interests, which now controlled the movement of goods. Crete's ports would thus have received shipments reflecting this new economic reality, whether they chose to adopt them or not. Some percentage of the Cretan clientele might have ardently desired Italian Sigillata bowls in an effort to keep up with the trends established by the new Power – at Gortyn, for instance, while other customers may simply have needed a bowl or dish. That functional necessity was more important than cultural significance as a product of the Roman marketplace is confirmed not only by the wide distribution of this pottery across Crete, but also by the lack of contemporary development in other aspects of Roman lifestyle and culture.

The question can now be posed: does the evidence from Crete indicate globalization in the century or so after conquest? A cautiously positive answer may be proposed, but Crete reflects a more passive version of the term. The Roman pottery stands alone as a 'marker' of *Romanitas*, but does not, *a priori*, indicate a deliberate desire to become Roman or an acceptance of Roman ways. The degree to which the acquisition of Roman pottery was deliberate and designed to align the buyer with Roman practices cannot be known, especially for sites where no other evidence for a change to or adoption of Roman culture can be documented.

A globalized Crete can be more securely argued for the island from the late 1st century CE onwards, when Crete became an active participant in the Roman economy, and what had been regional production with minimal impact outside the island was transformed into a centralized, international, economic powerhouse that produced amphora-borne exports circulating around the Roman world for nearly eight centuries.[74] Contemporary with this expansion was the Cretan exploitation of Roman architectural forms and materials, many of which testify to the adoption of Roman cultural practices by locals, such as baths and entertainment venues like the amphitheater at Gortyn, and the island's many theaters.[75] The 2nd century sees Crete importing expensive colored marbles for decor and architectural purposes, the erection of lavish villas, and commemorative statuary in public and private contexts, and it is clear that the island supported a wealthy, elite upper class eager for the finer things in life. The population of the island, which must have included native Cretans as well as settlers who had arrived at any point since Crete's transformation into a Roman province, were realizing and exploiting the benefits of Roman power and money.

The other side of Roman Crete, the areas that did not so thoroughly – or at all – adopt Roman ways, reveals information about the island's insularity. Crete is the third largest Mediterranean island, but its topographical regionalism, noted even in the Bronze Age, has no less of an impact in later periods and was not obliterated by Roman rule.[76] The island's mountains, gorges, broad arable plains, peninsulas, cliffs, and sandy shores divide Crete into north and south, but also east, central, and west. These divisions can clearly be read in the archaeological record, especially in the distribution of local pottery. More research and publication is needed, but numerous ceramic workshops dating to the Roman period are known across Crete, and fabric analysis has provided information about the use of local clay resources.[77] Crete produced some distinctive pottery, aside from its transport amphorae, but much of this did not travel particularly far from its source: for example, eastern wares, like East Cretan Cream Wares, did not leave eastern Crete; vessels made in Gortyn are largely found in the area of the city; very small amounts of pottery from Knossos appear elsewhere; and material from Eleutherna stays around there.[78]

The relative physical isolation that encourages this limited distribution may also be partially responsible for the ongoing consistency in vernacular architecture, especially at rural and inland sites. Isolated agricultural workers may not have been aware of urban trends, or they may have felt that monumental civic structures, including even the numerous aqueducts and cisterns that dotted the rural landscape, had little to do with their daily existence. This was the population for whom Roman baths and games at an amphitheater sponsored by a local grandee meant next to nothing, instilled no civic pride, and encouraged no conformity to Roman norms. They were unable to contribute to inscriptions, provide financial support for reconstructions or buildings, erect commemorative monuments, and if they traveled to cities to see entertainments or visit baths, they left no evidence for such activities.

Further insularity can be posited on the basis of Crete's relationship with its provincial partner, Cyrenaica. Modern scholars have tended to consider these two land masses, separated only by the Libyan Sea individually, and for good reason: they had almost nothing to do with each other throughout their union.[79] Only small numbers of Cretan amphorae and Cretan-made ceramic oil lamps bridge the gap.

Reasons for this are unknown, but the administrative connection of these regions, not to mention their physical proximity, recommends much more contact than can be documented historically or archaeologically. Cretan wine and other products were regularly exported to markets much farther away than Cyrenaica, and while most of the island's primary harbors were located on the north, it did not lack for south-coast ports directly facing its provincial partner.[80] This separation was certainly deliberate and it effectively cut Crete off from interaction with North Africa, a situation that ceased when Diocletian administratively severed the province in 298; from this point, the ceramic record on Crete begins to show more numerous imports, especially of African Red Slip and North African amphorae.[81]

The pattern of Crete's interaction with the other half of its senatorial province, along with the retention of Greek for the majority of inscriptions, the continuation of old burial practices, and the persistence of traditional architectural practices, recommend an interpretation of the island as conservative and relatively insular. Yet Crete's long contribution to the international economy and its adoption at many cities and towns of monumental and expensive aspects of Roman cultural practices clearly demonstrate an adherence to and acceptance of Rome. This duality illustrates well the reality of Roman Crete, which teems with contradictions – north versus south, east versus central and west, urban versus rural, coastal versus inland, which would have been continuously shifting and changing over the eight centuries or so of Roman rule on the island. Even within such fluctuations, however, harbor sites continued to act as constant hubs providing external contact and communication in multiple directions.

It is also difficult to recreate or understand with any authenticity the attitude of the Cretans to the Romans, or even the ethnicities of its residents, which would have affected individual, family, or group reactions to Rome.[82] Such responses would have changed over time, subject to any number of external and internal factors. For instance, a beekeeper in central Crete may produce a surplus of honey that, after passing through numerous hands, was sold in Pompeii; because of this outcome, and perhaps because he owns a Çandarlı Ware bowl, he may think of himself as thoroughly Roman and part of the global community. His neighbor may be a subsistence farmer with no imported pottery, for whom the Romans are an unrealized and unseen entity. An urban trader living in a grand house with marble walls and mosaic floors, who travels on paved streets and yet is a fervent devotee to Britomartis, may view his adoption of *Romanitas* as necessary to his personal and economic well-being but still consider himself a Cretan at heart. And a Cretan living on the coast will have had different experiences with the Romans than someone living inland, who may never see Roman merchant ships or the arrival of foreign cargoes and people. It is even more difficult to understand the mindsets of Crete's foreign populations, some of whom, in varying degrees, may have embraced local traditions, while others retained aspects of their own traditional practices.[83] More informative in this regard would be the attitude of the rest of the Roman world to

Crete, but evidence for this is lacking, save the oft-repeated adage that all Cretans are liars.[84]

Conclusion

It is thus not possible to conclude that Roman Crete was either entirely globalized or insular; it was both, but it was also regional, conservative, wealthy, strained, and peaceful. The islanders do not seem to have had any island-wide concept of self, although research on the Roman response to the Minoan past may alter this; current information indicates that local identities mattered more.[85] That Crete engaged in no active rebellions against the Romans and the island never supported a standing army indicates a passive acceptance of Roman governance, with the benefits accrued outweighing 'going it alone'. Memory of the Hellenistic Wars may have remained strong, and no unified self-identity to guide subversive anti-Roman activity was thus required. The Romans, for their part, adopted a laissez-faire attitude towards Crete, and the islanders reciprocated by doing what was required of them, which in many cases was exactly what they had been doing before.

Notes

1 I would like to thank Anna Kouremenos and Jody Michael Gordon for the invitation to participate in the 2017 AIA panel on which this research is based. Thanks also to George Harrison, Martha Baldwin Bowsky, and Matt Buell.

2 The bibliography on Hellenistic Crete is growing; for general outlines of the pre-Roman state of the island, see, for example, Sanders 1982, 3–6; Chaniotis 2008, 2004; Sweetman 2013, 7–9. For an overview of the battles during the Roman conquest, see Sanders 1982, 3–4.

3 The date for the formation of the province of *Creta et Cyrenaica* remains unclear: see Harrison 1985, 368–369; Sweetman 2007, 67; Chevrollier 2016; Kouremenos 2018; .

4 It is assumed that at least some of the colonists at Knossos came from Italy; see Rigsby 1976; Paton 2004, 1994; Baldwin Bowsky 2011. Gortyn's Roman administrative function is discussed, for instance, in Di Vita 2010, 61–62 and Lippolis 2016.

5 Sanders 1982, 6–7; Sweetman 2013, 10; Chevrollier 2016, 22–23.

6 On the 365 CE earthquake, see Stiros and Papageorgiou 2001; Stiros 2010. The bibliography for early Christian Crete is substantial; recently, Sweetman 2004a; 2004b; 2005; 2013. For the Arab attacks on Crete, see Brookes 1913; Christides 1981; 1984.

7 A distinction is made in this paper between native Cretans whose families were well entrenched on the island by the time Rome showed interest in the island, and those who spent time or settled on Crete but came from elsewhere, regardless of how 'Cretanized' they may have become over time. Although this division is difficult to trace archaeologically, traces of origins for the latter group may appear in the use of Latin or in Roman family names on inscriptions. See Baldwin Bowsky 1999 for instances of Roman citizens on Crete, although some of these may have come from the first group.

8 See, for instance, Haggis 1996; Baldwin Bowsky 1999; 2004; 2017; Grigoropoulous 2004; Sweetman 2004a; 2007; 2011; Litinas 2008; Romeo 2010; Pałuchowski 2011; Kelly 2013; Kouremenos 2013; 2018; Gallimore 2014; Poulou-Papadimitriou and Nodarou 2014; Chevrollier 2015; Martin-Arroyo *et al.* 2016; Francis 2017.

9 The gazetteer of Roman sites in Sanders (1982, 135–175) has recently been updated by Sweetman 2013, 290–309. For more comprehensive research, see Harrison 1993; Livadiotti and Simiakaki 2004; Francis and Kouremenos 2016.

10 Two centuries of war on Crete and mercenary service took a toll on manpower and social structure and may have made Crete easier to conquer; at the same time, the Roman presence discouraged the resurrection of old quarrels.

11 For the appearance of early Eastern Sigillata A (ESA) forms on Crete, see, for example, Hayes 1971, 252, 257, 263; Sackett 1992, 151; Lippolis 2001, 26–29; Forster 2009, 78–79; Gallimore 2015, 113–117, 277–280.

12 It is at present impossible to present quantified statistics for ESA on Crete, as few complete assemblages have been published and the early forms tend to have a long lifespan; Gallimore's research at Hierapytna counts 73 ESA vessels, but only publishes 11 (2015, 115–116). On the other hand, the early Forms 3 and 4 are dwarfed at Knossos by later shapes, and in the Augustan period, ESA far overwhelms the numbers of other fine wares (Sackett 1992, 163, fig. 2). At the Praetorium Excavations at Gortyn, only a single Form 2A and two fragments of Form 4A represent the early phase (Lippolis 2001, 26–29).

13 Late series Rhodian and Koan amphorae have been identified at Knossos (Hayes 1971, 261, nos 42–44); for early Italian amphorae, see Portale and Romeo 2001, 267–268. A good summary of Hellenistic imports to eastern Crete is Gallimore 2015, 271–274; for central Crete, see Englezou 2005; for Lyttos, Englezou 2000. Crete's importation pattern at this time seems to reflect that of other Mediterranean centers; see Mazurek in this volume.

14 This is the case at Hierapytna, as noted by Gallimore 2015, 277. Raab (2001, 9–16) discusses the Cretan economy and trade in the Hellenistic and Roman periods for the Akrotiri peninsula.

15 Cretan decorated tablewares are not fully understood; production sites and distribution patterns are not well known, as is the relationship between the Cretan shapes and decorative schemes and primary workshop products. Many sites seem to have been making their own to supplement imported wares, but the market for this pottery remains elusive. Knossos preserves a reasonably sized assemblage (Hayes 1971, 266, nos 25–39; Sackett 1992, 161–63; Forster 2009, 114–115), while Hierapytna, in east Crete, sees the continuation in use of a well-defined Hellenistic locally made pottery (East Cretan Cream Ware) alongside imitations of Roman products; see Gallimore 2015, 91–100, for both Hellenistic and Roman-phase examples.

16 The following references are not intended to form an exhaustive list but merely present some of the distribution at well-published sites for the various shapes and wares, as identified and published. Eastern Sigillata B: Coldstream 1973, 48, nos 15–16 (Knossos); Sackett 1992, 156–58; Forster 2001, 143; Lippolis 2001, 30–33 (Gortyn); Gallimore 2015, 117–122, nos 128–42 (Hierapytna). Italian Sigillata: Sackett 1992, 186 A2, 24–31 (Knossos); Eiring 2004; Gallimore 2015, 122–126, nos 143–153 (Hierapytna). Cypriot Sigillata: Sackett 1992, 182, A1, 2, 185, A2, 15–23 (Knossos); Rizzo 2001 (Gortyn); Gallimore 2015, 126–127 (Hierapytna); the Cypriot source of this ware has not been confirmed (*pro*: Slane 1989, 222, n. 20; Gomez *et al.* 2002, 32; *contra*: Gunneweg *et al.* 1983, 15); see also Lund 2015, 166–167. Lead Glazed: Sackett 1992, 186, A2, 32–33 (Knossos). Thin-walled: De Tommaso 2001, 21–24 (Gortyn). Pompeian Red Ware: Sackett 1992, 168, 189, A2, 84 (Knossos); Gallimore 2015, 199–201, nos 369–373 (Hierapytna).

17 See, for example, Spanish amphorae: Forster 2001, 161 (Knossos); Portale and Romeo 2001, 284–285, no. 27 (Gortyn). Italian amphorae: Sackett 1992, 183, A1, 30 (Knossos); Portale and Romeo 2001, 267–268, nos 5, 6 (Gortyn).

18 On the presence of Italian Sigillata at Knossos, see Sackett 1992, 153–156; Forster 2009, 82–87; 2001, 141–142. For Gortyn, see Martin 1997b, 125–26; Rizzo 2001, 36–38; Baldwin Bowsky 2011; 2016.

19 Not all large-scale Cretan cities of the early (or later) empire have been excavated and published; little is known, for instance, of the Roman ceramic record for Chersonisos, Lyttos, Kissamos,

or Kydonia. Surveys with identified, inland Roman sites include Sphakia (Moody *et al.* 1998), Vrokastro (Harrison and Hayden 2005), Moni Odigitria (Francis 2010a), Gournia (Vogeikoff-Brogan 2012), and Galatas (Gallimore 2017a, 105–117, 235–240). See also Francis 2012 for an examination of coastal versus inland Roman sites on Crete. For the relationship between the sea, ports, and the hinterland, see Mazurek in this volume.

20 Even the coins from the island's administrative center, Gortyn, continue to be inscribed in Greek; see Burnett *et al.* 1992, 216–217. The main resource for Cretan coins remains Svoronos 1890, but see also Price 1992, for Knossos, and publications of the coins from Gortyn (Di Vita 1988; Garraffo 1997; 1999; 2001). Many of Crete's pre-Roman coin images reflect the island's mythological history, such as Europa at Gortyn and the Minotaur at Knossos, but few of these motifs survive the change to Roman numismatic control; an exception is the retention of the labyrinth on Knossian coins. Some specifically Cretan images are altered to a more traditionally Roman iconography, such as the Artemis Diktynna, who is turned into Artemis Ephesia (see Burnett *et al.* 1992, 217); see also Sweetman 2007, 110–111.

21 The lack of architectural activity in early Roman Crete has been briefly noted by Sweetman (2007, 68) and Kelly (2013, 133–135), and observed in Raab's survey of the Akrotiri Peninsula (2001, 141); see also Sanders on Aptera (1982, 167, Site 17/2).

22 Strabo (1.462) refers to the Ptolemaic financial support for Gortyn's reconstruction; see also Di Vita 2010, 59, 60, 147–150; Lippolis 2016, 157, 160, 161, 167.

23 This interpretation is based on current evidence, but the precise dating of site phases and individual structures from architecture alone is extremely problematic on Crete due to a lack of a securely dated *corpus* and few published examples. Ceramic evidence remains the best chronological indication of a site or individual building.

24 Sweetman 2007.

25 On the excavations of Roman material at Eleutherna, see Themelis 2000; 2009; Stampolidis 2004.

26 So little is known of Hellenistic architecture on Crete that some of these structures identified as Roman may be earlier, but this dating does not contradict the statements above, that the Cretans did not immediately adopt Roman building types or materials.

27 Metellus: *IC* II.xxiii.14; Croz 2002, 141–142; Lagogianni-Georgarakos 2002, 15; Martinez Fernandez 2012, 104–105, no. 16; Karanastasi 2016, 101. Agrippa: Baldwin Bowsky 2007; Tzifopoulos 2007; Karanastasi 2016, 101. Both these inscriptions are in Greek; only four inscriptions dating to the late 1st century BCE, all from Gortyn, are written in Latin (*IC* IV.290, IV.327, IV.328, IV.426). The practice of public commemoration with portraits, which originated in the Greek east, is also not common in pre-Roman Crete; see Rose 1997, 3–4.

28 For instance, the possible portraits of Gaius Caesar (Herakleion, Arch. Mus. 66: Portale 1998, 295–304, no. 3, pls. 38, 73b ; Lagogianni-Georgakarakos 2002, 56–57, no. 13, pl. 14) and Livia (Athens, Nat. Mus. 355: Portale 1998, 304–310, no. 4; Lagogianni-Georgakarakos 2002, 70–71, no. 35, pl. 39). A portrait head of the Prima Porta Augustus type, without findspot, is housed in the Herakleion Museum (507); see Lagogianni-Georgakarakos 2002, 47–48, no. 1, pl. 1. Again, dynastic commemoration with portraiture of the type discussed by Rose (1997) cannot be proven for Crete.

29 For the *trapezophoros* now built into a church in Foedele, see Lassithiotakis 1951; Cohon 1984, 213, no. 49; Karanastasi 2016, 101–102. On the Neo-Attic krater, see Karanastasi 2016, 102, pl. 18, with references.

30 Hellenistic Cretan transport amphorae seem to have been produced at a number of centers on the island, but their characteristics and distribution remain ill defined. While future research, like the recently published Hellenistic kiln site at Loutro, near Rethymnon (Tsatsaki and Nodarou 2014), should clarify the island's economy in this period, available evidence suggests that Crete was not an active participant in international trade, despite the arrival of foreign goods through probable trans-shipment at some coastal sites (Chaniotis 2005, 97–98; Gallimore

2015, 269–274); *contra* Vogeikoff-Brogan (2004, 217), who states that the lack of focused and widespread research on Hellenistic ceramics on Crete does not provide an accurate picture of trade in this period; also Harris 1999, 357.

31 On East Cretan Cream Ware, see Gallimore 2015, 71–90 (Hierapytna) and Vogeikoff-Brogan 2000, 70–72; 2014, 28–29 (Mochlos).

32 Research and publication on Cretan Roman amphora production and export has reinforced the role of Cretan wine in the Roman economy, but there is also evidence that Crete was exporting its honey as early as the 3rd century BCE (Hanson 1972, 164–165; see also Gallimore 2015, 271). In the Roman period, *dipinti* indicating honey on several Cretan amphorae found in Italy confirm the ongoing practice (Peña 2007, 103–105, with citations). For the epigraphical, numismatic, and literary references to *passum*, see Marangou-Lerat 1995, 5–34; see also Gallimore 2017b. The production of olive oil is confirmed by finds of olive presses, such as the twelve identified in the Gournia Survey area (Vogeikoff-Brogan 2012, 87; Gallimore 2015, 283) and at Mochlos (Vogeikoff-Brogan 2014), but it is unknown whether such installations produced surplus sufficient for trade. The cultivation, processing, and export in invisible products from Crete such as salt (Francis 2010b) and aromatic and medicinal herbs (Gallimore 2015, 271) is documented in the late Hellenistic/early Roman era but probably began much earlier.

33 For instance, Theophrastus (9.16.1) on Cretan dictamus; see also Rackham and Moody 1996; Kouremenos forthcoming.

34 Theatres on Crete: Hierapytna (Belli, cited in Falkener 1854, 14; Sanders 1982, 57–59; Gallimore 2015, 19–20); Chersonisos (Belli, cited in Falkener 1854, 14; Sanders 1982, 59–61); Lyttos (Belli, cited in Falkener 1854, 18; Sanders 1982, 61), Gortyn (Di Montali 2006; Vita 2010, 271–272, 272–228, 289–293, with references), Aptera (Niniou-Kindeli and Chatzidakis 2016), Knososs (Hood and Smythe 1981, 23), Kouphonisi (Leonard 1972). Amphitheaters are known at Gortyn (Di Vita 2010, 294–298), possibly at Knossos (Hood and Smythe 1981, 23) and Hierapytna, although this has not been located and is cited only by Belli (in Falkener 1854, 12–13). Gortyn built the island's only odeion (Di Vita 2010, 108–119). Baths have been identified at 52 sites on Crete (Kelly 2013).

35 Terracotta subterranean pipes are common at Cretan sites (*e.g.* Gortyn: Di Vita 2010, 177); arched aqueduct lines are well preserved, if briefly, outside Chersonisos to Lyttos (Oikonomaki 1986; Kelly 2018); on the Gortyn aqueduct and water systems, see Pagano 2007, 1992; Di Vita 2010, 231–39; Giorgi 2016; for hydraulics in west Crete, see Christodoulakos 2011. Nymphaea have been excavated at Gortyn (*e.g.* Di Vita 2010, 224–230). Chersonisos preserves a singular pyramidal fountain (Massara 2013). Cisterns are common; see, for example, Zaros (Sanders 1982, 155, Site 10/1), Kastelliana (Sanders 1982, 151, Site 7/30), Aptera (Andreadaki-Vlasaki 1997, 47), and the Diktynnaion Sanctuary (Welter and Jantzen 1951); see also Mays *et al.* 2013, 1923–1925.

36 Gortyn boasts a particularly splendid road system (Lippolis 2016, 164–165). The best-preserved Roman road on Crete leads to the Diktynnaion Sanctuary in the west (unpublished); the ancient road system of the island is indicated on the Tabula Peutinger (Pazarli *et al.* 2007). Distance markers have been published from Aptera (Baldwin Bowsky and Niniou-Kindeli 2006) and Hierapytna (Baldwin Bowsky 2006).

37 The list of buildings with brick and concrete is substantial; for well-preserved examples, see the Villa Dionysos at Knossos (Paton 1998), the probable warehouse at Tholos (Haggis 1996), and the cisterns at Kastelliana (Sanders 1982, 151, Site 7/30, fig. 55). See Brandon *et al.* 2005, for the use of hydraulic concrete in the harbor at Chersonisos.

38 On foreign marbles and building materials on Crete, see Sackett and Jones 1979; Paton and Schneider 1999; Lambrugo 2011; Antonelli *et al.* 2017.

39 Sanders 1982, 37–38; the interpretation of the locations and extent of the Imperial Cult on Crete continues to be problematic. Britomartis appears on Roman coins across Crete and was

assimilated to Diktynna in the west (*e.g.* Svoronos 1890, 249, nos 1–5). The Diktynna sanctuary in west Crete seems to have received abundant support for refurbishment in the Hadrianic period but remains woefully underexplored (Welter and Jantzen 1951; Sanders 1982, 39, 174, Site 20/29). The cult of Zeus Cretagenes may have been based in the Idaean Cave; see Sapouna 1998; for inscriptions, see *IC* I.xii.1–8.

40 On the architecture of the Villa Dionysos, see Sanders 1982, 69–70; Paton 1998. The pottery has been published by Hayes (1983); on the mosaics, see Sweetman 2013, 157–169.

41 Sackett and Jones 1979; Sackett *et al.* 1992, 37–47.

42 Markoulaki 2012; 2015; Kouremenos 2013, 144–162.

43 Papadakis 1986, 31–39.

44 See Sweetman 2013, 83–89, on the distribution of Roman mosaics on Crete.

45 Several examples of *trapezophoroi* are attested: for example, Karanastasi 2016, 101–102; Milidakis and Papadaki 2016.

46 Karanastasi (2016) provides a good overview of Roman sculpture in Crete; also Romeo (1998) for the ideal sculpture from Gortyn. At present nothing is known about the source of the marble or any trade to/from Crete in stone for sculpture. Crete has marble, but not of sufficient quality for sculpture (*e.g.* Durkin and Lister 1983; Harrison 1990).

47 On the group of Artemis and Niobe with her youngest daughter from the Inatos villa (Herakleion, Archaeological Museum 265, 266), see Marinatos 1934–1935. For sculpture from Kissamos, see Markoulaki 2009; Kouremenos 2013, 147, 158.

48 This linguistic distinction is even more strongly confirmed by numismatic inscriptions: nine Cretan cities minted coins in the Imperial period with Greek inscriptions (Axos, Kydonia, Eleutherna, Gortyn, Gierapytna, Lappa, Lato, Lyttos, Polyrrhenia), compared to only Knossos with Latin. The coins of the Cretan Koinon also bore inscriptions in Greek. See the catalogue of Svoronos (1890) for individual examples as well as Burnett *et al.* 1992.

49 For instance, of the eight inscriptions published by Baldwin Bowsky (1995), all but one are written in Greek.

50 Knossos Greek: *IC* I.viii.20–21, 23–25, 27, 30, 41–42; Knossos Latin: *IC* I.viii.48–50, 53–54.

51 The entire fourth volume of *Inscriptiones Creticae* is dedicated to the Gortyn inscriptions.

52 Lyttos Greek: *IC* I.xviii.11, 14–52, 64–71, 73–75, 77–84, 86–87, 89–96, 98–106, 109–118, 120–121, 123–135, 137–139, 141–144, 146–157, 159–163, 166–187; Latin: *IC* I.xviii.188–189. Hierapytna Greek: *IC* III.iii.7, 11–12, 14–20, 22–23, 25–30, 32, 36, 38–39, 42, 45–49, 51–53, 57–64.

53 A comprehensive analysis of Cretan surveys is Gkiasta 2008, to which can be added the Gournia Survey (Watrous *et al.* 2012) and the Galatas Survey (Watrous *et al.* 2017).

54 For instance, the rural sites on the Frangokastello Plain in east Sphakia employ traditional stone-built architecture until well into the late antique period; see Francis 2017, 519–520; see also Raab 2001, 82.

55 Many Roman sites on Crete are identified solely on the basis of Roman concrete, but their original function and size cannot be estimated; see, for example, Khoumeri (Hood *et al.* 1964, 55–56, site 2/3; Sanders 1982, 163, site 13/10) and Asomatos (Hood *et al.* 1964, 76, site 27/5; Sanders 1982, 161, site 12/9).

56 The use of pozzolana with pumice, probably from Italy, in the harbor at Chersonisos is noteworthy; the method of analysis employed for this identification has not been applied to any other site on Crete (Brandon *et al.* 2005) and other instances of this material are at present unknown.

57 On burials in general, see Sanders 1982, 40–43. Cist graves: Sanders 1982, 152, Site 8/1 (Herakleion), 155, Site 9/15 (Ano Asites), 170, Site 18/18 (Cydonia), 173, Site 20/15 (Drapania); Sweetman 2013, 300 (Kissamos), 294 (Elounda), 296 (Gortyn). Tile graves are frequent: *e.g.* Sanders 1982, 137, Site 1/14 (Episkopi), 144, Site 6/4 (Gournes), 154, Site 9/8 (Gazi), 159, Site

10/23 (Lebena), 169–170 (Cydonia); Sweetman 2013, 294 (Elounda), 303 (Knossos). Shaft graves: Sweetman 2013, 294 (Elounda), 296 (Gortyn). The best-known chamber tombs are at Matala (Sanders 1982, 41, fig. 7); for other examples, see Sanders 1982, 152, Site 8/1 (Herakleion), 150–151, Site 7/23 (Velouli), 155, Sitei 9/16 (Prinias Patela), 164, Site 14/16 (Amnatos), 168, Site 17/18 (Asi Gonia); on Knossos, Hood and Smyth 1981, 24–26; Carrington Smith 1982; Sanders 1982, 152–153, Site 8/4; Raab 2001, 82–83; Wardle and Wardle 2004; Sweetman 2013, 303.

58 Lippolis *et al.* 2015.

59 Lissos: Sanders 1982, 42–43, fig. 10; Sweetman 2013, 305. Lasaia: Blackman and Branigan 1975, 28–21, Site SC10; Sanders 1982, 160, Site 10/25. Phoinix-Loutro: largely unpublished; mentioned by Francis 2017, 510, and discussed by Price 2006.

60 Grave stelai with relief decoration are scattered across Crete. Funerary scenes occur, but the representation of symbolic objects is more common. For the former, see, *e.g.* a farewell scene of unknown provenience (Herakleion, Arch. Mus. 187), a funerary banquet scene on a relief from Herakleion (Arch. Mus. no inv. number), a seafaring scene from Tymbaki (Herakleion, Arch. Mus. no inv. number), and a scene of the deceased from Gras (Sanders 1982, 136, Site 1/8; *IC* III. ix.3). For symbolic objects, see a stele with a mirror from Koutsouras (Sanders 1982, 136, Site 1/9), a relief of a comb and mirror from Maronia (Sanders 1982, 137, Site 1/18), of agricultural equipment from Armacha, Embaros, and Partira (Sanders 1982, 149, Site 6/30; 149–150, Site 6/37; 151, Site 7/24), and of a double axe from Tarrha (Kouremenos 2016, 54, fig. 5.20). See also Sporn 2012.

61 Niniou-Kindeli and Christodoulakos 2004, 316–319; Karanastasi 2016, 113, fig. 8.25.

62 Sanders (1982, 47–48) cites 13 sarcophagi from Crete, including examples now located in museums off the island (pls. 8, 10). See also Coulson and Leventi 1998, 224, pl. 36a, b (Chersonisos); Sanders 1982, 139–140, Site 2/8 (Hierapytna); 142, Site 4/15 (Psykro); 144–146, Site 6/7; 147, Site 6/20 (Mallia); 171–72, Site 19/18 (Lissos); Sweetman 2013, 296 (Gortyn); Gallimore 2015, 575, fig. 13.

63 Karanastasi (2016, 108) has noted the sculptural emphasis in the Augustan and Julio-Claudian periods. A portrait of a youth from Gortyn may represent Gaius Caesar Germanicus, or Drusus (Herakleion, Arch. Mus. 66: Portale 1998, 295–304, no. 3, pls 38, 73b; Lagogianni-Georgakarakos 2002, 56–57, no. 13, pl. 14). Two portraits of Tiberius come from Lissos (Chania, Arch. Mus. Λ 138, Λ139: Stavridis 1985, 106, pl. 9.4–6 and 105–106, pl. 9.1–3) and one from Gortyn (Herakleion, Arch. Mus. 65: Portale 1998, 310–318, no. 5, pls. 40, 73a ; Lagogianni-Georgakarakos 2002, 48–49, no. 3, pl. 3). Gortyn preserves two portraits of Caligula (Herakleion, Arch. Mus. 64: Portale 1998, 325–31, no. 7, pl. 42, 331–336, no. 8, pl. 43; Lagogianni-Georgakarakos 2002, 49–51, nos 3, 4, pls. 3, 4).

64 One portrait of Trajan comes from Lyttos (Herakleion Arch. Mus. 317: Lagogianni-Georgakarakos 2002, 51–52, no. 6, pl. 8); another is without findspot (Chania, Arch. Mus. Λ 140: Stavridis 1985, 108, pl. 16.1). Portraits of Hadrian are more common, perhaps because of the emperor's interest in Crete, his possible sponsorship of the renovations of the Diktynnaion Sanctuary, and the inclusion of Hierapytna, Gortyn, and Lyttos in the emperor's Panhellenion League; also Romeo 2002. For the cuirass statue of Hadrian from Hierapytna, now in Istanbul (Arch. Mus. 50), see Mendel 1914, 316–320, no. 316. For other representations of Hadrian: Kissamos, from the theatre (Kissamos, Arch. Mus. Λ 30: unpublished but mentioned in Markoulaki (2009, 339–340, n. 11); Herakleion (Louvre Ma 3131: Lagogianni-Georgakarakos 2002, 52–53, no. 8, pl. 9; Louvre Ma 3132: Lagogianni-Georgakarakos 2002, 52, no. 7, pl. 9); Knossos (Villa Ariadne: 91, no. 71, pl. 75); Gortyn (Herakleion, Arch. Mus. 5: Portale 1998, 445–451, no. 33, pl. LXIII; Lagogianni-Georgakarakos 2002, 89–91, no. 70, pls 72–74); and the Diktynnaion Sanctuary (Chania, Arch. Mus. 82: Andreadaki-Vlazaki 1997, 63–65, fig. 74); a further portrait is without findspot (Herakleion, Arch. Mus. 341: Lagogianni-Georgakarakos 2002, 53–54, no. 9, pl. 10). Karanastasi (2012–2013) provides an analysis of these portraits.

65 For the portrait of Marcus Aurelius (Herakleion, Arch. Mus. 574), see Portale 1998, 364–370, no. 17, pl. XLIX; Lagogianni-Georgakarakos 2002, 54–55, no. 10, pl. 11. For Caracalla (Herakleion, Arch. Mus. 409), see Portale 1998, 406–410, no. 23, pl. LVI; Lagogianni-Georgakarakos 2002, 55–56, no. 11, pl. 12. The Itanos inscription is recorded in *IC* 3.iv.20. The Constantinian re-worked head from Kydonia is in Istanbul (Arch. Mus. 273: Mendel 1914, III, 344–345, no. 1107; L'Orange 1984, 69, pl. 48c; Portale 1998, 426, n. 905; Prusac 2011, 147–148, no. 310; Karanastasi 2016, 109); for the Gortyn example, see Portale 1998, 424–430, no. 26, pl. LIX; Lagogianni-Georgakarakos 2002, 70, no. 33, pl. 38; Karanastasi 2016, 109).

66 For portraits of unknown Romans – presumably local grandees and family members, see, for example, Lagogianni-Georgakarakos 2002, 28–34, 67–70, cats 12–34 and 71–87, cats 36–67.

67 The degree to which the irregular erection of portraits on Crete was prompted by either a gift or a promised benefaction is unknown but this practice might be suspected for Gortyn; note the dynastic group of the Julio-Claudians; Portale 1998, 293–318.

68 See Forster 2001, 153 for ongoing traditions at Knossos. A probable mortarium comes from the Villa Dionysos at Knossos (Hayes 1983, 162, A39).

69 Leatham and Hood 1958–1959; Davaras 1974; Mylona 2003; Francis 2010b; Mourtzas 2012a; 2012b.

70 On the re-use of fish-sauce amphorae, see Peña 2007, 66–68.

71 See also Gallimore 2015, 278.

72 For example, two examples from the Villa Dionysos (Knossos) excavations (Hayes 1983, 146, A41–42), and those from Gortyn (*e.g.* Portale and Romeo 2001, 284–285, nos 26–27).

73 For example, late 2nd-century BCE coins appeared in mixed Roman (C2), Neronian (N3), and Tiberian (T1) deposits; see Price 1992, 324, nos 53, 54, 57. Whether these coins were still in circulation at the time of their deposition is unknown.

74 Scholarship on Cretan transport amphorae and their role in the island's Roman economy continues to grow: De Caro 1992–1993; Marangou-Lerat 1995; Marangou 1999; 2000; Portale and Romeo 2000; Williams 2003; De Aloe 2009; Portale 2014; Poulou-Papadimitriou and Nodarou 2014; Sazanov 2014; Gallimore 2015, fig. 10.6; 2016; 2017b; 2018.

75 Onorio Belli documented the theatres of Roman Crete, many of which have not survived (Falkener 1854); more recently, for example, see Sanders 1982, 57–67; Harrison 2016; Niniou-Kindeli and Chatzidakis 2016.

76 For regionalism reflected in Bronze Age Crete, see Wilson and Day 1994; Murphy 2011.

77 On the state of fabric analysis for Cretan projects, see Yangaki 2016, 202–203. Fabric information is available for Roman pottery from Sphakia (Moody *et al.* 2003), Knossos (Forster 2009, 72–76), Gortyn (Martin 1997a, 293–95), Hierapytna (Gallimore 2015, 93–94, 152–153, 178–80, 206–208, 252–253), Eleutherna (Aloupi *et al.* 2000; Vogt 2000; Yangaki 2005, 36–37), Itanos (Xanthopoulou *et al.* 2014), Chania and the Akrotiri Peninsula (Raab 2001, 61–73). Kiln sites active in the Roman period continue to be excavated, such as that in Chania (Limantzaki 2011) but information about the range of distribution for their products remains elusive.

Fabric analysis remains the primary means for identifying pottery sources on Crete, but lack of consistent application, methodologies, and publication has resulted in only vaguely usable definitions for regional workshop products. Nonetheless, major centers with identified 'local' fabrics, like Gortyn, Eleutherna, and Knossos, provide rudimentary comparative information, which confirms the limited regional distribution of these specific wares. A well-attested example is the Hellenistic and early Roman production of East Cretan Cream Ware, which was made in Hierapytna and circulated throughout the Bay of Mirabello area (*e.g.* Eiring 2000, 54; Vogeikoff-Brogan 2000, 70–2; Vogeikoff-Brogan *et al.* 2008, 330–333; Gallimore 2015, 72–90).

78 Francis 2017. Some of the sites on the Frangokastello Plain in southwest Sphakia eloquently indicate the conservative values and practices that continued well into the late Roman period, with only Roman imported pottery – and probably the identity of the entity to whom they sold their products or which collected taxes – marking changes from earlier times.

79 Gallimore 2015, 280–281; Chevrollier 2016. The lack of interaction between the two parts of the province is all the more curious since the south coast provided Crete's only winter harbor (Phoinix-Loutro) and ancient *testimonia* confirms the passage of commercial ships along this route and thus its utility (Francis 2018). On the other hand, this was also the location of St Paul's shipwreck (*Acts* 27.8).

80 South coast ports exploited in the Roman era include Hierapytna, Phoinix-Loutro, and Matala.

81 On trade between the two areas, see, recently, Chevrollier 2016. For African Red Slip (ARS) deposits see, for example, Dello Preite 1984; Yangaki 2016, 204. For a survey of North African amphorae on Crete, see Gallimore 2015, 233–236; Yangaki (2016, 217–218) presents late antique examples.

82 The bibliography on contemporary responses to the imposition of Roman rule and culture is growing; see, for example, Woolf 1998.

83 There is very little evidence for foreigners resident on Crete. Inscriptions name various individuals as coming from Cyrenaica and Egypt, some of whom acted as *proxenoi*. Eight or nine private monuments, like grave stelai, commemorate Libyans living on the island. For a discussion of this evidence, see Baldwin Bowsky 1999; Chevrollier 2016, 18–21; also n. 7 above.

84 Ascribed to Epimenides, from Knossos; also, for example, Callimachus, *Hymn to Zeus* I.4–9; see also St Paul, *Titus* 1.12.

85 Alcock 2002.

Bibliography

Alcock, S. (2002) *Archaeologies of the Greek Past*. Cambridge: Cambridge University Press.

Aloupi, E., Kilikoglou, V., Day, P. and Joyner, L. (2000) Provenance and Technological Characterisation of Fine Tableware (with Appendix: Petrographic Analysis of Domestic Pottery from Byzantine Eleutherna). In *Πρωτοβυζαντινή Ελεύθερνα, τομέας* I.2, edited by P.G. Themelis. Rethymnon Panepistemio Kretes, 207–235.

Andreadaki-Vlasaki, M. (1997) *The County of Khania through its Monuments*. Athens: Ministry of Culture, Archaeological Receipts Fund.

Antonelli, F., Bonetto, J., Lazzarini, L., Salvo, G. and Fabrini, M.G. (2017) The Use of White Marbles for Sculptures in Roman Gortyn (Crete) as Revealed by Archaeometric Analyses. *Archaeological and Anthropological Sciences* 9, 579–589.

Baldwin Bowsky, M.W. (1995) Eight Inscriptions from Roman Crete. *Zeitschrift für Papyrologie und Epigraphik* 108, 263–280.

Baldwin Bowsky, M.W. (1999) The Business of Being Roman: The Prosopographical Evidence. In *From Minoan Farmers to Roman Traders. Sidelights on the Economy of Ancient Crete*, edited by A. Chaniotis. Heidelberger Althistorische Beiträge und Epigraphische Studien 29. Stuttgart: Franz Steiner, 305–347.

Baldwin Bowsky, M.W. (2004) Of Two Tongues: Acculturation at Roman Knossos. In *Colonie Romane nel Mondo Greco* (Minima Epigraphica et Papyrologica, Suppl. 3), edited by G. Salmeri, A. Raggi and A. Baroni. Rome: L'Erma Bretschneider, 94–150.

Baldwin Bowsky, M.W. (2006) Highways and Byways of Roman Hierapytna (Crete): Four New Claudian Road Inscriptions. *Annuario della Scuola Archeologica di Atene* 84, 551–580.

Baldwin Bowsky, M.W. (2007) From Piracy to Privileged Status: Lappa (Crete) and the Romans. In *XII Congressus Internationalis Epigraphiae Graecae et Latinae. Provinciae Imperii Romani Inscriptionibus Descriptae: Barcelona, 3–8 Septembris 2002*, edited by M. Mayer i Olivé, G. Baratta and A. Guzmán. Barcelona: Institut d'Estudis Catalans, 197–202.

Baldwin Bowsky, M.W. (2011) *Colonia Iulia Nobilis Cnosus*, The First 100 Years: The Evidence of Italian Sigillata Stamps. In *Roman Colonies in the First Century of their Foundation* edited by R.J. Sweetman. Oxford: Oxbow Books, 117–134.

Baldwin Bowsky, M.W. (2016) A Context for Knossos: Italian Sigillata Stamps and Cultural Identity Across Crete. In *Roman Crete: New Perspectives*, edited by J.E. Francis and A. Kouremenos. Oxford: Oxbow Books, 27–41.

Baldwin Bowsky, M.W. (2017) Normalization at Knossos: Material and Non-material Evidence. In *L'Héritage grec des Colonies Romaines d'Orient: interactions culturelles dans les provinces hellénophones de l'empire romain: actes du colloque de Strasbourg (8–9 novembre 2013)*, edited by C. Brélaz. Paris: Éditions De Boccard, 291–307.

Baldwin Bowsky, M.W. and Niniou-Kindeli, V. (2006) On the Road Again: A Trajanic Milestone and the Road Connections of Aptera, Crete. *Hesperia* 75, 405–433.

Blackman, D.J. and Branigan, K. (1975) An Archaeological Survey on the South Coast of Crete. *Annual of the British School at Athens* 70, 17–36.

Brandon, C., Hohlfelder, R.L., Oleson, J.P. and Stern, C. (2005) The Roman Maritime Concrete Study (ROMACONS): The Harbour of Chersonisos in Crete and its Italian Connection. *Méditerranée* 104, 25–29.

Brookes, E.W. (1913) The Arab Occupation of Crete. *The English Historical Review* 28, 431–443.

Burnett, A., Amandry, M. and Ripollés, P.P. (1992) *Roman Provincial Coinage. Vol. I.* London and Paris: British Museum Press with Bibliothèque Nationale Paris.

Carrington Smith, J. (1982) A Roman Chamber Tomb on the South-East Slopes of Monasteraki Kephala, Knossos. *Annual of the British School at Athens* 77, 255–291.

Chaniotis, A. (2004) From Communal Spirit to Individuality: The Epigraphic Habit in Hellenistic and Roman Crete. In *Creta Romana e Protobizantina. Atti del Congresso Internzionale (Iraklion, 23–30 settembre 2000)*, edited by M. Livadiotti and I. Simiakaki. Padua: Bottega d'Erasmo, 75–87.

Chaniotis, A. (2005) Inscribed Instrumenta Domestica and the Economy of Hellenistic and Roman Crete. In *Making, Moving and Managing: The New World of Ancient Economies*, edited by Z.H. Archibald, J.K. Davies and V. Gabrielsen. Oxford: Oxbow Books, 92–116.

Chaniotis, A. (2008) What Difference did Rome Make? The Cretans and the Roman Empire. In *The Province Strikes Back: Imperial Dynamics in the Eastern Mediterranean*, edited by B. Forsen and G. Salmeri. Helsinki: Suomen Ateenan-instituutin säätiö, 83–105.

Chevrollier, F. (2015) Épigraphie et Identité. Autour de quelques Lieux de Mémoire dans la Crète d'Époque Romaine. In *Afti inè i Kriti! Identités, altérités et figures crétoises*, edited by P. Louvier, P. Monbrun and A. Pierrot. Scripta Receptoria 4. Bordeaux: Ausonius Éditions, 219–230.

Chevrollier, F. (2016) From Cyrene to Gortyn. Notes on the Relationship between Crete and Cyrenaica under Roman Domination (1st century BC–4th century AD). In *Roman Crete: New Perspectives*, edited by J.E. Francis and A. Kouremenos. Oxford: Oxbow Books, 11–26.

Christides, V. (1981) The Raids of the Moslems of Crete in the Aegean Sea: Piracy and Conquest. *Byzantion* 51, 76–111.

Christides, V. (1984) *The Conquest of Crete by the Arabs (ca. 824): A Turning Point in the Struggle between Byzantium and Islam.* Athens: Akademia Athenon.

Christodoulakos, G. (2011) Ρωμαϊκά υδραγωγεία της Δυτικής Κρήτης. In *Πεπραγμένα του Ι' Διεθνούς Κρητολογικού Συνεδρίου (Χανιά, 1–8 Οκτωβρίου 2006)*, A2, edited by M. Andrianakis. Chania: Philologikos Syllogos 'O Chrystostomos', 171–193.

Cohon, R. (1984) *Greek and Roman Stone Table Supports with Decorative Reliefs.* Unpublished Ph.D. thesis, New York University.

Coldstream, J.N. (1973) *Knossos: The Sanctuary of Demeter.* BSA Suppl. 8. London: British School of Archaeology at Athens; Thames and Hudson.

Coulson, W.D.E. and Leventi, I. (1998) A Roman Head in the American School of Classical Studies at Athens. *Hesperia* 67, 223–229.

Croz, J.F. (2002) *Les portraits sculptés de Romains en Grèce et en Italie de Cynoscéphales à Actium 197–31 av. J.C.: essai sur les perspectives idéologiques de l'art du portrait.* Paris: Editions L'Harmattan.

Davaras, C. (1974) Rock-Cut Fish Tanks in Eastern Crete. *Annual of the British School at Athens* 69, 87–93.

De Aloe, I. (2009) Le Terme a sud del Pretorio di Gortina. Produzione e Circolazione dei Contenitori da Trasporto. *Lanx*, 38–43.

De Caro, S. (1992–93) Vino di Cnosso dei Campani: Un Nuovo Documento Epigrafico per la Storia del Vino Cretese in età Romana. *Annuario della Scuola Archeologica di Atene* 70–71, 307–312.

Dello Preite, A. (1984) Le Importazioni di Ceramica Fine a Gortina e Creta tra il IV e il VII sec. D.C. *Annuario della Scuola Archeologica di Atene* 46, 177–198.

De Tommaso, G.D. (2001) Ceramica a Pareti Sottili. In *Gortina V.3. Lo Scavo del Pretorio (1989–1995) t. 1. I Materiali*, edited by A. Di Vita. Monografie della scuola archeologica Italiana di Atene e delle missioni Italiane in oriente XII. Padua: Bottega d'Erasmo, 21–24.

Di Vita, A. (1988) Monete. In *Gortina I*, edited by A. Di Vita. Monografie della scuola archeologica Italiana di Atene e delle missioni Italiane in oriente III. Rome: L'Erma Bretschneider, 153–164.

Di Vita, A. (2010) *Gortina di Creta: Quindici Secoli di Vita Urbana*. Rome: L'Erma Bretschneider.

Durkin, M.K. and Lister, C.J. (1983) The Rods of Digenis: An Ancient Marble Quarry in Eastern Crete. *Annual of the British School at Athens* 78, 69–96.

Eiring, J. (2000) Hellenistic Pottery from Pyrgos at Myrtos. In *E'Επιστημονική Συναντηση για την Ελληνιστική Κεραμική. Χρονολογικα Προβληματα. Κλειστα συνολα-εργαστηρια. Πρακτικά. Κείμεναln*, edited by S. Drogou, E. Zerboudaki, L. Maragkou and G. Touratsoglou. Athens: Ekdose tou Tameiou Archaiologikon Poron kai Apallotrioseon, 53–60.

Eiring, J. (2004) The Earliest Italian Sigillata at Knossos. In *Early Italian Sigillata. The Chronological Framework and Trade Patterns. Proceedings of the First International ROCT-Congress, Leuven, May 7 and 8, 1999*, edited by J. Poblome, P. Talloen, R. Brulet and M. Waelkens. Leuven: Peeters, 71–72.

Englezou, M. (2000) Ελληνιστική κεραμική από την αρχαία Λύττο. In *E'Επιστημονική Συναντηση για την Ελληνιστική Κεραμική. Χρονολογικα Προβληματα. Κλειστα συνολα-εργαστηρια. Πρακτικά. Κείμεναln*, edited by S. Drogou, E. Zerboudaki, L. Maragkou and G. Touratsoglou. Athens: Ekdose tou Tameiou Archaiologikon Poron kai Apallotrioseon, 61–68.

Englezou, M. (2005) *Ελληνιστική Κεραμική Κρήτης: Κεντική Κρήτη*. Athens: Tameio archaiologikon poron kai apallatrioseon.

Falkener, E. (1854) *Description of Some Important Theatres and Other Remains in Crete: from a ms. History of Candia by Onorio Belli in 1586*. London: Trübner.

Forster, G. (2001) The Roman Period. In *Knossos Pottery Handbook: Greek and Roman*, edited by J.N. Coldstream, L.J. Eiring and G. Forster. BSA Studies 7. London: British School at Athens, 137–167.

Forster, G. (2009) *Roman Knossos: The Pottery in Context. A Presentation of Ceramic Evidence Provided by the Knossos 2000 Project (1993–95)*. Unpublished Ph.D. Thesis, University of Birmingham.

Francis, J. (2010a) Appendix: Roman Pottery. In *Moni Odigitria: A Prepalatian Cemetery and its Environs in the Asterousia, Southern Crete*, edited by A. Vasilakis and K. Branigan. INSTAP Prehistory Monographs 30. Philadelphia: INSTAP Academic Press, 28–46.

Francis, J. (2010b) A Re-Evaluation of Rock-Cut Fish Installations in Roman Crete. *Creta Antica* 11, 255–275.

Francis, J. (2012) What's so Rural about the Landscape of Roman Crete? In *Comparative Issues in the Archaeology of the Roman Rural Landscape*, edited by P. Attema and G. Schoerner. Journal of Roman Archaeology Suppl. 88. Portsmouth: Journal of Roman Archaeology, 91–106.

Francis, J. (2017) Roman Influence on Greek Sphakia. In *From Maple to Olive. Proceedings of a Colloquium to Celebrate the 40th Anniversary of the Canadian Institute in Greece*, edited by D.W. Rupp and J.E. Tomlinson. Publications of the Canadian Institute in Greece 10. Athens: Canadian Institute in Greece, 505–533.

Francis, J. (2018) Coast and Hinterland in Graeco-Roman Sphakia (West Crete). Abstract in 19th International Congress of Classical Archaeology, Cologne/Bonn, 22–26 May 2018, http://www.aiac2018.de/programme/sessions/#5-3_5.

Francis, J.E. and Kouremenos, A. (eds) (2016) *Roman Crete: New Perspectives*. Oxford: Oxbow Books.

Gallimore, S. (2014). An Interpretation of the Chersonesos Ostraca, O.Cret.Chers. *Zeitschrift für Papyrologie und Epigraphik* 190, 203–209.

Gallimore, S. (2015) *An Island Economy. Hellenistic and Roman Pottery from Hierapytna, Crete.* New York: Peter Lang.

Gallimore, S. (2016) Crete's Economic Transformation in the Late Roman Empire. In *Roman Crete: New Perspectives*, edited by J.E. Francis and A. Kouremenos. Oxford: Oxbow Books, 175–188.

Gallimore, S. (2017a) Abandonment and Assimilation in the Roman Period. In *The Galatas Survey. Socio-Economic and Political Development of a Contested Territory in Central Crete During the Neolithic to Ottoman Periods*, edited by L.V. Watrous, D.M. Buell, E. Kokinou, P. Soupios, A. Sarris, S. Beckman, G. Rethemiotakis, L.A. Turner, S. Gallimore and M.D. Hammond. INSTAP Prehistory Monographs 55. Philadelphia: INSTAP Academic Press, 105–117.

Gallimore, S. (2017b) Food Surplus and Archaeological Proxies: A Case Study from Roman Crete. *World Archaeology* 49, 138–150.

Gallimore, S. (2018) The Relationship Between Agricultural Production and Amphora Manufacture on Roman Crete. *Journal of Roman Archaeology* 31, 373–386.

Garraffo, S. (1997) Monete. In *Gortina II. Pretorio. Il Materiale degli Scavi Coloni 1970-1977*, edited by A. Di Vita and A. Martin. Monografie della scuola archeologica di Atene e delle missioni Italiane in oriente 7. Padua: Bottega d'Erasmo, 77–110.

Garraffo, S. (1999) Le Monete. In *Gortina III. Le Fortificazioni di eta Ellenistica*, edited by N. Allegro and M. Ricciardi. Monografie della scuola archeologica di Atene e delle missioni Italiane in oriente 10. Padua: Bottega d'Erasmo, 270–274.

Garraffo, S. (2001) Monete. In *Gortina V.3. Lo Scavo del Pretorio (1989-1995), t. II. I Materiali*, edited by A. Di Vita. Monografie della scuola archeologica Italiana di Atene e delle missioni Italiane in oriente XII. Padua: Bottega d'Erasmo, 655–720.

Giorgi, E. (2016) *Archeologia dell'Acqua a Gortina di Creta in età Protobizantina.* Oxford: Access Archaeology.

Gkiasta, M. (2008) *The Historiography of Landscape Research on Crete.* Archaeological Studies 16. Leiden: Leiden University Press.

Gomez, B., Neff, H., Rautman, M.L., Vaughan, S.J. and Glascock, M.D. (2002) The Source Provenance of Bronze Age and Roman Pottery from Cyprus. *Archaeometry* 44, 23–36.

Grigoropoulos, D. (2004) Tomb robbing and the transformation of social memory in Roman Knossos. In *TRAC 2003: Proceedings of the Thirteenth Annual Theoretical Roman Archaeology Conference which took place at the University of Leicester 3-6 April 2003*, edited by B. Croxford, H. Eckhardt, J. Meade and J. Weekes. Oxford: Oxbow Books, 62–77.

Gunneweg, J., Perlman, I. and Yellin, J. (1983) *The Provenience, Typology, and Chronology of Eastern Terra Sigillata.* Jerusalem: Institute of Archaeology, Hebrew University of Jerusalem.

Haggis, D.C. (1996) The Port of Tholos in Eastern Crete and the Role of a Roman Horreum along the Egyptian 'Corn Route'. *Oxford Journal of Archaeology* 15, 183–209.

Hanson, A. (1972) A Ptolemaic List of Aromata and Honey. *Transactions of the American Philological Association* 103, 161–166.

Harris, W.V. (1999) Crete in the Hellenistic and Roman Economies: A Comment. In *From Minoan Farmers to Roman Traders: Sidelights on the Economy of Ancient Crete*, edited by A. Chaniotis. Heidelberger althistorische Beiträge und epigraphische Studien 2. Stuttgart: Franz Steiner, 353–358.

Harrison, G.W.M. (1985) The Joining of Cyrenaica to Crete. In *Cyrenaica in Antiquity*, edited by G. Barker, J. Lloyd and J. Reynolds. BAR International Series 236. Oxford: British Archaeological Reports, 365–373.

Harrison, G.W.M. (1990) A Roman Marble Quarry in Eastern Crete. *Cretan Studies* 2, 147–150.

Harrison, G.W.M. (1993) *The Romans and Crete.* Amsterdam: A.M. Hakkert.

Harrison, G.W.M. (2016) Theatres, Plays, and the '3rd Century Crisis'. In *Roman Crete: New Perspectives*, edited by J.E. Francis and A. Kouremenos. Oxford: Oxbow Books, 189–197.

Harrison, G.W.M. and Hayden, B.J. (2005) Roman Pottery Summary. In *Reports on the Vrokastro Area, Eastern Crete. Volume 3: The Vrokastro Regional Survey project: Sites and Pottery*, edited by B.J. Hayden. University Museum Monographs 123. Philadelphia: University of Pennsylvania Museum of Archaeology and Anthropology, 57–79.

Hayes, J.W. (1971) Four Early Roman Groups from Knossos. *Annual of the British School at Athens* 66, 249–275.

Hayes, J.W. (1983) The Villa Dionysos Excavations, Knossos: The Pottery. *Annual of the British School at Athens* 73, 97–169.

Hood, S. and Smyth, D. (1981) *Archaeological Survey of the Knossos Area*. BSA Suppl. 14. London: British School at Athens.

Hood, S., Warren, P. and Cadogan, G. (1964) Travels in Crete, 1962. *Annual of the British School at Athens* 59, 50–99.

Karanastasi, P. (2012–13) Hadrian im Panzer. Kaiserstatuen zwischen Realpolitik und Philhellenismus. *Jahrbuch des Deutschen Archäologischen Instituts* 127/128, 323–391.

Karanastasi, P. (2015) New Evidence about Roman Eleutherna. In *Αρχαιολογικο Εργο Κρητης 3. Πρακτικά της 3ης Συνάντησης, Ρέθυμνο, 5-8 Δεκεμβρίου 2013. Τομος Β' Χανια - Ρεθυμνο - Λασιθι*, edited by P. Karanastasi, A. Tzigounaki and C. Tzigonaki. Rethymnon: Faculty of Letters Publications, University of Crete, Ministry of Culture and Sports - Ephorate of Antiquities of Rethymnon, 417–428.

Karanastasi, P. (2016) Roman Imperial Sculpture from Crete: A Reappraisal. In *Roman Crete: New Perspectives*, edited by J.E. Francis and A. Kouremenos. Oxford: Oxbow Books, 101–118.

Kelly, A. (2013) Roman Bathhouses on Crete as Indicators of Cultural Transition: The Dynamics of Roman Influence. In *Creating Ethnicities & Identities in the Roman World*, edited by A. Gardner, E. Herring and K. Lomas. BICS Suppl. 120. London: Institute of Classical Studies, School of Advanced Study, University of London, 313–367.

Kelly, A. (2018) A Roman Aqueduct Through the Cretan Highlands – Securing the Water Supply for Elevated Lyttos. In *Great Waterworks in Roman Greece. Aqueducts and Monumental Fountains. Function in Context*, edited by G.A. Aristodemou and T.P. Tassios. Oxford: Archaeopress, 147–169.

Kouremenos, A. (2013) *Houses and Identity in Roman Knossos and Kissamos, Crete: A Study in Emulative Acculturation*. Unpublished DPhil Thesis, University of Oxford.

Kouremenos, A. (2016) The Double Axe (Λάβρυσ) in Roman Crete and Beyond: The Iconography of a Multi-Faceted Symbol. In *Roman Crete: New Perspectives*, edited by J.E. Francis and A. Kouremenos. Oxford: Oxbow Books, 43–58.

Kouremenos, A. (2018) In the Heart of the Wine-Dark Sea: Cretan Insularity and Identity in the Roman Period. In *Insularity and Identity in the Roman Mediterranean*, edited by A. Kouremenos. Oxford: Oxbow Books, 41–64.

Kouremenos, A. (forthcoming) *Origanum Dictamnus* (Dittany of Crete): Testaments, Uses, and Trade of a Sacred Plant in Antiquity. In *Change and Transition on Crete: Interpreting the Evidence from the Hellenistic Through to the Early Byzantine Period. Papers Presented in Honour of G.W.M. Harrison*, edited by M. Curtis and J.E. Francis. Oxford: Archaeopress.

Lagogianni-Georgakarakos, M. (2002) *Die römischen Porträts Kretas. I. Bezirk Heraklion. Corpus signorum Imperii Romani. Grèce*, fasc. 1. Athens: Akademie von Athen.

Lambrugo, C. (2011) I Marmi Annullati: Calcare a Gortina. *Lanx* 8, 120–135.

Lassithiotakis, K. (1951) Ο ναός των Εισοδίων και μια παλαιότερη βασιλική στο Φόδελε. *Kretika Chronika* 1, 76–86.

Leatham, J. and Hood, S. (1958–59) Sub-Marine Exploration in Crete, 1955. *Annual of the British School at Athens* 53–54, 263–280.Leonard Jr., A. (1972) Kouphonisi Revisited. *Archeologia Classica* 24, 353–363.

Limantzaki, L. (2011) Κεραμικοί κλίβανοι της εποχής της ρωμαιοκρατίας στην Κυδωνιία. In *Πεπραγμένα του Ι' Διεθνούς Κρητολογικού Συνεδρίου (Χανιά, 1-8 Οκτωβρίου 2006)*, A2, edited by M. Andrianakis. Chania: Philologikos Syllogos 'O Chrystostomos', 263–276.

Lippolis, E. (2001) Terra Sigillata Orientale. In *Gortina V.3. Lo scavo del Pretorio (1989–1995o, t.I, I Materiali*, edited by A. Di Vita. Monografie della Scuola archeolgica di Atene e delle missioni italiane in Oriente 12. Padua: Bottega d'Erasmo, 25–35.

Lippolis, E. (2016) Roman Gortyn: from Greek Polis to provincial Capital. In *Roman Crete: New Perspectives*, edited by J.E. Francis and A. Kouremenos. Oxford: Oxbow Books, 155–174.

Lippolis, E., Sassu, R., Giatti, C. and Calio, L.M. (2015) Gortys. Archaeological Excavations of New Mausoleums in the Praetorium Area. In *Αρχαιολογικο Εργο Κρητης 3. Πρακτικά της 3ης Συνάντησης, Ρέθυμνο, 5-8 Δεκεμβρίου 2013. Τομος Β' Χανια* - Ρεθυμνο - Λασιθι, edited by P. Karanastasi, A. Tzigounaki and C. Tzigonaki. Rethymnon: Faculty of Letters Publications, University of Crete, Ministry of Culture and Sports - Ephorate of Antiquities of Rethymnon, 537–552.

Litinas, N. (2008) *Greek Ostraca from Chersonesos, Crete: Ostraca Cretica Chersonesi (O.Cret.Chers.)* Tyche, Suppl. 6. Vienna: Holzhausen.

Livadiotti, M. and Simiakaki, I. (eds) (2004) *Creta Romana e Protobizantina. Atti del Congresso Internzionale (Iraklion, 23–30 settembre 2000)*. Padua: Bottega d'Erasmo.

L'Orange, H.P. (1984) *Das spätantike Herrscherbild von Diokletian bis zu den Konstantin-Söhnen 294–361 n. Chr.* Das Römische Herrscherbild III.4. Berlin: Mann.

Lund, J. (2015) *A Study of the Circulation of Ceramics in Cyprus from the 3rd Century BC to the 3rd Century AD*. Aarhus: Aarhus University Press.

Marangou, A. (1999) Wine in the Cretan Economy. In *From Minoan Farmers to Roman Traders: Sidelights on the Economy of Ancient Crete*, edited by A. Chaniotis. Heidelberger althistorische Beiträge und epigraphische Studien 29. Stuttgart: Franz Steiner, 269–278.

Marangou, A. (2000) The Wine-trade between Crete and Egypt: A First Account. In *Κρήτη- Αίγυπτος: Πολιτισμικοί δεσμοί τριών χιλιετιών*, edited by A. Karetsou. Athens: Herakleion Archaeological Museum, 250–253.

Marangou-Lerat, A. (1995) *Le vin et les amphores de Crète de l'époque classique à l'époque impériale*. Athens: Ecole Française d'Athènes and Thessalonike: Fondation Fany Boutari.

Marinatos, S. (1934–35) Αι Νιοβίδαι της Ινάτου. *Archaiologike Ephemeris*, 1–17.

Markoulaki (2009) 'Αριστοκρατικές' αστικές επαύλεις στην ελληνορωμαϊκή Κίσαμο. In *Ubi Dubium Ibi Libertas*, edited by C. Loukos, N. Xifaras and N. Pateraki. Rethymnon: Ekdoseis Philosophikes Scholes Panepistemiou Kretes, 337–380.

Markoulaki, S. (2012) Ένα νέο ενυπόγραφο ψηφιδωτό Μενάνδρου από την αρχαία Κίσαμο. In *Αρχαιολογικό Έργο Κρήτης 2*, edited by M. Andrianakis, P. Barthalitou and I. Tzachili. Rethymnon: Faculty of Letters Publications, University of Crete, 562–575.

Markoulaki, S. (2015) Dining with Menander in West Crete (Greece): A New Mosaic Pavement in Kissamos. In *XII Colloquio AIEMA. Venezia, 11–15 settembre 2012. Atti*, edited by G. Trovabene and A. Bertoni. Paris: Scripta edizioni, 281–288.

Martin, A. (1997a) Ceramica Comune: Vasi da Mensa e da Dispensa. In *Gortina II. Pretorio. Il Materiale degli Scavi Coloni 1970–1977*, edited by A. Di Vita and A. Martin. Monografie della scuola archeologica di Atene e delle missioni Italiane in oriente 7. Padua: Bottega d'Erasmo, 291–345.

Martin, A. (1997b) Sigillata Italica. In *Gortina II. Pretorio. Il Materiale degli Scavi Coloni 1970–1977*, edited by A. Di Vita and A. Martin. Monografie della scuola archeologica di Atene e delle missioni Italiane in oriente 7. Padua: Bottega d'Erasmo, 125–126.

Martín-Arroyo, D., Prignano, L., Morer, I., Rull, G., García-Sánchez, M., Díaz-Guilera A. and Remesal, J. (2017) The Wine Trade of Roman Crete: Construction of Onomastic and Geographical Network. In *Insularity, Identity and Epigraphy in the Roman World*, edited by J. Velaza. Cambridge: Cambridge Scholars Publishing, 177–194.

Martinez Fernandez, A. (2012) *Επιγραφές Πολυρρήνιας*, *Archaiologikon Deltion*. Μελέτες 103. Athens: Hellenic Ministry of Culture and Tourism.

Massara, D. (2013) La Decorazione a Mosaica della Fontana Romana di Chersonissos (Creta). *Lanx* 15, 51–73.

Mays, L., Antoniou, G.P. and Angelakis, A.N. (2013) History of Water Cisterns: Legacies and Lessons. *Water* 5, 1916–1940.

Mendel, G. (1914) Musées Impériaux Ottomans. *Catalogue des Sculptures. Grecques, Romaines et Byzantines*. Constantinople: n.p.

Milidakis, M. and Papadaki, C. (2016) An Attic Marble Table Support (τραπεζοφόρον) in Relief from Roman Kissamos: Preliminary Remarks. In *Roman Crete: New Perspectives*, edited by J.E. Francis and A. Kouremenos. Oxford: Oxbow Books, 120–126.

Montali, G. (2006) *Il Teatro Romano di Gortina*. Studi di archeologia cretese 4. Padua: Bottega d'Erasmo.

Moody, J., Nixon, L. and Price, S. (1998) Surveying Poleis and Larger Sites in Sphakia. In *Post Minoan Crete: Proceedings of the First Colloquium on Post-Minoan Crete held at the British School at Athens and the Institute of Archaeology, University College London, 10–11 November 1995*, edited by W. Cavanagh and M. Curtis. BSA Studies 2. London: British School at Athens, 87–95.

Moody, J., Robinson, H.L., Francis, J., Nixon, L. and Wilson, L. (2003) Ceramic Analysis and Survey Archaeology: The Sphakia Survey. *Annual of the British School at Athens* 98, 37–105.

Mourtzas, N.D. (2012a) Archaeological Indicators for Sea Level Change and Coastal Neotectonic Deformation: The Submerged Roman Fish Tanks of the Gulf of Matala, Crete, Greece. *Journal of Archaeological Science* 39, 884–895.

Mourtzas, N.D. (2012b) Fish Tanks of Eastern Crete (Greece) as Indicators of the Roman Sea Level. *Journal of Archaeological Science* 39, 2392–2408.

Murphy, J.M.A. (ed.) (2011) *Prehistoric Crete: Regional and Diachronic Studies on Mortuary Systems*. Philadelphia: INSTAP Academic Press.

Mylona, D. (2003) Fishing in Late Antiquity: The Case of Itanos, Crete. In *Zooarchaeology in Greece: Recent Advances*, edited by E. Kotjabopoulou, Y. Hamilakis, P. Halstead, C. Gamble and P. Elefanti. BSA Studies 9. London: British School at Athens, 103–110.

Niniou-Kindeli, V. and Chatzidakis, N. (2016) The Roman Theatre at Aptera: A Preliminary Report. In *Roman Crete: New Perspectives*, edited by J.E. Francis and A. Kouremenos. Oxford: Oxbow Books, 127–153.

Niniou-Kindeli, V. and Christodoulakos, G. (2004) Ρωμαϊκή Απτέρα. Μία πρώτη προσέγγιση. In *Creta Romana e Protobizantina. Atti del Congresso Internazionale (Iraklion, 23–30 settembre 2000)* II, edited by M. Livadiotti and I. Simiakaki. Padua: Bottega d'Erasmo, 313–334.

Oikonomaki, N.E. (1986) Το θδραγωγέιο της Χερσονήσος. *Lyktos* 2, 50–98.

Pagano, M. (1992) Recherches sur l'aqueduc romain de Gortyne (Crete). In *L'eau et les hommes en Méditerranée et en mer Noire dans l'Antiquité de l'époque mycénniene au règne de Justinien: actes du congrès international, Athènes, 20–24 mai 1988*, edited by G. Argoud. Athens: Centre national de recherches sociales, 279–292.

Pagano, M. (2007) Ricerche sull'Acquedotto e sulle Fontane Romane e Bizantine di Gortina (Creta). *Creta Antica* 8, 330–400.

Pałuchowski, A. (2011) La Romanisation de l'Île de Crète. In *Studia Lesco Mrozewicz ab Amicis et Discipulis Dedicata* (Publikacje Instytutu Historii UAM 103), edited by C. Balbuza and C. Królczyk. Poznań: Inst. Historii UAM, 299–322.

Papadakis, N. (1986) *Ierapetra: Bride of the Libyan Sea*. Translated by J.M. Kafetzaki. Ierapetra: Ierapetra Town Council.

Paton, S. (1994) Roman Knossos and the Colonia Julia Nobilis Cnossus. In *Knossos: A Labyrinth of History. Papers Presented in Honour of Sinclair Hood*, edited by D. Evely, H. Hughes-Brock and N. Momigliano. Athens: British School at Athens, 141–153.

Paton, S. (1998) The Villa Dionysos at Knossos and its Predecessors. In *Post Minoan Crete: Proceedings of the First Colloquium on Post-Minoan Crete Held at the British School at Athens and the Institute of Archaeology, University College London, 10–11 November 1995*, edited by W.G. Cavanagh and M. Curtis. BSA Studies 2. London: British School at Athens, 123–128.

Paton, S. (2004) Knossos: An Imperial Renaissance. In *Knossos: Palace, City, State*, edited by G. Cadogan, E. Hatzaki and A. Vasilakis. BSA Studies 12. London: British School at Athens, 451–455.

Paton, S. and Schneider, R.M. (1999) Imperial Splendour in the Province: Imported Marble on Roman Crete. In *From Minoan Farmers to Roman Traders: Sidelights on the Economy of Ancient Crete*, edited by A. Chaniotis. Heidelberger althistorische Beiträge und epigraphische Studien 29. Stuttgart: Franz Steiner, 279–304.

Pazarli, M., Livierator, E. and Boutoura, C. (2007) Road Network of Crete in Tabula Peutingeriana. *E-Perimetron* 2.4, 245–260.

Peña, J.T. (2007) *Roman Pottery in the Archaeological Record*. Cambridge: Cambridge University Press.

Portale, E.-C. (1998) I Ritratti. In *Gortina III. Le Sculture*, edited by I. Romeo and E.-C. Portale. Monografie della Scuola archeologica di Atene e delle missioni italiane in oriente 8. Padua: Bottega d'Erasmo, 280–512.

Portale, E.C. (2014) The Sunset of Gortyn: Amphorae in the 7th–8th Centuries AD. In *LRCW 4. Late Roman Coarse Wares, Cooking Wares and Amphorae in the Mediterranean. Archaeology and Archaeometry. The Mediterranean: A Market without Frontiers*, edited by N. Poulou-Papadimitriou, E. Nodarou and V. Kilikoglou. BAR International Series 2616. Oxford: Archaeopress, 477–489.

Portale, E.-C. and Romeo, I. (2000) Le Anfore Locali di Gortina Ellenistica e Romana. *Rei Cretariae Romanae Fautorum Acta* 36, 417–426.

Portale, E.-C. and Romeo, I. (2001) Contenitori da Trasporto. In *Gortina V.3. Lo Scavo del Pretorio (1989–1995) t. 1. I Materiali*, edited by A. Di Vita. Monografie della scuola archeologica Italiana di Atene e delle missioni Italiane in oriente 12. Padua: Bottega d'Erasmo, 260–410.

Poulou-Papadimitriou, N. and Nodarou, E. (2014) Transport Vessels and Maritime Trade Routes in the Aegean from the 5th to the 9th C. AD. Preliminary results of the EU funded 'Pythagoras II' project: The Cretan Case Study. In *LRCW 4. Late Roman Coarse Wares, Cooking Wares and Amphorae in the Mediterranean. Archaeology and Archaeometry. The Mediterranean: A Market without Frontiers*, edited by N. Poulou-Papadimitriou, E. Nodarou and V. Kilikoglou. BAR International Series 2616. Oxford: Archaeopress, 873–883.

Price, M.J. (1992) The Coins. In *Knossos: From Greek City to Roman Colony. Excavations at the Unexplored Mansion II*, edited by L.H. Sackett. BSA Suppl. 21. London: British School of Archaeology at Athens; Thames and Hudson, 323–331.

Price, S.R.F. (2006) The Loutro Peninsula and its Resources in Context. In *Ι' Διεθνές Κρητολογικό Συνεδρίο (Χανιά, 1–8 Οκτωβρίου 2006), Περιλήψεις*. Chania, 85–86.

Prusac, M. (2011) *From Face to Face: Recarving of Roman Portraits and the Late-Antique Portrait Arts*. Leiden: Brill.

Raab, H. A. (2001) *Rural Settlement in Hellenistic and Roman Crete*. BAR International Series 984. Oxford: Archaeopress.

Rackham, O. and Moody, J. (1996) *The Making of the Cretan Landscape*. Manchester: Manchester University Press.

Rigsby, K.J. (1976) Cnossus and Capua. *Transactions of the American Philological Association* 106, 313–330.

Rizzo, M.A. (2001) Terra Sigillata Cipriota. In *Gortina V.3. Lo Scavo del Pretorio (1989–1995) t. 1. I Materiali*, 39, edited by A. Di Vita. Monografie della scuola archeologica Italiana di Atene e delle missioni Italiane in oriente 12. Padua: Bottega d'Erasmo.

Romeo, I. (2002) The Panhellenion and Ethnic Identity in Hadrianic Greece. *Classical Philology* 97, 21–40.

Romeo, I. (2010) Europa's sons: Roman Perceptions of Cretan Identity. In *Local Knowledge and Microidentities in the Imperial Greek World*, edited by T. Whitmarsh. Cambridge: Cambridge University Press, 69–85.

Rose, B.C. (1997) *Dynastic Commemoration and Imperial Portraiture in the Julio-Claudian Period*. Cambridge: Cambridge University Press.

Sackett, L.H. (1992) Roman Pottery. In *Knossos: From Greek City to Roman Colony. Excavations at the Unexplored Mansion II*, edited by L.H. Sackett. BSA Suppl. 21. London: British School of Archaeology at Athens; Thames and Hudson, 147–256.

Sackett, L.H. and Jones, J.E. (1979) Knossos: A Roman House Revisited. *Archaeology* 32, 18–27.

Sanders, I.F. (1982) *Roman Crete. An Archaeological Survey and Gazetteer of Late Hellenistic, Roman, and early Byzantine Crete*. Warminster: Aris and Phillips.

Sapouna, P. (1998) *Die Bildlampen römischer Zeit aus der Idäischen Zeusgrotte auf Kreta*. BAR International Series 696. Oxford: Archaeopress.

Sazanov, A. (2014) Cretan Amphorae from the Northern Black Sea Region: Contexts, Chronology, Typology. In *LRCW 4. Late Roman Coarse Wares, Cooking Wares and Amphorae in the Mediterranean. Archaeology and Archaeometry. The Mediterranean: A Market without Frontiers*, edited by N. Poulou-Papadimitriou, E. Nodarou and V. Kilikoglou. BAR International Series 2616. Oxford: Archaeopress, 399–409.

Slane, K.W. (1989) Corinthian Ceramic Imports: The Changing Pattern of Provincial Trade in the First and Second Centuries AD. In *The Greek Renaissance in the Roman Empire*, edited by S. Walker and A. Cameron. London: Institute of Classical Studies, 219–225.

Sporn, K. (2012) Römische Grabreliefs auf Kreta. In *Κλασική παράδοση και νεωτερικά στοιχεία στην πλαστική της ρωμαϊκής Ελλάδας*, edited by T. Stefanidou-Tiberiou, P. Karanastasi and D. Damaskos. Thessaloniki: University Studio Press, 451–466.

Stampolidis, N.C. (ed.) (2004) *Eleutherna: Polis-Acropolis-Necropolis*. Athens: Museum of Cycladic Art.

Stavridis, A. (1985) Römische Porträts im Archäologischen Museum von Chania. *Boreas* 8, 105–110.

Stiros, S.C. (2010) The 8.5+ Magnitude, AD 365 Earthquake in Crete: Coastal Uplift, Topography Changes, Archaeological and Historical Signature. *Quaternary International* 216, 54–63.

Stiros, S.C. and Papageorgiou, S. (2001) Seismicity of Western Crete and the Destruction of the Town of Kisamos at AD 365: Archaeological Evidence. *Journal of Seismology* 5, 381–397.

Svoronos, I.N. (1890) *Numismatique de la Crète ancienne*. Macon: Imprimerie Protat Frères.

Sweetman, R.J. (2004a) Late Antique Knossos. Understanding the City: Evidence of Mosaics and Religious Architecture. *Annual of the British School at Athens* 99, 315–354.

Sweetman, R.J. (2004b) The Changing Nature of Knossos: Roman to Late Antique – Some Problems. In *Knossos: Palace, City, State*, edited by G. Cadogan, E. Hatzaki and A. Vasilakis. BSA Studies 12. London: British School at Athens, 481–488.

Sweetman, R.J. (2005) Knossos Medical Faculty Site: Late Antique Graves and Other Remains. *Annual of the British School at Athens* 100, 331–386.

Sweetman, R.J. (2007) Roman Knossos: The Nature of a Globalized City. *American Journal of Archaeology* 111, 61–81.

Sweetman, R.J. (2011) Domus, Villa, and Farmstead: The Globalization of Crete. In *Stega: The Archaeology of Houses and Households in Ancient Crete*, edited by K.T. Glowacki and N. Vogeikoff-Brogan. Hesperia, Suppl. 44. Princeton: American School of Classical Studies at Athens, 441–450.

Sweetman, R.J. (2013) *The Mosaics of Roman Crete*. Cambridge: Cambridge University Press.

Sweetman, R.J. and Becker, M.J. (2005) Knossos Medical Faculty Site: Late Antique Graves and Other Remains. *BSA Annual of the British School at Athens* 100, 331–386.

Themelis, P.G. (ed.) (2000) *Προτοβυζαντινή Ελεύθερνα, τομέας 1, Β' τόμος*. Rethymnon: Panepistemio Kretes.

Themelis, P.G. (2009) *Ancient Eleutherna: sector I*, Vol. I. Athens: Scripta.

Tsatsaki, N. and Nodarou, E. (2014) A New Hellenistic Amphora Production Centre in West Crete (Loutra, Rethymnon): Study and Petrographic Analysis of the Pottery Assemblage *Annual of the British School at Athens* 109, 287–315, 431–437.

Tzifopoulos, Y. (2007) The Archive of Inscriptions of the Rethymnon Prefecture: Results, Prospects and New Discoveries in Lappa, Crete. In *XII Congressus Internationalis Epigraphiae Graecae et Latinae. Provinciae Imperii Romani Inscriptionibus Descriptae: Barcelona, 3–8 Septembris 2002*, edited by M. Mayer i Olivé, G. Baratta and A. Guzmán. Barcelona: Institut d'Estudis Catalans, 1461–1466.

Vogeikoff-Brogan, N. (2000) Late Hellenistic Pottery from Mochlos in East Crete. In *Ε' Επιστημονική Συνάντηση για την Ελληνιστική Κεραμική: Χρονολογικά προβλήματα – Κλειστά σύνολα – Εργαστήρια. Πρακτικά, Χανιά, 1997*, edited by S. Drogou, E. Zerboudaki, L. Maragkou and G. Touratsoglou. Chania: Ekdose tou Tameiou Archaiologikon Poron kai Apallotrioseon, 69–74.

Vogeikoff-Brogan, N. (2004) The Late Hellenistic Period in East Crete. In *Crete Beyond the Palaces: Proceedings of the Crete 2000 Conference*, edited by L. Preston Day, M.S. Mook and J.D. Muhly. INSTAP Prehistory Monographs 10. Philadelphia: INSTAP Academic Press, 213–220.

Vogeikoff-Brogan, N. (2012) Hellenistic and Roman Periods: Expansion of the Isthmus in an International Era. In *An Archaeological Survey of the Gournia Landscape*, edited by L.V. Watrous, D.C. Haggis, K. Nowicki, N. Vogeikoff-Brogan and M. Schultz. INSTAP Prehistory Monographs 39. Philadelphia: INSTAP Academic Press, 81–96.

Vogeikoff-Brogan, N. (2014) *Mochlos III. The Late Hellenistic Beam-Press Complex*. INSTAP Prehistory Monographs 48. Philadelphia: INSTAP Academic Press.

Vogeikoff-Brogan, N., Nodarou, E. and Boileau, M.-C. (2008) New Evidence for Amphora Production in East Crete in the Hellenistic Period. An Integrated Approach of Typology and Thin-Section Petrography. In *Proceedings of the 4th Symposium of the Hellenic Society for Archaeometry*, edited by G. Facorellis, N. Zacharias and K. Polikreti. BAR International Series 1746. Oxford: Archaeopress, 327–334.

Vogt, C. (2000) The Early Byzantine Pottery. In *Πρωτοβυζαντινή Ελεύθερνα, τομέας I.2*, edited by P.G. Themelis. Rethymnon: Panepistemio Kretes, 39–199.

Wardle, K.A. and Wardle, D. (2004) Glimpses of Private Life: Roman Rock Cut Tombs of the First and Second Centuries AD at Knossos. In *Knossos: Palace, City, State*, edited by G. Cadogan, E. Hatzaki and A. Vasilakis. BSA Studies 12. London: British School at Athens, 473–480.

Watrous, L.V., Buell, D.M., Kokinou, E., Soupios, P., Sarris, A., Beckman, S., Rethemiotakis, G., Turner, L.A., Gallimore, S. and Hammond, M.D. (2017) *The Galatas Survey. Socio-Economic and Political Development of a Contested Territory in Central Crete during the Neolithic to Ottoman Periods*. INSTAP Prehistory Monographs 55. Philadelphia: INSTAP Academic Press.

Watrous, L.V., Haggis, D.C., Nowicki, K., Vogeikoff-Brogan, N. and Schultz, M. (eds) (2012) *An Archaeological Survey of the Gournia Landscape*. INSTAP Prehistory Monographs 39. Philadelphia: INSTAP Academic Press.

Welter, G. and Jantzen, U. (1951) Das Diktynnaion. *Forschungen auf Kreta 1942*. Berlin: W. de Gruyter, 106–117.

Williams, D. (2003) Cretan Wine in Roman Britain. *Journal of Roman Pottery Studies* 10, 26–31.

Wilson, D.E. and Day, P.M. (1994) Ceramic Regionalism in Prepalatial Central Crete: The Messara Imports at EM I to EM II Knossos. *Annual of the British School at Athens* 89, 1–87.

Woolf, G. (1994) Becoming Roman, Staying Greek: Culture, Identity and The Civilizing Process of the Roman East. *Proceedings of the Cambridge Philological Society* 40, 116–143.

Xanthopoulou, M., Nodarou, E. and Poulou-Papadimitriou, N. (2014) Local Coarse Wares from Late Roman Itanos (East Crete, Greece). In *LRCW 4. Late Roman Coarse Wares, Cooking Wares and Amphorae in the Mediterranean. Archaeology and Archaeometry. The Mediterranean: A Market without Frontiers II*, edited by N. Poulou-Papadimitriou, E. Nodarou and V. Kilikoglou. BAR International Series 2616. Oxford: Archaeopress, 811–817.

Yangaki, A. (2005) *La céramique des IVe–VIIIe siècles ap. J.-C. d'Eleutherna*. Athens: Scripta.

Yangaki, A. (2016) Pottery of the 7th–early 9th Centuries on Crete: The Current State of Research and New Directions. In *Roman Crete: New Perspectives,* edited by J.E. Francis and A. Kouremenos. Oxford: Oxbow Books, 199–234.

Chapter 9

From the Land of the Paphian Aphrodite to the Busy Christian Countryside: Globalization, Empire, and Insularity in Early and Late Roman Cyprus

Jody Michael Gordon and William R. Caraher

Introduction

Cyprus, as the Mediterranean Sea's third largest island, has often functioned as a self-sufficient 'matchbox continent' endowed with valuable mineralogical and agricultural resources.[1] Moreover, its strategic location at the crux of eastern, western, and Anatolian sailing routes has historically facilitated interactions with external agents. Cypriots then, have often experienced changing levels of connectivity to regional networks in response to economic, political, and cultural 'push-pull' factors. These emic and etic social pressures have ranged from market forces, to imperialist politics, to religious proselytism. Cyprus' sea-girt nature has also allowed its inhabitants to manipulate their insularity, that is, their sense of identity conditioned by living on an island, when faced with heightened levels of cross-cultural interaction. The archaeology of Cyprus, as the physical residue of such practices, thus offers fascinating insights into how islanders have historically mediated their relationships with outsiders as parts of 'global' networks where time and space are compressed and people become increasingly interdependent.

This chapter's goal is to explore archaeologically how Cypriot culture changed in the face of globalizing pressures during two of the most connected periods in the island's history, the Early (c. 30 BCE–293 CE) and Late Roman (c. 293–649 CE).[2] As van Dommelen and Knapp have argued, a 'diachronic perspective provides important insights into how new senses of place are created and how new identities are forged'.[3] Here, we aim to compare how these periods' increased, yet variegated, levels of connectivity affected the identities of people living on the same island across time through an analytical lens that draws on globalization theory, empire studies, and island archaeology.[4]

Following a brief overview of our theoretical approach and how Cyprus' long-term geohistorical features influenced 'cycles of social complexity', we present two case studies that explore how changing levels and orientations of connectivity affected local practices as expressed through mainly numismatic, ceramic, and architectural remains.[5] Such remains reflect an alteration of the island's cultural landscapes as Cyprus was transformed from a pagan land of the Paphian Aphrodite (the island's patron goddess, and the title of a seminal archaeological monograph), to a busy Christian countryside (which references not only Cyprus' transition to monotheism, but also another pioneering study).[6] Lastly, we review how a globalization approach to cultural change during eras of imperial rule can be particularly useful to understanding how connectivity and 'push-pull' forces shape the ways islanders identify themselves.

Towards a Globalized Archaeology of Imperial Insularity for Early and Late Roman Cyprus

As argued in this volume's introduction, globalization theory has recently become an effective tool for interrogating the archaeological remains of cultural change on sea-girt islands since these landforms were some of the most connected Mediterranean places.[7] Indeed, Cyprus' long-term insular character, from its strategic maritime location, to its ports, to its natural resources all played a role in creating the 'push-pull' forces that shaped how and when Cypriots were connected to interdependent socio-economic systems, such as empires.[8] It was arguably following disruptive events like imperial (re)integration that islanders' connectivity to external groups were gradually expanded, and when their senses of time and space were compressed through cross-cultural interactions that created social tensions akin to modern processes of globalization.[9] Tamar Hodos has defined globalization as 'processes of increasing connectivities that unfold and manifest as social awareness of these connectivities'.[10] She has also stressed that a globalization approach to societies situated at the crux of inter-regional relations 'rehabilitates competing, sometimes oppositional perspectives on the nature of connectivity'.[11] Hodos' statements seem salient to this chapter because the archaeologies of Early and Late Roman Cyprus reveal punctuated levels and new forms of connectivity that were created through 'oppositional' processes of cultural change between islanders and extra-insular actors, including grobalization (a form of acculturation), glocalization (a form of hybridization), and the re-embedding of local culture (a form of constructive-resistance).[12]

Based on the similarities between how pre-modern empires and modern entities, from nation states to corporations, seek to connect people for political and economic gain, we propose that ancient imperialism was a globalizing force.[13] Imperialism is typically defined as a social process involving an expansive polity's coercive integration of a region(s) for political or economic gain followed by the top-down imposition of external social norms on the passive colonized.[14] More recently, however, postcolonial approaches to understanding imperialism have complicated traditional accultarative models and emphasized the diverse processes of cultural change suggested by globalization theory. In this context, imperialism emerges as a special type of colonial encounter where people actively negotiate their senses of belonging (*i.e.* their identities) in relation to local power structures, which are often reorganized by imperial states.[15] Redefining imperialism as a globalizing process recognizes empires' ability to increase connectivity, while also providing the colonized with local agency in relation to geohistorical factors, including insularity.[16] Such a perspective offers insights for Early and Late Roman Cyprus because the expanded connectivity witnessed in the archaeological record may have occurred *specifically because* the Roman state provided unprecedented levels of maritime security that fostered social change.[17]

A final theoretical idea to consider is how Cypriots could connect to imperial networks in unique ways *specifically because* they were islanders living on a 'matchbox continent' that could both link them to or insulate them from the wider world.[18] Cyprus' status as a large island with significant natural resources situated on maritime trading routes influenced how Rome and Constantinople strategically viewed the island, and how Cypriots understood their sense of place.[19] Thus, during the first half of the 1st millennium CE when sea travel offered the most efficient means of transport, living on an island *mattered*.[20] Insularity, as a social identity shaped by living on an island in a specific location and time, 'may be,' as Bernard Knapp has argued, 'adopted or adapted as individual or wider social concerns dictate'.[21] For islanders, insularity can act as a source of social power that allows them to connect or disconnect with networks of agents who initiate change, from traders to administrators to pilgrims. Thus, any examination of how Cypriot culture changed during heightened eras of connectivity needs to consider how islanders' notions of their insularity influenced their connections to global networks.

In this chapter, we demonstrate that a globalized archaeology of imperial insularity presents a productive approach to understanding how Cypriots were integrated into the Early and Late Roman empires. This theoretical perspective allows us to move beyond simplistic interpretations of how connectivity affects island life and to appreciate how islanders actively shape their identities over time at the nexus of complex local and global influences.

The Insular Geography of Cyprus: 'Push-Pull' Factors, Connectivity, and Globalization

Cyprus' history reveals a series of long-term geohistorical factors that cyclically affected how islanders were connected to the Mediterranean world by pushing Cypriots outward and pulling external groups inward. Maria Iacovou has referred to these 'push-pull' forces as 'island-specific invariable factors', which played a key role nurturing 'cycles of social complexity' that altered *mentalités* (*sensu* Bintliff).[22] For Iacovou then, 'no Cypriot polity could maintain its status for long if it was cut off from the Mediterranean trading systems'.[23] This observation emphasizes the critical correlations between the island's 'push-pull' factors manifest in Cypriots' relationship to external groups and how such connections transformed the material manifestation of their *mentalitiés*. Hence, before examining the political nature of Cypriots' integrations into Roman and Byzantine networks, it is useful to briefly review the long-term geohistorical factors that shaped such connections.

Cyprus' strategic location and natural resources represent two unique factors that connected islanders to outside groups. Cyprus is one of the Mediterranean's largest islands and is within easy sailing distance of Cilicia and Syria (Figs 49 and 50).[24] This strategic location brought Cypriots under the hegemony of the Assyrians, Persians, and Macedonian Greeks, even before the Roman conquest during the late 1st century BCE. In some cases, these imperial states may have been pulled to Cyprus for *realpolitik* purposes linked to expansion or defense, or so that they could exploit Cyprus' natural resources, such as copper and timber from the Troodos Massif, or agricultural goods from the expansive plain of the Mesaoria.[25] In other cases, access to imperial markets may have pushed Cypriots outward in order to import luxury items (*e.g.* ivory, fine pottery, or marble), foods, or metals (*e.g.* gold or tin), or so that they could find

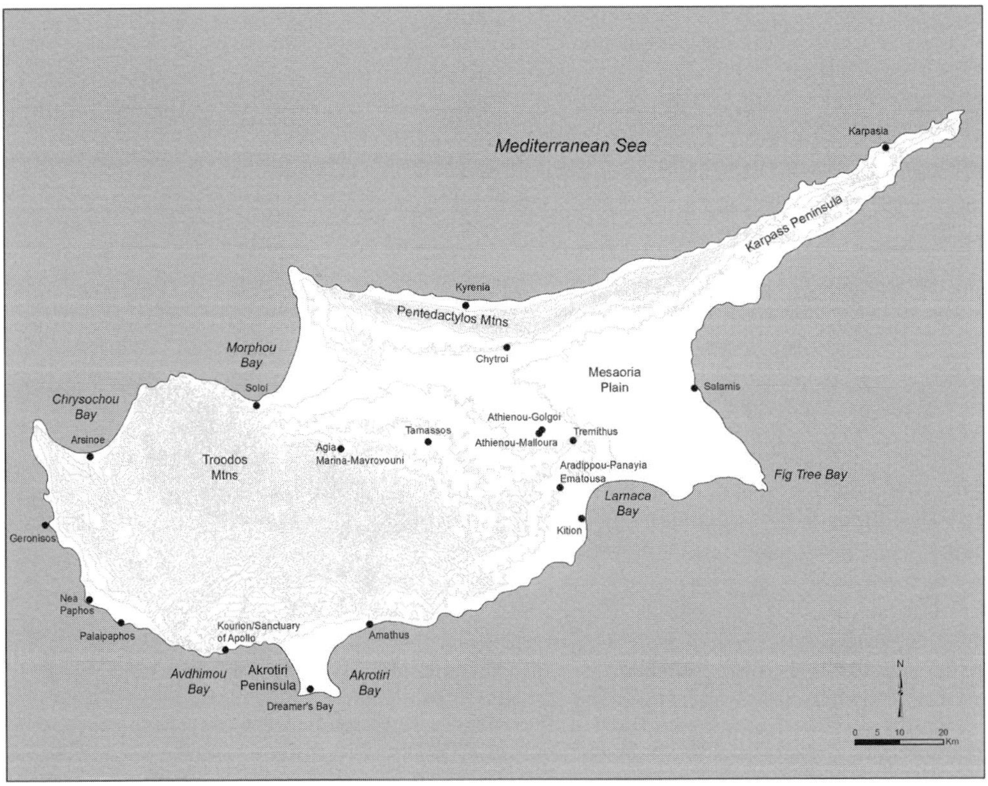

Figure 49: Map of Cyprus showing key geographical features and ancient cities in the Early and Late Roman period (created by and with the permission of Brandon Olson).

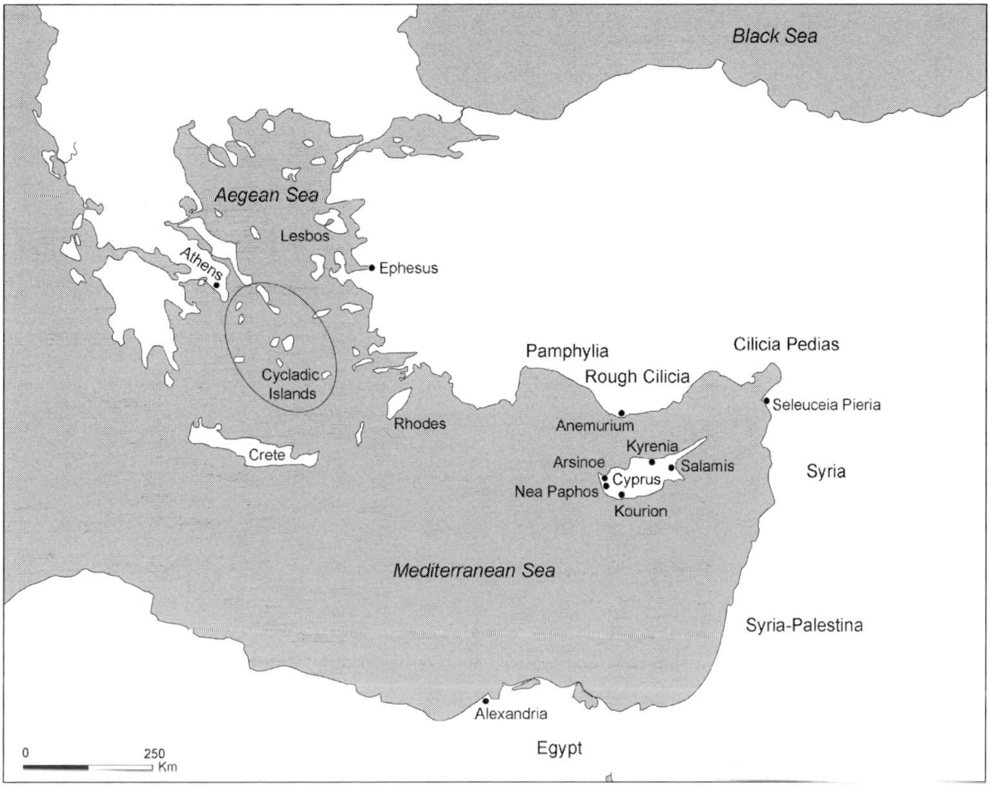

Figure 50: Map showing Cyprus' strategic location within the eastern Mediterranean (created by and with the permission of Brandon Olson).

their fortunes elsewhere (*e.g.* as traders, mercenaries, or religious leaders).[26] Finally, Cyprus could also function as a 'matchbox continent' capable of self-sustenance when external connections proved unprofitable or impossible, although such episodes of discontinuity were relatively infrequent.[27]

Cyprus' natural resources were also tied to the island's unique topography, geology, and Mediterranean climate. The island has a seasonally well-watered, large agricultural plain, the Mesaoria (producing wheat in particular), which is located between two mountain ranges, the Kyrenia range in the north and the Troodos Massif in the west. Some coastal river basins in the south-central region, such as the Vasilikos or Kouris, along with various sections of the Troodos foothills (useful for olive and grape cultivation) also provided additional agricultural zones. Yet, Cyprus' agricultural landscapes could also be cyclically marginal and may have pushed people to nucleate in central locations or emigrate.[28] During the Early and Late Roman periods, however, the climatic evidence suggests that conditions were favorable for high yields, which in turn facilitated demographic and economic growth.[29] Besides the socially disruptive menace of earthquakes, economic conditions in Cyprus were

Figure 51: View of the Cypriot coastline looking west from the ancient city of Kourion (photo: authors).

favorable during most of the first half of the 1st millennium CE.[30] These economic conditions were enhanced, ultimately, by Cyprus' sea-girt nature as an island. The sea served as a connecting force that – when combined with the large island's strategic location, valuable resources, and Cypriots' long experience as seafarers – made Cyprus a key network node during cycles of globalization (Fig. 51).[31] Overall, it was these 'push-pull' factors, along with the middle-term geopolitical events discussed below (such as the rise of the Roman empire or the expansion of Christianity), which spurred the globalizing processes that diachronically shaped Cypriot insularity and identity.

Early Roman Cyprus: From Regional Possession to Globalized Province

After over two centuries of Ptolemaic rule, Cyprus came under Roman Republican control in 58 BCE following Pompey the Great's conquest of the east, and Metellus' takeover of Crete.[32] Rome's initial annexation, however, seems to have been initiated by a mixture of political infighting and *realpolitik* as opposed to a grander political strategy.[33] Clodius, the tribune and ally of the First Triumvirate, ordered Cato the Younger to annex Cyprus mainly because with Cato removed from the capital, it would be easier to exile Cicero, one of the Triumvirate's opponents (Plut. Cat. 34.2.–35.2, 36.1–37.2, 38.1–3, 40.1–2; Dio Cass. 39.22.1–23.4).[34] Given these circumstances, Cyprus was clearly not considered of great strategic value (it was originally managed at arm's length from Cilicia), and so the fact that Julius Caesar returned the island to Ptolemaic rule under Cleopatra VII is unsurprising.

Octavian's eventual reconquest of Cyprus following his defeat of the Ptolemies in 30 BCE was an example of offensive imperialism. The Ptolemaic garrisons were removed, and Cypriots were treated as non-citizen *dediticii*.[35] In 23 BCE, Cyprus was made a senatorial province governed by an annual proconsul. Provincial coinage was minted in the capital city of Nea Paphos, and the proconsul controlled the administration of justice and taxation, assisted by a coterie of epigraphically attested officials. No Roman colonies are known, nor any military contingents other than those assigned to the proconsul.[36] Even if Rome's initial 'pull' towards Cyprus was offensive, they soon realized that Cypriots would not prove restive. As Gallimore has recently recognized for Roman Crete, Rome's conquest of Cyprus was not an 'event' that sparked immediate socio-cultural change.[37] Instead, the *realpolitik* goals of Augustus' conquest likely allowed several pre-Roman social and cultural structures to remain in place once the province was initially pacified. As a result, other push-pull processes, such as globalization via Cypriots' gradual integration into new imperial trading networks, likely played a greater role in gradually transforming local practices than externally enforced acculturation.[38]

Early Roman Cyprus: The Busy Coastscape

Over the last 25 years, new studies of Early Roman Cyprus' archaeology have transformed our views about Cypriots' connections to the wider Mediterranean. Traditional epigraphic and historical views of Cyprus as colonized somnolent backwater have been replaced with an image of well-connected and prosperous island whose people had the freedom to socially and economically interact with outsiders.[39] Such a transformation of thought has been possible through the theoretically-nuanced analysis of ceramics, architecture, and other material remains. These objects are valuable because they reveal the mobility and agency of objects, people, and symbols, and can be used to explore the *mentalités* islanders developed as they leveraged Cyprus' 'island-specific invariable factors' to negotiate with outside groups as globalizing pressures increased following the Roman conquest.[40]

The archaeological evidence dating to Early Roman times for seafaring, coastal development, and changing islandscapes all reflect Hodos' definition of globalization as 'processes of increasing connectivities that unfold and manifest as social awareness of these connectivities'.[41] This dynamic era reveals a punctuated rise in the number of Mediterranean shipwrecks, and it seems that Cyprus, as a strategically-located island, was not left out of this 'cycle of social complexity'.[42] Justin Leidwanger's studies of ports and shipwreck cargos from the southwest coast of Turkey have illustrated that the number of regional shipwrecks increased from the 1st century BCE to the 1st century CE.[43] Although the shipwreck evidence around Cyprus is more meager, he also excavated the remains of a small 2nd-century CE ship off the east coast near Salamis. The Fig Tree Bay ship contained a 5–6 ton cargo made up mainly of Cilician Pseudo-Cos en cloche (Agora M54) amphorae, as well as some Gauloise 4 (likely from the west), some Cilician Dressel 30 amphorae, and a few Ras al Bassit amphorae from Syria.[44] This shipwreck is significant because it shows that traders coasting Cyprus carried cargos that reflect the importance of elite goods like wine within increasingly global modes of maritime interaction.

John Leonard has identified two major trade routes involving Cyprus in Roman times.[45] One route led east from Alexandria and followed the coast of the Levant and then that of Anatolia, whereas another possible route was a central one that crossed the open sea from Alexandria to Paphos and onwards to points west including, eventually, Rome. When ships passed near Cyprus, they typically circumnavigated the island in a counterclockwise fashion supported by prevailing winds and currents.[46] The increased maritime traffic in the Early Roman eastern Mediterranean was pulled towards Cyprus not only because of its location, but also because of its ports and resources. During the Early Roman period, existing coastal settlements were expanded and redeveloped while other sites began to flourish for the first time, illustrating that enhanced maritime connectivity could push people towards the coasts creating transitory spaces of globalized interaction.[47]

The two largest port cities, Nea Paphos in the west and Salamis in the east, became Cyprus' largest urban sites.[48] Their large-scale harbors provided havens for ships ten times the size of the Fig Tree Bay wreck, including those within Rome's *annona* fleet, which sailed to and from Alexandria.[49] Such connections transformed these ports into cosmopolitan, marble-clad gateway cities connected to Cyprus' internal road system, which, by the 2nd century CE both circumnavigated and traversed the island.[50] Secondary port towns, like Kourion, Amathus, and Soloi, also reached new levels of urban sophistication at this time, while transshipment points, like Dreamer's Bay (located between Kourion and Amathus), began to emerge as strategically-situated trading centers marked by *horrea* and extensive breakwaters.[51] A final type of haven was the smaller village harbor or anchorage, such as those at Pyla-*Koutsopetria*, Drousha-*Kioni*, or Avdhimou that permitted shelter for small crafts likely engaged in cabotage between larger ports.[52]

Outside of the coastal cities, settlement expansion has been noted across the island in Early Roman times. As the results of several pedestrian surveys have revealed, site density in most rural areas increased; however, the prevailing trend of urbanization was relegated to the coasts.[53] With meager evidence of comparable spatial growth and monumentality at former kingdom sites, like Tamassos, Idalion, and Golgoi, and the decline in use of open-air sanctuaries, likely in preference for outward-looking, newly monumentalized coastal ones at Palaipaphos, Kourion, or Nea Paphos, the predominant hinterland site type appears to be resource processing centers, such as the smelting site of Agia Marina-*Mavrovouni* in the Troodos, or the farming complex of Aradippou-*Panayia Ematousa* near Kition with small or only seasonal populations.[54] These sites and the rural landscapes around them lack the vestiges of social development found in coastal cities, like marble statues, prostyle temples, or mosaic-clad villas.[55] However, they do provide ceramic evidence for imported finewares, suggesting that materials imported to the coastal gateways were traveling to the hinterland via an extensive Roman-era road system, likely in exchange for processed resources, such as copper, olive oil, or wine.[56]

Shipwrecks, expanded coastal settlements, and a decrease in the size and social complexity of interior sites indicate that a socio-economic reorientation towards a 'busy coastscape' occurred in Cyprus during the Early Roman period.[57] This reorientation was mutually beneficial to both Cypriots and the external peoples with whom they interacted. Cypriots, who were pushed to the coasts, could manipulate their insularity to insert themselves into new long-distance trade routes, while seafarers moving between Alexandria and Rome were pulled to Cyprus as a safe haven or as a source of wine, ceramics, copper, or timber. In addition, particularly loyal Cypriots who manipulated the island's resources could go to Rome as 'ambassadors to the emperor', while inquisitive scholars like Galen could research the Troodos mines, and the future emperor Titus could honor Cyprus' matron goddess, at the Sanctuary of Aphrodite at Palaipaphos.[58] Taken together, Rome's control of the seas and Cypriots' manipulation of their island's 'invariable factors' brought globalizing economic and cultural influences to Cyprus' coastal settlements where a paradoxically cosmopolitan, yet locally meaningful, material record was forged.

Early Roman Cyprus: Becoming a Roman Islander

According to Justin Jennings, some of the hallmarks of globalization include time-space compression, standardization, homogeneity, and deterritorialization.[59] Cypriots' connections to Roman networks, especially in coastal port cities, seem to have introduced these globalizing forces on to the island as evidenced by coins, ceramics, and architecture.

During the Ptolemaic era, several port cities, including Nea Paphos, Kition, and Salamis, minted gold, silver, and bronze royal coinage. However, under the Romans, the mint was centralized in Nea Paphos, and standardized, homogenous bronze denominations, which Danielle Parks stated 'fall into the provincial category', became the dominant specie.[60] Cyprus' new connection to a distant western Mediterranean empire was starkly expressed through the first coins minted following the conquest (Fig. 52).[61] These coins replaced the imagery of Zeus Ammon and the Ptolemaic Eagle with Augustus' head, on the obverse, and Nike standing on a globe, on the reverse.[62] In addition, the language of the legends was changed from Greek to Latin. 'Of King Ptolemy' in Greek on the Ptolemaic reverse was replaced with 'IMP CAESAR DIVI F AVGVSTVS' in the Latin script, while the reverse Latin legend celebrates Augustus' ninth year as consul designate, 26 BCE.

Figure 52: Bronze semis (avg. diameter: 17–20 mm; weight: 8.2 g) of Augustus minted in Cyprus c. 26 BCE. Obverse: IMP CAESAR DIVI F AVGVSTVS; Augustus' head facing right. Reverse: COS OCTAVO DESIG IX; Nike advancing left (image courtesy of the American Numismatic Society).

Although we can only speculate how Cypriots may have reacted to these coins, it is fair to assume that they may have felt tensions associated with globalization, including deterritorialization and time-space compression. Since the earliest coins bear the name of the emperor, it should be assumed that they were minted on his authority.[63] As a result, these coins appear to have been forced on their users by colonizing administrators from an imperial capital most islanders would never see. They also utilized a script rarely used on the island, Latin, to introduce Cypriots to their new external ruler. Moreover, the Ptolemaic divine imagery of Zeus was replaced with the youthful head of the 'son of a god', Augustus, while the image of Nike astride a globe, that is, a symbol of the inhabited 'orbis terrarum', was used to 'project Rome's claim to a universal hegemony'.[64]

For Cypriots, these early Roman coins may have invited them to grapple with a form of Roman *gro*balization that was aimed at integrating conquered peoples into imperial economic and political systems. The use of novel scripts and symbols of external imperial power may have acclimated Cypriot users into realizing that they were now connected to a larger state. However, the empire's minting of these local coins also represents an attempt to connect Cyprus, and especially its port cities, like Nea Paphos, into standardized Roman systems of economic exchange.[65] The first coins minted in Roman Cyprus thus show how large-scale states like empires could use homogenized and standardized material culture to effectively begin the process of globalizing island cultures. As Carla Sinopoli has argued, 'Imperial integration entails varying and changing emphases on coercion, rewards, structural transformations, cooption, and accommodation.'[66] In the case of the Roman Cypriot coinage, it seems like the first provincial coins were aimed at coercing Cypriots to recognize their new rulers, and then, once Cypriots' loyalty was assured, the right to mint could become a more integrative process, as will be discussed below.

The deterritorialization and homogenization promoted by Roman provincial coins was also likely felt by Cypriots when they encountered imported ceramics in the island's coastal cities during the 1st and 2nd centuries CE. John Lund in his exhaustive study of Cypriot ceramic circulation patterns has shown that Cyprus was involved in a range of 'long-distance exchanges' with imported vessels arriving from Italy, the Aegean, Anatolia, the Levant, and Egypt, particularly in the gateway port of Nea Paphos.[67]

The variety of long-distance imports to Nea Paphos has also been expanded in the work of Anthi Kaldeli, as well as that of Meyza and Baginska. At Nea Paphos, Kaldeli has analyzed the remains of western transport amphorae from Italy, Gaul, Spain, Tripolitania, and Portugal, indicating that the provincial capital likely lay directly on imperial trade routes, including those plied by *annona* grain ships.[68] Meyza and Baginska's research also identified Italian and Spanish amphorae, along with Adriatic vessels.[69] For regional wares at Nea Paphos, Kaldeli, as well as Meyza and Baginska, have stressed the presence of Aegean, Cilicia, and Levantine amphorae showing that the capital was also a hub of regional commerce. Nea Paphos' domineering connectivity does not mean that Cyprus' smaller harbors were disconnected from wider commercial trends. Imported products from both west and east arrived at Dreamer's Bay, Amathus, and Pyla, although, as both Leidwanger's and Kaldeli's work suggest, the mechanisms for such exchanges may have been indirect and supported by local cabotage.[70] In general, the wide range of imported materials discovered in Cyprus indicates that Cypriots, as islanders who could manipulate the connectivity of their ports, would have been exposed to a disparate variety of tablewares and food products that signaled the globalized nature of the imperial world they now inhabited.

In major coastal cities like Nea Paphos, where proconsuls and other officials from Rome minted provincial coins and imported fine wines from as far afield as Spain, the architectural remains also indicate a local desire to emulate the globalized décor and aesthetic tastes found in port cities as close as Antioch and as far away as Pompeii. At Nea Paphos, several large villas illustrate a knowledge of cosmopolitan domestic ground plans and the latest trends in floor mosaic décor. For example, the 2nd-century CE House of Dionysos was a large (over 2000 m^2) elite residence that, in the words of Christine Kondoleon, 'incorporates the cultural habits of Rome in a Greek eastern setting' by taking the centralizing units of Roman peristyle atrium houses and arranging them into progressively exclusive sectors for entering and working, entertaining, and private living.[71]

The house's most impressive architectural feature is its intricate floor mosaics, which feature scenes from Greco-Roman mythology (including the eponymous Triumph of Dionysos, Fig. 53), symbolic natural imagery (*e.g.* the seasons), and geometric designs. Many of the mosaics seem inspired by houses in North Africa (*e.g.* hunting scenes) or Syria (especially Antioch). Yet, according to Michaelides, the unique style that emerges betrays the existence of local workshops led either by Cypriots acquainted with insular traditions or by mosaicists from nearby regions.[72] Given the house's location in a gateway port city, it seems like globalizing forces may have led its owner to make design choices that could be understood by external visitors who shared a similar elite ethos. As Kondoleon has suggested, 'The Paphian House – its plan and pavements – reflects a trend among provincial notables in the Greek east to express their *Romanitas* in the selection of the design elements of their homes.'[73]

Figure 53: Floor mosaic from the House of Dionysos, Nea Paphos, showing the Triumph of Dionysos (photo: authors).

Early Roman Cyprus: Remaining Cypriot within a Roman World

A cursory overview of the numismatic, ceramic, and architectural evidence from Cyprus' port cities, reveals an island that was closely connected to Roman imperial economic and social systems by the 2nd century CE. However, Cyprus' long-term 'island-specific invariable factors' also conditioned Cypriots' connectivity to global systems in ways that would permit *glocal*ized and conflicting responses to Roman cultural influences. The roots for such reactions may lie in the differing accessibility of certain groups of Cypriots to external peoples and objects and in the way that elite Cypriots transformed symbols of local significance into cosmopolitan emblems that could improve their social status 'globally'.

By the early 2nd century CE, Cypriots had integrated themselves into the multi-scalar systems of infra-insular and networked economic exchange protected by the Roman empire. However, this process was more gradual than some of the early homogenous material culture would suggest, such as the initial Augustan era coinage. Instead the transformation of Cypriot culture into a globalized Roman provincial one seems to have taken place over several generations. Such a gradual rate of imperial integration is comparable to Gallimore's analysis of Roman Crete where globalization processes may have mediated the rate of material culture change.[74] Since there is meager evidence for Roman settlers on Cyprus and no evidence of imperial control of resources beyond the copper mines, the island's economic system must have involved the participation of local people. Through their management of agricultural estates, their knowledge of resource extraction and seafaring, and their public loyalty to Rome, these entrepreneurial islanders were poised to negotiate new forms of material culture.[75] Case in point might be Sergius Sulpicius Pancles Veranianus, a Cypriot granted Roman citizenship who was wealthy enough to pay for the imported ceramics or mosaic-clad houses discovered in port cities like Nea Paphos or his hometown of Salamis.[76] It was these coastal centers which prospered financially and grew demographically due to an economy that pushed people and natural resources from the Cypriot interior towards globalized seaborne markets.[77] As a result, this economic system created new islandscapes whose material culture and its semiotics reveal innovative responses to globalization.

Returning to the Early Roman coinage, elite Cypriots' contributions to the island's prosperity began to appear in the decade after Actium with the replacement of hegemonic symbols, like Nike astride a globe, with local ones that could also reflect imperial loyalty: the tripartite temple of Aphrodite at Palaipaphos (Fig. 54) and the sacred Statue of Zeus from Salamis.[78] These symbols' use may indicate that elites from Nea Paphos and Salamis were now considered integrated enough to help create a hybrid, Cypro-Roman coin that not only honored Cyprus' most famous sanctuaries, but also two tutelary gods of the ruling Julio-Claudian dynasty, Venus, the mother of Aeneas (progenitor of the Julii), and Zeus, the god of kings.[79] Such progressive hybridization of the coinage continued during the reign of Claudius when bronze coins in three denominations (as, dupondius, and sestertius) were minted that united the emperor's

Figure 54: Bronze quadrans (avg. diameter: 15–17 mm; weight: 3.67 g) of Augustus minted in Cyprus c. 26 BCE. Obverse: IMP CAESAR DIVI F; Augustus' head facing right. Reverse: A. PLAVTIVS PROCOS; Temple of Aphrodite at Palaipaphos, containing conical xoanon, in front, paved semi-circular courtyard (image courtesy of the American Numismatic Society).

image and name on the obverse with the name of the '*Koinon Kyprion*', the league of Cypriot cities, within a laurel wreath on the reverse.[80] The most striking feature of these coins is that they mark a hybridizing linguistic transition. The obverses retain Latin to write the emperor's names and titles, while the reverses utilize *Greek* to write the new issuing authority's name: 'KOINON KYΠPωN'. Since epigraphy indicates that the *Koinon* played a key role in imperial cult worship, these coins suggest that by the 40s CE, Cypriot elites were so integrated into imperial culture that they were given control of local minting, a concordat that would remain in place for the next two centuries.[81] This numismatic transition may reveal the level to which Cypriot culture had been glocalized following 70 years of Roman rule.

In Early Roman times, Cypriots imported wine amphorae and finewares from locations as far afield as Spain and Gaul. Although these imports reflect Cyprus' integration into wider Roman networks, their influence on local ceramic traditions was mixed, reflecting both acculturation and the re-embedding of local practices. In terms of local production, the acculturative force of imported ceramics was powerful. These objects may have resulted in the globalization of local ceramic types through what Kaldeli has called the 'transfer of symbolism through stylistic similarities'.[82] This process is evident in possible local imitations of Dressel 2–4 wine amphorae that Cypriots perhaps believed exuded the social status linked to imported vessels.[83] A similar argument could be made about 'Cypriot sigillata', if it was indeed made somewhere near Nea Paphos.[84] According to Lund, the advent of Eastern Sigillata A (ESA), which was probably produced somewhere near the Gulf of Iskenderun, led to a decline in local fineware production in some eastern Mediterranean regions.[85] However, Cypriots may have tried to keep up or compete with global trends by producing Cypriot sigillata and other local variants of red-slipped wares, which, in any case, may have also simply continued some earlier Cypriot Hellenistic color-coated fineware traditions.[86] In addition, imported mold-made oil lamps also seem to have been emulated locally.[87] Thus, although the ceramic evidence is admittedly complex, Cypriot potters may have responded to elite consumers' demands by producing wares that emulated the status-symbol ceramics entering Cypriot ports.

At the same time, Lund's analysis of ceramic circulation on the island may hint at the continuity of regional relations that pre-date the Roman period.[88] According to his study of the distribution of Eastern Sigillata A finewares as well as pinched-handle and Pseudo-Cos en cloche amphorae, regional connections between the following areas have been revealed: i) Rough Cilicia and Western Cyprus, ii) Eastern Rough Cilicia, Smooth Cilicia, and Eastern/Southeastern Cyprus, and iii) Northwestern Syria and Eastern Cyprus.[89] Such connections show that despite their interest in emulating global styles, Cypriots continued to trade with their most immediate neighbors, likely for regional foodstuffs, like wine or olive oil, or for pottery produced in regional kilns like ESA, ESB (likely from western Asia Minor), and Cypriot sigillata.[90] These observations further hint at how Cyprus' insular economy, based on its unique topography, local sailing conditions, and its strategic, subcontinental location may have re-embedded longstanding modes of regional trade even in the face of new long-distance forms of global connectivity.

The hybridization and re-embedding of local culture in the face of imperial integration is also visible in Cyprus' Early Roman architectural remains. One key locus of cross-cultural interaction was in connected coastal contexts where sacred traditions came into contact with globalizing trends. Most impressive are the remains from the sanctuary sites of Kourion and Amathus where impressive prostyle podium temples were erected.[91] The Temple of Apollo Hylates at Kourion (Fig. 55) was rebuilt, likely during the mid–late 1st century CE, at an ancient site using local limestone to fashion a prostyle tetrastyle design that featured plain-faced Cypro-Corinthian columns that evoke Nabataean sites.[92] Arguably, Cypriots' new connections to the wider Roman world influenced the design of temples that could speak not only to local pilgrims, but also to those brought to Cyprus via the island's expanded maritime connections to east and west. Yet, sometimes the value of local cultural capital in the face of globalizing pressures could influence the appearance of sacred Cypriot spaces.[93] The most famous temple that retained its pre-Roman form was the Temple of Aphrodite at Palaipaphos, which commemorated the mythic location of the goddess' birth. None of the temple's remains are extant, however, its representation on Cypriot bronze coins (see Fig. 54) provides a good insight into its design.[94] The temple was represented as a tripartite shrine preceded by a semi-circular forecourt that housed an aniconic baetyl, which may have symbolized the goddess.

The architectural choices revealed through these sacred sites should be understood as part of wider globalizing, socio-political dialogues that were occurring as Cypriots attempted to identify themselves as members of a wider imperial world.

Figure 55: The (partially reconstructed) Early Roman-era Temple of Apollo at the Sanctuary of Apollo Hylates near the ancient city of Kourion (photo: authors).

Such dialogues seem particularly vociferous at Kourion and Palaipaphos where epigraphic evidence also hints at the linked worship of local deities and the imperial cult.[95] However, the presence of these sacred sites in outward-facing coastal locations reveals what seems a key trend in Early Roman Cyprus: the closer a site was to the coast, the more globalized the architecture might be. Although the road network connected coastal and hinterland sites, and some evidence (such as the over life-size bronze statue of Septimius Severus from inland Chytroi) shows that significant shrines may have existed, the lack of Early Roman monumental architecture in rural contexts is striking.[96] The ceramic evidence indicates that people still lived in places like Idalion, the Malloura Valley, or Aradippou-*Panayia Ematousa*; however, there is little evidence for the marble and mosaic splendor found in Paphian villas or the imposing podia of prostyle temples.[97] In sum, enhanced maritime connectivity and the manipulation of local resources for export via coastal centers combined to globalize the *mentalités* of Cypriot islanders, a process that is arguably reflected in the material culture that characterizes the island's unique islandscapes during Early Roman times.

Connectivity, Insularity, and Bridging the Gap Between Early and Late Roman Cyprus

In Cypriot archaeology, the Early and Late Roman periods are typically viewed as distinct 'cycles of social complexity' and not as a 'long' Roman one. When and how the periods are divided depends on the scholar and the evidence under analysis, and so a range of dates and terms (Late Roman/Early Byzantine) have been proposed.[98] However, the transitional phase between the eras seems to fall somewhere within the century between the 230s–340s CE where archaeology and history combine to reveal a gradual reorientation of the effects of globalization on island life.[99]

From 235–284 CE the Roman empire experienced a breakdown of political and economic stability typically referred to as the Third Century Crisis.[100] In terms of Cypriot history, few events are recorded beyond an attempted Gothic invasion of 269 CE, while the archaeological evidence exhibits a similar dearth of data.[101] Regional shipwrecks are unknown, landscape surveys reveal settlement decline, inscriptions cease, and familiar ceramic types, like sigillatas and common amphorae, like Dressel 2–4, disappear from the record.[102] The latest provincial coins are dated to Severus Alexander's reign and the last stylistically Early Roman mosaics can be dated to around the same time.[103] Cyprus' economy and society thus seem to have been affected by heightened levels of *dis*connectivity unseen for generations as Rome's protection of Mediterranean connectivity broke down.[104]

Reconnections to imperial administrative networks began to occur, however, with Diocletian's political reorganization of the empire, and Cyprus' assignment to the Diocese of the East in 293 CE.[105] At this point, imperial inscriptions reappear in Cyprus' archaeology, and by the early 4th century, following the shift of the imperial capital to Constantinople in 330 CE, Cyprus' reintegration into maritime exchange networks becomes apparent.[106] Ammianus Marcellinus (fl. 4th century; Amm. Marc. 14.8.14), speaks of Cyprus as an 'insula portuosa' that makes its own ships, while the evidence for shipwrecks, imported ceramics, and a brand-new type of architecture, the Christian basilica, begins to emerge.[107] The most ostentatious examples of these religious structures were especially found at major port sites that lay on pilgrimage routes, like Salamis, which was renamed Constantia in 346 CE and made the island's capital, likely due to its proximity to Antioch, the seat of the *Comes Orientis*.[108] Thus, despite Cyprus' disconnection from Roman networks during the 3rd century, the island's self-sufficient and sea-girt nature allowed some Early Roman cultural traditions to survive (*e.g.* the use of mosaics and red-slipped ceramics), albeit in different forms, as Cypriots' *mentalités* were shaped by new globalizing forces, the most significant of which was Christianity.[109] This religion would evolve as a potent ethos that could fuse imperial and local cultural practices as Cypriots leveraged their centralized location and seafaring knowledge to connect with the ideas and markets found in the imperial capital of Constantinople, the Holy Land, and the eastern patriarchates.[110]

Late Roman Cyprus: A Composite Crossroads of Mediterranean Influences

The Late Roman period on Cyprus shows so many of the hallmarks of globalization that it is tempting to read the Cypriot landscape as a series of premodern non-places to appropriate the term that Marc Augé coined to describe the indistinguishable character of hotels, airports, and shopping malls in the globalized contemporary world.[111] Indeed, G. Bowersock noted that the brilliant series of Late Roman mosaics from the House of Aion at Paphos depicting the life of Dionysos reflect a pan-Mediterranean fascination with Dionysos echoed in the 6th-century epic poem of Nonnos of Panopolis.[112] In later late antiquity, Derek Krueger read the 7th-century world of Leontios of Cyprus' Life of St Symeon the Holy Fool and Life of St John the Almsgiver as leveraging a range of economic and political realities common to the wider Eastern Roman world.[113] As a result, this text produced a landscape that would be familiar to literate residents of Leontios's native Neapolis on Cyprus, in St Symeon's Emesa, and St John's Alexandria where his lives were certainly read. The regular transit of bishops, pilgrims, and other Romans across the island ensured that the Late Roman cities of Cyprus's south coast formed part of a familiar landscape connecting Egypt, North Africa, and the Levant with the Aegean. It is difficult to avoid the impression that whatever aspects of a distinctly Cypriot culture persisted into the Early Roman period, by late antiquity, Cyprus emerged as a composite crossroads of Mediterranean influences.[114]

Late Roman Cyprus: The Busy Countryside

The archaeological evidence from the island likewise reflects the global character of Cyprus during late antiquity. While there is no doubt that the basic settlement pattern that originally emerged over the course of the Cypriot Iron Age persisted into the 5th, 6th, and even 7th century, a new constellation of villages, ex-urban, and suburban settlements came to complement the densely urbanized southern coast of the island.[115] Many of these settlements appear to have supported the place of Cyprus within the economy of the Late Roman Mediterranean.[116]

The ex-urban site of Ayios Georgios-*Peyias* near Paphos, for example, features warehouses that the excavator suspects to have supported the *annona* route from Egypt to Constantinople.[117] The remarkable ceramic scatter and architectural remains at Pyla-*Koutsopetria* may have emerged as a harbor supporting the *quaestura exercitus* instituted in the mid-6th century.[118] The site at Dreamer's Bay appears to be another significant entrepôt on the south coast of the island, and recent work excavating warehouses promises to contribute to how we understand the island's economic relationship with the wider region.[119] The presence of kilns for Late Roman 1 amphorae on the coast near the village of Zigi provides more evidence for the role of ex-urban coastal sites within networks of large-scale agricultural production and exchange during Cypriot late antiquity.[120] Inland village sites, such as Kalavassos-*Kopetra*, situated in intermediate zones between the ore bearing Troodos mountains and coast also flourished in the 6th and 7th centuries and complemented ongoing extraction of copper from long-worked veins.[121] A parallel development in the Karkotis valley documented by the Troodos Archaeological and Environmental Survey Project (TAESP) seems to have supported mines in the region of Skouriotissa.[122] Rural settlement on Cyprus appears to have expanded in the Late Roman period leading Marcus Rautman to remark on the 'busy countryside of Late Roman Cyprus', which appears to have prospered into the late 6th century.[123] The intensity of settlement in the Cypriot landscape during late antiquity finds parallels across the Mediterranean world from the well-known 'deserted village' of the limestone massif in Syria to the valleys of the Peloponnesus.[124]

Late Roman Cyprus: A Plurality of Global Influences

At a glance, the material culture of Cyprus tells a similar story. Cyprus saw a regular flow of imported fine or tablewares, particularly African Red Slip (ARS) and Phocaean Ware (or Late Roman C/LRC ware) to the island. Archaeologists long thought that Cypriot Red Slip (Late Roman D/LRD ware) was manufactured on the western side of the island, perhaps near production sites of the earlier Cypriot Sigillata, but it now appears that most forms of Cypriot Red Slip were manufactured in Psidia in Asia Minor.[125] These fine wares, whatever their provenience, remain common in assemblages from across the eastern Mediterranean, Egypt, and the Levant. It remains difficult to identify the provenience of the ubiquitous Late Roman 1 amphora on Cyprus, but it appears likely that a substantial percentage of this common form originated in the Aegean or Anatolia. The same can be said for its successor, the globular Late Roman 13 amphora, which also saw production on Cyprus, but appeared extensively in 7th- and 8th-century assemblages in the Aegean and, most famously, Constantinople.[126] Cyprus manufactured cooking pots as well, including the well-known Dhiorios type known from kilns excavated by Hector Catling at the site of Dhiorios from which these pots get their name.[127] Paul Reynolds and his colleagues have noted that cooking pots both in fabrics common to Beirut and elsewhere in the Levant appeared in common 'Dhiorios' forms as early as the mid-6th century and circulated widely.[128]

In sum, the standard components of Cypriot ceramic assemblages throughout late antiquity were common not just on Cyprus, but across the eastern Mediterranean and Aegean at least through the end of the 7th century or the first decades of the 8th century. If the Cypriot landscape follows a pattern common to economic expansion across the eastern Mediterranean at the end of antiquity, the ceramic assemblages suggest that the local economies were either integrated at a regional level or at least sufficiently related for common ceramic forms to appear from multiple, contemporary production sites in the Aegean, Asia Minor, and the Levant. Thus, in a similar manner to the Early Roman period, Cypriots continued to participate in local and regional networks of exchange. Certain products, most notably fine tablewares and wine containers, signified inclusion in a globalized social hierarchy that was regional and that had meaning beyond the island's port cities.

Ecclesiastical architecture from the 5th through the 7th century presents a similar picture on Cyprus.[129] The ecclesiastical sites on the island reflect a remarkably globalized variation of ground plans and décor indicating contact with the Aegean basin, the Levant, and Egypt.[130] Traditionally, historians have argued that Cypriot church designs remained inward-facing and provincial until it was drawn into the expanding orbit of Constantinopolitan authority in the 6th and 7th centuries.[131] Recent scholarship though has served to complicate that picture by arguing for influences ranging from Levantine centers in Syria, Palestine, and Egypt without neglecting clear evidence for Aegean and Constantinopolitan forces at play on Cyprus.[132] Most of these arguments, while carefully wrought, rely on stylistic dating for many of the major churches on the island and reflect the rather incomplete publication status of many of these buildings. As a result, many of the chronological arguments for the history of influences on Cyprus' Early Christian architecture remain difficult to assess. What remains clear, however, is that the long-standing narrative of insularity or Constantinopolitan influence is no longer sufficient for understanding architecture on the island.

*Figure 56: General view of the architectural remains of Basilica A at Ayios Giorgios-*Peyias *(photo: authors).*

Churches like the massive basilica currently being excavated at Katalymata ton Plakaton on the coast of the Akrotiri Peninsula with its western apse and massive transept may have evoked the pilgrimage church of Abu Mina or even old St Peter's in Rome.[133] In either case, the eastern atrium and associated buildings make a strong case for the church's status as a pilgrimage site for pilgrims traveling to and from the Holy Land along the south coast of the island or even Christian traders unloading their wares at nearby Dreamer's Bay. In contrast, the central basilica at Ayios Georgios-*Peyias* (Fig. 56) was almost certainly the seat of a bishop in this coastal settlement.[134] It clearly bears the marks of Aegean influence from

Figure 57: View of the central nave in the Campanopetra Basilica at Salamis-Constantia (photo: authors).

Figure 58: General view of the architectural remains of the Basilica of St Epiphanios at Salamis-Constantia (photo: authors).

its prominent low stylobates marking the division between the nave and the aisles, its use of Proconnesian marble, and its central ambo.[135] In Salamis-Constantia, scholars have argued that the St Epiphanios and Campanopetra basilicas have parallels with the 4th-century churches of the Holy Land. At Campanopetra (Fig. 57), Roux suggested that the rectangular court to the east of the main apse had parallels with similar features in the Church of the Holy Sepulchre in Jerusalem and the Church of the Nativity in Bethlehem.[136] Richard Maguire has argued that the three eastern apses in the Epiphanios basilica (Fig. 58) not only invoked Trinitarian theology, but also the design of the basilica of Mt Sion in Jerusalem.[137] The plurality of influences on Cypriot church architecture in late antiquity belies earlier arguments for the island's 'provincial' or 'insular' character and proposes a more complex picture informed by the island's role in Christological debates, pilgrimage, and regular movement between the eastern Mediterranean and Egypt.[138]

Late Roman Cyprus: An Island of Distinct Places

Ceramics and Early Christian architecture represent only two ways to understand Cyprus as a globalized island in late antiquity. Moreover, they tend to reflect certain methodological biases in how we understand the material landscape of the island. Our tendency to juxtapose the global with the insular often pushes us to oscillate between regional and local parallels and to categorize architectural styles as either metropolitan or provincial. Luca Zavagno has similarly noted our tendency to see the later history of Cyprus as a decline from cosmopolitan prosperity in the 5th and 6th centuries to economic, political, and cultural isolation in the late 7th and 8th.[139] It goes without saying that these two polarized narratives have shaped our reading of the evidence for church architecture on the island and our willingness to identify trends that are distinctive to Cyprus.

The remains of the three-aisled South Basilica at the site of Late Roman Arsinoe (modern Polis tis Chrysochous; Fig. 59) offers a window into the range of influences present in Late Roman Cyprus. In its first phase, the 'South Basilica' lacked a narthex and was likely a simple wood-roofed building that underwent a major reconstruction which added not only a narthex, but also a south porch and, at the same time,

Figure 59: Aerial view of the South Basilica at Late Roman Arsinoe (Polis tis Chrysochous) from the north (courtesy of the Princeton Cyprus Expedition).

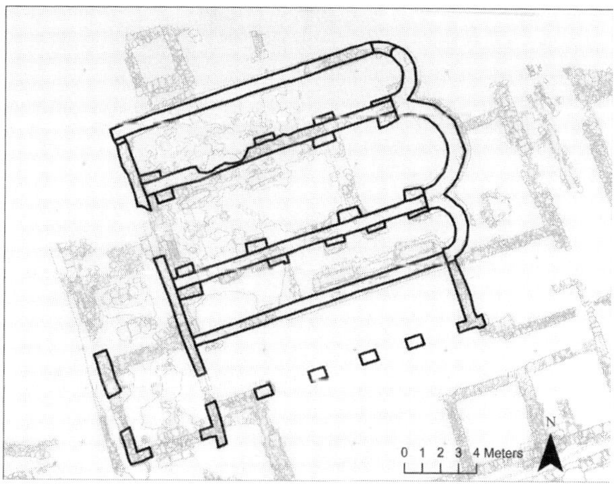

Figure 60: Plan of the South Basilica at Late Roman Arsinoe (Polis tis Chrysochous) in its second phase. Base plan courtesy of the Princeton Cyprus Expedition (modified by W.R. Caraher).

barrel vaulting over the nave. The modified church (Fig. 60) with its south porch opening onto a courtyard may reflect the influence of the slightly earlier Amathus Acropolis basilica located on the island's south coast.[140] The transformation, likely at the end of the 7th or early 8th century, reflects an architectural intervention characteristic of a series of basilicas in the neighborhood of Salamis and the Karpas peninsula which underwent a similar transformation.[141] Scholars have often proposed that the conversion from wood-roofed to locally inspired barrel-vaulted basilicas coincided with political turmoil brought to Cyprus after the Arab raids or economic and demographic decline in the 8th and 9th centuries.[142] It seems equally possible, however, to argue that such changes to basilicas on Cyprus trace lines of influence from the episcopal see of Salamis-Constantia to the congregation at Polis or even the movement of pilgrims from the island's western port at Polis via the Acropolis basilica at Amathus and the important churches of Salamis and the Karpas. The influence of the episcopal see's architecture on other insular sites seems particularly convincing, given the fact that the Archbishop of Cyprus, who presided over Constantia's main church, wielded significant island-wide power following the confirmation of his autocephaly by the Ecumenical Council of Ephesus in 431 CE.[143]

Local trends also appear in the distribution of ceramics across the island. While understanding local fabrics and forms present in Late Roman Cyprus remains in its relative infancy, the variations in the assemblages of imported ceramics suggest that communities across the island had varying relationships with the region. For example, a large assemblage of fineware from a recently published assemblage from Polis-Arsinoe was 97% Late Roman D or, Cypriot Red Slip ware.[144] It lacked significant quantities of African Red Slip and Phocaean Red Slip (or Late Roman C wares) which represent the most commonly imported finewares on the island. The only forms of these ceramic types present are the later African Red Slip, forms 104 and 105, which probably date to the mid-6th to mid-7th century, and the common Phocaean Ware form 3, which dates a half century earlier.

The assemblage from the site of Pyla-*Koutsopetria* derived from several seasons of intensive pedestrian survey and largely came from the coastal plain beneath the heights of Vigla and Koutsopetria.[145] Like the assemblage at Polis, Late Roman D ware dominated the finewares present, but only constituted 70% of the Late Roman fineware assemblage from across the site. Phocaean Ware, particular forms 3 and the later for 10, constituted almost 20% of the Koutsopetria assemblage, and a very diverse assemblage of the later forms of African Red Slip another 10%. Another coastal site, Maroni-*Petrara*, located some 50 km to the west of Koutsopetria at the mouth of the Kalavassos valley, produced a similar assemblage that was approximately 80% Cypriot Red Slip.[146] The similarities between these coastal sites is perhaps not surprising.

Inland sites, however, reveal more diverse assemblages. For example, at the nearly contemporary site of Kalavassos-*Kopetra* Phocaean Ware made up 37% of the assemblage and African Red Slip less than 10% with the remaining 50% or so being Late Roman D ware.[147] The published ceramics from the Athienou Archaeology Project's Maloura Valley Survey on the Mesaoria produced similar percentages.[148] The site of Aradippou-*Panayia Ematousa*, which is about 10 km inland from Koutospetria, produced an even greater percentage of Phocaean ware, which constituted almost 60% of the assemblage.[149] Cypriot Red Slip made up 20% of the material and African Red Slip 15%.

John Hayes, in his study of the ceramics from the Episcopal precinct of Kourion, proposed that African Red Slip became more common on the island only the in 7th century with Late Roman D ware and Phocaean wares being more common in earlier periods.[150] John Lund makes a similar argument for the presence of late forms of African Red Slip at *Panayia Ematousa* observing that the peak of African Red Slip appears in the mid-6th century.[151] That being said, it remains difficult to disentangle 6th-, 7th-, and early 8th-century ceramic assemblages on the island.[152] In fact, the presence of late forms of African Red Slip, Late Roman D, such as the so-called 'well form', and Phocaean Ware, such as Form 10, suggest that these sites continued to have access to all major forms of Late Roman fineware until the end of their production in the mid-7th century.

The differences in assemblages of finewares at sites across Cyprus suggests intra-insular variation with inland sites seeming to produce a comparatively higher proportion of North African and Aegean wares. This observation may, of course, reflect the rather small sample of sites across the island, the character of the assemblages being compared, and our still developing understanding of Late Roman finewares. The reasons for this apparent discrepancy might also be chronological, although it is hard to imagine a scenario where coastal sites through which imports moved declined before their inland destinations.[153] Finally, it might reflect variations in taste among communities across the island as different groups assigned different values to material culture. The role of slipped fineware in public displays such as dining may have served to distinguish one community from another. The constituent parts of these assemblages reflect the global character of table ware in Late Roman Cyprus, but the way in which the table is set suggests that local interests produced variation across the island in ceramics just as it did in church architecture.[154] Even at its most globalized, Cyprus remained an island of distinct places.

Becoming Roman on a Distinct Island: Insularity, Connectivity, and the Globalization of Culture in Early and Late Roman Cyprus

> Once there was a great famine [in Salamis], no bread could be found in the marketplace ... when Epiphanios was praying to God on behalf of those who were suffering, God's voice came to him and said, 'Epiphanios, do not be disturbed'. And he said, 'Lord, what is it?' And the voice said to him, 'Go to the temple which is called the sanctuary of Zeus, the seals of its doors will be loosed and upon entering you will find a large amount of gold. Take it, purchase all the wheat and barley of Phaustinianos [a dealer who was withholding grain from the people], and give it for food to those in need.'
>
> *Vita of St Epiphanios*[155]

This passage from the Life of St Epiphanios describes a 5th-century landscape where ancient pagan monuments could still be visited by those who were called to convert Cypriots to the nascent global faith of Christianity. Epiphanios, in fact, was a model globalized proselytizer. Born near Jerusalem, he lived as a monk in Egypt and the Holy Land until he was chosen to be Bishop of Salamis-Constantia, and eventually, Archbishop of Cyprus. He also spoke five languages and represented the island at church councils at Antioch and Rome.[156] Yet, he was not the first saint to preach Christ's word to Salamis' pagans. That honor falls to St Paul of Tarsus, also a globalized traveler, who traversed the island during the 1st century with Cyprus' own St Barnabas and converted the Roman proconsul, Sergius Paullus. The examples of Saints Epiphanios and Paul illustrate the types of globalized trampers, traders, and pilgrims who were 'pulled' towards Cyprus' outward-looking port cities during two of its most connected periods, the Early and Late Roman.

This chapter's goal has been to explore archaeologically how Cypriots like Barnabas might have interacted with representatives of globalized imperial cultures, such as Sergius Paullus, during two 'cycles of social complexity' on an island whose strategic location and ample resources pushed its inhabitants outwards and pulled outsiders inwards. However, since Cyprus' *histoire événementielle* rarely appears in written narratives, a comparative globalized archaeology of imperial insularity has been employed to show how Cypriots leveraged their island home to meet the enhanced connectivity accompanying imperial integration.

As Pitts and Versluys have stated, globalization involves, 'processes by which localities and people become increasingly interconnected and interdependent.'[157] During both the Early and Late Roman periods, Cypriots, and especially those living in coastal cities linked to maritime networks, became connected to and dependent on a wide range of globalizing influences emanating both directly and indirectly from Rome and Constantinople. In reference to Cyprus in the Early Middle Ages, Zavagno has argued that the sea-girt island was a centrally-located 'middle ground, based upon the idea that cultures stem from the creative interaction of human populations and never from isolation'.[158] Such a connected 'middle ground' concept might be applied to Cyprus in these earlier eras as well. Yet, because the orientations of trade routes, the nature of political rule, and the cultural forces of empire, like religion, had changed between the 3rd and 4th centuries, these periods' archaeology reveals different processes of imperial integration, connectivity, and globalization, even on the same island. Moreover, these processes were actively conditioned by Cypriots who, as islanders, strategically leveraged their insularity in ways that fit the changing social, economic, and political climates. According to Bernard Knapp:

> Insularity poses special restraints but at the same time offers special opportunities; it demands risks, provides benefits, and can modify social and politico-economic developments in unique and often unpredictable ways. What is important is the way that people manipulate insularity, in distinctive ways, in different times and places.[159]

Given the archaeological evidence for the creation of unique forms of material culture that blended global trends and local traditions as well as for economic prosperity and settlement expansion, it seems that Cypriots successfully manipulated their insularities in ways that, for the most part, positively transformed society.[160]

The Early Roman era began with a form of cultural grobalization as the new Roman rulers of Cyprus issued coins in the Latin script featuring *Mare Nostrum's* new ruler, Augustus, and an image of Rome's ecumenical aspirations with Nike astride a globe. Within a decade or so, however, glocalized images of Cyprus' famous pagan shrines appeared on coin reverses, and within two generations, Greek legends overtook Latin with the *Koinon Kyprion* taking control of minting. Early Roman Cyprus was also clearly integrated into Roman imperial trade routes that stretched from Spain to Egypt. Numerous shipwrecks have been found in the region dating to the 1st and 2nd centuries, and amphorae and finewares discovered at major port cities, such as the capital of Nea Paphos, indicate that elite Cypriots appreciated imported wines and red-slipped plates. Moreover, architectural remains, such as the House of Dionysos, reveal a mosaic-clad décor influenced by subject matters and designs found in several other provinces.

As with the coinage, local hybridization of imperial ceramic (*e.g.* Cypriot sigillata, or at least its use along with ESA) and architectural types (such as Kourion's

'Nabataean'-style podium temple) also occurred after two or three generations of participation in Rome's globalized maritime world. In addition, globalization also resulted in the re-embedding of local culture as the 'Land of the Paphian Aphrodite' retained the tripartite form of the patron goddess' famous temple at Palaipaphos. Another aspect of local continuity was the maintenance of regional circulation patterns for goods in preference to long-distance shipping, a practice that likely reflected pre-Roman relationships. Globalization in Early Roman Cyprus also resulted in uneven development as a 'busy coastscape' was created even as hinterland sites shrunk in size, lacked monumentality, and focused on resource processing for an export-oriented, coastal economy.

With the emperor Diocletian's stabilization of the imperial administration and economy following the Third Century Crisis, Cyprus was (re)connected to imperial trading and cultural networks that were reoriented towards the new political capital in Constantinople and spiritual region of the Holy Land. Such enhanced levels of connectivity transformed Cyprus into a middle-ground, composite crossroads of the Mediterranean where a globalized Christian culture intersected with, and eventually replaced, the remnants of a pagan sacred landscape that had existed for centuries.[161] The ceramic evidence reveals connections to Africa, Anatolia, and Syria, and Christian basilicas emerged to form the nuclei of villages dotting the 'busy countryside of Late Roman Cyprus', as indicated at inland sites like Kalavassos-*Kopetra*.[162] At the same time, however, the island's unique geography and local Christian history, which stretched back to Paul and Barnabas, permitted the development of distinct places. For example, the South Basilica at Late Roman Arsinoe could take its stylistic lead from local insular traditions, such as those found at Epiphanios' church at Salamis-Constantia, as opposed to the more 'imperial' forms found at other sites, like Ayios Georgios-*Peyias*, where Constantinopolitan influences prevailed. Overall, Late Roman Cyprus was also a globalized island, yet such processes of cultural change occurred in novel ways that differed from the Early Roman era.

As Ian Morris has argued, 'Geography did not lock in history, because geographical advantages are always ultimately self-defeating. They drive up social development, but in the process social development changes what geography means.'[163] During the Late Roman period, Cyprus' insular geography was perhaps more valuable than it had been in the Early Roman period. By the 4th century, the locus of imperial power had shifted eastward from Rome to Constantinople, and Cyprus was now administered by the *Comes Orientis* in Antioch. Furthermore, the island's capital city was transferred to Salamis-Constantia, which catered to ships from Antioch and those returning from the Holy Land or the Patriarchate of Alexandria. As a result of its strategic position situated on maritime sea routes directly between these political and spiritual poles, Cyprus increased in geographical value, which likely resulted in enhanced processes of globalization.[164]

It is not surprising that Christianity, as both the prevalent regional and state religion, seems to have spread relatively quickly (within a century or so) on Cyprus, and that it provided those who converted with access to maritime networks of exchange that would help develop the 'busy countryside' and the monumental basilicas that would, in turn, spiritually sustain the people.[165] Cyprus occupied a more centralized position in Late, as opposed to Early, Roman times and this location enhanced islanders' ability to connect with external political and social trends, a situation which fostered a local plurality of global influences. Indeed, the importance of these external connections is made plain when one compares the Early *or* Late Roman period to eras of relative disconnectivity, such as during the 3rd century, or the island's time as a 'borderland' between the Byzantine and Islamic empires in the Early Middle Ages.[166] Although Zavagno has recently argued that this latter era was one of continuity and economic stability, one must admit that, at least archaeologically, the countryside appears much less 'busy' and interdependent than in earlier eras.[167] The Early and Late Roman periods in Cyprus then, when viewed diachronically as related, yet reoriented, hyperconnected periods of 'social complexity', show how globalization theory sheds light on the nature of cultural change on islands located at the heart of imperial maritime networks.

Notes

1 For the term 'matchbox continent', see Held 1989.
2 For a complementary analysis of the development of Cypriot cultural landscapes during these eras and into the Early Middle Ages, see Vionis and Papantoniou 2019.
3 Knapp and van Dommelen 2010, 7.
4 For more on the analytical value of comparing colonial encounters, see Stein 2005. For more on the analytical value of comparing empires, see Alcock *et al.* 2001 and Morris and Scheidel 2009.
5 For 'cycles of social complexity', see below and Iacovou 2013, 17.
6 For the 'Land of the Paphian Aphrodite', see Sørensen *et al.* 1993. For the 'Busy Cypriot Countryside', see Rautman 2003.
7 See *Introduction*, this volume. For the particularly connected nature of islands in antiquity due to the facility of sea travel over land travel, see Knapp 2008, 20.
8 Knapp 2013, 36–37; Gordon 2016, 144–150.
9 Gordon 2018a, 16–19.
10 Hodos 2017, 4.
11 Ibid., 7.
12 Ibid., 6–7. For the re-embedding of local culture, see also Jennings 2017, 15.
13 See also Pitts and Versluys 2015; Terpstra 2019, 3.
14 For a thoughtful discussion of definitions of empire, see Morrison 2001, 1–3. For the Roman period in particular, see Mattingly 1997. For more on why empires establish colonies, see Stein 2005, 10. The reader may notice that we have avoided discussing the debated process of Romanization in terms of cultural change here and elsewhere in this chapter. This omission stems from the realization that the use of Romanization as a grand theory aimed at explaining most cultural change under Roman rule is now clearly untenable. We do address imperial and religious expansion as a form of grobalization below; but unlike Romanization, which often denotes top-down acculturation, grobalization can be a more inclusive and negotiated process that includes both local and imperial actors and can take place in multiple phases, even though it ultimately results in expanded imperial power. For more on the current status of the Romanization debate, see Versluys 2014 and the accompanying articles in *Archaeological Dialogues* 21(1).

15 van Dommelen 1998, 16; Stein 2005.
16 Hingley 2005; Pitts and Versluys 2015.
17 In reference to the Mediterranean islands, Cosentino (2013, 94) sees more of a 'long Roman period' with a 'long period of peace and prosperity under Roman rule, which lasted roughly from the 1st century BC until the second half of the 7th century AD'. For Rome's protection of maritime trade and its consequences, see Leidwanger 2017, 598; Terpstra 2019, 10. For the applicability of globalization theory to both the Early *and* Late Roman periods, see Dark 2006.
18 Knapp 2008, 24; Leidwanger and Knappett 2018, 5–6.
19 For the concepts of 'colonial programs' or 'imperial strategies', whereby 'homeland ideologies' structure 'interaction, accommodation, and resistance' in local contexts, see Stein 2005.
20 Knapp 2008, 20; Wilson 2011, 39; Gordon 2018a, 34; Terpstra 2019, 5.
21 Knapp 2008, 14.
22 Bintliff 1991, 10; Iacovou 2013, 18.
23 Iacovou 2013, 24; see also Knapp 2008, 20, 24.
24 For an informative overview of Cyprus' biogeographical features, see Knapp 2013, 3–19.
25 For a useful review of the archaeological and historical evidence for Assyrian and Egyptian influences on Archaic Cyprus, see Reyes 1994. For a critical analysis of the archaeology of Persian Cyprus, see Zournatzi 2005. For a postcolonial revision of the Greek, Persian, and Phoenician influences on the Cypriot Classical era, see Maier 1985. One of the most relevant studies of the *realpolitik* factors that drew the Ptolemies to Cyprus is Hauben 1987. Michaelides 1996 assembles the literary evidence for Cyprus' resources in Hellenistic and Roman times, while Kassianidou 2012 provides a concise overview of the exploitation of Cyprus' most historically significant resource, the copper of the Troodos mountains.
26 Although the evidence for Cypriots traveling abroad in most periods is sparse, it is likely that Archaic era Cypriots may have traveled to Assyria and Persia, there were Kitians in Piraeus in Greece by Late Classical times, Cypriots are detected in Ptolemaic papyri in Egypt, Tacitus and epigraphy tell us that Cypriots served as ambassadors to the emperor in Roman times, and saints *vitae* describe the many Cypriots who traveled throughout the eastern Mediterranean region during the late antique period. In addition to Cypriots traveling abroad, Cyprus' natural resources must have served as a key trading commodity from the Late Bronze Age onwards that permitted the import of the high-status items found in the 'royal tombs' at Salamis or the marble-clad Roman era *agorai*.
27 That is, with the possible exception of the Ceramic Neolithic and Chalcolithic Periods (7000–2700 BCE). According to Knapp (2013, 260), from the end of the Aceramic Neolithic to the Late Chalcolithic, 'people living on the island of Cyprus seem to have had somewhat limited contacts with the surrounding peoples and cultures of the eastern Mediterranean'.
28 Iacovou 2013, 19–21; Papantoniou and Vionis 2017.
29 Harper 2017, 39–54.
30 For more on the possible effects of earthquakes on Cypriot society, see Davis 2010.
31 For more on the importance of the sea as a key connective conduit between islanders and the wider world, see Knapp 2008, 26.
32 For a critical historical analysis of the Roman conquest of Cyprus and its administration, see Potter 2000. Mitford's (1980) study should also still be consulted as a synthesis of his life-long work on Roman epigraphy.
33 Badian 1965 examines the entire incident in great detail.
34 Potter (2000, 773, 775) suggests that there was 'no reason, aside from the ambition of P. Clodius Pulcher, for Rome to annex the island'. The abbreviations for ancient writers and their works used in this chapter are primarily based on those found in the third edition of the *Oxford Classical Dictionary*, xxix–liv.
35 See Mitford 1980, 1290, 1296.

36 See Mitford 1980, 1296. Mitford (1980, 1345) does mention epigraphic evidence for the presence of a cohort of Roman troops in the northeastern Mesaoria, but this situation seems isolated. For Cypriots possibly serving in the Roman military, see Bekker-Nielsen 2002.
37 Gallimore 2019, 595.
38 For similar processes in Roman Crete, see Gallimore 2019, 601.
39 Colonialist interpretations of Roman Cyprus include Hill 1972 and Mitford 1980. For more recent interpretations of the Roman period on Cyprus, see Parks 1999; 2004; Leonard 2005; Gordon 2012, 13–22; Hussein 2014; Gordon 2016; Christodoulou 2018. For a brief introduction to the interpretive context of Cypriot archaeology, see Knapp 2013, 28–33.
40 Iacovou 2013, 18. For the importance of 'materiality' and 'the role that "things" may play in restructuring old or formulating new identities', see Knapp 2008, 381.
41 Hodos 2017, 4. For the concept of islandscapes, see Broodbank 2000, 21–25; Knapp 2008, 25–27. For more on the importance of including 'archaeologies of the sea' and 'maritime cultural landscapes' in island archaeologies, see Rainbird 2007; Westdahl 2011; Leidwanger and Knappett 2018, 6.
42 Wilson 2011; Terpstra 2019.
43 Leidwanger 2017.
44 Leidwanger 2013.
45 Leonard 2005, 341–343.
46 Ibid., 349.
47 See Gordon 2018b; Vionis and Papantoniou 2019, 262.
48 Rupp 1997, 244.
49 For Nea Paphos' harbor, see Hohlfelder 1995. Less is known about Salamis' facilities, but Leonard (2005, 148) suggests that there were few major constructions before Late Roman times when the city had become the capital and renamed Constantia. Before that, large ships would have anchored off-shore and ferried their goods to the city. For *annona* ships traveling via Cyprus, see Rickman 1980, 266; Kaldeli 2013, 131–132. For the importance of harbors in the Roman era, see Terpstra 2019, 11.
50 Gordon 2018b.
51 For Kourion's breakwater, see Leonard 1995, 236–238. For Amathus' harbor, see Aupert 1996, 164–169. For the extensive remains at Dreamer's Bay, see Leonard and Demesticha 2004, 194; James *et al.* 2018.
52 For Pyla-*Koutsopetria* in the Early Roman era, see Caraher *et al.* 2014, 290. For Drousha-*Kioni*, see Leonard 1995, 236. For Avdhimou, see Leidwanger 2014, 63–64.
53 See Lund 1993, 141; Rupp 1997, 257–259; Rautman 2003, 248–255.
54 For the decline in extra-urban sacred sites in Roman times on Cyprus, see Papantoniou 2013, 50. For Panayia Ematousa, see Sørensen 2006, 57–61. For Agia Marina-*Mavrovouni*, see Graham *et al.* 2006. Knapp (2013, 36) also points out that on large islands like Cyprus, where interior sites are at a distance from the sea, there were always people who may have been unaware that they were 'islanders'. The changes in elevation on Cyprus may have also contributed to creating an 'interior insular world' of people who rarely visited the coast. See also Gordon 2018b on hinterland vs. coastal life in Cyprus, and Vionis and Papantoniou 2019, 260 fig. 11.1 where they present a map of Cyprus showing the 'Beyond Seascape' zone.
55 Two exceptions to the rule might be the over life-size bronze statue of Septimius Severus discovered at Chytroi (although how it got there or was displayed is unknown), and the recently discovered mosaic-clad villa at Akaki, which likely dates to the 4th century CE. Both of these sites are in the central Mesaoria plain, relatively close to Nicosia today.
56 Lund 2006, 182–186; Winther Jacobsen 2013, 64–65. For the road system of Roman Cyprus, see Bekker-Nielsen 2004.
57 For more on the concept of coastscape, see Tartaron 2013, 188–190.

58 For more on Cypriot ambassadors to the emperor, see Fujii 2013, 104–105. For Galen's visit to Cyprus see, Galen De *Temp. Fac. Simp. Med.* 9. For Titus' visit to Palaipaphos, see Tac. Hist. 2.2–4; Suet. Tit. 5.
59 Jennings 2017, 14–15.
60 Parks 2004, 35.
61 Parks 2004, 37–39. We would like to extend our thanks to the American Numismatic Society for permission to publish these coins from Roman Cyprus.
62 For the bronze coins of late Ptolemaic Cyprus, see Nicolaou 1990, 54–62.
63 Parks 2004, 35.
64 Hingley 2005, 1; Dark 2006, 12.
65 Terpstra 2019, 5.
66 Sinopoli 2003, 195.
67 Lund 2015, 208–210.
68 Kaldeli 2013.
69 Meyza and Baginska 2013.
70 Leonard and Demesticha 2004, 191–195; Kaldeli 2013, 132; Caraher *et al.* 2014; 286–287; Leidwanger 2014, 64–65.
71 Kondoleon 1995, 9.
72 Michaelides 1992, 4.
73 Kondoleon 1995, 320.
74 Gallimore 2019, 595.
75 Potter 2000, 849; Leonard 2005, 945–959.
76 Potter 2000, 838–839.
77 Gordon 2018b; Terpstra 2019, 8.
78 Parks 2004, 39–43.
79 Such semiotic linkages between Cypriot and Roman imperial deities are also witnessed in the so-called 'Oath of Allegiance to Tiberius', an inscription discovered at the Sanctuary of Aprhodite at Palaipaphos, where the members of the *Koinon Kyprion* swear to obey Tiberius by both Roman and Cypriot gods. For more on the Oath, see Mitford 1960 and Fujii 2013, 77–91. For representations of Aphrodite and Zeus in the Roman sculpture of Cyprus, see Gordon 2018a, 28–29.
80 Parks 2004, 68–72.
81 For more on the *Koinon Kyprion*, see Mitford 1960, 78; Potter 2000, 817–23; Fujii 2013, 15. For the *Koinon's* role as a 'bearer of a unifying ideology', see Vionis and Papantoniou 2019, 262.
82 Kaldeli 2009, 378.
83 Kaldeli 2013, 126. For a discussion of regional imitations of other imported wine vessels, such as Dressel 30 amphorae, see Leidwanger 2013.
84 Lund 2015, 167.
85 Ibid., 219.
86 Ibid., 102.
87 Bailey 1965, 13–17; Gordon and Cova 2010, 282.
88 *cf.* also Lund 2015, 208–209.
89 Lund 2015, 178.
90 Lund 2013, 95.
91 For the Amathus temple, see Aupert 1996, 123–129.
92 For a detailed discussion of the temple's design and excavation, see Soren 1987.
93 See Woolf 2010, 200 for a discussion of how local Greek histories were 'integral' to the empire's 'global culture' and 'how deeply interconnected macro- and microidentities were'.
94 Parks 2004, 40–41.
95 See Fujii 2013, 61–65; 79–85.

96 Based on its ostentatious size and likely cost, the life-size bronze of Septimius Severus probably stood in some kind of privileged location or shrine. Evidence for such imperial cult shrines is known from Lapethos on Cyprus' north coast where an Adrastos, son of Adrastos, erected an epigraphically-attested temple and statue dedicated to Tiberius. For the inscription describing the temple, see Fujii 2013, 27–28.

97 For the diachronic development of the Malloura Valley, see Gordon *et al.* 2012.

98 Davis and Stewart 2014.

99 Michaelides 1990, 125.

100 Drinkwater 2005; for a recent analysis of this crisis era with regard to the possible influence of climatic events and accompanying disease, see Harper 2017, 129–145.

101 Potter 2000, 854; Vionis and Papantoniou 2019, 262.

102 See Lund 1993, 142.

103 Michaelides 1992, 5–6; Parks 2004, 135.

104 For the Middle Roman decline in shipping in the eastern Mediterranean, see Leidwanger 2017, 612.

105 Michaelides 1990, 125; Cosentino (2013, 95) highlights how the 3rd century CE also marked the 'militarisation of Roman society', which in turn helped to shape social organization in late antiquity and may have led to increased prosperity in some island contexts, including 7th-century CE Cyprus.

106 Lund 1993, 143; Caraher *et al.* 2014, 287; Leidwanger 2015; Leidwanger 2017, 613.

107 Rautman 2003, 253; Gordon and Caraher 2019, 476; Vionis and Papantoniou 2019, 263–265.

108 Michaelides 1990, 128. For more of the role of smaller basilicas as local central places in the Late Roman Cypriot countryside, see Vionis and Papantoniou 2019, 270.

109 Dark 2006, 14.

110 For a recent review of Cyprus' Early Christian archaeology, see Gordon and Caraher 2019. Vionis and Papantoniou (2019, 263) further suggest that, 'The official establishment of Christianity, the economic prosperity that Cyprus started enjoying, and the shift of political control (at the local level) from imperial families to Christian elites and bishops contributed to the transformation of the sacred townscapes and landscapes of Cyprus.'

111 Augé 2008.

112 Bowersock 1990, 49–53.

113 Krueger 1996.

114 For a broader consideration of Late Roman Cyprus, see Metcalf 2009; Zavagno 2017. For Cypriot connectivity in late antiquity, see Caraher and Pettegrew 2016, 182–184.

115 Rupp 1997. Interestingly, the Early to Late Roman transition had a different effect on the western Mediterranean, with decreased numbers of rural sites witnessed in places like Mallorca, see Mas Florit and Cau Ontieveros 2011.

116 For an overview of the economy of Late Roman Cyprus, see Papacostas 2001.

117 Bakirtzis 1995; Cosentino 2013.

118 Caraher *et al.* 2014.

119 Leonard and Demesticha 2004; James and Score 2018.

120 Manning *et al.* 2000.

121 Rautman 2003; Given *et al.* 2013; for the 13 ha inland 'agro-town' site of Kofinou-*Panagia*, which was located 12 km from *Kopetra* and which had a three-aisled church in the 6th and 7th centuries, see Vionis and Papantoniou 2019, 266–267.

122 Given *et al.* 2013; Rautman 2014.

123 Rautman 2000; 2003.

124 For Greece, see Pettegrew 2007; Caraher and Pettegrew 2016.

125 Jackson *et al.* 2012.

126 Hayes 1992.

127 Catling 1972; for the recently discovered Late Roman ceramic workshop at Kofinou, see Vionis and Papantoniou 2019, 267–268.
128 Catling 1972; Reynolds *et al.* 2005.
129 Gordon and Caraher 2019, 476–483.
130 For a comparison between Cypriot church designs and those in Crete, Lycia, and the Peloponnese in relation to maritime connectivity, see Sweetman 2017.
131 Megaw 1974.
132 See Maguire 2012, and the various contributions to Horster *et al.* 2018.
133 Maguire 2012; Procopiou 2014.
134 Maguire 2012, volume 2, 54.
135 Michaelides 2001.
136 Roux 1998, 240–242; Maguire 2012, volume 1, 65.
137 Maguire 2012, volume 1, 81–96.
138 See also Sweetman 2017, 35–36.
139 Zavagno 2017.
140 Caraher *et al.* 2019.
141 Megaw 1946; Stewart 2010.
142 Megaw 1946; Dikigoropoulos 1961; Stewart 2010.
143 Rapp 2014, 35.
144 Caraher *et al.* 2019.
145 Caraher *et al.* 2014.
146 Manning *et al.* 2002.
147 Rautman 2003.
148 Moore and Gregory 2012.
149 Sørensen and Jacobsen 2006.
150 Hayes 2007.
151 Lund 2006.
152 Zavagno 2017, 161.
153 For more on issues of rural and urban abandonment at the beginning of the Early Middle Ages, see Vionis and Papantoniou 2019, 274.
154 Caraher and Pettegrew 2016, 189–190.
155 *Vita of St. Epiphanios* 53 (364 A–C); Pohlsander 1999, 16.
156 Rapp 2014, 30–31. For a recent study of St Epiphanios within his Late Roman context, see Kim 2015.
157 Pitts and Versluys 2015, 11.
158 Zavagno 2017, 4–5.
159 Knapp 2008, 22.
160 For more on Cypriots' fashioning their insularity in late antique times, see Vionis and Papantoniou 2019, 258–259. For the positive transformation of society during the Roman era, see Terpstra 2019, 3 who refers to it as 'an extraordinary episode in the economic progress of man' and suggests that 'economic activity reached levels not seen again until the High Middle Ages or the start of the Early-Modern Period'.
161 Rautman 2001; Nicolaou 2001; Hauben 2004; Panayides 2016; Deligiannakis 2018.
162 Vionis and Papantoniuou 2019, 270.
163 Morris 2010, 33.
164 See also Dark 2006 11–14; Leidwanger 2017, 613.
165 Rapp 2014, 29–30.
166 *cf.* Vionis and Papantoniou 2019, 276 who refer to Cyprus as a 'buffer zone' of 'cross-imperial interaction' as opposed to a 'cultural barrier between antagonistic empires'.
167 Cosentino 2013, 99–100; Zavagno 2017, 8; Vionis and Papantoniou 2019, 274.

Bibliography

Alcock, S.E., D'Altroy, T.N., Morrison, K.D. and Sinopoli, C. (eds) (2001) *Empires: Perspectives from Archaeology and History*. Cambridge: Cambridge University Press.

Augé, M. (2008) *Non-Places: An Introduction to Supermodernity.* Translated by J. Howe. London: Verso.

Aupert, P. (ed.) (1996) *Guide d'Amathonte*. École Française d'Athènes, Sites et monuments 15. Athens: École Française d'Athènes and Fondation A.G. Leventis.

Badian, E. (1965) M. Porcius Cato and the Annexation and Early Administration of Cyprus. *Journal of Roman Studies* 55(1/2), 110–121.

Bailey, D.M. (1965) Lamps in the Victoria and Albert Museum. *Opuscula Atheniensia* VI, 1–83.

Bakirtzis, C. (1995) The Role of Cyprus in the Grain Supply of Constantinople in the Early Christian Period. In *Cyprus and the Sea: Proceedings of the International Symposium, Nicosia, 25-26 September 1993*, edited by V. Karagheorgis and D. Michaelides. Nicosia: University of Cyprus, 247–254.

Bekker-Nielsen, T. (2002) Cypriots in the Roman Army. *Report of the Department of Antiquities, Cyprus*, 317–322.

Bekker-Nielsen, T. (2004) *The Roads of Ancient Cyprus*. Copenhagen: Museum Tusculanum Press, University of Copenhagen.

Bintliff, J.L. (1991) *The Annales School and Archaeology*. Leicester: Leicester University Press.

Bowersock, G. (1990) *Hellenism in Late Antiquity.* Ann Arbor: University of Michigan Press.

Broodbank, C. (2000) *An Island Archaeology of the Early Cyclades*. Cambridge: Cambridge University Press.

Caraher, W.R., Moore, R.S. and Papalexandrou, A. (2019) The South Basilica at Polis on Cyprus. *Hesperia* 88(2), 319–364.

Caraher, W.R., Moore, R.S. and Pettegrew, D.K. (eds) (2014) *Pyla-Koutsopetria I: Archaeological Survey of an Ancient Coastal Town*. American Schools of Oriental Research Archaeological Reports 21. Boston: The American Schools of Oriental Research.

Caraher, W.R. and Pettegrew, D.K. (2016) Imperial Surplus and Local Tastes: A Comparative Study of Mediterranean Connectivity and Trade. In *Across the Corrupting Sea: Post-Braudelian Approaches to the Ancient Mediterranean*, edited by C. Concannon and L. Mazurek. London: Routledge, 165–191.

Catling, H. (1972) An Early Byzantine Pottery Factory at Dhiorios in Cyprus. *Levant* 4, 1–82.

Christodoulou, S. (2018) Ρωμαική Κύπρος (30 π.Χ.–284 μ.Χ) [Roman Cyprus (30 BC–284 AD]. In *Ιστορία της Κύπρου* [History of Cyprus], Τόμος Α΄[Volume 1], edited by S. Neocleous. Nicosia: Ecumenical Hellenism Foundation, 142–177.

Cosentino, S. (2013) A Longer Antiquity? Cyprus, Insularity, and Economic Transition. *Cahier du Centre d'Études Chypriotes* 43, 93–102.

Dark, K. (2006) Globalizing Late Antiquity: Models, Metaphors And The Realities Of Long-Distance Trade And Diplomacy. *Reading Medieval Studies* XXXII, 3–14.

Davis, T. (2010) Earthquakes and the Crises of Faith: Social Transformation in Late Antique Cyprus. *Buried History* 46, 3–14.

Davis, T. and Stewart, C. (2014) A Brief History of Byzantine Archaeology on Cyprus. In *Cyprus and the Balance of Empires: Art and Archaeology from Justinian I to the Coeur de Lion*, edited by T. Davis and C.A. Stewart. Archaeological Reports 20. Boston: American Schools of Oriental Research, 17–28.

Deligiannakis, G. (2018) From Aphrodite(s) to Saintly Bishops in Late Antique Cyprus. In *Authority and Identity in Emerging Christianities in Asia Minor and Greece*, edited by C. Breytenbach and J.M. Ogereau. Leiden: Brill, 326–346.

Dikigoropoulos, A. (1961) Cyprus 'betwixt Greeks and Saracens' AD 674–965. PhD Dissertation, Oxford University.

Drinkwater, J. (2005) Maximinus to Diocletian and the 'Crisis'. *Cambridge Ancient History* 12, 28–66.

Fujii, T. (2013) *Imperial Cult and Imperial Representation in Roman Cyprus.* Heidelberger althistorische Beiträge und epigraphische Studien 53. Stuttgart: Franz Steiner Verlag.

Gallimore, S. (2019) An Island in Crisis? Reconsidering the Formation of Roman Crete. *American Journal of Archaeology* 123(4), 589–617.

Given, M., Knapp, A.B., Knoller, J.S., Sollars, L. and Kassianidou, V. (eds) (2013) *Landscape and Interaction: the Troodos Archaeological and Environmental Survey Project, Cyprus. Volume 1: Methodology, Analysis and Interpretation*. Levant Supplementary Series 14. Oxford: Oxbow Books.

Gordon, J.M. (2012) *Between Alexandria and Rome: A Postcolonial Archaeology of Cultural Identity in Hellenistic and Roman Cyprus*. PhD Dissertation, Department of Classics, University of Cincinnati.

Gordon, J.M. (2016) To Obey by Land and Sea: Empires, the Mediterranean, and Cultural Identity in Hellenistic and Roman Cyprus. In *Across the Corrupting Sea: Post-Braudelian Approaches to the Ancient Mediterranean*, edited by C. Concannon and L. Mazurek. London: Routledge, 133–164.

Gordon, J.M. (2018a) Insularity and Identity in Roman Cyprus: Connectivity, Complexity, and Cultural Change. In *Insularity and Identity in the Roman Mediterranean*, edited by A. Kouremenos. Oxford: Oxbow Books, 4–40.

Gordon, J.M. (2018b) Transforming Culture on an Insula Portunalis: Port Cities a Central Places in Early Roman Cyprus. In *Central Places and Un-Central Landscapes: Political Economies and Natural Resources in the Longue Durée*, edited by G. Papantoniou and A.K. Vionis. *Land* 7(4) https://doi.org/10.3390/land7040155.

Gordon, J.M. and Caraher, W.R. (2019) The Holy Island: An Archaeology of Early Christian Cyprus. In *The Oxford Handbook of Early Christian Archaeology*, edited by D.K. Pettegrew, W.R. Caraher and T.W. Davis. Oxford: Oxford University Press, 473–494.

Gordon, J.M. and Cova, E. (2010) Romanesis in Cyprus: A Lamp from Athienou-Malloura. *Cahier du Centre d'Études Chypriotes* 40, 277–294.

Gordon, J.M., Kardulias, P.N. and Toumazou, M.K. (2012) The Historical Background: Regional Chronology and Local History. In *Crossroads and Boundaries: The Archaeology of Past and Present in the Malloura Valley, Cyprus*, edited by M.K. Toumazou, P.N. Kardulis and D.B. Counts. AASOR 65. Boston: American Schools of Oriental Research, 35–44.

Graham, A., Winther Jacobsen, K. and Kassianidou, V. (2006) Agia Marina *Mavrovouni*. Preliminary Report on the Roman Settlement and Smelting Workshop in the Central Northern Foothills of the Troodos Mountains, Cyprus. *Report of the Department of Antiquities, Cyprus*, 345–367.

Harper, K. (2019) *The Fate of Rome: Climate, Disease, and the End of an Empire*. Princeton: Princeton University Press.

Hauben, H. (1987) Cyprus and the Ptolemaic Navy. *Report of the Department of Antiquities, Cyprus*, 213–226.

Hauben, H. (2004) Christ Versus Apollo in Early Byzantine Kourion? With a Note on the So-called 'Panayia Aphroditissa' in Paphos. In *Philomathestatos. Studies in Greek Patristic and Byzantine Texts Presented to Jacques Noret for his Sixty-Fifth Birthday*, edited by B. Janssens, B. Roosen and P. van Deun. Orientalia Lovaniensia Analecta 137. Leuven: Peeters, 269–284.

Hayes, J.W. (1992) *Excavations at Saraçhane in Istanbul, Vol. II: The Pottery*. Princeton: Princeton University Press.

Hayes, J.W. (2007) Pottery. In *Kourion: Excavations in the Episcopal Precinct*, edited by A.H.S. Megaw. Dumbarton Oaks Studies 38. Cambridge, MA: Dumbarton Oaks Research Library and Collection, 435–475.

Held, S. (1989) Colonization Cycles on Cyprus 1: The Biogeographic and Paleontological Foundations of Early Prehistoric Settlement. *Report of the Department of Antiquities, Cyprus*, 7–28.

Hill, G.F. (1972) *A History of Cyprus*. Cambridge: Cambridge University Press.

Hingley, R. (2005) *Globalizing Roman Culture: Unity, Diversity and Empire*. London: Routledge.

Hodos, T. (2017) Globalization: Some Basics. An Introduction to *The Routledge Handbook of Archaeology and Globalization*. In *The Routledge Handbook of Archaeology and Globalization*, edited by T. Hodos. London: Routledge, 3–11.

Hohlfelder, R. (1995) Ancient Paphos Beneath the Sea: A Survey of the Submerged Structures. In *Proceedings of the International Symposium Cyprus and the Sea*, edited by V. Karageorghis and D. Michaelides. Nicosia: University of Cyprus, 191–208.

Horster, M., Nicolaou, D. and Rogge, S. (eds) (2018) *Church Building in Cyprus (4th–7th Centuries): A Mirror of Intercultural Contacts in the Eastern Mediterranean.* Schriften des Instituts für Interdisziplinäre Zypern-Studien 12. Münster: Waxmann.

Hussein, E. (2014) *Power and Identity in Roman Cyprus.* PhD Dissertation, University of Warwick.

Iacovou, M. (2013) Cyprus's Political Geography in the Iron Age. *Bulletin of the American Schools of Oriental Research* 370, 1–39.

Jackson, M., Zelle, M., Vandeput, L. and Köse, V. (2012) Primary Evidence for Late Roman D Ware Production in Southern Asia Minor: A Challenge to 'Cypriot Red Slip Ware'. *Anatolian Studies* 62, 89–114.

James, S. and Score, V. (2018) Akrotiri-Dreamer's Bay (Nissarouin) Excavation and Survey Spring 2018 Interim Report. Leicester: University of Leicester, https://www2.le.ac.uk/departments/archaeology/research/projects/ancient-akrotiri/images/DreamersBay2018MarAprinterim.pdf/view.

Jennings, J. (2017) Distinguishing Past Globalizations. In *The Routledge Handbook of Archaeology and Globalization*, edited by T. Hodos. London: Routledge, 12–28.

Kaldeli, A. (2009) Trade and the Transmission of Roman Values to Cyprus, as Evidenced by the Amphorae. *Cahier du Centre d'Études Chypriotes* 39, 365–386.

Kaldeli, A. (2013) Early Roman Amphorae from Cyprus as Evidence of Trade and Exchange in the Mediterranean. In *The Transport Amphorae and Trade of Cyprus*, edited by M.L. Lawall and J. Lund. Gösta Enbom Monographs 3. Aarhus: Aarhus University Press, 123–132.

Kassianidou, V. (2012) Natural Resources and the Importance of Copper. In *Ancient Cyprus: Cultures in Dialogue: Exhibition Catalogue*, edited by D. Pilides and N. Papdimitriou. Nicosia: Department of Antiquities, Cyprus.

Kim, Y.R. (2015) *Epiphanius of Cyprus: Imagining an Orthodox World.* Ann Arbor: University of Michigan Press.

Knapp, A.B. (2008) *Prehistoric and Protohistoric Cyprus: Identity, Insularity, and Connectivity.* Oxford: Oxford University Press.

Knapp, A.B. (2013) *The Archaeology of Cyprus: From Earliest Prehistory through the Bronze Age.* Cambridge: Cambridge University Press.

Knapp, A.B. and van Dommelen, P. (2010) Material Connections: Mobility, Materiality, and Mediterranean Identities. In *Material Connections in the Ancient Mediterranean: Mobility, Materiality and Mediterranean Identities*, edited by P. van Dommelen and A.B. Knapp. London: Routledge, 1–18.

Kondoleon, C. (1995) *Domestic and Divine: Roman Mosaics in the House of Dionysos.* Ithaca: Cornell University Press.

Krueger, D. (1996) *Symeon the Holy Fool: Leontios' Life and the Late Antique City.* Berkeley: University of California Press.

Leidwanger, J. (2013) Between Local and Long-Distance: a Rome Shipwreck off Fig Tree Bay of SE Cyprus. *Journal of Roman Studies* 26.1, 191–208.

Leidwanger, J. (2014) Integrating an Empire: Maritime Trade and Agricultural Supply in Roman Cyprus. *Skylla* 13, 59–66.

Leidwanger, J. (2015) Late Roman and Early Byzantine Cyprus: A View from the Sea. In *Maritime Studies in the Wake of the Byzantine Shipwreck at Yassıada, Turkey*, edited by D.N. Carlson, J. Leidwanger, and S.M. Kampbell. College Station: Texas A&M University Press, 156–165.

Leidwanger, J. (2017) From Time Capsules to Networks: New Light on Roman Shipwrecks in the Maritime Economy. *American Journal of Archaeology* 121(4), 595–619.

Leidwanger, J. and Knappett, C. (2018) Maritime Networks, Connectivity, and Mobility in the Ancient Mediterranean. In *Maritime Networks in the Ancient Mediterranean World*, edited by J. Leidwanger and C. Knappett. Cambridge: Cambridge University Press, 1–21.

Leonard, J. (1995) Evidence for Roman Ports, Harbours and Anchorages in Cyprus. In *Proceedings of the International Symposium Cyprus and the Sea*, edited by V. Karageorghis and D. Michaelides. Nicosia: University of Cyprus, 211–227.

Leonard, J. (2005) *Roman Cyprus: Harbors, Hinterlands, and 'Hidden Powers'*. PhD Dissertation, State University of New York at Buffalo.

Leonard, J. and Demesticha, S. (2004) Fundamental Links in the Economic Chain: Local Ports and International Trade in Roman and Early Christian Cyprus. In *Transport Amphorae And Trade In The Eastern Mediterranean: Acts Of The International Colloquium At The Danish Institute At Athens, September 26–29, 2002*, edited by J. Eiring and J. Lund. Monographs of the Danish Institute at Athens 5. Aarhus: Aarhus University Press, 189–202.

Lund, J. (1993) Pottery of the Classical, Hellenistic, and Roman Periods. In *The Land of the Paphian Aphrodite*, edited by L. Wriedt Sørensen, D. Rupp and P. Guldager Bilde. *Studies in Mediterranean Archaeology* 104, 2. Göteborg: Paul Åströms Förlag, 79–155.

Lund, J. (2006) Ceramic Fine Wares from the 4th Century BC to the 7th Century AD. In *Panayia Ematousa: A Rural Site in South-Eastern Cyprus I*, edited by L. Wriedt Sørensen and K. Winther Jacobsen. Monographs of the Danish Institute at Athens Vol. 6.1. Athens: Danish Institute at Athens, 182–230.

Lund, J. (2013) Connections Between Rough Cilicia and Northwestern Cyprus Between About 200 BC and AD 200: The Ceramic Evidence. In *Rough Cilicia: New Historical and Archaeological Approaches*, edited by M.C. Hoff and R.F. Townsend. Oxford: Oxbow Books, 189–198.

Lund, J. (2015) *A Study of the Circulation of Ceramics in Cyprus from the 3rd Century BC to the 3rd Century AD*. Gösta Enbom Monographs 5. Aarhus: Aarhus University Press.

Maguire, R. (2012) *Late Antique Basilicas on Cyprus Sources, Contexts, Histories*. PhD Dissertation, University of East Anglia.

Maier, F.-G. (1985) Factoids in Ancient History: The Case of Fifth-Century Cyprus. *Journal of Hellenic Studies* 105, 32–39.

Manning, S.W., Manning, A., Tomber, R., Sewell, D., Monks, S.J., Ponting, M.J. and Ribeiro, E.C. (2002) *The Late Roman Church at Maroni-Petrera: Survey and Salvage Excavations 1990–1997, and Other Traces of Roman Remains in the Lower Maroni Valley, Cyprus*. Nicosia: A.G. Leventis Foundation.

Manning, S.W., Monks, S.J., Sewell, D.A. and Demesticha, S. (2000) Late Roman Type 1a Amphora Production at the Late Roman Site Of Zygi-*Petrini*, Cyprus. *Report of the Department of Antiquities, Cyprus*, 233–257.

Mas Florit, C. and Cau Ontiveros, M.Á. (2011) From Roman to Byzantine: The Rural Occupation of Eastern Mallorca (Balearic Islands). *Journal of Mediterranean Archaeology* 24(2), 191–217.

Mattingly, D.J. (1997) Dialogues of Power and Experience in the Roman Empire. In *Dialogues in Roman Imperialism: Power, Discourse, and Discrepant Experience in the Roman Empire*, edited by S.E. Alcock and D.J. Mattingly. JRA Suppl. Ser. 23. Portsmouth, RI: Journal of Roman Archaeology, 7–24.

Megaw, A.H.S. (1946) Three Vaulted Basilicas in Cyprus. *Journal of Hellenic Studies* 66, 48–56.

Megaw, A.H.S. (1974) Byzantine Architecture and Decoration in Cyprus: Metropolitan or Provincial? *Dumbarton Oaks Papers* 28, 57–88.

Metcalf, M. (2009) *Byzantine Cyprus 491–1191*. Nicosia: Cyprus Research Centre.

Meyza, H. and Baginska, D. (2013) Roman Amphorae from the Polish Excavations at Nea Paphos, Maloutena: An Overview. In *The Transport Amphorae and Trade of Cyprus*, edited by M.L. Lawall and J. Lund. Gösta Enbom Monographs 3. Aarhus: Aarhus University Press, 134–153.

Michaelides, D. (1990) The Roman Period. In *Footprints in Cyprus: An Illustrated History*, edited by D. Hunt. London: Trigraph, 110–135.

Michaelides, D. (1992) *Cypriot Mosaics*. Nicosia: Department of Antiquities, Cyprus.

Michaelides, D. (1996) The Economy of Cyprus During the Hellenistic and Roman Periods. In *The Development of the Cypriot Economy: From the Prehistoric Period to the Present Day*, edited by V. Karageorghis and D. Michaelides. Nicosia: Lithographica, 139–152.

Michaelides, D. (2001) The Ambo of Basilica A at Cape Drepanon. In *Mosaic: Festschrift for A.H.S. Megaw*, edited by J. Herrin, M. Mullett and C. Otten-Froux. British School at Athens Studies 8. Athens: British School at Athens, 43–56.

Mitford, T.B. (1960) A Cypriot Oath of Allegiance to Tiberius. *Journal of Roman Studies* 50, 75–79.

Mitford, T.B. (1980) Roman Cyprus. *Aufstieg und Niedergang der römischen Welt* 2(7.2), 1285–1384.

Moore, R.S. and Gregory, T.E. (2012) Athienou Archaeological Project Survey Pottery. In *Crossroads and Boundaries: The Archaeology of Past and Present in the Malloura Valley, Cyprus*, edited by M. Toumazou, P.N. Kardulias and D.B. Counts. The Annual of the American Schools of Oriental Research 65. Boston: American Schools of Oriental Research, 203–213.

Morris, I. (2010) *Why the West Rules - for Now: The Patterns of History, and What They Reveal About the Future*. New York: Farrar, Straus and Giroux.

Morris, I. and Scheidel, W. (eds) (2009) *The Dynamics of Ancient Empires: State Power from Assyria to Byzantium*. Oxford Studies in Early Empires. Oxford: Oxford University Press.

Morrison, K.D. (2001) Sources, Approaches, Definitions. In *Empires: Perspectives from Archaeology and History*, edited by S.E. Alcock, T.N. D'Altroy, K.D. Morrison and C. Sinopoli, Cambridge: Cambridge University Press, 1–9.

Nicolaou, I. (1990) *The Coins from the House of Dionysos*. Paphos 2. Nicosia: Department of Antiquities, Cyprus.

Nicolaou, I. (2001) The Transition from Paganism to Christianity as Revealed in the Mosaic Inscriptions of Cyprus. In *Mosaic: Festschrift for A.H.S. Megaw*, edited by J. Herrin, M. Mullett and C. Otten-Froux. British School at Athens Studies 8. Athens: British School at Athens, 13–17.

Panayides, P. (2016) *The Fate of Statues: A Contextualised Study of Sculpture in Late Antique Cyprus*. PhD Dissertation, 2 vols, Durham University.

Papacostas, T. (2001) The Economy of Late Antique Cyprus. In *Economy and Exchange in the East Mediterranean in Antiquity, Proceedings of a conference at Somerville College, Oxford - 29th May, 1999*, edited by S. Kingsley and M. Decker. Oxford: Oxbow Books, 107–128.

Papantoniou, G. (2013) Cyprus from Basileis to Strategos: A Sacred-Landscapes Approach. *American Journal of Archaeology* 117(1), 33–57.

Papantoniou G. and Vionis, A.K. (2017). Landscape Archaeology and Sacred Space in the Eastern Mediterranean: A Glimpse from Cyprus. *Land* 6(2) https://doi.org/10.3390/land6020040.

Parks, D.A. (1999) *Burial Customs of Roman Cyprus: Origins and Development*. PhD Dissertation, University of Missouri.

Parks, D.A. (2004) *The Roman Coinage of Cyprus*. Nicosia: Cyprus Numismatic Society.

Pettegrew, D. (2007) The Busy Countryside of Late Roman Corinth: Interpreting Ceramic Data Produced by Regional Archaeological Surveys. *Hesperia* 76(4), 743–784.

Pitts, M. and Versluys, M.J. (eds) (2015) *Globalisation and the Roman World: World History, Connectivity and Material Culture*. Cambridge: Cambridge University Press.

Pohlsander, H. (1999) *Greek Texts of the Fourth to Thirteenth Centuries*. Sources for the History of Cyprus 7. Altamont: Greece and Cyprus Research Center, SUNY Albany.

Potter, D.S. (2000) Η Κύπρος επαρχία της Ρωμαϊκής αυτοκρατωρίας [Cyprus as a Province of the Roman Empire]. In *Ιστορία της Κύπρου* [History of Cyprus], Vol. 2, pt. 1, edited by T. Papadopoullos. Nicosia: Archbishop Makarios III Foundation, 763–864.

Procopiou, E. (2014) The Katalymata ton Plakoton: New Light from the Recent Archaeological Research in Cyprus. In *Cyprus and the Balance of Empires: Art and Archaeology from Justinian I to the Coeur de Lion*, edited by T. Davis and C.A. Stewart. Archaeological Reports 20. Boston: American Schools of Oriental Research, 69–98.

Rainbird, P. (2007) *The Archaeology of Islands*. Cambridge: Cambridge University Press.

Rapp, C. (2014) Christianity in Cyprus in the Fourth to Seventh Centuries: Chronological and Geographical Frameworks. In *Cyprus and the Balance of Empires: Art and Archaeology from Justinian*

I to the Coeur de Lion, edited by T. Davis and C.A. Stewart. Archaeological Reports 20. Boston: American Schools of Oriental Research, 29–38.

Rautman, M. (2000) The Busy Countryside of Late Roman Cyprus. *Report of the Department of Antiquities, Cyprus*, 317–331.

Rautman, M. (2001) From Polytheism to Christianity in the Temples of Cyprus. In *Ancient Journeys: A Festschrift in Honour of Eugene Numa Lane*. Stoa Consortium, https://www.stoa.org/texts/2001/01/0014.

Rautman, M.L. (ed.) (2003) *A Cypriot Village of Late Antiquity: Kalavasos-Kopetra in the Vasilikos Valley*. JRA Suppl. Ser. 52. Portsmouth, RI: Journal of Roman Archaeology.

Rautman, M.L. (2014) The Troodos in Twilight: A Provincial Landscape in the Time of Justinians. In *Cyprus and the Balance of Empires: Art and Archaeology from Justinian I to the Coeur de Lion*, edited by T. Davis and C.A. Stewart. Archaeological Reports 20. Boston: American Schools of Oriental Research, 39–56.

Reyes, A.T. (1994) *Archaic Cyprus: A Study of the Textual and Archaeological Evidence*. Oxford Monographs on Classical Archaeology. Oxford: Clarendon Press.

Reynolds, P. (2005) Levantine Amphorae from Cilicia to Gaza: A Typology and Analysis of Regional Production Trends from the 1st to 7th Centuries. In *LRCW I. Late Roman Coarse Wares, Cooking Wares and Amphorae in the Mediterranean. Archaeology and Archaeometry*, edited by J.M. Gurt i Esparraguera, J. Buxeda I Garrigós and M.Á. Cau Ontiveros. BAR International Series 1340. Oxford: Archaeopress, 563–611.

Rickman, G.E. (1980) The Grain Trade under the Roman Empire. In *The Seaborne Commerce of Ancient Rome: Studies in Archaeology and History*, edited by J.H. D'Arms and E.C. Kopff. Memoirs of the American Academy in Rome 36. Ann Arbor: University of Michigan Press, 261–275.

Roux, G. (1998) *La Basilique de la Campanopétra*. Salamine de Chypre XV. Paris: Boccard.

Rupp, D. (1997) 'Metro' Nea Paphos: Suburban Sprawl in Southwestern Cyprus in the Hellenistic and Earlier Roman Periods. In *Urbanism in Antiquity: From Mesopotamia to Crete*, edited by W.E. Aufrecht, N.A. Mirau and S.W. Gauley. Journal for the Study of the Old Testament. Suppl. Ser. 244. Sheffield: Sheffield Academic Press, 236–262.

Sinopoli, C. (2001) Imperial Integration and Imperial Subjects. In *Empires: Perspectives from Archaeology and History*, edited by S.E. Alcock, T. D'Altroy, K.D. Morrison and C. Sinopoli. Cambridge: Cambridge University Press, 195–200.

Soren, D. (ed.) (1987) *The Sanctuary of Apollo Hylates at Kourion, Cyprus*. Tucson: University of Arizona Press.

Sørensen, L.W. (2006) Introduction: Stratigraphy and Summary of the Site Analysis. In *Panayia Ematousa: A Rural Site in South-Eastern Cyprus I*, edited by L.W. Sørensen and K. Winther Jacobsen. Monographs of the Danish Institute at Athens Volume 6.1. Athens: Danish Institute at Athens, 34–63.

Sørensen, L.W., Rupp, D. and Guldager Bilde, P. (eds) (1993) *The Land of the Paphian Aphrodite*. SIMA 104, 2. Göteborg: Paul Åströms Förlag.

Sørensen, L.W. and Winther Jacobsen, K. (eds) (2006) *Panayia Ematousa: A Rural Site in South-Eastern Cyprus*. 2 vols. Monographs of the Danish Institute at Athens Vol. 6. Athens: Danish Institute at Athens.

Stein, G. (2005) Introduction: The Comparative Archaeology of Colonial Encounters. In *The Archaeology of Colonial Encounters: Comparative Perspectives*, edited by G. Stein. School of American Research Advanced Seminar Series. Santa Fe: School of American Research Press, 3–32.

Stewart, C.A. (2010) The First Vaulted Churches in Cyprus. *Journal of the Society of Architectural Historians* 69(2), 162–189.

Sweetman, R. (2017) Networks and Church Building in the Aegean: Crete, Cyprus, Lycia, and the Peloponnese. *British School at Athens Annual*, 1–60.

Tartaron, T. (2013) *Maritime Networks in the Mycenaean World*. Cambridge: Cambridge University Press.

Terpstra, T. (2019) *Trade in the Ancient Mediterranean: Private Order and Public Institutions*. Princeton: Princeton University Press.
van Dommelen, P. (1998) *On Colonial Grounds: A Comparative Study of Colonialism and Rural Settlement in First Millennium BC West Central Sardinia*. Archaeological Studies Leiden University 2. Leiden: Faculty of Archaeology, University of Leiden.
Versluys, M. (2014) Understanding Objects in Motion. An Archaeological Dialogue on Romanization. *Archaeological Dialogues* 21(1), 1–20 doi:10.1017/S1380203814000038.
Wilson, A. (2011) Developments in Mediterranean Shipping and Maritime Trade from the Hellenistic Period to AD 1000. In *Maritime Archaeology and Ancient Trade in the Mediterranean*, edited by D. Robinson and A. Wilson. Oxford Centre for Maritime Archaeology 6. Oxford: Institute of Archaeology, University of Oxford, 33–60.
Vionis, A.K. and Papantoniou, G. (2019) Economic Landscapes and Transformed Mindscapes in Cyprus from Roman Times to the Early Middle Ages. In *Change and Resilience: The Occupation of Mediterranean Islands in Late Antiquity*, edited by M.Á. Cau Ontiveros and C. Mas Florit. Joukowsky Institute Publication 9. Oxford: Oxbow Books, 257–284.
Westdahl, C. (2011) The Maritime Cultural Landscape. In *The Oxford Handbook of Maritime Archaeology*, edited by A. Katsambis, B. Ford and D.L. Hamilton. Oxford: Oxford University Press, 733–762.
Winther Jacobsen, K. (2013) Hellenistic and Roman Landscapes. In *Landscape and Interaction: Troodos Archaeological and Environmental Research Project, Cyprus. Vol 1*, edited by M. Given, A.B. Knapp, J. Noller, L. Sollers and V. Kassianidou. Levant Supplementary Series 14. Oxford, Oxbow Books, 328–334.
Woolf, G. (2010) Afterword: The Local and the Global in the Graeco-Roman East. In *Local Knowledge and Microidentities in the Imperial Greek World,* edited by T. Whitmarsh. Cambridge: Cambridge University Press, 189–200.
Zavagno, L. (2017) *Cyprus Between Late Antiquity and the Early Middle Ages (ca. 600–800): An Island in Transition*. Birmingham Byzantine and Ottoman Studies. Oxford: Routledge.
Zournatzi, A. (2005) *Persian Rule in Cyprus: Sources, Problems, Perspectives*. Meletemata 44. Athens: De Boccard.

Afterword

P. Nick Kardulias

Most scholars would agree that there is abundant evidence for numerous links among Mediterranean societies in both historic and prehistoric periods. At times those connections have been due to the presence of overarching political structures, most notably perhaps the Roman empire over a period of some five centuries, but with economic ties even in less centralized epochs. A key research question has been how best to characterize the nature of those links. We must keep in mind that the ancient residents at times recognized the region as a cultural unit (the *mare nostrum* of the Romans), or at least as a major transit route for the exchange of goods or an avenue to facilitate colonization by the Greeks and Phoenicians. It is important, therefore, to include as much as possible the ancient conception of the region (*e.g.* the Braudelian mentalities discussed in the paper by Gordon and Caraher) in constructing our models for understanding how people utilized the sea, surrounding landmasses, and the islands. It is the effort to bring together the ancient perception and the modern observation of relevant data with which the contributors to this volume have grappled. In so doing, they present an array of concepts and frameworks in an attempt to understand cultural interaction in the Mediterranean from the Bronze Age to the early medieval period. These efforts display the vitality of theorizing that has come to characterize the archaeology of late prehistoric and historic periods in the Mediterranean over the past four decades, moving beyond the culture historical approach that dominated the discipline through the mid-20th century.

In order to comment usefully on the various chapters, it is important to start with the definition of some of the key concepts that the authors employ. Insularity is particularly relevant to the Mediterranean because of the abundance of islands that can be found throughout its expanse. As several contributors note, islands simultaneously possess the traits of both isolation and connection (to other islands and the landmasses). Because of physical separation from the landmasses, access could be gained only by sea. The spatial separation and intervening water meant that establishing connections required technological and temporal adjustments. The former went from rafts to ships with oars and sails, with a concomitant increase in size and ability to carry cargo. The timing of travel prior to steamships was limited to periods when waters were calmer, and when prevailing winds blew in the direction one wanted to go. In addition, some islands had numerous insular neighbors and/or were close to continental coasts, thus minimizing travel time and increasing the frequency of off-island transit. This relative ease of access to neighbors is particularly evident among offshore islands such as those near the west coast of Asia Minor or the east coast of the Adriatic Sea. In addition, there are a few pockets where islands are densely packed (*e.g.* the Aegean), making it relatively easy to hop from one to another and avoid the hazards of long trips over open water. Finally, the largest islands (*e.g.* Sicily, Sardinia, Cyprus, Corsica) are in some cases quite close to the mainland and offer habitats that share at least some mainland traits and supported substantial populations, reducing internal isolation to some extent. Even for those islands separated by only short distances from other islands or the mainland, internal connections would probably have been the norm of daily life, and this trait would have been enhanced for the more remote ones. The development of cultural idiosyncrasies in customs and language fostered by isolation was tempered by the occasional influx of outside influences, even on those most remote or desolate islands. In general, the smaller the island, the more likely it was that people looked to the sea for their livelihood because arable land was very limited. In so doing they often exhibited a truly entrepreneurial spirit as they devised or entertained innovations out of necessity.

The other key term that appears throughout the volume is globalization. The work of archaeologists in general, and of the contributors to the volume in particular, demonstrates one of the ways that study of the past can help us come to a fuller, clearer understanding of forces affecting modern life. Today, globalization typically refers primarily to forces that have created a multinational or transnational network in which the world economy has become highly interdependent. The system involves the extraction of raw materials, their transformation into usable forms, and the assembly of the individual components into finished products, with the various stages undertaken in different locations. The system also involves the movement of capital and labor (migration) at unprecedented levels and speed. Reallocation of jobs is a major feature of the system, with automobiles formerly manufactured in the US now produced in Mexico and imported to be sold in the Midwest. Some also argue that globalization leads to economic and cultural homogenization as people in different countries acquire similar objects (*e.g.* cell phones, high-definition televisions, etc.), with accompanying practices, making the world 'smaller'. Many envision globalization as a phenomenon of the modern world, but archaeology provides the additional time depth and data from a range of cultural settings that can enrich our understanding of both the geographical and temporal extent of globalization. Archaeology reveals long-term patterns of interaction that help us understand the general nature of the process. It is in this way that the present volume can address those who often ask what lessons the ancient world holds for life in the 21st century. We see that globalization is not temporally confined, a point made strongly by Jennings,[1] Hall, and many of the present contributors. As Chase-Dunn and Lerro state, 'The lessons we can learn from studying the earlier waves of global integration and disintegration are entirely relevant for understanding the problems of the twenty-first century.' They further argue that '...the changes in human societies over the past 12,000 years can be understood as constituting a single complicated earth-wide event of spiraling globalization'.[2] This approach encompasses all of the time periods examined in this book, providing a broad base for comparisons among an array of cultures.

In examining the interplay of insularity and globalization, the contributors deal explicitly with the idea of connectivity in order to address how exactly ancient Mediterranean societies were linked.[3] This issue draws from several scholarly traditions that include organizing principles or approaches such as hybridity, network analysis, and the notion of small worlds. Each author attempts to illustrate the general features that tied together various groups through trade, exchange of styles, and other practices that highlight commonalities, while at the same time pointing out the variation and idiosyncratic nature of the individual cultures and sites involved in complex networks. The various studies show that while there are some general trends across the entire region, the process is not exactly the same for each subsection. For example, Russell suggests that the development of Nuragic society on Sardinia in the Late Bronze Age was due more to internal (emic) rather than global factors. Gorogianni makes a similar argument for the Cyclades; while there was greater sharing of features here due to developments in transportation and the proximity of the various islands compared to the more isolated Sardinia, there is also evidence for heterogeneity in individual cultures. Her concern that 'macro-level approaches, no matter how illustrative they may be, obscure the agency of individuals and objects' is shared by many of the contributors. Smith suggests a similar variability during the Iron Age in the Balearic Islands. There is, however, evidence of more homogeneity in Mediterranean cultures during the later historical periods. Mazurek presents evidence for some degree of uniformity in the Hellenistic period as reflected in the representations of Isis in coastal communities in particular. She advances a compelling argument by emphasizing the specific relationship between mainland ports and islands, with the latter holding more important positions than often recognized. Francis demonstrates the dual nature of connectivity and insular distinctiveness on Roman Crete. As a large island with both a substantial coast that provides excellent harbors, and an interior that can be remote even in recent times, Francis demonstrates this dual nature for Crete. Gordon and Caraher correctly suggest that residents of Cyprus, and other islands, were not passive recipients of external forces, but played active roles. Cyprus is of particular interest because of its size and its proximity to the major venues of civilization (Levant, Egypt, Asia Minor) that clearly had an impact on the native culture over a number of millennia. Nonetheless, the residents of the island exhibited a strong tendency to be selective in the adoption of outside influences, and in the process formed a uniquely Cypriot culture. While Greek features are perhaps dominant from the Bronze Age and later, there is still significant impact from Phoenician and Egyptian societies. It is perhaps this adaptive malleability that makes it possible for the ready adoption of many features of Roman society, and the subsequent relatively smooth transition to late antique culture and the Christianization of the island.

The contributors have consulted an array of authors who have presented concepts and approaches that speak to the key issues of globalization, insularity, and connectivity. Among the authors cited in several chapters are Jennings and Hold on globalization and Knapp on insularity. The contributors make good use of these ideas, demonstrating the utility of the concepts to their particular geographic focus while also testing the ideas with specific data and to some extent providing useful additions or modifications based on their research. The work of Jennings receives deserved mention in all the chapters, with Russell, Lieberman, Mazurek, and Gordon and Caraher utilizing his definition of globalization most directly. The list of defining characteristics of globalization that Jennings provides is a useful tool that all of the chapters employ explicitly or implicitly, providing a unity of purpose to the volume. The establishment of colonies in the Archaic and extensive contacts in other periods represent the surges of interaction that Jennings discusses. One way that the contributors to this volume, and by implication Jennings, could expand their research is to consider also the work of world-systems analysts who have demonstrated the ability of peripheral groups to negotiate with economically more potent intruders. Tom Hall has discussed this issue for over 30 years, with a special emphasis on the nature of interaction in border or frontier areas,[4] a concentration that is especially relevant to many of the studies in this volume. Chase-Dunn and Hall have also explored in detail the variable nature of incorporation, from weak to strong.[5] At the initial contact between indigenous people and outside colonists/intruders, the former often have considerable leverage because of their familiarity with the terrain and its resources, and the attenuated nature of colonial power due to the distance from the mother city or culture. It is typically at this time that the native people are most able to negotiate the conditions of their relationship with the newcomers.[6] Russell suggests something similar in the way that Nuragic culture on Sardinia remained largely an independent entity despite some contact with BA people from the eastern Mediterranean. Francis presents a mixed picture, with some clear evidence of urban Cretans adopting major aspects of Roman culture, while other segments of the island did not.

The concept of insularity that is another central theme is important for understanding the interplay between island and mainland cultures, and between indigenous people on the one hand, and Greek, Phoenician, and other colonists on the other in all its complexity. The contributors take an expansive view of insularity by exploring the valences of contact (intra-island, inter-island, island-mainland) that islanders managed. Barnett and Ugarković give us a fascinating view of the colonists on Dalmatian islands, relatively late arrivals, but ones that facilitated Corinth's trade with the northern Adriatic. Mazurek links the particular styles of Isis sculptures to migrations during the Hellenistic period, demonstrating the religious and symbolic face of connectivity. In addition, she emphasizes the key role of island ports in the interaction with their mainland counterparts, reversing the direction of influence. Gorogianni tackles the issue of directional influence in her discussion of Minoanization, arguing more for local decision-making as opposed to imposition from the outside (Crete). Her discussion links with that of several others on Romanization. What the several studies make clear is that Minoanization and Romanization should now be thought of as specific examples of a more general process of globalization, but with internal factors that regulate the degree of participation in or adoption of outside elements. Another concept from world-systems analysis is the contested periphery, which is an area in the interstices between major states over which the latter fight for control.[7] Some islands held this status as they moved from being controlled by one empire to another. For example, Cyprus was at various times under the control of the Assyrians, Macedonians, Romans, Byzantines, Franks, Venetians, and Ottomans. Sicily, because of its size, presents a particularly interesting case as a periphery over whose hegemony Greeks and Carthaginians struggled (Smith, this volume). As several of the contributors have noted, one of the key pieces that we lack is evidence about the indigenous people on the colonized islands. To help rectify this problem, Russell and Gorogianni make good use of ethnographic analogy, exploring the anthropological literature to fill in gaps. The concept of small worlds, dealing with localized but significant interactions, is mentioned in only one chapter (Gorogianni), but is implied by all of the contributors. An examination of the manner in which world-systems analysts have used this approach would enrich the conversation in the volume as the various authors continue their investigations. The world-systems approach to small worlds focuses on prehistoric foragers to demonstrate that the difference between pre-state and state level societies in terms of interaction networks is a matter of scale, not of kind. The detailed examination of the Wintu in northern California by Chase-Dunn and Mann provides guidelines for how we who work in the Mediterranean could structure the investigation of small local indigenous networks, and how the intrusion of state-sponsored colonists (Greeks, Phoenicians, and others) reoriented the preexisting interaction sphere.[8]

The editors are to be commended for producing a volume that explores globalization and insularity as ideas that build on the work of previous scholars while adding depth and nuance to our understanding of how the people of the ancient Mediterranean interacted with one another. The broad geographic coverage invites the reader to entertain with greater clarity the degree to which one can talk about the unity of the Mediterranean as a culture area. The time range, from the Bronze Age to the medieval era, demonstrates, I think, the manner in which the global and insular forces ebbed and flowed in a cyclical manner. While local factors dominated at various times, external contacts intruded in the form of archaeologically recognizable elements such as pottery. In other periods, especially the first half of the 1st millennium AD, globalizing forces in the form of commerce and political control drew the various areas into a tighter web. What we can draw from these studies is a view that global and local forces were always in play, with swings more strongly in one direction or the other over time. The vital lesson to draw for our world is that the events we are witnessing are not new – globalization has been with us for thousands of years, and people try now to draw what benefits they can while maintaining as much control as possible over their lives, just as did the ancestral people of the Mediterranean.

Notes

1 Jennings 2011; Hall 2018; see also Hall *et al.* 2011.
2 Chase-Dunn and Lerro 2014, xxii.
3 LaBianca and Scham 2006.
4 Hall 1986; Chase-Dunn and Hall 1997; Hall and Fenelon 2009.
5 Chase-Dunn and Hall 1997.
6 Kardulias 2007.
7 Allen 1996.
8 Chase-Dunn and Mann 1998.

Bibliography

Allen, M. (1996) *Contested Peripheries: Philistia in the Neo-Assyrian World-System.* Unpublished Ph.D. dissertation, University of California, Los Angeles.

Chase-Dunn, C. and Hall, T.D. (1997) *Rise and Demise: Comparing World-Systems.* Boulder: Westview Press.

Chase-Dunn, C. and Lerro, B. (2014) *Social Change. Globalization from the Stone Age to the Present.* Boulder: Paradigm Press.

Chase-Dunn, C. and Mann, K.M. (1998) *The Wintu and Their Neighbors: A Very Small World-System in Northern California.* Tucson: University of Arizona Press.

Hall, T.D. (1986) Incorporation in the World-System: Toward a Critique. *American Sociological Review* 51, 390–402.

Hall, T.D. (ed.) (2018) *Comparing Globalizations: Historical and World-System Approaches.* Cham, Switzerland: Springer International.

Hall, T.D. and Fenelon, J.V. (2009) *Indigenous Peoples and Globalization.* Boulder: Paradigm Press.

Hall, T.D., Kardulias, P.N. and Chase-Dunn, C. (2011) World-Systems Analysis and Archaeology: Continuing the Dialogue. *Journal of Archaeological Research* 19, 233–279.

Jennings, J. (2011) *Globalizations and the Ancient World.* Cambridge: Cambridge University Press.

Kardulias, P.N. (2007) Negotiation and Incorporation on the Margins of World-Systems: Examples from Cyprus and North America. *Journal of World-Systems Research* 13(1), 55–82.

LaBianca, Ø.S. and Scham, S.A. (eds) (2006) *Connectivity in Antiquity: Globalization as a Long-term Historical Process.* London: Equinox.

Index